PIPELINED AND PARALLEL COMPUTER ARCHITECTURES

PIPELINED AND PARALLEL COMPUTER ARCHITECTURES

Sajjan G. Shiva
University of Alabama, Huntsville

HarperCollinsCollegePublishers

To My Students
1971 to 1996

Sponsoring Editor: Michael Slaughter
Project Editor and Composition Management:
  Proof Positive/Farrowlyne Associates, Inc.
Design Administrator: Jess Schaal
Text Design: Jeanne Calabrese
Cover Design: Jeanne Calabrese
Cover Illustration/Photo: Dominique Sarraute/The Image Bank
Production Administrator: Randee Wire
Compositor: Interactive Composition Corporation
Printer and Binder: R. R. Donnelley & Sons
Cover Printer: Phoenix Color Corporation

Pipelined and Parallel Computer Architectures

Copyright © 1996 by Sajjan G. Shiva

HarperCollins® and ■® are registered trademarks of HarperCollins Publishers Inc.

*For information about any HarperCollins title, product, or resource, please visit our World Wide Web site at **http://www.harpercollins.com/college**.*

All rights reserved. Printed in the United States of America. No part of this book may be used or reproduced in any manner whatsoever without written permission, except in the case of brief quotations embodied in critical articles and reviews. For information address HarperCollins College Publishers, 10 East 53rd Street, New York, NY 10022.

Library of Congress Cataloging-in-Publication Data

Shiva, Sajjan G.
  Pipelined and parallel computer architectures / Sajjan G. Shiva.
    p. cm.
  Includes bibliographical references and index.
  ISBN 0-673-52093-5
  1. Computer architecture. 2. Computers, Pipeline. 3. Parallel
computers. I. Title.
QA76.9.A73S455 1996
004'.35—dc20   95-33024
                                                     CIP

95 96 97 98 9 8 7 6 5 4 3 2 1

Contents

PREFACE   ix
INTRODUCTION   1

I.1   Computing Paradigms   2
I.2   The Need for Pipelined and Parallel Processing   4
I.3   Overview   5
      References   8

CHAPTER 1
Uniprocessor Architecture Overview   9

1.1   A Uniprocessor Model   9
1.2   Enhancements to the Uniprocessor Model   12
1.3   Two Architecture Styles   20
1.4   Performance Evaluation   23
1.5   Cost Factor   27
1.6   Example Systems   28
1.7   Summary   49
      References   49
      Problems   50

CHAPTER 2
Styles of Architecture   52

- 2.1   Parallel Processing Models and Terminology   53
- 2.2   Flynn's Taxonomy   58
- 2.3   Skillcorn's Taxonomy   64
- 2.4   Duncan's Taxonomy   75
- 2.5   Summary   85
        References   85
        Problems   87

CHAPTER 3
Pipelining   88

- 3.1   Pipeline Model   89
- 3.2   Pipeline Control and Performance   99
- 3.3   Other Pipeline Problems   108
- 3.4   Dynamic Pipelines   118
- 3.5   Example Systems   124
- 3.6   Summary   128
        References   129
        Problems   130

CHAPTER 4
Vector Processors   132

- 4.1   Vector Processor Models   133
- 4.2   Memory Design Considerations   137
- 4.3   Architecture of the Cray Series   141
- 4.4   Two Other Architectures   151
- 4.5   Performance Evaluation   157
- 4.6   Programming Vector Processors   159
- 4.7   Summary   164
        References   165
        Problems   166

CHAPTER 5
Array Processors   168

- 5.1   SIMD Organization   169
- 5.2   Data Storage Techniques and Memory Organization   174
- 5.3   Interconnection Networks   180
- 5.4   Performance Evaluation and Scalability   195
- 5.5   Programming SIMDs   199
- 5.6   Example Systems   200

5.7	Systolic Arrays	218
5.8	Summary	232
	References	233
	Problems	235

CHAPTER 6
Multiprocessor Systems 237

6.1	MIMD Organization	240
6.2	Memory Organization	243
6.3	Interconnection Networks	247
6.4	Operating System Considerations	255
6.5	Programming	266
6.6	Performance Evaluation and Scalability	271
6.7	Example Systems	277
6.8	Summary	312
	References	313
	Problems	316

CHAPTER 7
Dataflow Architectures 318

7.1	Dataflow Models	319
7.2	Dataflow Graphs	323
7.3	Dataflow Languages	326
7.4	Example Systems	329
7.5	Performance Evaluation	346
7.6	Summary	353
	References	355
	Problems	357

CHAPTER 8
Current Directions 358

8.1	Computer Networks and Distributed Processing Systems	361
8.2	Japan's Fifth Generation Computer Systems (FGCS) Project	363
8.3	The Sixth Generation	367
8.4	Optical Computing	375
	References	379

Index 385

Preface

Recent advances in hardware and software technologies have enabled us to build very powerful computer systems. Along with the improved performance of these machines, the variety of applications for which they are utilized has also widened. With performance requirements for these applications increasing continuously, one approach to meeting these performance demands has been to build the most powerful single processor system that the technology enables us to build, at any given time. When such a system does not meet the performance requirements, overlapped (pipelined) and parallel processing structures have been employed. These structures utilize a multiplicity of processing elements in the design of the system. This book is an introduction to pipelined and parallel processing architectures.

Ideally, in order to take full advantage of multiple processor architectures, one has to (1) devise algorithms with the highest possible degree of parallelism the application exhibits, (2) translate these algorithms into programs that retain the degree of parallelism, (3) compile these programs into machine code that retains the degree of parallelism, and (4) run the object code on the hardware structure that allows execution at the appropriate degree of parallelism. In practice, the first three steps are heavily influenced by the type of hardware available, except in those rare cases where we have the luxury of designing the hardware structure to suit the application. It is my belief that a good grasp of the capabilities and limitations of underlying hardware structures makes an application developer more efficient. Thus, the book introduces pipelined and parallel processing concepts with an emphasis on corresponding hardware architectures.

This book is designed for a second course in computer architecture, and as such assumes a background in basic architectural concepts of single processor systems. These concepts are reviewed in the first two chapters of the book. Chapters 3 and 4 concentrate on pipelined architectures. Chapters 5, 6, and 7 deal with parallel processing architectures, and Chapter 8 concludes the book with a discussion of current trends. Each chapter describes the most generic hardware aspects followed by supporting details on corresponding programming languages, data structures, and operating systems.

Each chapter also provides details of several commercially available systems. The field of multiple processing systems is a dynamic one, in the sense that new systems are being introduced at a rapid rate. At the same time, the lives of these systems tend to be short, either because they get replaced by a more powerful system or because the manufacturer goes out of business due to the small market for the system. As such, no textbook can be completely up to date in describing these systems. Manufacturers' manuals and open literature are the best sources for the most current details.

The field of parallel processing has seen continuous experimentation in building systems over the last few years. Most of these systems have remained laboratory curiosities. As such, I have stayed away from complete descriptions of experimental architectures, although I have utilized the pertinent concepts utilized in these systems to reinforce the material presented.

This book is a result of my teaching a sequence of courses in computer architecture over the last twenty years to computer science and engineering students. It can be used for a semester course in either of these curricula, at the senior or beginning graduate level. It can also be used in an advanced graduate level course, for which the book provides the material needed for about one-half to three-fourths of the course. The remaining part of the course is typically based on readings from journal articles or projects based on the hardware available. The book can also be used as a reference by practicing computer scientists and engineers.

I owe much to a number of people who have contributed to this work. In particular, I thank all the students in my computer architecture classes over the last few years for their thoughts, comments, and tolerance during the evolution of this book. Thanks to Rajiv Virmani and Girish Budibetta for their contributions to the development of Chapters 6 and 7 and Beth Allen for her contributions to the Solutions Manual. It is a pleasure to acknowledge the contributions of the following reviewers, whose suggestions have made the book what it is today: Dharma P. Agrawal, *North Carolina State University;* Shakil Akhtar, *Central Michigan University;* Erik Brunvard, *University of Utah;* Michael A. Driscoll, *Portland State University;* Moshen Javadian, *Texas Southern University;* Peter M. Maurer, *University of South Florida;* Amos Olagunju, *Delaware State College;* Fred Petry, *Tulane University.*

My thanks to all the manufacturers of machines I have used as examples in the book for their permission to use this material. Thanks to Dan Weiskopf of Proof Positive/Farrowlyne Associates for superb editing support, and Michael Slaughter and all the other staff at HarperCollins for their patience and support. The preparation of the manuscript became a family project. I thank my wife Kalpana and daughters Sruti and Sweta for their continuing support, love, and encouragement.

Sajjan G. Shiva

Introduction

This book is about the architecture of high performance computer systems. Architecture is the "art or science of building; a method or style of building" according to *Webster's*. Computer architecture comprises both the art and the science of designing new and faster computer systems to satisfy the ever increasing demand for more powerful systems. A computer architect specifies the modules that form the computer system at a functional level of detail and also specifies the interfaces between these modules to achieve the desired performance-to-cost ratio. Traditionally, these modules were thought to be hardware elements consisting of processors, memories, and input/output devices. With the advances in hardware and software technologies it is now possible to formulate efficient structures for each module using hardware, software, firmware, or a combination of the three. As such, at the architecture level, consideration of the detailed functional characteristics of each module is more important than the implementation details of the module. The exact mix of hardware, software, and firmware used to implement the module depends on the performance requirements, cost, and availability of the hardware, software, and firmware components.

    Progress in hardware and software technologies provides new choices each year. The architect not only has to base his or her decisions on the choices available today, but also has to keep in mind the expected changes in technology during the life of the system. An architectural feature that provides the optimum performance-to-cost ratio today may not be the best feature for tomorrow's technology.

Performance and **cost** are the two major parameters for evaluation of architectures. The aim is to maximize the performance while minimizing the cost (i.e., maximize the performance-to-cost ratio). Performance is usually measured as the maximum number of operations performed per second, be they arithmetic operations, logical inferences, or input/output (I/O) operations. In addition to these, other measures, such as maximum program and data size, ease of programming, power consumption, weight, volume, reliability, and availability, have also been used to evaluate architectures.

Most of the performance enhancements achieved so far have been due to advances in hardware technology. In fact, the four **generations** of computer systems are identified with improvements in hardware technology, namely vacuum tubes, transistors, medium scale integrated (MSI) circuits, and large scale integrated (LSI) circuits. It is also interesting to note that the first three **waves** of computing are also based on hardware technology. The first wave in the 1960s was dominated by mainframes. The second wave in the 1970s belonged to the minicomputer systems, and the third wave in the 1980s was that of microcomputers. Because these generations and waves were primarily based on their improvements in hardware technology, they are considered **evolutionary** approaches to building high performance machines.

While early generations of computer hardware were more or less accompanied by corresponding changes in computer software, since the mid-seventies, hardware and software have followed divergent paths. While the introduction of minicomputers, workstations, and personal computers has changed the way hardware and software are made available to end users, programming methodologies and types of software available to end users have followed a path independent of the underlying hardware.

It is often said that the limits of semiconductor technology have already been reached and no significant performance improvements are possible by technology improvements alone. History has always proven this statement to be false. We always make the most out of the existing technology. When the technology improvements alone cannot yield the desired performance, pipelined and parallel processing architectures can be used. These processing structures produce performance improvements based on the existing technology without the need to wait for the next generation.

Parallel processing is considered the **fourth wave** of computing. Parallel processing architectures utilize a multiplicity of processors and provide for building computer systems with orders-of-magnitude performance increases. To utilize parallel processing architectures efficiently, an extensive redesign of algorithms and data structures (as utilized in the nonparallel implementation of the application) is needed. As such, these are considered **revolutionary** approaches for high performance computer system architecture.

This book covers both the above approaches, starting with the introduction of the three common computing **paradigms** (models) in the next section.

I.1 COMPUTING PARADIGMS

Computing structures can be broadly represented by three paradigms: serial, pipelined, and parallel. These paradigms are illustrated by the following example.

I.1 COMPUTING PARADIGMS

EXAMPLE I.1

Figure I.1 shows the three models with reference to the task of building an automobile. This task can be broadly partitioned into the following subtasks: assembling the chassis, attaching the engine, attaching the body, and painting and cleaning.

Figure I.1(a) shows the **serial** paradigm. Here all four subtasks are performed at one station; that is, there is a single server and the four subtasks are done in sequence for each automobile. Only one automobile is worked on at a time. If each of these subtasks takes T minutes to complete, $4T$ minutes are needed to assemble each automobile and, hence, $4NT$ minutes are needed to assemble N automobiles.

Figure I.1(b) shows the **pipelined** processing paradigm, which resembles the standard automobile assembly line. Here the assembly is done in four stages. Each stage is specialized to perform one subtask. Once an automobile leaves stage 1 and moves to stage 2, the next automobile will be worked on by stage 1. The other three stages also work in this **overlapped** manner. This means it takes $4T$ minutes to fill the assembly line with work. The first automobile is complete at the end of $4T$ minutes and from then on one automobile is completed every T minutes. It still takes $4T$ minutes to assemble an automobile. But to assemble N automobiles, it takes $4T + (N-1)T$ minutes. The **speedup** achieved by the pipeline is thus:

$$\frac{4NT}{4T + (N-1)T} \tag{I.1}$$

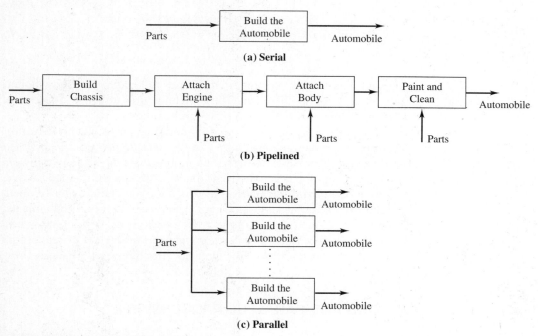

Figure I.1 Three Paradigms

For large N, the speedup is four times that of serial architecture. In general, an ideal pipeline with P stages provides a speedup of P compared to a serial architecture. This ignores the overhead required to manage the stages of the pipeline.

Figure I.1(c) shows the **parallel** paradigm. Here, P stations, each capable of performing all the four subtasks, are used. All the P stations operate simultaneously, each working on a separate automobile. It still takes $4T$ minutes to complete one automobile, but P automobiles are produced in $4T$ minutes. Thus to assemble N automobiles it takes $4NT/P$ minutes. The speedup achieved by this architecture is P times that of serial architecture. To achieve the P-fold speedup, note that the hardware complexity has increased by P-fold compared to the serial paradigm. Also, each of the P stages could have been implemented as a pipeline as in (b), thus enhancing the throughput further, although at the cost of increased hardware complexity.

The four subtasks in this application must be performed in sequence to complete the task. There is no way to perform all the subtasks simultaneously on the same automobile. The application is not parallelizable, and hence, we had to use P identical production lines to enhance the throughput.

EXAMPLE I.2

As another example, consider the computation of the column-sum of an $N \times N$ matrix. In the serial (single processor) implementation of this task, the processor takes N time units to compute the sum of each column and hence requires N^2 time units to complete the task. In the parallel implementation of this task, N processors are used. Each processor accumulates elements of a column in N time units. Because all the processors operate simultaneously, the total time for the completion of the task is N. Thus the throughput is enhanced N-fold.

The pipelined and parallel processing architectures in general provide a higher throughput compared to serial architecture. These architectures utilize multiple processors and are more complex compared to serial architectures.

The key attribute of the application is that it should be partitionable into subtasks that can be executed simultaneously to make the parallel processing possible. When such partitioning is not possible (as in the automobile assembly example above), the pipeline mode of computation is adopted. The matrix computation example above is the case of the so-called **trivial parallelism** in which the job could be partitioned into independent tasks. That is, the subtasks do not exchange data (i.e., communicate with each other) during the computation. In practice, such clean partitioning is not always possible and there will be a considerable communication and task coordination overhead associated with the parallel and pipelined structures that reduces their throughput. This overhead is ignored in the above illustrations.

I.2 THE NEED FOR PIPELINED AND PARALLEL PROCESSING

Enhancement of speed of computations is the main reason for parallel and pipelined processing. The fastest supercomputers of today can perform about 20 billion operations per second. But such speed is not adequate for many scientific applications.

Geophysicists, for example, need a computer system that is 1000 times faster than today's supercomputers for reliable climate modeling. With the computing power available today, weather forecasting can be accurate to only the next five days. Extending it to eight to ten days requires much higher computation rates than currently possible. Applications such as materials analysis, protein folding, earthquake prediction, aircraft design, and so forth require machines capable of performing 1 trillion operations per second.

The U.S. Office of Science and Technology Policy's Committee on Physical, Mathematical and Engineering Sciences produced a report titled "Grand Challenges: High Performance Computing and Communications (HPCC)" in 1991. This report correlates the performance requirements of various computational tasks and the corresponding computing power, as summarized in Figure I.2. As can be seen, the major challenge of the 1990s is to build machines that use 10 billion words (10 gigawords) of memory and are capable of providing 1 trillion operations per second (teraops).

As stated earlier, the important attribute of the application to make it suitable for parallel processing implementation is that it should be possible to partition the application into subtasks that can be executed simultaneously (i.e., in parallel). In practice, these subtasks communicate with each other during their execution. The overall processing speed thus depends on two factors: the **computing** speed of the processors and the **communication** speed of their interconnection structure. The communication overhead is a function of the **bandwidth** (i.e., the number of units of

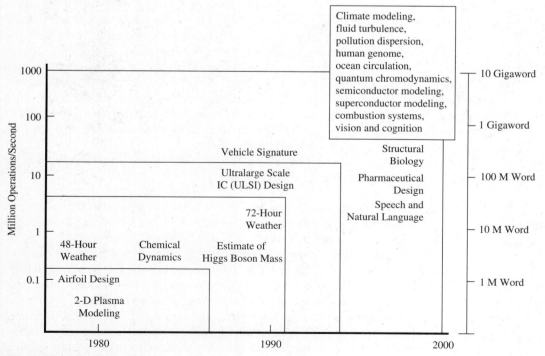

Figure I.2 Grand Challenges

data that can be transmitted per second) and the **latency** (how long it takes to transmit data from a source to a destination) of the interconnection structure.

Obviously, it is better to implement the application on a single processor architecture if it provides the required performance in a cost-effective manner because it eliminates the communication overhead. The supercomputers of today provide for this implementation mode and are suitable for applications that cannot be easily partitioned into a large number of parallel subtasks. They offer very high speeds utilizing a relatively small number of functional units (4 to 16) and extensive pipelining. Their price, however, is approaching a range affordable by only a small number of users.

The performance-to-cost characteristics of serial computers over the last few decades have shown an interesting trend. The characteristic remains linear at the lower performance levels. As the performance level increases, the cost becomes exorbitantly high for small increments in performance. With the advances in very large scale integrated circuit (VLSI) technology, it is now possible to build very fast, low-cost microprocessors. The speed of the current day microprocessors is within an order of magnitude of the speed of the fastest serial processor on the market. Because the cost of microprocessors is low, it is possible to utilize a large number of them to build low-cost, high-performance systems.

There are applications that can be partitioned to run on architectures that utilize thousands of inexpensive microcomputers (workstations or personal computers) interconnected by a network. For instance, consider a VLSI design environment in which each engineer performs part of the design at his or her workstation and accesses the shared database and design information (sparingly) over the network. Each workstation provides the speed needed for the engineer's tasks while the communication speeds of the network are adequate for the interaction requirements.

There are applications in which the communication speed of the above network architecture becomes a bottleneck. The processors need to be more closely coupled to attain a very high communication speed. Some examples are the applications mentioned in the HPCC Grand Challenge, requiring top level performance. Such performance is expected to be achieved by **massively parallel processor** (MPP) architectures consisting of a large number of processors interconnected by a high bandwidth, low-latency network structure.

The major issues of concern in the effective utilization of pipelined and parallel computing architectures are:

- Hardware: The hardware structure should allow **scale-up** to a large number of processors, allowing fast computation and communication speeds. With the advances in hardware technology, it is now practical to build such structures.
- Algorithms: In general, an algorithm that is efficient for serial computation need not be efficient for parallel implementation. Development of parallel algorithms has been an active area of research over the past decade.
- Languages: The language should allow programming of parallel algorithms. New languages are being developed, and sequential languages are being modified to accommodate parallel programming constructs.
- Compilers and other programming tools: Compilers that translate parallel language programs into object code while retaining the parallelism expressed

in the programs are being developed. Another area of activity has been the development of parallelizing compilers that extract the parallelism from serial programs. Several programming environments and tools, such as simulators and debuggers, are being developed.
- Operating systems: The multiplicity of processors and processing paradigms makes the control of a parallel processing architecture more complex compared to its serial counterpart. Existing operating systems are being extended, and newer operating systems are being designed.
- Performance evaluation: Methods that allow the evaluation of the speedup obtained, the scale-up characteristics, the algorithm efficiency and resource (processor, memory, interconnection structure, etc.) utilization are being developed.

All these issues are addressed in subsequent chapters of this book.

I.3 OVERVIEW

This book follows the progression in architecture technology that started with uniprocessor architectures. Enhancements were made to the uniprocessor architecture to improve its performance. Pipelined architectures were introduced as a natural way of enhancing performance by utilizing the overlapped processing mode. Architectures up to this point basically adopted the serial processing paradigm. The 1990s saw the introduction of parallel architectures that attempt to exploit the parallelism in application algorithms in order to meet the performance requirements. The book consists of the following parts:

- PART 1: Preliminaries (Chapters 1 and 2)
- PART 2: Pipelined Architectures (Chapters 3 and 4)
- PART 3: Parallel Architectures (Chapters 5 and 6)
- PART 4: Experimental Architectures (Chapters 7 and 8)

Chapter 1 briefly traces the evolution of digital computer architectures starting from the von Neumann single processor structure to the now common multiple processor structures.

Chapter 2 introduces the most basic models for serial, pipelined, and parallel processing applications and the corresponding terminology. Along with the evolution of architectures, several architectural classification schemes have also been attempted over the years. A representative set of classification schemes are utilized in this chapter as a means of introducing popular styles of architecture. The purpose of this chapter is not to exhaustively cover classification schemes, but to introduce the most popular processing structures.

As mentioned earlier, the first effort toward parallel processing was through pipeline architectures, although such architectures offer more of an overlapped processing mode rather than a strictly parallel processing mode. Pipelined structures were viewed as speed enhancement schemes for single processor architectures. Chapter 3 covers pipeline processing.

Pipeline concepts are extensively used in creating architectures suitable for array- or vector-oriented computations. These architectures, known as **pipelined array processors** or **vector processors,** are covered in Chapter 4.

Chapter 5 describes **synchronous array processor** architectures. These architectures are based on parallelism in data and hence are suitable for computations with array-oriented data. There are several common interconnection structures used to connect the subsystems of a multiple processor system. Interconnection structures suitable for array processor architectures are also described in Chapter 5.

Chapter 6 covers multiprocessor architectures. These are the most generalized parallel processing structures.

Chapter 7 is a brief description of data flow computers. This is a non–von Neumann experimental architecture style.

Chapter 8 concludes the book with a brief description of the current architectural trends.

The field of computer architecture is a dynamic one. The characteristics of architectures not only keep changing, but architectures fade away and new ones appear at a fast rate. Therefore, the example architectures in this book are current as of this writing and the reader is referred to the manufacturers' manuals for the latest details.

Only commercially available architectures are selected as examples throughout this book. This book does not include details on several prominent experimental architectures because these experiments tend to be special-purpose in nature and may or may not result in commercial production. The reader is referred to magazines such as *IEEE Computer, IEEE Spectrum, Computer Design, Byte,* and *Proceedings of the Symposium on Computer Architecture* (held annually) for details on these architectures.

REFERENCES

Burks, A. W., H. H. Goldstine, and J. von Neumann. 1946. *Preliminary discussion of the logical design of an electrical computing instrument.* U.S. Army Ordnance Department Report.

Goldstine, H. H. 1972. *The Computer from Pascal to von Neumann.* Princeton: Princeton University Press.

IEEE Spectrum. 1992. *Special issue on supercomputers,* September.

Shiva, S. G. 1991. *Computer design and architecture,* 2d ed. Glenview, Il.: HarperCollins.

CHAPTER 1

Uniprocessor Architecture Overview

The pipelined and parallel processing architectures utilize multiple processors and can be considered as enhancements of modern day uniprocessor (or single processor) architectures. All commercially successful uniprocessor architectures are based on the digital computer model proposed by von Neumann in the 1940s. There have been several enhancements to this model. Readers not familiar with the von Neumann model and enhancements thereof are referred to Shiva (1991) and Hennessey and Patterson (1990). In order to provide a baseline for the modern day uniprocessor architecture, a brief review of the von Neumann uniprocessor model is provided in Section 1 and a listing of advances in architecture as enhancements to this model is given in Section 2. Section 3 describes the effects of hardware and software technologies on architectures in terms of the evolution of reduced instruction set computers (RISC) and high level language (HLL) architectures. Section 4 provides a brief description of performance evaluation methodologies, and Section 5 describes the cost factors and economics pertinent to computer architectures. Section 6 provides a brief description of three contemporary architectures (Digital Equipment Corporation's Alpha, Intel Corporation's i860 and MIPS Computer System's R4000) along with a summary of characteristics of other popular processors.

1.1 A UNIPROCESSOR MODEL

Figure 1.1 shows the structure of a typical uniprocessor computer system consisting of the memory unit, the arithmetic logic unit (ALU), the control unit, and the I/O unit.

The memory unit is a single port device consisting of a memory address register (MAR) and a memory buffer register (MBR)—also called a memory data register

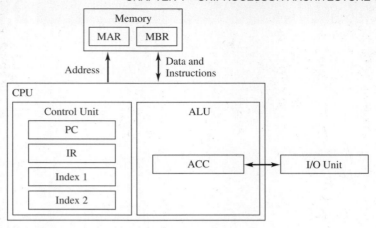

Figure 1.1 Von Neumann Architecture

(MDR). The memory cells are arranged in the form of several memory words where each word is the unit of data that can be read or written. All the read and write operations on the memory utilize the memory port.

The ALU performs the arithmetic and logic operations on the data items in the accumulator (ACC) and/or MBR, and typically the ACC retains the results of such operations.

The control unit consists of a program counter (PC) that contains the address of the instruction to be fetched and an instruction register (IR) into which the instructions are fetched for execution from the memory. A set of index registers are included in the structure. These allow easier access to subsequent locations in the memory. They can also be used to expand the direct addressing range of the processor.

For simplicity, the I/O subsystem is shown to input to and output from the ALU subsystem. In practice the I/O may also occur directly between the memory and I/O devices without utilizing any processor registers.

The components of the system are interconnected by a multiple bus structure on which the data and addresses flow. The control unit manages this flow through the use of appropriate control signals.

Figure 1.2 shows a more generalized computer system structure representative of modern day architectures. The processor subsystem (i.e., the central processing unit—CPU) now consists of the ALU and control unit and various processor registers. The processor, memory, and I/O subsystems are interconnected by the system bus, which consists of data, address, and control lines.

Practical systems may differ from the single bus architecture of Figure 1.2 in the sense that they may be configured around multiple buses. For instance, there may be a memory bus that connects the processor to the memory subsystem and an I/O bus to interface I/O devices to the processor, forming a two-bus structure. Further, it is possible to configure a system with several I/O buses wherein each bus may interface one type of I/O device to the processor. Because multiple bus structures allow simultaneous operations on the buses, a higher throughput is possible compared to single bus architectures. But because of the multiple buses, the system complexity increases. Thus, a speed-for-cost tradeoff is required to decide on the system structure.

1.1 A UNIPROCESSOR MODEL

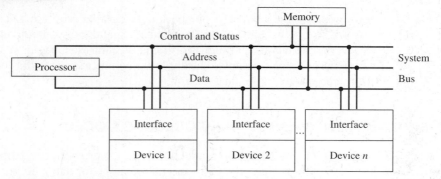

Figure 1.2 General Computer System Structure

It is important to note the following characteristics of the above von Neumann model that make it inefficient:

1. Programs and data are stored in a single sequential memory, which can create a memory access bottleneck.
2. There is no explicit distinction between data and instruction representations in the memory. This distinction has to be brought about by the CPU during the execution of programs.
3. High level language programming environments utilize several data structures (such as single and multidimensional arrays, linked lists, etc.). The memory, being one dimensional, requires that such data structures be linearized for representation.
4. The data representation does not retain any information on the type of data. For instance, there is nothing to distinguish a set of bits representing floating-point data from that representing a character string. Such distinction has to be brought about by the program logic.

Because of the above characteristics, the von Neumann model is overly general and requires excessive mapping by compilers to generate the code executable by the hardware from the programs written in high level languages. This problem is termed the *semantic gap*. In spite of these deficiencies, the von Neumann model has been the most practical structure for digital computers. Several efficient compilers have been developed over the years that have narrowed the semantic gap to the extent that it is almost invisible for a high level language programming environment.

Early enhancements to the von Neumann model mainly concentrated on increasing the speed of the basic hardware structure. As the hardware technology progressed, efforts were made to incorporate as many high level language features as possible into firmware and hardware in an effort to reduce the semantic gap.

Note that the hardware enhancements alone may not be sufficient to attain the desired performance. The architecture of the overall computing environment starting from the algorithm development to execution of programs needs to be analyzed to arrive at the appropriate hardware, software, and firmware structures. If possible, these structures should exploit the parallelism in the algorithms themselves. Thus, performance enhancement is one reason for parallel processing. There are also other reasons, such as reliability, fault tolerance, expandability, modular development, and so forth, that dictate parallel processing structures. Chapter 2 further introduces parallel processing concepts. The hardware enhancements to the von Neumann model are traced briefly in the next section.

1.2 ENHANCEMENTS TO THE UNIPROCESSOR MODEL

Note that the von Neumann model of Figure 1.1 provides one path for addresses and a second path between the CPU and the memory for data and instructions. An early variation of this model is the **Harvard architecture** shown in Figure 1.3. This architecture provides independent paths for data addresses, data, instruction addresses, and instructions. This allows the CPU to access instruction and data simultaneously. The name *Harvard architecture* is due to Howard Aiken's work on Mark-I through Mark-IV computers at Harvard University. These machines had separate storage for data and instructions. Current Harvard architectures do not use separate storage for data and instructions but have separate paths and buffers to access data and instructions simultaneously.

The remainder of this section highlights the major performance attributes of each subsystem in the above uniprocessor model. A brief discussion of the important architectural features that are found in practical computer systems and that enhance one or more of the performance attributes is also provided.

1.2.1 Arithmetic Logic Unit

The major performance parameters for an ALU are:

    a. the variety of arithmetic and logic functions it can perform (i.e., the functionality) and

    b. the speed of operation.

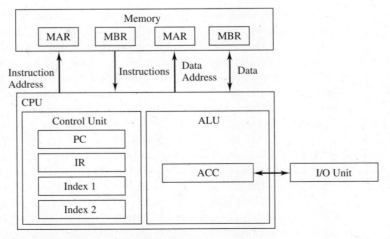

Figure 1.3 Harvard Architechure

1.2 ENHANCEMENTS TO THE UNIPROCESSOR MODEL

In the early 1960s when hardware costs were high, a minimum set of arithmetic (add, subtract) and logic (shift) operations were implemented in hardware. The other required operations were implemented in software. As the progress in integrated circuit (IC) technology yielded cost effective and compact hardware, several fast algorithms were devised and implemented in hardware. Multifunction ALUs, fast multipliers, and other ICs that aid the design of versatile ALUs are now available off the shelf. The ALU subsystem has thus been enhanced in the following ways:

- **a.** Faster algorithms for ALU operations and corresponding hardware implementations (carry lookahead adders, fast multipliers, hardware division, etc.).
- **b.** Use of a large number of general purpose registers in the processor structure wherein most of the ALU operations are on the data items residing in those registers. This reduces the number of accesses to the memory and hence increases the speed of the ALU.
- **c.** Stack-based ALUs increased the speed of operation because operands and intermediate results could be maintained in stack registers, thus reducing the memory access requirements. Note that this concept refers to the so-called **zero-address machines,** in which the arithmetic and logic operations always refer to the operands on the top one or two levels of a stack. A set of registers in the processor are interconnected to form a stack.
- **d.** The speed of ALU was further enhanced by implementing it as a pipeline with several stages when the ALU operations allow such multiple stage execution. Example I.1 introduced the concept of the pipeline. Chapter 3 describes this concept further.
- **e.** Implementation of the processing unit with multiple functional units, where each unit is dedicated to a single arithmetic or logic operation (such as add, shift, multiply, etc.), was used in machines built as early as the 1960s (e.g., Control Data Corporation's 6600). This implementation allows the simultaneous execution of several functions thereby enhancing the processing speed.
- **f.** As the hardware became more cost-effective, systems with multiple ALUs became common. Here each ALU is capable of performing all required arithmetic logic functions and all the ALUs operate simultaneously. The array processor attachments (such as Floating-Point Systems' 5000 series) and the arithmetic coprocessors for various microprocessors available today are examples of these architectures.

1.2.2 Memory

The major parameters of interest for the memory subsystem are:

- **a.** the access speed,
- **b.** the capacity, and
- **c.** the cost.

In general, the memory subsystem should provide the highest access speed and the largest capacity at the lowest cost per bit of storage. The speed is measured in terms of two parameters: the bandwidth and the latency. The **bandwidth** is a measure of the number of data units that can be accessed per second. It is a function of the **access time** (i.e., time between a read request and the arrival of data at the memory output) and the **cycle time** (i.e., the minimum time between requests to memory). The memory **latency** is a measure of how fast the requested data arrive at the destination. It is a function of the bandwidth of the memory, the memory hierarchy, and the speed of the interconnection structure between the memory and the device accessing the memory. Other parameters, such as power consumption, weight, volume, reliability, and error detection/correction capability, are also important depending on the application.

Several hardware technologies with varying speed-to-cost characteristics have been used in building the memory subsystem. Magnetic core memories were used extensively as the main memory of the systems built through the late 1960s. They are still being used in some space and defense applications where their non-volatile characteristic is important. But semiconductor memories have now displaced them almost completely and offer better speeds and lower cost. Static memory devices offer higher speeds compared to dynamic memories, while dynamic memories offer higher chip densities. Access speeds and chip capacities of semiconductor memories have continued to increase due to progress in IC technology.

The following architectural features have been used over the years to enhance the bandwidth and capacity of memory subsystems while maintaining the lower cost:

1. Wider word fetch
2. Blocking (interleaved and banked organizations)
3. Instruction/data buffers
4. Cache memories
5. Virtual memory schemes
6. Multiport memories

The memory subsystem is usually built out of several physical modules (or blocks). The size of the module is dependent on the technology and the sizes offered by that technology, as illustrated by the following example.

EXAMPLE 1.1

If a 128K words ($1K = 2^{10} = 1024$) memory with 32 bits/word (i.e., 128K $\times$ 32 memory) is required and the technology offers 1K $\times$ 8 chips, several memory organizations are possible. Some of these are shown below.

Chips per block	Block capacity	Blocks
4	1K $\times$ 32	128
8	2K $\times$ 32	64
16	4K $\times$ 32	32
64	16K $\times$ 32	8

1.2 ENHANCEMENTS TO THE UNIPROCESSOR MODEL

> Typically, each block has its own port (i.e., MAR/MBR) and read/write control circuits and can be accessed independently. As such, it is possible to access several modules simultaneously.

One of the earliest speed enhancement techniques used in memory systems was the **wider word fetch.** Here, several memory blocks utilize a common MAR and each block has its own MBR. This organization allows access to multiple memory words per memory cycle. Obviously, this requires external buffering of the multiple words accessed from the memory.

Another speed enhancement technique is memory **interleaving,** which distributes the memory addresses such that concurrent accesses to memory blocks are possible. In **low-order interleaving** the blocks are organized such that the consecutive memory addresses lie in consecutive physical blocks with each block having its own port and read/write controls. That is, if the memory contains 2^n words arranged in 2^m blocks, the low-order m bits of the address selects a block and the remaining $n - m$ bits select a word within that block. This organization allows overlapped access to successive memory locations because the read/write access to the block containing a word can be initiated well before the access to the previous block is completed. This increases the speed of instruction fetch during program execution.

In **high-order interleaving** (also called **banking**) technique the consecutive addresses lie in the same physical bank. That is, the high-order m bits of the address select a physical block and the remaining $n - m$ bits select a word within that block. This allows the data and instruction segments of the program to be located in different physical blocks that can be accessed simultaneously because each block has its own port and read/write control.

When any of the above speed enhancement techniques are used, a buffer is needed between the memory and the processor to hold the instructions or data. These buffers can take the form of a simple queue where the memory feeds the data or instructions from one end and the processor retrieves it at the other end. It is possible to allow the input to and output from the buffer to occur in parallel as long as proper controls are exercised.

The **cache** memory scheme can be considered as an extension of the idea of memory buffers where a fast memory block (typically, 10 to 100 times faster than the main memory) is inserted between the primary memory and the processor. The motivation for the cache memory was not to buffer data between the processor and the memory, but to take advantage of temporal locality in memory references during program execution keeping those blocks of memory referenced most recently in the cache, thus decreasing the effective access time. That is, the processor accesses instructions and/or data from the cache as far as possible. When the cache does not contain the needed data or instruction, an appropriate main memory block is brought into the cache. Almost all modern architectures utilize cache memory mechanisms. Some have separate data and instruction caches, some utilize caches only for instruction retrieval, and some use a single cache for both data and instruction retrieval. Most of the modern single-chip processors have on-chip cache structures. In addition, it is possible to include an off-chip (second level) cache.

Virtual memory is used to increase the apparent capacity of the primary memory. Here, a large low-cost secondary memory device (usually magnetic or optical disks or low-speed semiconductor memories) is included in the memory system. The operation of virtual memory systems is similar to that between the cache and the main memory. Only the immediately needed blocks from the secondary memory are brought into the primary memory for execution. The blocks in the primary memory (i.e., pages) are replaced with those from the secondary memory as and when needed. This organization allows the programmer to assume that the system memory is as large as the secondary memory. The virtual memory operation is transparent to the programmer.

Modern memory architectures are organized in a hierarchy consisting of processor registers, cache, main memory, and secondary memory. The lowest cost (per bit) and speed characteristics are offered by the secondary memory, and the highest cost (per bit) and speed are offered by processor registers. Memory architecture thus involves the selection of appropriate devices and capacities at each level in the hierarchy to minimize the cost and maximize the speed.

Multiport memory ICs are now available. These devices contain multiple ports and individual port controls that allow simultaneous access to data stored in the memory. That is, one port can be reading from a memory location while the other could be writing into another location or several ports can be reading from the same location. But when multiple ports try to write to the same location, only one of the ports (i.e., the one with the highest priority among them) will be successful.

As described later in this book, multiport memories are useful in building multiple processor systems because the memory subsystem resolves the memory contention problem brought about by the multiplicity of processors accessing the memory simultaneously. Note that large capacity multiport memories are not generally a viable option because of the packaging costs and pin-bandwidth limitations.

1.2.3 Control Unit

The major parameters of interest for control units are:

    a. speed,
    b. complexity (cost), and
    c. flexibility.

The design of the control unit must provide for the fastest execution of instructions possible. Instruction execution speed obviously depends on the number of data paths (i.e., single versus multiple buses) available in the processor structure; the complexity of the instruction itself (number of memory addresses, number of addressing modes, etc.); and the speeds of hardware components in the processor. The control unit design should minimize the instruction cycle time (i.e., the time to fetch and execute an instruction) for each instruction.

The complexity of the control unit is predominantly a function of the instruction set size, although factors such as the ALU complexity, the register set complexity, and the processor bus structure influence it. Machines built in the early 1960s had small instruction sets because of the complexity and hence the high cost of hardware. As IC technology progressed, it became cost-effective to implement complex control units in hardware. Thus, machines with large instruction sets (i.e., complex instruction set computers—CISCs) were built. It was noted that in IC implementation of the CISC, the control unit would occupy 60% to 75% of the total silicon area. It was also observed that on an average 20% to 30% of the instructions in an instruction set are not commonly used by application programmers, and it is difficult to design high level language compilers that can utilize a large instruction set. These observations led to the development of the reduced instruction set computer (RISC). The RISCs of the early 1980s had relatively small instruction sets (i.e., 50 to 100 instructions). But the instruction sets of the modern day RISCs have around 200 instructions.

The IC technology is currently progressing at such a rapid rate that newer and more powerful processors are quickly introduced to the market. This forces the computer manufacturers to introduce their enhanced product rapidly enough so that the competition does not gain an edge. To make such rapid introduction possible, the design (or enhancement) cycle time for the product must be as short as possible. The control unit, being the most complex component of the computer system, consumes the largest part of the design cycle time. Therefore it is important to have a flexible design that can be enhanced rapidly with a minimum number of changes to the hardware structure.

Two popular implementations of the control unit are:

a. hardwired and
b. microprogrammed.

Note that each instruction cycle corresponds to a sequence of micro-operations (or register transfer operations) brought about by the control unit. These sequences are produced by a set of gates and flip-flops in a hardwired control unit, or from the microprograms located in the control read only memory (ROM) in a microprogrammed control unit. Thus, changing these sequences requires only changing the ROM contents in the case of a microprogrammed control unit while it requires a redesign of a hardwired control unit.

The microprogrammed control units offer flexibility in terms of tailoring the instruction set for a particular application. The hardwired implementations, on the other hand, offer higher speeds.

Almost all hardwired control units are implemented as synchronous units whose operation is controlled by a clock signal. Synchronous control units are relatively simpler to design compared to asynchronous units. Asynchronous units do not have a controlling clock signal. The completion of one micro-operation triggers the next in these units. If designed properly, asynchronous units provide faster speeds.

A popular scheme for enhancing the speed of execution is the overlapped instruction execution where the control unit is designed as a pipeline consisting of several stages (Fetch, Decode, Compute address, Execute, etc.). Chapter 3 provides further details on pipelined control units.

1.2.4 I/O Subsystem

The major performance parameter of the I/O subsystem is the speed. This subsystem should provide for the fastest transfer of data between the processing system and the application environment.

The I/O interface needs to be general in the sense that it should be easy to interface newer devices with characteristics that differ from the system. Several bus standards and I/O protocols have evolved over the years. The I/O subsystem should accommodate such standards easily.

The most popular I/O structures are:

a. programmed I/O,
b. interrupt mode I/O,
c. direct memory access,
d. channels, and
e. I/O processors.

In the **programmed** I/O structure, the CPU initiates the I/O operation and waits for either the input device to provide the data or the output device to accept the data. Because I/O devices are slow compared to the CPU and the CPU has to wait for the slow I/O operations to be completed before continuing with other computations, this structure is inefficient. It is possible to increase the efficiency if the processor is made to go off and perform other tasks, if possible, while the I/O devices are generating or accepting data. Either way, the processor has to explicitly check for the availability or acceptance of data. This is the simplest of the I/O structures because it requires a simple I/O device controller that can respond to the control commands from the CPU and all the I/O protocol is handled by the CPU. In this structure typically one or more processor registers are involved in data transfer.

In the **interrupt mode I/O,** some of the I/O control is transferred from the CPU to the I/O device controller. The CPU initiates the I/O operation and continues with other tasks, if any, and the I/O device interrupts the CPU once the I/O operation is complete. This I/O mode enhances the throughput of the system because the CPU does not idle during the I/O. This mode of I/O is required in applications such as real-time control where the system has to respond to the changes in inputs that occur at unpredictable times.

The **direct memory access** (DMA) mode of I/O allows I/O devices to transfer data to and from the memory directly. This mode is useful when large volumes of data need to be transferred. In this structure the CPU initiates the DMA controller to perform an I/O operation and continues with its computational tasks. The DMA controller acquires the memory bus as needed and transfers data directly to and from the memory. The CPU and the DMA controllers compete for the memory access through the memory bus. The I/O control is thus transferred completely to the I/O device relieving the CPU from the I/O overhead. Note also that this structure does not require that CPU registers be involved in I/O operations as in other structures described earlier.

I/O channels are enhanced DMA controllers. In addition to performing data transfer in the DMA mode, they perform other I/O-related operations such as error detection and correction, code conversion, and control of multiple I/O devices. There are two types of I/O channels. **Selector channels** are used with high speed devices (such as disk and tape) and **multiplexer channels** are used with slow speed devices (such as terminals). Large computer systems of today typically have several I/O channels.

I/O channels were traditionally specially designed hardware elements to suit a particular CPU. With the advent of very large scale integration (VLSI), low-cost microprocessors came into being. The I/O channels were then implemented using microprocessors programmed to perform the I/O operations of the channel. As the capabilities of microprocessors were enhanced to make them suitable for general purpose processing, channels became **I/O processors** that handled some computational tasks on the data in addition to I/O.

The structure of modern day systems thus consists of a multiplicity of processors: a central processor and one or more I/O processors or **front-end processors.** With such multiple processor structure, the computational task is partitioned such that the subtasks are executed, as far as possible, on various processors simultaneously. This is a simple form of parallel processing.

1.2.5 Interconnection Structures

The subsystems of the computer system are typically interconnected by a bus structure. The function of this interconnection structure is to carry data, address, and control signals. Thus the bus structure can be organized either to consist of separate data, control, and address buses, or as a common bus carrying all the three types of signals or several buses (carrying all three types of signals) each interconnecting a specific set of subsystems. For instance, in multiple bus structures it is common to see buses designated as memory buses and I/O buses.

The registers and other resources within the CPU are also interconnected by either a single or a multiple bus structure. But data transfer on these buses does not involve elaborate protocols as on buses that interconnect system elements (CPU, memory, I/O devices).

The major performance measure of the bus structure is its **bandwidth,** which is a measure of number of units of data it can transfer per second. The bandwidth is a function of the bus width (i.e., number of bits the bus can carry at a time), the speed of the interface hardware, and the bus protocols adopted by the system.

The advantage of multiple bus structures is the possibility of simultaneous transfers on multiple buses, thereby providing a high overall bandwidth. The disadvantage of this structure is the complexity of hardware.

Single bus structure provides uniform interfacing characteristics for all devices connected to it and simplicity of design because of the single set of interface characteristics. Because this structure utilizes a single transfer path, it can result in higher bottlenecks for transfer operations compared to multiple bus structures.

As computer architectures evolved into systems with multiple processors, several other interconnection schemes with varying performance characteristics have been introduced. Several such interconnection structures are described in later chapters of this book.

1.2.6 System Considerations

All enhancements outlined in this section were attempts to increase the throughput of the uniprocessor system. As hardware technology moved into the VLSI-era, more and more functions were implemented in hardware rather than in software. Large instruction sets, large numbers of general purpose registers, and larger memories became common. But the basic structure of the machine remained that proposed by von Neumann.

With the current technology, it is possible to fabricate a complex processing system on a chip. Processors with 32-bit architectures along with a limited amount of memory and I/O interfaces are now fabricated as single chip systems. It is expected that the complexity of systems fabricated on a chip would continue to grow.

With the availability of low-cost microprocessors, the trend in architecture has been to design systems with multiple processors. It is common to see a CPU and several coprocessors in such multiple processor architectures. The CPU is usually a general purpose processor dedicated to basic computational functions. The coprocessors tend to be specialized. Some popular coprocessors are numeric coprocessors that handle floating-point computations working with an integer-oriented CPU; I/O processors dedicated to I/O operations; and memory management units (MMU) that coordinate the main memory, cache, and virtual memory interactions.

There are also multiple processor architectures in which each processor is a general CPU (i.e., the CPU/coprocessor distinction does not exist). There are many applications that can be partitioned into subtasks that can be executed in parallel. For such applications the multiple processor structure has been proved to be very cost-effective compared to building systems with a single powerful CPU.

Note that there are two aspects of the multiple processor structures described above that contribute to their enhanced performance. First, each coprocessor is dedicated for a specialized function and, as such, it can be optimized to perform that function efficiently. Second, all the processors in the system could be operating simultaneously (as far as the application allows it), thereby providing a higher throughput compared to single processor systems. Due to the second aspect, these multiprocessor systems can be called **parallel processing** architectures. Thus, trends in technology have forced the implementation of parallel processing structures. There are other motivations for parallel processing covered later in this book.

1.3 TWO ARCHITECTURE STYLES

There are two processor architecture styles that try to reduce the semantic gap but conflict in their hardware implementation strategy:

1. reduced instruction set computers (RISC), and
2. high level language (HLL) architectures.

The aim of RISCs, discussed earlier, is to implement a powerful processor while maintaining a small instruction set. These architectures depend on the compilers for the reduction of the software semantic gap. That is, an HLL program has to be translated into the machine primitives represented by the small instruction set. HLL architectures, on the other hand, tend to reduce the semantic gap by making the primitives available in the instruction set identical to those in the HLL. That is, the hardware interprets the HLL constructs directly.

1.3 TWO ARCHITECTURE STYLES

1.3.1 High Level Language (HLL) Architectures

When high level languages (HLL) are used for programming computers, the programs must be converted into the object code (or machine language program) before the program execution begins. In conventional architectures, the translation from the HLL source to machine language is performed by software means (i.e., compilers) and the execution is performed by the hardware. Introduction of block-structured languages helped the speed-up of the compilation process. Machine hardware supported the translation process of such languages by stack organizations. As the hardware costs came down with the improvements in hardware technology, more complex instructions (e.g., block move, loop) were added to the assembly language instruction sets to provide a more direct translation capability.

Several modes of program translation and execution have evolved over the years. Figure 1.4 shows the evolution starting from the compilation mode in (a). In the interpretive mode of (b), the source program is first converted into an intermediate form (a set of tables, or reverse polish notation), and this form in turn is interpreted by the hardware. Two variations of this mode are shown in (c) and (d). In (c), the

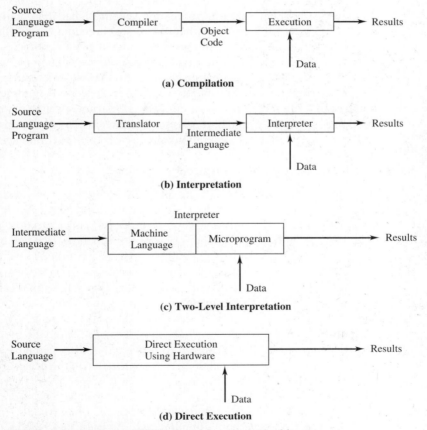

Figure 1.4 Evolution of High Level Language Architectures

intermediate form is first converted into machine language and then interpreted by microprograms. In (d), the microprogram or hardware is designed to interpret the source language form directly. This mode of interpretation results in a **direct execution language (DEL) architecture** or **language corresponding architecture.**

In a DEL architecture, microprograms interpret HLL constructs rather than machine language constructs, as they do in conventional machines. As such, microprograms to interpret each HLL must be designed individually. A well-known DEL architecture is that of the EULER machine, in which a subset of ALGOL-60 constructs were directly executed by microprogramming an IBM 360. The intermediate language used was the reverse polish string. Other FORTRAN, ALGOL, APL, and Pascal architectures exist.

In DEL architectures, the translation from source HLL to intermediate language is performed by the software. In an HLL architecture like the one shown in (d), the hardware is specifically designed for translating and subsequently executing the source HLL program. A well-known architecture of this type is the SYMBOL machine developed at Iowa State University in 1971 to directly execute a high level language called Symbol Programming Language.

The advantage of HLL architectures is a very high translate-load speed. It has not been proven that they offer execution speeds higher than conventional architectures. A further disadvantage is that only one source language for which the machine is designed can be used in programming the machine. For an architecture to be commercially successful, it has to be general purpose enough to suit a large number of applications, thus increasing the number of units sold and reducing the cost per unit. As such, HLL architectures have never been successful commercially. The most popular DEL architectures today are Texas Instruments's Explorer and Symbolics' 3600 series. These machines are designed to execute list processing (LISP) language and are extensively used in symbolic processing (artificial intelligence) applications.

1.3.2 Reduced Instruction Set Computers (RISC)

As mentioned earlier, the advent of VLSI technology provided the capability to fabricate a complete processor on an IC chip. An analysis of such ICs indicates that implementation of the control unit of the processor consumes 60% to 70% of the chip area, thereby limiting the number of processor functions that can be implemented on the chip. Because the control unit complexity is proportional to the number of instructions in the instruction set, an obvious way to reduce the control unit complexity is to reduce the number of instructions in the instruction set. Simplification of the control unit to enable building a complete processor on an IC chip was the prime motivation behind the RISC designs first initiated at IBM in 1975 and in 1980 at the University of California, Berkeley. Obviously, the most frequently used instructions were selected and the control unit was optimized to provide the fastest possible execution.

The progress in IC technology also contributed to the design of complex instruction set computers (CISC), as mentioned earlier. Several high level language constructs became part of the machine instruction set. But designing compilers that utilize these high level constructs in the production of object code from the high level language program became a complex task. Because most of the compilers utilized only 60% to 70% of the constructs found in the instruction set, implementation of elaborate instruction sets was deemed unnecessary, supporting the idea of simpler control units.

Consider, for example, the instruction set of Digital Equipment Corporation's (DEC) VAX-11, a CISC architecture. It consists of 304 instructions with 16 addressing modes utilizing 16 registers. It supports a considerable number of data types (6 types of integers, 4 types of floating-points, packed decimal and character strings, variable length bit fields, etc.) and variable length instructions (2 to 25 bytes) with up to 6 operand specifiers.

A RISC is expected to have much less than 304 instructions and a much simpler instruction environment. There is no consensus about the number of instructions in a RISC instruction set. The Berkeley RISC-I had 31, the Stanford University MIPS had over 60, and the IBM 801 had over 100. The simplification is achieved also by reducing the number of addressing modes and the number of instruction formats.

RISC designs with more than 100 instructions are now on the market, and the characteristics that distinguish a RISC from a CISC are becoming blurred. Nevertheless the following items provide a framework to characterize RISC architectures:

a. A relatively low number of instructions (around 100)
b. A small number of addressing modes (around three)
c. A small number of instruction formats (mostly fixed length)
d. Fast execution of all instructions by utilizing a large number of parallel data paths and overlapping the fetch and execute phases of successive instructions (i.e., pipelined execution)
e. Minimized memory access by utilizing a large number of registers and mostly register-to-register instructions. Memory access is performed by only load and store instructions
f. Support for most frequently used operations in the application inherently in the machine design by a judicious choice of instructions and optimizing compilers.

1.4 PERFORMANCE EVALUATION

The performance of the machine is measured by the bandwidth provided by its memory (i.e., the number of bits per second the memory can deliver); processor (i.e., the number of instructions per second it can execute); and the I/O subsystem (i.e., the number of bits per second it can transfer).

Several measures of performance have been used in the evaluation of computer systems. The most common ones are: million instructions per second (MIPS), million operations per second (MOPS), million floating-point operations per second (MFLOPS or megaflops), and million logical inferences per second (MLIPS). Machines capable of billion floating-point operations per second (GFLOPS or gigaflops) are now available, and the current direction is to build machines capable of trillion floating-point operations per second (teraflops).

The measure used depends on the type of operations one is interested in for the particular application for which the machine is being evaluated. As such, any of these measures have to be based on the mix of operations representative of their occurrence in the application.

EXAMPLE 1.2

If the instruction mix in an application and instruction execution speeds of a hypothetical machine are as follows:

Instruction	Speed (cycles)	Occurrence
ADD	8	30%
SHIFT	4	20%
LOAD	12	30%
STORE	12	20%

The average instruction speed is $(8 \times 0.3 + 4 \times 0.2 + 12 \times 0.3 + 12 \times 0.2) = 8.2$ cycles. If the clock frequency is 1 MHz (i.e., 1 million cycles per second), the machine performs 1/8.2 MIPS. This rating is more representative of the machine performance than the maximum rating (1/4 MIPS) computed by using the speed of execution (4 cycles) of the fastest instruction (SHIFT).

Thus, the performance rating could be either the **peak rate** (i.e., the MIPS rating the CPU cannot exceed) or the more realistic **average or sustained rate.** In addition, a **comparative** rating that compares the average rate of the machine to that of other well-known machines (for example, IBM MIPS, VAX MIPS, etc.) is also used.

In addition to the performance, other factors considered in evaluating architectures are: **generality** (how wide is the range of applications suited for this architecture), **ease of use,** and **expandability** or **scalability.** One feature that is receiving considerable attention now is the **openness** of the architecture. The architecture is said to be **open** if the designers publish the architecture details so that others can easily integrate standard hardware and software systems to it. The other guiding factor in the selection of an architecture is the **cost.** Some of the factors contributing to the cost parameter are explored in Section 5.

Several analytical techniques are used in estimating the performance. All these techniques are approximations, and as the complexity of the system increases, most of these techniques become unwieldy. A practical method for estimating the performance in such cases is by using benchmarks.

1.4.1 Benchmarks

Benchmarks are standardized batteries of programs run on a machine to estimate its performance. The results of running a benchmark on a given machine can then be compared with those on a known or standard machine, using criteria such as CPU and memory utilization, throughput and device utilization, and so forth.

1.4 PERFORMANCE EVALUATION

Benchmarks are useful in evaluating hardware as well as software and single processor as well as multiprocessor systems. They are also useful in comparing the performance of a system before and after certain changes are made.

As a high level language host, a computer architecture should execute efficiently those features of a programming language that are most frequently used in actual programs. This ability is often measured by benchmarks. Benchmarks are considered to be representative of classes of applications envisioned for the architecture.

Common benchmarks fall into the following categories:

1. **Kernel Benchmarks:** They are code fragments extracted from real programs in which the code fragment is responsible for most of the execution time. They have the advantage of small code size and long execution time. Examples are Linpack and Lawrence Livermore loops. The **Linpack** measures the MFLOPS rating of the machine in solving a system of equations in a Fortran environment. The **Lawrence Livermore loops** measure the MFLOPS rating in executing 24 common Fortran loops operating on data sets with 1001 or fewer elements.
2. **Local Benchmarks:** These are programs that are site specific. That is, they include in-house applications that are not widely available. Because the user is most interested in the performance of the machine for his or her applications, local benchmarks are the best means of evaluation.
3. **Partial Benchmarks:** These are partial traces of programs. It is in general difficult to reproduce these benchmarks when the portion of benchmarks that was traced is unknown.
4. **Recursive Benchmarks:** These are programs that implement recursive algorithms, such as the Towers of Hanoi or Nine Queens problems.
5. **Unix Utility and Application Benchmarks:** These are programs that are widely employed by the Unix-user community. The **SPEC** (System Performance Evaluation Cooperative Effort) benchmark suite belongs to this category and consists of ten scenarios taken from a variety of science and engineering applications. This suite developed by a consortium of computer vendors is for the evaluation of workstation performance. The performance rating is provided in **SPECmarks**.
6. **Synthetic Benchmarks:** These are small programs constructed specially for benchmarking purposes. They do not perform any useful computation, but statistically approximate the average characteristics of real programs. Examples are **Dhrystone** and **Whetstone** benchmarks.

    The Whetstone benchmark in its original form was developed in ALGOL 60. Whetstone reflects mostly numerical computing, using a substantial amount of floating-point arithmetic. It is now chiefly used in a Fortran version. Its main characteristics are as follows.

    a. A high degree of floating-point data and operations, because the benchmark is meant to represent numeric programs.
    b. A high percentage of execution time is spent in mathematical library functions.

    c. Use of few local variables because the issue of local versus global variables was hardly being discussed when these benchmarks were developed.
    d. Instead of local variables, a large number of global variables are used. Therefore, a compiler in which the most heavily used global variables are used as register variables (as in C) will boost the Whetstone performance.
    e. Because the benchmark consists of nine small loops, Whetstone has an extremely high code locality. Thus, a near 100% hit rate can be expected even for fairly small instruction caches.

    The distribution of the different statement types in this benchmark were determined in 1970. As such, the benchmark cannot be expected to reflect the features of more modern programming languages (e.g., record and pointer data types). Also, recent publications on the interaction between programming languages and architecture have examined more subtle aspects of program behavior (e.g., the locality of data references—local versus global) that were not explicitly considered in earlier studies.

    In early efforts dealing with the performance of different computer architectures, performance was usually measured using some collection of programs that happened to be available to the user. However, following the pioneering work of Knuth in the early 1970s, an increasing number of publications have been providing statistical data about the actual usage of programming language features. The **Dhrystone benchmark** program set is based on these recent statistics, particularly in systems programming. Its main features are as follows:
    a. It contains a measurable quantity of floating-point operations.
    b. A considerable percentage of execution time is spent in string functions. In the case of C compilers this number goes up to 40%.
    c. Unlike Whetstone, Dhrystone contains hardly any loops within the main measurement loop. Therefore, for processors with small instruction caches, almost all the memory accesses are cache misses. But as the cache becomes larger, all the accesses become cache hits.
    d. Only a small amount of global data is manipulated, and the data size cannot be scaled.

7. **Parallel Benchmarks:** These are for evaluating parallel computer architectures. The 1985 workshop at the National Institute of Standards (NIST) recommended the following suites for parallel computers: Linpack, Whetstone, Dhrystone, Livermore loops, Fermi National Accelerator Laboratory codes used in equipment procurement, NASA/Ames benchmark of 12 Fortran subroutines, John Rice's numerical problem set, and Raul Mendez's benchmarks for Japanese machines.

    Another popular benchmark set is the **Stanford Small Programs.** Concurrent with the development of the first RISC systems John Hennessy and Peter Nye at Stanford's Computer Systems Laboratory collected a set of small C programs. These programs became popular because they were the basis for the first comparisons of RISC and CISC processors. They have now been collected into one C program containing eight integer programs (Permutations, Towers of Hanoi, Eight Queens,

Integer Matrix Multiplication, Puzzle, Quicksort, Bubble Sort, and Tree Sort) and two floating-point programs (matrix multiplication and fast fourier transform).

The PERFormance Evaluation for Cost-Effective Transformations (**PERFECT**) benchmark suite consists of 13 Fortran subroutines spanning four application areas (signal processing, engineering design, physical and chemical modeling, and fluid dynamics). This suite consists of complete applications (with the input/output portions removed) and hence constitutes significant measures of performance.

The Scalable, Language-Independent, Ames Laboratory, One-Minute Measurement (**SLALOM**) is designed to measure the parallel computer performance as a function of problem size. The benchmark always runs in one minute. The speed of the system under test is determined by the amount of computation performed in one minute.

There are many other benchmark suites in use, and more are being developed. Refer to Weicker (1990) and Simpson (1990) for a survey of common benchmarks.

It is important to note that the benchmarks provide only a broad performance guideline. It is the responsibility of the user to select the benchmark that comes close to his or her application and further evaluate the machine based on scenarios expected in the application for which the machine is being evaluated.

1.5 COST FACTOR

The unit cost of the machine is usually expressed as dollars per MIPS (or MFLOPS). It is important to note that the cost comparison should be performed on architectures of approximately the same performance level. For example, if the application at hand requires a performance level of N MIPS, it is usually an overkill to select an architecture that delivers M MIPS where M is far greater than N, even though the unit cost of the latter system is lower. On the other hand, an architecture that offers N/X MIPS at a lower unit cost would be better for the application at hand if it is possible to attain N MIPS by using Y such systems (where $Y \geqq X$) with a lower total cost compared to the architecture delivering N MIPS. Of course, if an architecture consisting of multiple machines each delivering N/X MIPS cannot deliver N MIPS, then it is not a candidate for comparison. This is obviously an oversimplification because configuring multiple machines to form a system typically requires other considerations, such as partitioning of application into subtasks, reprogramming the sequential application into parallel form, overhead introduced by the communication between multiple processors, and so forth. These considerations are discussed later in this book.

The cost of a computer system is a composite of its software and hardware costs. The cost of hardware has fallen rapidly as the hardware technology progressed while the software costs are steadily rising as the software complexity grows, despite the availability of sophisticated software engineering tools. If this trend continues, the cost of software would dictate the cost of the system while the hardware would come free once the software is purchased.

The cost of either hardware or software is dependent on two factors: an upfront development cost and a per unit manufacturing cost. The development cost is amortized over the life of the system and distributed to each unit produced. Thus, as the number of systems produced increases, the development component of the cost decreases.

The production cost characteristics of the hardware and software differ. Production of each unit of hardware requires assembly and testing, and hence, the cost of these operations will never be zero even if the cost of hardware components tends to be negligible. In the case of software, if we assume that there are no changes to the software once it is developed, resulting in zero maintenance costs, the production cost becomes almost zero as the number of units produced is large. This is because producing a copy of the software system and testing it to make sure it is an accurate copy of the original (by bit-by-bit comparison) is not an expensive operation. But the assumption of zero maintenance costs is not realistic because the software system always undergoes changes and enhancements are requested by the users on a continual basis.

There are other effects of progress in hardware and software technologies on the cost of the system. Each technology provides a certain level of performance, and as the performance requirements increase, we exhaust the capability of a technology and hence will have to move to a new technology. Here we are assuming that the progress in technology is user driven. In practice, the technology is also driving the user's requirements in the sense that the progress in technology provides systems with higher performance at lower cost levels thereby making older systems obsolete faster than before. That means that the life spans of systems are getting shorter bringing an additional burden of recuperating development costs over a shorter period of time.

The cost considerations thus lead to the following guideline for a system architect: make the architecture as general purpose as possible in order to make it suitable for a large number of applications, thus increasing the number of units sold and reducing the cost per unit.

1.6 EXAMPLE SYSTEMS

This section provides a brief description of three contemporary architectures. These architectures incorporate most of the features described in this chapter. The Digital Equipment Corporation (DEC) Alpha is the fastest RISC architecture on the market as of this writing. This and the MIPS Computer Systems R4000 represent the 64-bit family. The Intel i860, on the other hand, represents the 32-bit CPU design.

The thrust of this section is to list the main features of the three processor architectures. All three processors utilize pipeline and parallel structures in their design. Because these structures are described in remaining chapters of this book, it may not be possible to understand all the details in this section at the first reading. I suggest revisiting these processor descriptions after reading other chapters of the book. Manufacturers' manuals provide further details on these processors.

1.6.1 Digital Equipment Corporation's (DEC) Alpha

The DEC Alpha is the fastest RISC chip on the market today. This chip, conceived in 1988, is a 64-bit architecture running at a clock speed of 200 MHz. While designing Alpha, DEC considered several alternatives including: a subset of DEC's popular

VAX architecture, a translated VAX, and an ultrapipelined VAX. These alternatives involved building translators or new microcodes to achieve the RISC performance. As such, DEC decided to build a new RISC from scratch with a few features to accommodate VMS, which is DEC's proprietary operating system.

One of the main goals that the architecture team set was longevity. To justify the time and expense of building the new chip from scratch, the executives at DEC had to be convinced that the final product would be able to grow in performance without large changes in hardware or software. Thus the objective was to build a chip that could increase in performance by a factor of 1000 over a span of 25 years. One of the ways this growth can come about is through increase in clock speeds. Hence, the chip was laid out so that a fast clock rate could be easily maintained throughout the chip. Over the span of 25 years, there will be a number of implementations that utilize the basic architecture. The initial versions of Alpha will eventually be replaced by future, more advanced implementations. This concept is similar to the one adopted by Motorola 680x0 and Intel ix86 architectures.

Another primary goal was to make the chip usable on a variety of operating systems. For this reason, an extra basic instruction format called PALcode (Privileged Architecture Library code) was included. These instructions refer to a group of callable routines for performing instructions unique to a particular operating system.

DEC has defined libraries for VMS and OSF/1, the two operating systems the Alpha chip will initially support. Each is comprised of two parts: privileged instructions, which are to be used only by the operating system, and unprivileged instructions, which can be used by the system and application programmers. These instructions call subroutines stored in the libraries and must run without interruption. Libraries can be created for any future operating system, and one is currently in the works for the WINDOWS-NT system.

ALPHA 21064

In December 1990, the first fully functional version of the chip (21064-AA) was ready for testing. In January 1991, the Ultrix (version 4) came up in what was referred to as a "hole in one" boot. This meant that the machine booted with the Alpha chip on the very first try with no errors. Table 1.1 shows the specifications, and Figure 1.5 shows the structure of the chip.

The Alpha 21064 fully implements the Alpha instruction set. Its internal structure is a full 64 bits wide and allows full scalability for multiprocessor implementations. It runs at 150 MHz (6.6 ns cycles) and has the ability to launch two instructions simultaneously.

The Alpha is a load/store RISC architecture. That is, the memory is accessed only through the load and store type instructions and all operations are performed between (or on) 64-bit registers.

Data is stored in the memory in the least significant byte to most significant byte order (i.e., little-endian representation). Memory is accessed via 64-bit addresses.

The basic addressable unit in the Alpha is the byte. A word is made of 2 contiguous bytes starting on a byte boundary. The preferred integer data formats are the longword and the quadword. The longword is 4 contiguous bytes starting on a byte boundary. The longword can be loaded and stored using sign-extended load/store instructions and can be operated using longword arithmetic instructions.

TABLE 1.1 DEC ALPHA 21064-AA CHARACTERISTICS

Clock Speed:	150 MHz
Transistor Count:	1.68 million
On-Chip Data Cache:	8 Kbyte, direct-mapped, write-through
On-Chip Instruction Cache:	8 Kbyte, direct-mapped
On-Chip Data Translation Buffer:	32 entry, fully associative with selectable 8K, 64K, 256K, or 4-Mbyte page size
On-Chip Instruction Translation Buffer:	8 entry, fully associative, 8-Kbyte page plus 4-entry fully associative, 4-Mbyte page
Floating-Point Unit:	On-chip, supports both IEEE and VAX floating-point
Bus:	Separate data and address buses. Data bus is 128 or 64 bit selectable
Virtual Address Size:	64-bits (currently only 43 are supported)
Physical Address Size:	34-bits
Pipelines	
Integer:	7-stage
Floating:	10-stage

Longwords are stored as two's-complement integers. The quadword is 8 contiguous bytes long starting on a byte boundary. The quadword is either interpreted as a two's-complement or as an unsigned integer.

The Alpha supports two of the three VAX floating-point types: F and G. The D type is partially supported by using the G-floating load and store instructions, but no D-floating arithmetic instructions exist. The F-floating datum is stored in memory as 2 contiguous words. The first word is defined as follows: Fraction Hi (bits 0–6); Exponent (bits 7–14); and Sign (bit 15). The second word consists of Fraction Lo. When read into a 64-bit register, an F-floating number is stored as follows: zero (bits 0–28); Fraction Lo (bits 29–44); Fraction Hi (bits 45–51); Exponent (bits 52–62); Sign (bit 63). Note that in the 64-bit representation the exponent portion has been expanded to 11 bits. The Alpha load does this, setting the low order bits to zero. When an F-floating number is read into a register, the result is compatible with the G-floating, therefore it is able to be manipulated by G-floating instructions.

The G-floating is an extension of the 32-bit F-floating to a 64-bit value. The first word is the same as described above, but the following 3 words are Fraction Midh, Fraction Midl, and Fraction Lo. The Alpha also supports the IEEE standard single and double formats for floating-point numbers.

There are 2 register sets (integer and floating-point), each with 32 registers. The integer instructions act only on the integer registers and the floating-point only on the floating-point registers. All instructions, floating-point as well as integer, act upon

1.6 EXAMPLE SYSTEMS

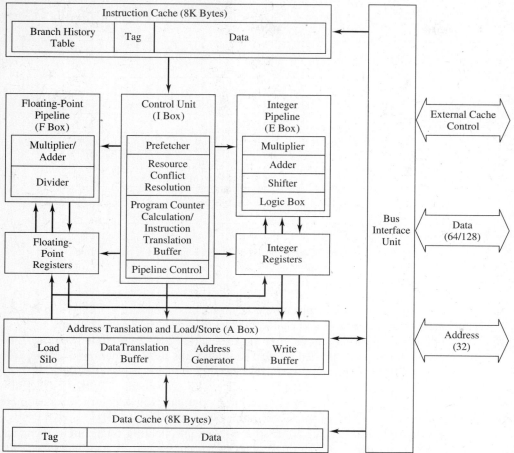

Figure 1.5 DEC Alpha Structure [Comerford, 1992] (Reprinted with permission from IEEE.)

quadwords. The integer registers are numbered R0 to R31, with R31 hardwired to zero. All writes to R31 are ignored. Similarly, the floating-point registers are numbered F0 to F31, with F31 hardwired to zero.

All Alpha instructions are 32 bits long. Because the Alpha reads 64 bits at a time, two instructions are read from the memory in a single fetch. There are only four instruction formats: PALcode, Branch, Memory, and Operate instructions shown in Figure 1.6. Here, Ra, Rb, and Rc are integer registers and Fa, Fb, and Fc are floating-point registers.

The PALcode instruction format is used to call "extended processor functions." The "Number" field specifies the extended operation, and the source and destination operands are in registers specified by the specific PALcode instruction.

Branch instructions are used for conditional branches as well as for program counter relative subroutine calls. Here, Ra is a target virtual address register, and the branch displacement is a longword offset. The data for the address register is com-

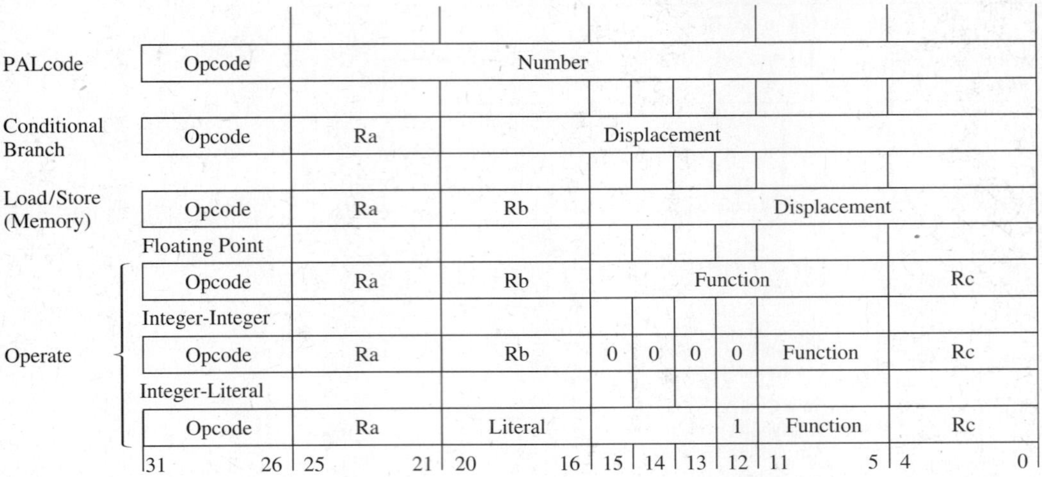

	PALcode	Opcode		Number							

PALcode	Opcode / Number
Conditional Branch	Opcode / Ra / Displacement
Load/Store (Memory)	Opcode / Ra / Rb / Displacement
Operate — Floating Point	Opcode / Ra / Rb / Function / Rc
Operate — Integer-Integer	Opcode / Ra / Rb / 0 0 0 0 / Function / Rc
Operate — Integer-Literal	Opcode / Ra / Literal / 1 / Function / Rc

Bit positions: 31 26 | 25 21 | 20 16 | 15 14 13 12 | 11 5 | 4 0

Figure 1.6 DEC Alpha Instruction Formats [Comerford, 1992] (Reprinted with permission from IEEE.)

puted by first shifting the displacement left by 2 bits (to address a longword offset), sign extend that value, and add that value to the current program counter.

In the memory instructions, Ra is the destination register, Rb is a byte offset, and the virtual address is computed by sign extending the displacement and adding it to the value in Rb. In some memory format instructions, the displacement can be used as a function, and the usage of the Ra and Rb fields are specified by the instructions. This format can also be used for certain jump commands in which the displacement field can be used for branch-prediction hints (Refer to Chapter 3.).

The operate instructions are further broken into floating-point, integer-integer, and integer-literal types. In floating-point operations, Fa and Fb are source registers and Fc is the destination register. The "function" is an 11-bit extended opcode. For integer operations Ra and Rb are the source registers and Rc is the destination. An 8-bit literal replaces Rb in the second format. This constant is a positive integer between 0 and 255, zero-extended to 64-bits.

Though the Alpha architecture is a true 64-bit architecture, the initial 21064 external bus interface is not. The 21064 can only access 34 bits of address space (i.e., 16 gigabytes of physical space). In addition, the virtual memory capability only handles 43 bits in the initial implementations. The future Alpha products are to improve upon these data and address widths.

Electrically, the 21064 runs using 3.3V logic. This voltage level reduces the power consumption of the chip (already a sizable 23W) while still able to run at 150 Mhz. Though powered by 3.3V, the chip does have the capability of interfacing to the standard 5V logic. It has a threshold input pin that determines the switching threshold voltage. This provides the system designer with great flexibility allowing interface with different technologies.

The external bus interface allows different speeds and sizing to further enhance its usability. The data bus can be interfaced in either a 64-bit size or 128 bits. The external interface provides two different clock signals for interface timing. The two clocks have the ability to be reduced in time base as well as skewed per clock cycle. All the above parameters are determined at bootup by the 21064, reading the inputs to the Interrupt Request inputs.

On system reset, the 21064 determines many of its operating parameters. After the reset input has been deactivated, the 21064 loads the entire contents of its internal instruction cache (Icache) with the contents of a serial ROM. After the instruction code is loaded, the machine jumps to address location 0 (which is the first location in the Icache) and starts execution. This initialization code is used to initialize the hardware of the 21064 and start the system bootstrap process.

The Icache is one of the three caches supported by the 21064. The other caches are the internal data cache (Dcache) and the external backup cache (Bcache). (See Figure 1.7.) The Dcache and Icache are the first level caches that are tested for data or instruction hits, respectively. The Bcache is the next level (optional) cache that can be utilized by the system designer.

The Icache is 8 Kbytes long with 32-byte line sizes. It can hold up to 64 individual instructions. All cache fills from memory are done in 32-byte increments. This means that all instruction fetches into the Icache are performed on the external data bus by multiple bus cycles.

The Dcache is also 8 Kbytes in size. It also utilizes the 32-byte line size requiring 32-byte line fills. In addition, the Dcache has write-through access that causes data written to the cache to also be written to external memory at the same time. (This write can go to either Bcache or to external memory.)

In attempting to provide for scalability, the Dcache facilitates cache coherency issues. (Refer to Chapter 6 for details on cache coherency.) It provides a backmapping ability to continuously store the address of data that is mapped into it. This store of addresses is kept external to the 21064 and allows for interrogation to determine what is in Dcache. This eliminates the bottleneck of interrogating the processor in testing for cache coherency.

The Bcache is mostly under the control of the 21064 processor. The processor does all cache searches and determines whether the address access is a hit or miss. The Bcache's control is passed to the external system logic on all external bus accesses. It is up to the external logic to perform Bcache loads during these external accesses.

The Bcache can be as small as 128 Kbytes and as large as 16 Mbytes. The size of the Bcache is determined when the BIU Control register is written to at system initialization. In addition, the BIU specifies timing parameters for cache accesses as well as disabling cache translation for certain areas of the memory bus. The latter is especially important for I/O memory addressing as well as shared memory systems with limited or no cache coherency checking. Like the other caches, the Bcache is sized in 32-byte lines.

All cache address translations are done off of physical addresses that have been translated from virtual addresses. The virtual addressing is handled internally to the chip by two separate translation buffers, one each for instructions and data. Each translation buffer is fully associative with page sizes ranging from 8 Kbytes to 4 Mbytes.

The structure of the Alpha system allows two instructions to be initiated at the same time. Because the integer and floating-point sections are isolated to a high degree, throughput can be substantially improved by interleaving floating-point and

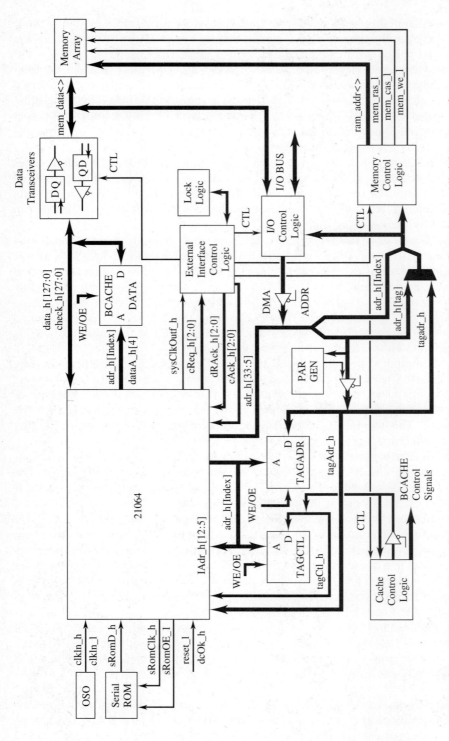

Figure 1.7 21064-Based System Block Diagram (Copyright © 1992, Digital Equipment Corporation. All rights reserved. Reprinted by permission.)

integer instructions. In doing this, the processor achieves a performance of two processors together, one doing solely integer manipulation and the other performing floating-point.

The Alpha architecture utilizes an asynchronous external bus interface. The type of cycle being initiated is indicated on the c_Req pins [0:2]. The cycle continues until a response is delivered back on the dRack [0:2] and cAck [0:2] pins. This handshake determines both that the cycle occurred correctly as well as that information was supplied back to be used in processor execution.

An example of the different types of bus cycle types is the code lock type cycle. In multitasking/multiprocessor systems, there is a requirement to provide a mechanism to guarantee uncorrupted access to a memory location. (This is often used for semaphore operations restricting access to different system resources. Refer to Chapter 6 for details.) Most processors lock the data bus utilizing a read-modify-write cycle to achieve this. The lock is effective until the instruction is completed, and no other device has access to the bus during that time.

The Alpha architecture takes a different approach to the code lock problem. It allows this sequence to be broken into multiple instructions. When the data is originally read, a lock is implemented by the bus system for the location read. The data is then manipulated after which the processor attempts to store the new data back in memory. During the store, the external bus interface determines whether the lock is still set and, if so, stores the data. If the lock is not set, the data is not stored and an indication of that fact is sent back to the processor. The lock is cleared by the external data bus interface if the locked memory location is written to or an exception occurs.

This lock mechanism provides a number of advantages. The action of read-modify-write is broken down into a number of simpler instructions, simplifying control unit design. The read-modify-write action no longer holds the bus inactive allowing other processors to access different locations in data while the read-modify-write is occurring.

The 21064 can manipulate byte level quantities yet cannot access them on the external data bus. The data bus is designed to access memory at a minimum of 32 bits though it best utilizes 64-bit data. It requires that the data be bounded to 32- or 64-bit page boundaries. Failure to do so can produce an alignment exception in the system.

Due to the pipelined nature of the Alpha architecture and the use of caching, access to data may appear out of order to other processors in a multiprocessor system. To ensure synchronization of data between processors the Alpha provides the memory barrier instruction. The memory barrier guarantees that any previous instruction writes and reads are fully completed before performing any successive instruction reads and writes. This allows data transfer between processors or processor and DMA to occur without the loss of data. Refer to Chapter 6 for further details on barriers.

The 21064 does not provide a distinct I/O bus. Instead it utilizes a concept known as a *mailbox*. The mailbox is set up with appropriate parameters for the desired transaction. After the data is set up, an external controller is activated that actually performs the transaction. This is much like a channel device.

The mailbox concept is not required in the 21064 system. Instead, I/O data may be memory mapped with possible offsets in addressing as appropriate. Addressing may be right shifted to bytewise access with only the low order bytes of data being utilized in I/O transactions. This decision is left to the designer.

The smart I/O controller mentioned above is utilized in DMA transfers. In addition, the 21064 comes with a bus master protocol to allow the DMA to take control of the bus. While it has the bus, the DMA has full control of the external memory and the Bcache. The 21064 bus accesses during DMA transfers are delayed causing the instruction pipelines to stall.

1.6.2 Intel Corporation's i860

In 1989, Intel announced its first full-scale RISC processor, the i860. Originally designed for high-performance graphics, this processor is implemented on a single chip consisting of more than one million transistors. There are nine components (shown in Figure 1.8) in the processor: the RISC core (integer unit), floating-point adder and multiplier units controlled by their own control unit, a memory management unit, a graphics unit, instruction cache, data cache, and a bus control unit.

Much of the i860's performance can be attributed to its three specialized ALUs: the floating-point multiplier unit, the floating-point adder unit, and the 3-D graphics unit. Each functional unit can operate in scalar (nonpipelined) or pipelined modes and in parallel with the RISC core unit. Further, the floating-point adder and multiplier can be linked together to perform vector operations.

The graphics unit incorporates many special graphics functions such as Z-buffering and Gouraud-Phong shading. This allows the processor to be used not

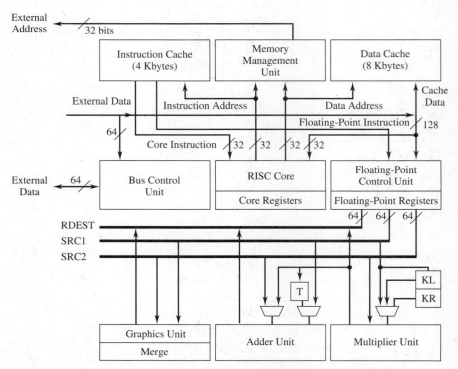

Figure 1.8 Intel i860 Processor Structure (Courtesy of Intel Corporation.)

1.6 EXAMPLE SYSTEMS

only as a stand-alone graphics chip, but also as the main processor of a supercomputer requiring graphics-rendering capabilities.

The RISC core unit is the master of the processor. It has the following functions:

    a. Fetching integer and floating-point instructions
    b. Executing loads and stores between memory and integer and floating-point registers
    c. Handling transfers between integer and floating-point registers
    d. Handling control register manipulations and cache configuration
    e. Performing arithmetic and logical operations on 32- and 64-bit integers
    f. Handling branching, using delayed transfers when possible to avoid breaks in the pipeline (Refer to Chapter 3 for details on delay transfer technique.)

Most RISC core instructions use registers as their operands rather than accessing external memory directly. There are 32 general purpose registers (Figure 1.9), a data breakpoint register, and two processor status registers. Nearly all integer instructions execute in one clock cycle.

The floating-point multiplier and adder units each accept two 64-bit inputs. The multiplier unit produces a 128-bit output while the adder unit produces a 64-bit output. Single- and double-precision adds and single-precision multiplies all execute in three clock cycles. Double-precision multiplies take four clock cycles. These units are organized as three-stage pipelines producing one result every cycle. Some instructions can activate the floating-point adder and the floating-point multiplier simultaneously. This allows an add to be executed along with a multiply with no performance degradation. Parallelism with the integer unit is also supported.

The graphics unit operates on 32- and 64-bit integers and supports long-integer arithmetic not handled in the core unit. It also supports 3-D graphics operations including 3-D shading for hidden surface elimination, distance interpolation, and pixel operations. An 8-byte MERGE register assists in parallelizing graphics algorithms. Like the floating-point multiplier and adder units, the 3-D graphics unit can also operate in parallel with the RISC core unit. High-level graphics functions are executed as machine level instructions in the RISC instruction set. This allows 3-D operations to execute up to ten times faster than the RISC core unit alone could manage.

The i860 views memory as a paged virtual address space of 2^{32} bytes. Data and instructions can be located anywhere within this address space, accessible as 8-, 16-, 32-, 64-, or 128-bit quantities. All address arithmetic is performed using 32-bit inputs, yielding 32-bit results. Memory access is limited to load and store instructions.

The memory management unit (MMU) performs address translation from virtual to physical addresses for both data and instructions. The i860 memory is comprised of 4 Kbyte pages with a two-level structure of page directories and page tables of 1K entries each. A virtual address refers indirectly to a physical address by specifying a page table, a page within that table, and an offset within that page. (See Figure 1.10.) The MMU also incorporates a translation look-aside Buffer (TLB), a 64-entry, 4-way set associative memory that caches translation information. The TLB spans the most recently accessed 64 pages (256 Kbytes) of the virtual memory space.

The i860 incorporates separate on-chip caches for instructions and data. Having the caches on chip saves a considerable amount of access time. The i860 aggregate

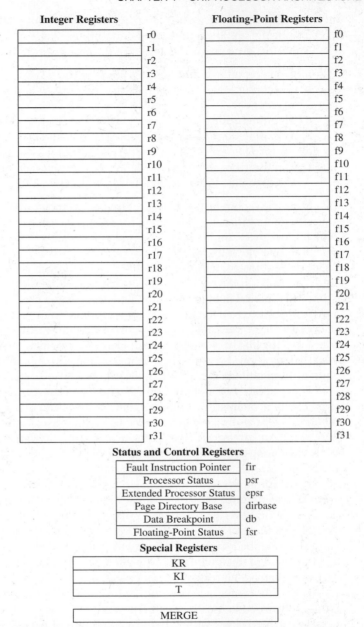

Figure 1.9 Intel i860 Register Set (Courtesy of Intel Corporation.)

transfer rate from the caches is 960 Mbytes per second at 40 MHz, a rate which would have been impossible with off-chip caches.

Instructions feed out of the 4 Kbyte, 64-bit wide instruction cache, a two-way set-associative memory with 32-byte blocks. This cache is capable of driving the CPU and the floating-point processor simultaneously through independent 32-bit instruc-

1.6 EXAMPLE SYSTEMS

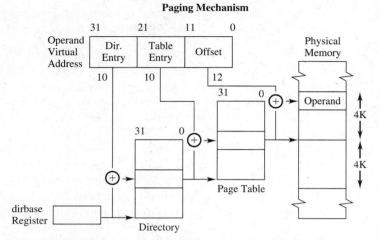

Figure 1.10 Intel i860 Virtual Address Parsing and Paging (Courtesy of Intel Corporation.)

tion buses. This is a sample of parallelism built into the i860, dual instruction mode.

Data feeds out of the 8 Kbyte, 128-bit wide data cache, a two-way set associative memory with 32 byte blocks. Besides writing data back to memory, this cache is capable of driving two long real arguments at a time to the adder, multiplier, or graphics unit. The i860 uses a write-back policy for the data cache. That is, modified cache is written to main memory only when the cache space is needed for other data. A random replacement algorithm is used to choose which line of a set of cache will be overwritten when a cache miss causes a line fetch. Similar replacement algorithms are used for the instruction cache and the address-translation cache (i.e., the TLB).

The i860 supports four data types: integer (32- and 64-bit), ordinal (32- and 64-bit unsigned), single (32-bit) and double precision (64-bit) real, and pixel (8-, 16-, or 32-bits).

The i860 supports 76 instructions. The instructions are 32 bits wide. There are three instruction formats: the REG and CTRL formats for core instructions and the floating-point instructions format.

When the floating-point adder and the floating-point multiplier are operating simultaneously, the i860 is said to be in dual operation mode. When the integer unit and either (or both) of the floating-point units are operating simultaneously, it is in dual instruction mode. The instruction set provides dual operation instructions.

As is the case for most RISCs, the i860 allows data access only through the load and store instructions; addresses are computed from the SRC1 and SRC2 fields of these instructions. SRC1 contains either the identifier of a 32-bit integer register or an immediate 16-bit address offset. SRC2 always specifies a register. Either SRC1 or SRC2 may be zero. Therefore, the following addressing modes are available:

  a. offset + register: Useful for accessing fields within a record, where register points to the beginning of the record; useful for accessing items in a stack frame where register is r3, the register used for pointing to the beginning of the stack frame

b. register: Useful as the end result of any arbitrary address calculation

c. offset: Absolute address into the first or last 32K of the logical address space

For floating-point load and store instructions, there is an auto increment addressing mode. This mode replaces SRC2 by the sum of SRC1 and SRC2 after performing the load or store. This mode is useful for array processing.

The i860 is considered very difficult to program. Because of some of the design choices made, the i860 did not achieve the close coupling of the compiler and the CPU design, a prime characteristic of all RISC architectures.

THE i860XP

In June of 1991 Intel announced i860XP, an enhanced version of the i860 running at 50 MHz. The i860XP, fabricated in Intel's three-metal process, contains over 2.5 million transistors. The major enhancements are to the cache units, the graphic unit, and the MMU.

The data and instruction caches, which are 4-way set associative and 32 bytes wide, can hold 16 Kbytes each. A line in the cache can be filled with a 4-transfer burst.

The i860XP's memory management system can mix both 4-Kbyte and 4-Mbyte pages in the same space. The 4-Kbyte page frames begin on 4-Kbyte boundaries and are fixed in size. The 4-Kbyte address transformation is compatible with that of the i386 and i486 microprocessors. This means that the i860 can share memory with the i386 or i486 processors when using the 4-Kbyte pages. The 4-Mbyte page frames are a new feature introduced in the i860XP. The 4-Mbyte pages are supported by a separate, 16-entry, 4-way set associative TLB dedicated to 4-Mbyte pages. Use of the 4-Mbyte pages will significantly improve the TLB hit rates and reduce the amount of time spent in address translation. Whether 4-Mbyte pages, 4-Kbyte pages, or some combination of the two are used, one page directory can cover the entire 4-Gbyte address space. Table 1.2 summarizes the characteristics of the i860XP.

SUPPORT CHIPS

Intel also has introduced a chip set that implements a second level cache subsystem. The chip set consists of a cache controller 82495XP and external cache static random access memories (SRAMs) 82490XP. The 82495XP provides the cache directory and control signals to the external cache SRAMs. The cache subsystem is a unified data and instruction cache that is transparent to system software. The advantages of using the subsystem include boosted performance, reduced memory bus load, speed scalability, and full multiprocessing support. The 82495XP controller can support up to 512 Kbytes of external cache SRAMs. As CPUs are added to multiprocessing systems, performance increases when the cache subsystem is used. The 82495XP subsystem also employs the same cache coherency protocol as the i860XP's on-chip caches. (Refer to Chapter 7 for details on cache coherency concepts.)

SOFTWARE

The i860 software, just like the i860 hardware, has gone through a period of significant change. Many companies are coming forward with software for the i860. This is due primarily to the major changes that were made to the hardware introduced

1.6 EXAMPLE SYSTEMS

TABLE 1.2 INTEL i860 XP CHARACTERISTICS

Clock Speed:	50 MHz
Transistor Count:	2.5 million
On-Chip Data Cache:	16 Kbyte, 4-way set associative, write-through, write-back, and write-once
On-Chip Instruction Cache:	16 Kbyte, 4-way set associative
On-Chip Memory Management Unit:	4-Kbyte and 4-Mbyte page sizes, Separate 4-way set associative TLBs
Floating Point Unit:	On-chip, IEEE floating-point
Bus:	Separate data and address buses. Data bus is 64 bit. Address bus is 32 bits
Virtual Address Size:	2^{32} bytes
Physical Address Size:	32-bits
Pipelines	
Floating Point Add:	3-Stage
Floating Point Multiply:	2- or 3-Stage

in the i860XP. Many of these changes have taken some of the bookkeeping requirements from the software and distributed it to the hardware. Probably the most significant hardware change, which has lifted some of the responsibility from the software, is the cache coherency unit described above. The following sections will chronicle just a few of the many software products that have surfaced in the last few months.

Software development tools include an assembler, linker, and debugger. C and FORTRAN compilers have a wide variety of features, including the capability for C and FORTRAN programs to call one another. The C compiler for UNIX System V Release 4 provides i860 CPU optimizations, including support for dual-operation instructions and dual instruction mode. Graphics libraries and interfaces that are supported include PHIGS, PHIGS+, and PEX. A full FORTRAN-77 math library with functions callable by FORTRAN or C is available. ANSI C functions, many written in i860 assembly language, are also provided. The i860XP contains a detached concurrency control unit that allows loop-level parallelism. This enables any application compiled with the Alliant PAX (Parallel Architecture eXtended), FORTRAN, and C compilers to run on a single or multiprocessor i860XP-based system. The Alliant compilers utilize multiprocessing system calls and hardware support for concurrency. Parallelized code optimized for i860XP is generated. This code can include instructions to the operating system describing how to schedule processors and how many processors are optimal for execution.

The only multiprocessing operating system that is currently being produced for the i860XP is multiprocessing Unix. This operating system makes use of the many hardware enhancements contained in the i860XP. Some of the enhancements that are helpful to the development of this operating system include the increase in the cache sizes, the development of a cache coherency unit, and the modified memory management unit. The multiprocessor interrupt controller chip is also of great assistance to the operating system considering the current hostile interrupt environment of the i860XP.

APPLICATIONS

The i860 has been used in a wide variety of implementations ranging from application accelerators, graphic subsystems, technical workstations to parallel supercomputers. The following paragraphs briefly describe some of these applications.

One popular use for the i860 CPU is to extend the capabilities of personal computers by adding an i860 as an applications accelerator. Because the i860 incorporates very high integer and floating-point performance, computation-intensive tasks may be off-loaded from the main processor to the i860, which may perform at levels 100 times faster. Specific applications that benefit the most include numeric or graphic intensive programs, such as imaging, 3-D modeling, or even financial analysis. Currently, there are numerous i860-based accelerators in the marketplace.

The i860's high-speed double precision floating-point capability, high bandwidth 64-bit data bus, and large numbers of floating-point registers provide capabilities that fit well the specifications of most graphics systems. The i860 can be used in single chip system implementation running both the graphics and operating system, as well as in the dedicated processor implementing the entire graphics subsystem. The Vistra 800 series workstations, built by Stardent Computer, Inc., for example, use a dedicated i860 for driving the graphics. In addition, a second i860 is utilized in high-end models to improve the graphics system further.

The balance of integer, floating-point, and graphics performance of i860 was specifically designed to meet the needs of the technical and scientific community. With i860's performance, 3-D visualization and real-time animation are possible in a price range and package size that is suitable for the desktop. As an example, the Intel workstation (i860 station), using a 40-MHz i860, is a high performance, turnkey software development platform for the i860. The Vistra 800, mentioned earlier, uses an i860 running at 40 MHz to run visualization software (numeric and graphics intensive).

Companies such as Alliant, IBM, and Intel Supercomputer Systems Division are building systems based on the i860 that match supercomputer performance at a fraction of the cost. For example, the Alliant FX parallel supercomputer uses multiple i860s to achieve its parallelism. Intel's Scientific Computer Group has developed a parallel supercomputer, called Paragon, which uses hundreds of i860s operating in parallel. The Paragon is capable of performing at rates approaching 32 GFLOPS.

1.6.3 MIPS R4000

The R4000 is the 64-bit successor to the R2000 and R3000 series of 32-bit processors from MIPS Computer Systems. There are three different versions of the chip available:

1. R4000PC (Lowest cost, 179-pin package, no secondary cache support or multiprocessor operation),
2. R4000SC (Single processor version, 447-pin package, secondary cache support), and
3. R4000MC (Full-featured 447-pin package).

1.6 EXAMPLE SYSTEMS

To achieve its 94 to 104 SPECmark rating, the R4000 utilizes on-chip floating-point capabilities, super pipelining (described later in this section), and a large cache along with the support for a large secondary cache. The internal clock speed is 100 MHz.

Table 1.3 summarizes the characteristics of the R4000, and Figure 1.11 shows the block diagram of the processor with the optional secondary cache. The input clock

TABLE 1.3 MIPS R4000 CHARACTERISTICS

Clock Speed:	50/100 MHz
Transistor Count:	1.3 million
On-Chip Data Cache:	8 Kbyte, direct mapped
On-Chip Instruction Cache:	8 Kbyte, direct mapped
Floating Point Unit:	On-chip, IEEE floating-point
Bus:	64-bit multiplexed
Virtual Address Size:	2^{64} bytes
Physical Address Size:	2^{36} bytes
Pipelines:	Floating-point Add/Multiply 4/8 stages

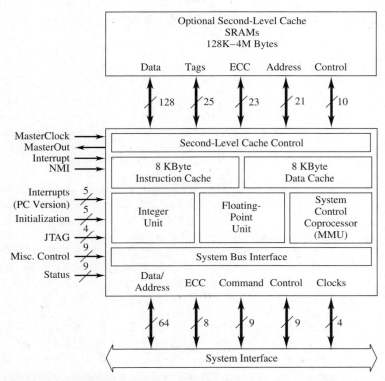

Figure 1.11 MIPS R4000 Processor (Reprinted with permission from *Microprocessor Report,* October 2, 1991.)

runs at 50 MHz. An on-chip phase-locked-loop multiplies the clock by two to produce the 100-MHz internal clock. The R4000 has three units in its internal processing configuration: integer, floating-point, and system control coprocessors. In addition, there is a separate controller for the secondary cache memory that monitors the transferring of data and instructions from the second chip.

The system coprocessor performs the controlling functions for the R4000. The address unit, program counter, and translation look-aside buffer (TLB) are held within the coprocessor, which fetches the instructions either from memory or cache, decodes them, and sends out the control signals either to the integer unit or the floating-point unit.

The integer unit has an ALU, registers, and the multiply/divide functions. This unit performs the indirect and indexing address computations and all the integer functions on the data.

The floating-point unit has its own registers for storing data, a status register, and the ability to multiply, add, divide, and do conversions and square roots.

The R4000 also has a specially designed interface control that manages the transfer of data between the processors and the rest of the system through the system interface bus. This bus allows 64-bit data and addresses to be multiplexed across the same channel. There are error correcting codes (ECC) used for the guaranty of data integrity during transfers.

The details of the R4000 bus structure are shown in Figure 1.12 with separate buses for data, secondary cache, and system interface. Each of these buses handles 64-bit data.

SUPERPIPELINING

High performance was a main goal of the R4000 processor. One definition of the performance is the average amount of time it takes a processor to complete a task. The run time R of a task containing N instructions on a processor that consumes on an average C cycles per instruction with a clock speed of T seconds per cycle is given by:

$$R = N \times C \times T$$

Thus, three factors determine the overall time to complete a task. The N is dependent upon the task, the compiler, and the skill of the programmer and therefore is not processor architecture dependent. The C and T are, however, processor dependent. The R4000 designers sought to reduce these two factors. Reduction of the T was accomplished simply through a high speed clock. The external masterclock input is 50 MHz. An on-chip phase-locked-loop multiplies this by 2 to get an internal clock speed of 100 MHz, the speed at which the pipeline runs. This 100 MHz can be divided by 2, 3, or 4 to produce interface speeds of 50, 33, or 25 MHz, thus allowing for some low end 50 MHz systems. However, the main reason for the adjustable clock speed is to make room for a 75- or 100-MHz external masterclock (150- or 200-MHz internal clock) while maintaining a 50-MHz system interface.

There are two popular techniques for reducing the C: **superpipelining** and **superscaling.** Superpipelining allows for fetching two instructions in one 50-MHz

1.6 EXAMPLE SYSTEMS

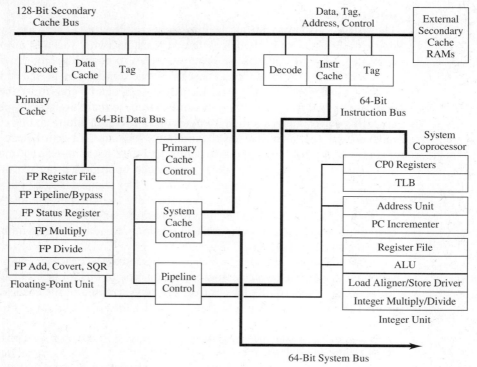

Figure 1.12 MIPS R4000 Bus Structure (Reprinted with permission from *Microprocessor Report,* October 2, 1991.)

clock cycle and then feeding them into the pipeline half a cycle apart. Superscaling also allows for multiple instructions per clock cycle but does this through multiple execution units rather than through pipelining. In order for superpipelining to work well, there must be a fast clock. In order for superscaling to work well, there must be good instruction dispatch and scoreboarding mechanisms. Because these are done in hardware, they take up a lot of chip real estate. MIPS decided that saving real estate for on-board cache is much more important.

Superpipelining techniques improve both integer and floating-point operations. Superscaling improves floating-point operation speed, but does not significantly improve integer operations speed due to the lack of parallelism in integer operations.

Superpipelining theoretically lacks scalability because current CMOS technology limits the pipeline at running twice as fast as the cache. Superscaling, however, could theoretically have an unlimited bus size and an unlimited number of execution units, and therefore, performance could be improved endlessly. In reality though, the multiple dispatch circuitry grows in complexity rapidly as one increases the dispatch multiplicity past 2. Also, the compiler complexity grows rapidly as one tries to avoid constant stalls with the multiple execution units.

Section 3.5 provides further details on R4000 pipeline operation.

CACHE MEMORY

The MIPS R4000 provides a flexible cache architecture. There are two on-chip primary caches and one off-chip secondary cache (with variable amount of storage capacity), thus allowing the tailoring of caches to particular implementations.

The instruction and the data cache are each 8 kilobytes in size and are controlled by the primary cache controller. Their line sizes can be chosen by the designer. The choices can be either 4 words or 8 words. Because there are 4 bytes per word on this chip, this corresponds to either 16 bytes or 32 bytes. In addition, this chip uses virtual indexing for the cache entries. This allows look up to begin before the address is actually translated. Both the instruction and data cache use direct mapping.

Figure 1.13 shows a typical data cache operation using 4 words per line. A physical memory of 64 gigabytes is assumed. This translates to 2^{36} physical addresses. Because the data area is 8 kilobytes and there are 16 bytes per line, the actual data area consists of 512 blocks. And because there are 2^{32} frames, $2^{32}/2^9 = 2^{23}$ frames map to each block. This makes the tag area 23 bits long. In addition, the number of addresses mapping to each block is $2^{36}/2^9 = 2^{27}$.

The optional secondary cache is connected to the processor chip via the 128-bit secondary cache bus, which contains 28 data bits, 25 bits for tag, 23 parity bits, 21 bits for addresses, and 10 bits for control. The physical area of the cache can vary in size from 128 kilobytes to 4 megabytes. Also, the line size can vary from 4, 8, 16, and 32 words.

Figure 1.14 shows a secondary cache with a line size of 4 words. The data area is 512 kilobytes. Therefore, there are $2^{19}/2^4 = 2^{15}$ blocks. The main memory is assumed to be 64 gigabytes (2^{36}). Thus, 2^{17} frames map to each block. As is the primary cache, the secondary cache is also direct mapped. But physical, instead of virtual, indexing is used.

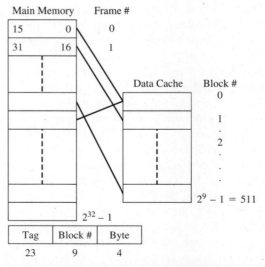

Figure 1.13 MIPS R4000 Cache Mechanism
(Courtesy of MIPS Computer Systems)

1.6 EXAMPLE SYSTEMS

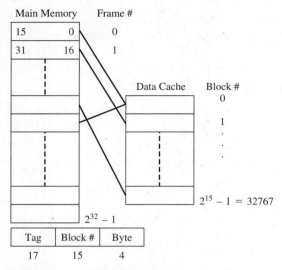

Figure 1.14 MIPS R4000 Virtual Memory (Courtesy of MIPS Computer Systems.)

VIRTUAL MEMORY

In the R4000, a 64-bit virtual address is mapped to a 36-bit physical address. Only 40 bits of the virtual address are translated. Figure 1.15 shows a virtual address configuration. The offset is 12 bits in the 4-kilobyte page size and 24 bits in the 16 megabyte page size. The page sizes can range from 4 kilobytes to 16 megabytes. The R4000 uses a translation look-aside buffer (TLB) that has 96 entries and holds the most recently referenced pages. The virtual address is broken into the page number and the displacement. The TLB checks to see if a recent translation for that page took place. If it did, then the TLB returns the address of the page and the mapping is done. A simultaneous search of the TLB and the page table are performed. If the page is in the TLB, then both searches stop.

Table 1.4 lists the characteristics of several contemporary RISC architectures. Probing further into the relative merits of these and other processors is left to the reader.

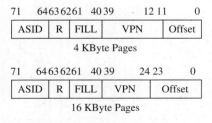

Figure 1.15 MIPS R4000 Virtual Address Configuration (Courtesy of MIPS Computer Systems.)

TABLE 1.4 CHARACTERISTICS OF CONTEMPORARY PROCESSORS

Processor	Clock frequency MHz	Execution units	Registers	On-Chip cache KBytes	Secondary cache KBytes	Instructions per cycle (Max)	SPECmarks integer	SPECmarks floating-point
DEC Alpha 21064	150, 200	IU, FPU BPU, LSU	32 64-bit GPR 32 64-bit FPR	8 INST 8 DATA	128–16000	2	84 at 150 MHz	160 at 150 MHz
MIPS R4400	75	IU, FPU	32 64-bit GPR	16 INST 16 DATA	128–4000	2	94	104
MOTOROLA PowerPC 601	50, 66	IU, FPU BPU	32 32-bit GPR 32 64-bit FPR	32 INST/ DATA	Not Applicable	3	60 at 66 MHz	80 at 66 MHz
INTEL Pentium	60, 66	2 IUs, FPU	8 32-bit FPS	8 INST 8 DATA	512	2	65 at 66 MHz	57 at 66 MHz
INTEL i860XP	50	IU, FPU GU	32 32-bit GPR	16 INST 16 DATA	Not Applicable	3	Not Available	Not Available
TEXAS INSTRUMENTS SuperSPARC	40, 50, 60	3IUs, FPU LSU	32 32-bit FPR Register File (8 Port, 8 Window)	20 INST 16 DATA	0–2000	3	76 at 60 MHz	96 At 60 MHz

IU   Integer unit   FPS   Floating-point stack   FPR   Floating-point register
FPU Floating-point unit   LSU   Load/store unit   GU   Graphics unit
BPU Branch processing unit   GPR   General purpose register

1.7 SUMMARY

The von Neumann single processor architecture was introduced in this chapter along with a review of the major enhancements made to this architecture. Details of three commercial architectures along with a listing of the major characteristics of other popular processors is given. Cost considerations and performance evaluation methods are also discussed. All these topics are necessarily brief. Refer to the books listed as references for further details. For details on latest processors and their characteristics, refer to corresponding manufacturers' manuals and magazines such as *IEEE Spectrum, IEEE Computer, EDN, Computer Design,* and *Byte*.

REFERENCES

Baer, J. L. 1980. *Computer systems architecture.* Rockwell, Md.: Computer Science Press.

Burks, A. W., H. H. Goldstine, and J. von Neumann. 1946. *Preliminary discussion of the logical design of an electrical computing instrument.* U.S. Army Ordnance Department report.

Comerford, R. 1992. How DEC developed Alpha. *IEEE Spectrum,* July.

Digital Equipment Corporation. 1992. *Alpha architecture handbook.* Maynard, Mass: Digital Equipment Corporation.

Digital Equipment Corporation. 1992. *Introduction to designing a system with the DEChip 21064 microprocessor.* Revision 1.1. Maynard, Mass: Digital Equipment Corporation.

Leibson, S. H. 1993. EDN's 20th annual microprocessor directory. EDN, November 25.

Goldstine, H. H. 1992. *The computer from Pascal to Von Neumann.* Princeton: Princeton University Press.

Flynn, M. J. 1966. *Very high speed computing systems.* Proceedings of IEEE, vol. 54, December, 1901–1909.

Hennessy, J. L. and D. A. Patterson. 1990. *Computer architecture: A quantitative approach.* San Mateo, Calif.: Morgan Kaufmann.

Hwang, K. and F. A. Briggs. 1984. *Computer architecture and parallel processing.* New York, N.Y.: McGraw-Hill.

Intel Corporation. 1990. *i860 64-Bit microprocessor hardware reference manual.* Order No. 240330-002. Beaverton, OR.

Intel Corporation. 1990. *Introducing the Intel i860 64-bit microprocessor, an innovation in power and performance.* Order No. 240438-001. Beaverton, OR.

IEEE Spectrum. 1992. Special issue on supercomputers, September.

Intel Corporation. 1990. *Overview of the i860 64-bit microprocessor.* Order No. 240888-001. Beaverton, OR.

Milutinovic, V. M. 1989. *High level language computer architecture.* New York: Computer Science Press.

Siewiorek, D. P., C. G. Bell, and A. Newell. 1982. *Computer structures: Principles and examples.* New York: McGraw-Hill.

Simpson, D. 1990. The trouble with benchmarks. *Systems Integration.* August, 37–45.

Shiva, S. G. 1991. *Computer design and architecture,* 2d ed. Glenview, Il.: HarperCollins.

Stone, H. S. 1989. *High-performance computer architecture,* 2d ed. Reading, Mass.: Addison-Wesley.

Weicker, R. P. 1990. *An overview of common benchmarks, IEEE Computer,* 23: 12, 65–75.

PROBLEMS

The following problems may require a literature search. For details on recent architectures consult magazines such as:

IEEE Computer (monthly), Los Alamitos, Calif.: IEEE Computer Society.

Byte (monthly), Peterborough, N.H.: McGraw-Hill.

Computer Design (semimonthly), Littleton, Mass.: PennWell.

1.1. Trace the history of any computer system you have access to. Describe why there is a family rather than a single machine. Trace the evolution of each feature and the reason for change as the family evolved.

1.2. Answer Problem 1.1 with respect to the following popular families of computers:
   a. Motorola 680X0 series
   b. Intel 80X86 series
   c. Digital Equipment Corporation's VAX-11
   d. International Business Machine Corporation's 370
   e. CRAY series from Cray Research Incorporated and Cray Computer Corporation
   f. Sun Microsystem's SUN workstations
   g. MIPS Computer's R3000 family

1.3. There are several coprocessors (I/O, numeric and memory management) available now. Study their characteristics and determine how they support the corresponding CPUs.

1.4. Define *von Neumann bottleneck*. To what degree has the bottleneck been minimized by the modern day structures?

1.5. There is no accepted definition of a RISC architecture to date. Trace the controversy.

1.6. Why did the following memory systems either prove to be unworkable or become obsolete?
   a. Magnetic bubble memories
   b. Magnetic drums
   c. Plated wire memories
   d. Magnetic core memories

1.7. Why did the following I/O devices become obsolete?
   a. Card reader
   b. Paper tape reader/punch
   c. Teletype

1.8. Look up the definitions of the following: *parallelism, pipelining,* and *overlapped processing.*

1.9. Look up the definitions of the following terms: *multiprogramming, multiprocessing, multitasking, batch processing,* and *time sharing.*

1.10. For each subsystem of a single processor computer system:
   a. Identify the forms of parallelism possible.
   b. List the hardware, software, and firmware support needed for each form.
   c. Identify commercially available systems that support each form.

1.11. Select a processor family you have access to and estimate the speedup obtained by using a floating-point coprocessor in the system, using an appropriate benchmark program.

1.7 SUMMARY

1.12. Show the schematic of a 16K × 16 memory system, built out of 1K × 8 memory modules using (a) high-order interleaving and (b) low-order interleaving.

1.13. Three memory chips are available with the following characteristics:

	Chip 1	Chip 2	Chip 3
Relative cost	1	2	4
Read/Write speed (clock pulses)	4	2	1

Assume that due to their low cost, a wider word-fetch scheme that fetches 4 and 2 words per cycle can be used with chips 1 and 2, respectively. Chip 3 implementation is cost effective only for single word-fetch. Also, assume that in 25% of the fetch cycles, half of the words fetched in wider word-fetch schemes are useless. Estimate the relative bandwidths of the three systems.

1.14. Assume that the cost of the CPU is 25% of the total cost of a computer system. It is possible to increase the speed of the CPU by a factor of 10 by increasing the cost also by 10 times. The CPU typically waits for I/O about 30% of the time. From a cost/performance viewpoint, is increasing the speed tenfold desirable?

CHAPTER 2

Styles of Architecture

Chapter 1 traced the evolution of architectures as enhancements to von Neumann's uniprocessor model. These enhancements employed several parallel and overlapped processing concepts. For instance, the DMA controller performing the I/O concurrent with the CPU's processing activities and the multiple functional units in the ALU subsystem operating concurrently are examples of parallel processing structures. The pipelined implementation of ALUs and control units is an example of overlapped processing structure. Although these structures enhance the performance of the computer system, it is still viewed as a serial system in the sense that the parallelism in the application is not completely exploited. That is, the hardware structures are designed to execute the application essentially in a serial mode while attaining the highest possible performance.

As mentioned in Chapter 1, there are applications that make the system throughput inadequate even with all the enhancements. The processing speed required by these applications cannot be achieved by the fastest CPU available. Therefore, newer architectures that can provide higher performance and circumvent the limits of technology have evolved. These parallel processing architectures are designed to better exploit the parallelism in the application.

This chapter introduces parallel processing concepts, terminology, and architectures at a gross level of detail. Subsequent chapters of this book provide further details on each of these architectures.

With the evolution of architectures, several architecture classification schemes (**taxonomies**) have also evolved. The intention of this chapter is not to cover the variety of taxonomies but to utilize a small set of those to introduce the most common architectures. The popular taxonomy due to Flynn (1960) is introduced first. Because this taxonomy does not adequately address many of the parallel processing structures that have now evolved, two extensions to Flynn's taxonomy are used to provide the framework for the description of popular architectures.

The next section introduces basic models for parallel processing and associated terminology. Section 2 introduces Flynn's taxonomy. Sections 3 and 4 introduce extensions to Flynn's taxonomy.

2.1 PARALLEL PROCESSING MODELS AND TERMINOLOGY

Chapter 1 considered uniprocessor architectures that have essentially a **single instruction stream** (i.e., a single control unit bringing about a serial instruction execution) operating upon a **single data stream** (i.e., a single unit of data being operated upon at any given time). Various enhancements were made to each of the subsystems of the uniprocessor system to enhance its performance. Another obvious way of increasing the performance is to use components from the fastest hardware technology available in the implementation of these subsystems.

Computer structures with multiple processors (CPU and one or more coprocessors) have now become practical. Because all the processors in such structures operate simultaneously, they are in a sense **parallel processing** architectures. The motivation behind these architectures is the enhancement of the throughput of the system by dedicating each processor to a particular function for which it is designed and by operating as many processors simultaneously as possible. Such partitioning of the application at hand is fairly straightforward; but tailoring the architecture to take advantage of the parallelism in the application itself offers a better cost-to-performance ratio.

2.1.1 Effect of Application on the Architecture

Suppose that the application allows the development of processing algorithms with a degree of parallelism A. The **degree of parallelism** is simply the number of computations that can be executed concurrently. Furthermore, if the language used to code the algorithm allows the representation of algorithms with a degree of parallelism L, the compilers produce an object code that retains a degree of parallelism C, and the hardware structure of the machine has a degree of parallelism H. Then, for the processing to be most efficient, the following relation must be satisfied:

$$H \geq C \geq L \geq A. \tag{2.1}$$

Here the objective is to minimize the computation time of the application at hand, which means that the processing structure that offers the least computation time is the most efficient one.

For the architecture to be most efficient, the development of the application algorithms, programming languages, compiler, operating system, and hardware structures must proceed together. This mode of development is only possible for a few special purpose applications. In the development of general purpose architectures, however, the application characteristics cannot be easily taken into account. But the development of other components should proceed concurrently as far as possible.

Development of algorithms with a high degree of parallelism is application dependent and basically a human endeavor. A great deal of research has been devoted to developing languages that contain parallel processing constructs, thereby enabling the coding of parallel algorithms. Compilers for these parallel processing languages retain the parallelism expressed in the source code during the compilation process, thus producing parallel object code. Also, compilers that extract parallelism from a serial program (thus producing a parallel object code) have been developed. Progress in hardware technology has yielded a large number of hardware structures that can be used in executing parallel code. Subsequent chapters of this book provide details of such parallel architectures along with pertinent programming language and compiler concepts.

2.1.2 Application Characteristics

In order to obtain the best possible performance from a parallel processing system, the application at hand should be partitioned into a set of **tasks** that can be executed concurrently. Each task accomplishes a part of the overall computation and typically requires some sort of communication (i.e., to transmit results, to request or provide data items that may be common to both tasks, etc.) with other tasks during execution.

In evaluating the performance of such implementations, four application characteristics are generally considered important:

1. granularity,
2. degree of parallelism,
3. level of parallelism, and
4. data dependency.

The **granularity** of an application module (task) is a function of R, the run time (execution time) of the task, and C, the communication time of the task, with other tasks. If R is large compared to C, the task granularity is said to be **coarse (large).** A coarse-grained task has the least communication overhead, and tasks in a coarse-grained application spend the most amount of time performing useful computations and the least amount of time communicating with each other. For **fine-grained** tasks, C dominates R; that is, the task performs a small amount of computation before requiring communication with other tasks. A **medium-grained** task is the compromise between the above two extremes.

The **degree of parallelism** (defined earlier) exhibited by the application is a measure of the number of **threads** of computation that can be carried out simultaneously.

The **level of parallelism** in a way dictates the granularity. The following levels (with decreasing granularity) are typically considered:

a. procedure level,
b. task level,
c. instruction level,
d. operation level, and
e. microcode level.

2.1 PARALLEL PROCESSING MODELS AND TERMINOLOGY

Here, the assumption is that the application is composed of several procedures that can be executed in parallel, thus resulting in procedure level parallelism. Each application is considered to have multiple tasks, which can be executed in parallel. Instruction level parallelism allows the concurrent execution of instructions in a given task. An instruction is composed of several operations.

EXAMPLE 2.1

The instruction

$$F = A * B + C * D, \qquad (2.2)$$

consists of two multiplication, one addition, and one assignment operations. Each operation is brought about by a set of micro-operations (microcode).

The order in which the procedure and task levels occur in the above list is sometimes reversed in the literature because there is no well-accepted *inclusion* between procedures and tasks. Furthermore, some do not distinguish between instruction and operation levels. In general, the microcode level of parallelism does not interest an application designer, but it does interest the hardware and microcode designer.

Consider again the computation in (2-2). Here, the two multiplications can be performed in parallel if two processors are available. However, the addition cannot be performed until the multiplications are completed and the assignment operation cannot be performed until the addition is complete. Even if the architecture has four processors available, the maximum number of processors that can be utilized concurrently for this application is two (i.e., the degree of parallelism is 2) because of the **precedence constraints** between the operations. These constraints are obeyed automatically in a single processor system because only one operation is executed at a time. When the application is split into several tasks to be implemented on a multiple processor system, a task requiring a data item will have to wait until another task producing it has indeed produced that item. If several tasks are updating a (shared) variable, the update sequence should be such that the result is the same as that which would be obtained when the application is executed by a single processor system. **Data dependencies** are the result of precedence constraints between operations (tasks or procedures) imposed by the application. Data dependencies also affect the granularity and the degree of parallelism of the application.

2.1.3 Performance

The main objective of multiple processor architectures is to minimize the computation time (i.e., to maximize the throughput of the system) of an application. Ideally, a computer system with N processors should provide a throughput of N times that of a single processor system. This requires that the degree of parallelism of the application is at most N.

In practice, the communication between tasks (due to data dependencies), allocation of tasks to processors, and control of the execution of multiple tasks generate considerable overhead. Hence, the N-fold speedup mentioned above is not possible in general.

There are applications, however, that can be partitioned such that there is no communication between tasks. These are called **trivially parallel** applications. If the system structure minimizes the task creation and execution overhead, an N-fold throughput can be achieved for these applications.

One obvious way of reducing the overhead is to partition the application into tasks with as large a granularity as possible. Although this minimizes the communication and task management overhead, it reduces the degree of parallelism because there are now fewer tasks that can be executed concurrently. To maximize the degree of parallelism, the application must be partitioned into as large a number of fine grain tasks as possible. This increases the execution overhead, and a compromise is needed between the granularity and the degree of parallelism to maximize the throughput of the system.

The above discussion assumes that throughput enhancement is the objective in building parallel architectures. Another common objective is to maximize the hardware utilization. In this context, the efficiency of the system is measured by the percentage of time during which all the processors are busy.

2.1.4 Processing Paradigms

There are a variety of ways in which an application can be modeled. The following are the most general ones:

1. completely serial,
2. serial-parallel-serial without data dependencies, and
3. serial-parallel-serial with data dependencies.

Figure 2.1 shows the model of a **completely serial** application. Here the degree of parallelism is 1. In (a) the application is implemented as a single task utilizing a single processor. The total computation performed (i.e., the total number of instructions or operations) by the task is W. In (b) the task is implemented as P sequential subtasks each performing a part (W_i) of the work W. Thus the total work is the sum of the work performed by the subtasks:

$$W = \sum_{i=1}^{P} W_i. \tag{2.3}$$

The latter model is useful when the task needs to be spread over multiple processors due to resource limitations of the individual processor in the system.

Figure 2.2 shows the **serial-parallel-serial** (without data dependencies) model. Here the first subtask initiates the computational task and spawns $P - 2$ subtasks. These subtasks are executed independently, and the results are combined by the last subtask. The total work W is now performed by P subtasks with $P - 2$ of them executing concurrently. This is the case of the so-called **easy** (or **trivial**) **parallelism** because the $P - 2$ subtasks can execute to completion once they are spawned. This

2.1 PARALLEL PROCESSING MODELS AND TERMINOLOGY

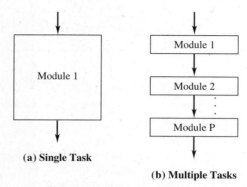

Figure 2.1 Completely Serial Application

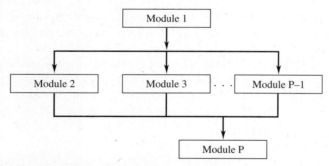

Figure 2.2 Serial-Parallel-Serial Application

model can also be viewed as a **supervisor/worker** model where task 1, the supervisor, spawns the $P-2$ worker tasks. The results produced by these workers are collected by the supervisor (as task P). The overhead introduced by this model is due to spawning and subtask creation, subtask allocation to processors, and orderly termination of the $P - 2$ subtasks. This model is ideal for applications that can be partitioned into subtasks with no data dependency between them. That is, the data structure is also partitioned such that each subtask has its own independent data to operate upon. There is no sharing of data between the concurrent subtasks.

Figure 2.3 shows the **serial-parallel-serial with data dependencies** model. Here subtasks communicate with each other passing messages to resolve data depen-

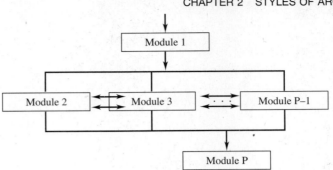

Figure 2.3 Serical-Parallel-Serial-Application with Data Dependencies

dencies. Typically, the processor executing the subtask can continue its processing for a while once a request for a data item is sent out. If the requested data does not arrive, the processor waits for it instead of switching to another task in order to minimize task switching overhead. This is also called the **communication-bound** model.

It is important to note that an application might exhibit all the above modes of computation in practice. An application can be partitioned into several procedures where the set of procedures might fit one of the above models. Each procedure in turn may be partitioned into tasks that again would fit one of the three models and so on. Such partitioning is obviously influenced by the architecture of the underlying hardware.

Several other parallel processing paradigms have evolved along with appropriate architectures over the years. The most common ones are described further in this and subsequent chapters starting with Flynn's taxonomy.

2.2 FLYNN'S TAXONOMY

Before providing the details of Flynn's taxonomy, it is interesting to examine the need for taxonomies, or classification schemes. Skillcorn (1988) provides three reasons for the classification of computer architectures:

1. The classification can answer questions such as what kind of parallelism is employed, which architecture has the best prospect for the future, and what has already been achieved by the architecture in terms of the particular characteristics one is interested in.
2. The classification reveals possible configurations that might not otherwise have occurred to the system architect. It allows a formal examination of possible design alternatives once the existing architectures have been classified.
3. The classification allows the building of useful models of performance thereby revealing the potential of a particular architecture for improvement in performance.

A taxonomy is usually based on one or more pertinent characteristics of the systems that are being classified. For example, Milutinovic (1989) combines the

2.2 FLYNN'S TAXONOMY

taxonomies by Treleaven (1982) and Myers (1982) to arrive at the following taxonomy based on what *drives* the computational flow of the architecture:

1. **Control-driven (control-flow) architectures**
   a. Reduced instruction set computers (RISC)
   b. Complex instruction set computers (CISC)
   c. High-level language architectures (HLL)
2. **Data-driven (data-flow) architectures**
3. **Demand-driven (reduction) architectures**

In **control-driven** or **control-flow architectures,** the instruction sequence (i.e., the program) guides the processing activity. The flow of computation is determined by the instruction sequence, and data are gathered as and when an instruction needs them. All architectures introduced in Chapter 1 and all commercial architectures to date belong to this category. Chapters 3 through 6 concentrate on this class of architectures.

A **data-driven** or **data-flow architecture** is controlled by the readiness of data. An instruction is executed (i.e., the control activity is invoked) when the data required by that instruction are ready to be operated upon. These experimental architectures are introduced later in this chapter and described further in Chapter 7.

In **reduction** or **demand-driven architectures,** an instruction is enabled for execution when its results are required as operands for another instruction that has already been enabled for execution. These experimental architectures are described further later in this chapter.

Flynn's taxonomy is based on the degree of parallelism exhibited by an architecture in its data and control flow mechanisms. He divides computer architectures into four main classes based on the number of instruction and data streams, as shown in Figure 2.4:

1. Single instruction stream, single data stream (SISD) machines, which are single processor systems (uniprocessor).
2. Single instruction stream, multiple data stream (SIMD) architectures, which are systems with multiple arithmetic-logic processors and a single control processor. Each arithmetic-logic processor processes a data stream of its own as directed by the single control processor. This classification includes **array processors.**
3. Multiple instruction stream, single data stream (MISD) machines in which the single data stream is simultaneously acted upon by a multiple instruction

		Data Stream	
		Single	Multiple
Instruction Stream	Single	SISD Uniprocessor	SIMD Array Processor
	Multiple	MISD Pipelined Processor?	MIMD Multiple Processor

Figure 2.4 Flynn's Architecture Classification

stream. This classification is considered an aberration because it is not practical to implement such an architecture. (Note that in pipelined processors multiple instruction streams exist. If the definition of the single data stream is stretched to include the conglomeration of all the data elements in pipeline stages, then pipelined processors fit this classification.)

4. Multiple instruction stream, multiple data stream (MIMD) machines, which contain multiple processors, each executing its own instruction stream to process the data stream allocated to it (i.e., a **multiprocessor system**). A computer system with a central processor and an I/O processor working in parallel is the simplest example of an MIMD architecture.

Chapter 1 provides the details of SISD architectures. Models for SIMD and MIMD classifications are provided below and further details on these architectures are provided in subsequent chapters.

2.2.1 SIMD

Figure 2.5 shows the structure of a typical SIMD machine. There are n arithmetic-logic processors (P_1 through P_n), each with its own memory block (M_1 through M_n). The individual memory blocks combined constitute the system memory. A bus is used to transfer instructions and data to the control processor (CP) from the memory blocks. The control processor decodes instructions and sends control signals to processors P_1 through P_n.

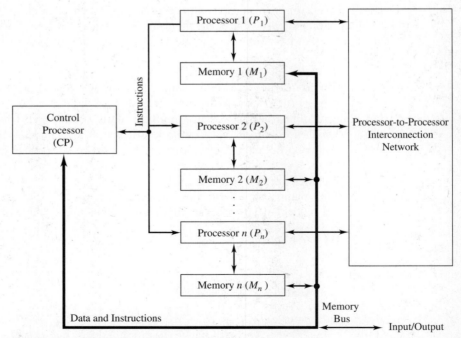

Figure 2.5 SIMD Structure

The control processor, in practice, is a full-fledged uniprocessor. It retrieves instructions from memory, sends arithmetic-logic instructions to processors, and executes control instructions (branch, stop, etc.) itself. Processors P_1 through P_n execute the same instruction, each on its own data stream. Based on arithmetic-logic conditions, some of the processors may be deactivated during certain instructions. Such activation and deactivation of processors is handled either by the control processor or by the logic local to each arithmetic processor.

Some computations on SIMD require that the data be exchanged between arithmetic processors. The processor interconnection network enables such data exchange. Chapters 5 and 6 provide further details on such networks.

The most important characteristic of SIMDs is that the arithmetic processors are synchronized at the instruction level. That is, they execute programs in a *lock-step* mode, where each processor has its own data stream. Hence this architecture is also called **data parallel architecture.**

SIMDs are special purpose machines albeit with a wide variety of suitable applications. They are called **array processors** because computations involving arrays of data are natural targets for this class of architecture. (Note that the term *array processor* has been used to describe architectures with an array of processors even though these processors are not synchronized at the instruction level.)

EXAMPLE 2.2

Consider the computation of the column sum of a matrix. Each column of the matrix can be assigned to one of the n arithmetic processors of an SIMD. The column sums of an $N \times N$ matrix can then be computed in N steps (where, $N \leq n$), rather than in N^2 steps required on an SISD machine.

As illustrated by the above example, SIMD systems can provide an n-fold speedup as long as the processing algorithm exhibits a high degree of parallelism at the instruction level.

ILLIAC-IV and Goodyear Aerospace's STARAN are SIMDs of historic interest. Thinking Machine Corporation's Connection Machine (models 1 and 2) and Maspar Corporation's MP series are examples of commercially available SIMDs.

Section 3 describes some variations of the above SIMD model, and Chapter 5 provides further details on SIMD machines.

2.2.2 MIMD

Figure 2.6 shows an MIMD structure consisting of p memory blocks, n processing elements, and m input/output channels.

The processor-to-memory interconnection network enables the connection of a processor to any of the memory blocks. Because all the memory blocks are accessible by all the processors, this is known as the **shared memory** MIMD architecture. Ideally, p should be greater than or equal to n and the interconnection network should allow p simultaneous connections in order that all the processors are kept busy. In addition, it should be possible to change these connections dynamically as the computation proceeds.

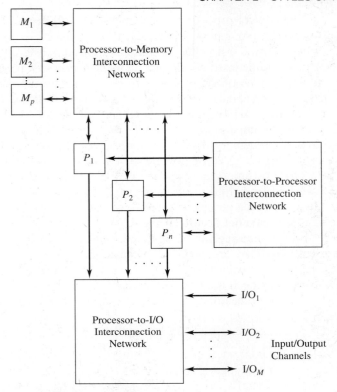

Figure 2.6 MIMD Structure

The processor-to-I/O interconnection network enables the connection of any I/O channel to any of the processors.

The processor-to-processor interconnection network is an interrupt network to facilitate data exchange between the processors. A processor generating data places them in the memory and interrupts the processor that requires that data through this network.

EXAMPLE 2.3

Consider the computation of the column sum of an $N \times N$ matrix. This can be partitioned into N tasks. The program to accumulate the elements in a column and the corresponding data form a task. Each task is assigned to a processor in the MIMD. If the MIMD contains N processors, all the N tasks can be performed simultaneously, thus completing the computation in N steps, rather than the N^2 steps needed by an SISD. If the number of processors p is less than N, p tasks are performed simultaneously in one cycle, requiring N/p such cycles to complete the computation. Tasks are assigned to processors as they become free after completing the task currently assigned to them. There is a considerable amount of coordination overhead required to execute tasks in this manner.

MIMDs offer the following advantages:

1. A high throughput can be achieved if the processing can be broken into parallel streams, thereby keeping all the processors active concurrently.
2. Because the processors and memory blocks are general purpose resources, a faulty resource can be easily removed and its work allocated to another available resource, thereby achieving a degree of fault tolerance.
3. A dynamic reconfiguration of resources is possible to accommodate varying processing loads.

MIMDs are more general purpose in application than SIMDs, but they are harder to program. The processors in an MIMD are not synchronized at instruction level as in an SIMD. But it is required that the processing algorithm exhibits a high degree of parallelism so that it can be partitioned into independent subtasks that can be allocated to processors concurrently.

Some issues of concern in the design of an MIMD system are:

1. Processor scheduling: efficient allocation of processors to tasks in a dynamic fashion as the computation progresses.
2. Processor synchronization: prevention of processors trying to change a unit of data simultaneously and obeying the precedence constraints in data manipulation.
3. Interconnection network design: Processor-to-memory and processor-to-processor interconnection networks are probably the most expensive elements of the system. Because of cost considerations, almost all MIMDs to date have not used a processor-to-I/O network, rather they dedicate I/O devices to processors.
4. Overhead: ideally an n processor system should provide n times the throughput of a uniprocessor. This is not true in practice because of the overhead processing required to coordinate the activities between the various processors and to resolve the contention for resources (such as memory and interconnection network).
5. Partitioning: Identifying parallelism in processing algorithms to invoke concurrent processing streams is not a trivial problem.

Several experimental MIMD systems have been built. Carnegie Mellon University's C.mmp and Cm*, New York University's Ultracomputer, University of Illinois's Cedar are some examples. Some popular commercial MIMD systems are BBN Butterfly, Alliant FX series, Thinking Machine Corporation's CM-5, and Intel Corporation's iPSc series. Many new MIMD systems are being introduced every year.

Section 3 describes other common models of MIMD machines, and Chapter 6 provides further details.

It is important to note that Flynn's architecture classification is not unique in the sense that a computer system may not clearly belong to one of the three classes. For example, the Cray series of supercomputers can be classified under all three classes based on their operating modes at a given time.

Although Flynn's taxonomy provides an initial framework for classification of architectures, it does not distinguish between the variety of SIMD and MIMD architectures proposed recently. The following sections describe the two most recent extensions to Flynn's taxonomy that accommodate some of the recent architectures.

2.3 SKILLCORN'S TAXONOMY

A computer system can be modeled at several levels of detail. Skillcorn (1988) considers the following levels:

a. Computation model: This is the most abstract level in which the primitive operations are the standard arithmetic and logic operations and the correct computational behavior is enforced by the programmer via the program. This level does not provide any insight into the structural details of the system.
b. Abstract machine model: This depicts the first level implementation of the computational model. It captures the essence of a particular architecture form for the computation model without distinguishing technologies and other implementation details. This is the programmer's level of description of the architecture in terms of various registers, arithmetic logic units, and other resources in the architecture.
c. Performance model: This level presents a logical structural view of the architecture in terms of the state transition structure of the machine. It need not necessarily concern only the technology used in the implementation of the machine.
d. Implementation model: This level reflects the actual implementation details in terms of technology used, speed characteristics, and so forth.

The abstract machine model forms the top level in Skillcorn's taxonomy, and the performance model forms the second (more detailed) level. This taxonomy uses four types of functional units to construct an abstract machine:

1. Instruction processor (IP), a functional unit that interprets the instructions (i.e., the control unit)
2. Data processor (DP), a functional unit that transforms data through arithmetic logic operations (i.e., the ALU)
3. A memory hierarchy that stores data (i.e., data memory—DM) and instructions (i.e. instruction memory—IM)
4. A switch that provides the connectivity between the functional units (i.e., the interconnection network)

Skillcorn's taxonomy classifies architectures at two levels of increasing detail. The first level classifies an architecture based on the following: the number of IPs, DPs, IMs, and DMs; the type of switch connecting IPs and IMs, DPs and DMs, IPs and DPs, and DPs to DPs. This level refines Flynn's SIMD and MIMD classifications. The second level refines the first level by specifying whether or not the processors can be pipelined and to what degree and by providing the state diagram for the processor.

2.3 SKILLCORN'S TAXONOMY

TABLE 2.1 POSSIBLE ARCHITECTURES (SKILLCORN, 1988). (REPRODUCED WITH PERMISSION FROM IEEE.)

Class	IPs	DPs	IP-DP	IP-IM	DP-DM	DP-DP	Name
1	0	1	none	none	1-1	none	reduct/dataflow uniprocessor
2	0	n	none	none	n-n	none	separate machines
3	0	n	none	none	n-n	n × n	loosely coupled reduct/dataflow
4	0	n	none	none	n × n	none	tightly coupled reduct/dataflow
5	0	n	none	none	n × n	n × n	
6	1	1	1-1	1-1	1-1	none	von Neumann uniprocessor
7	1	n	1-n	1-1	n-n	none	
8	1	n	1-n	1-1	n-n	n × n	Type 1 array processor
9	1	n	1-n	1-1	n × n	none	Type 2 array processor
10	1	n	1-n	1-1	n × n	n × n	
11	n	1	1-n	n-n	1-1	none	
12	n	1	1-n	n × n	1-1	none	
13	n	n	n-n	n-n	n-n	none	separate von Neumann uniprocessors
14	n	n	n-n	n-n	n-n	n × n	loosely coupled von Neumann
15	n	n	n-n	n-n	n × n	none	tightly coupled von Neumann
16	n	n	n-n	n-n	n × n	n × n	
17	n	n	n-n	n × n	n-n	none	
18	n	n	n-n	n × n	n-n	n × n	
19	n	n	n-n	n × n	n × n	none	Denelcor Heterogeneous Element Processor
20	n	n	n-n	n × n	n × n	n × n	
21	n	n	n × n	n-n	n-n	none	
22	n	n	n × n	n-n	n-n	n × n	
23	n	n	n × n	n-n	n × n	none	
24	n	n	n × n	n-n	n × n	n × n	
25	n	n	n × n	n × n	n-n	none	
26	n	n	n × n	n × n	n-n	n × n	
27	n	n	n × n	n × n	n × n	none	
28	n	n	n × n	n × n	n × n	n × n	

Table 2.1 shows the set of possible architectures with the restriction that the number of memories match the number of processors in each subsystem. Classes 1 through 5 are reduction/dataflow architectures that will be described further in this Section; Class 6 is an SISD; Classes 7 through 10 are SIMDs; Classes 11 and 12 can be considered MISDs although this architecture type is considered an aberration; and Classes 13 through 20 are conventional MIMDs with various types of interconnection schemes. Classes 21 through 28 are MIMD classes that are still unexplored.

This taxonomy thus extends Flynn's taxonomy by enhancing the discrimination between different kinds of parallel architectures. It captures the differences between architectures and reveals underlying relationships, if any. It also suggests other possible architectures for future exploration. More detailed treatment of common architectures as viewed by this taxonomy follows.

2.3.1 SISD

Figure 2.7 shows the abstract machine level model of an SISD architecture using the above functional units. The IP determines the label (address) of the instruction in the instruction memory (IM) to be fetched next, fetches the instruction, decodes it and

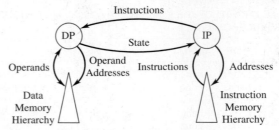

Figure 2.7 Skillcorn's Abstract Level Representation of an SISD (Skillcorn, 1988) (Reproduced with permission from IEEE.)

informs the DP of the operation required, determines the addresses of the operands and passes them to the DP, and receives the state information (condition codes) after the completion of the operations. The DP receives the instruction type and the operand addresses from the IP, instructs the memory hierarchy to provide the data values, receives and transforms the data values, returns the results to the memory hierarchy, and provides state information to the IP. Separate instruction and data memory hierarchies are shown in this model. The function of the memory hierarchy is to retain the next piece of data required by the processor attached to it at the topmost level where the access time is the smallest. The pyramid structure of memory hierarchy thus depicts the standard memory hierarchy in which the data stored closest to the processor has the smallest access time and that farthest from the processor will have the largest access time. A switch-type functional unit is not needed for the SISD model.

Figure 2.8 shows the implementation level details of the SISD structure. In (a) the operation of the IP is depicted in the form of a state diagram, thereby implying the specific sequence in which the IP performs its functions. Similarly, (b) shows the sequence of operations of the DP. The dotted arrows on these state diagrams indicate

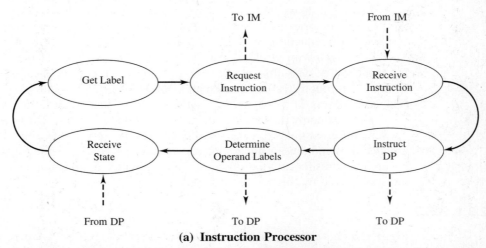

Figure 2.8 Internal Structure of SISD (Skillcorn, 1988) (Reproduced with permission from IEEE.)

2.3 SKILLCORN'S TAXONOMY

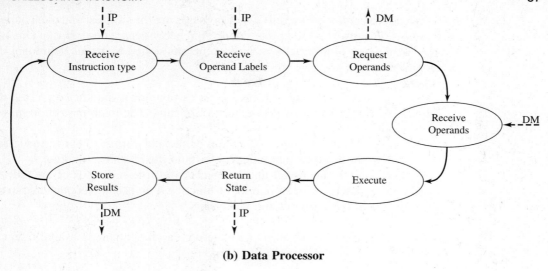

(b) Data Processor

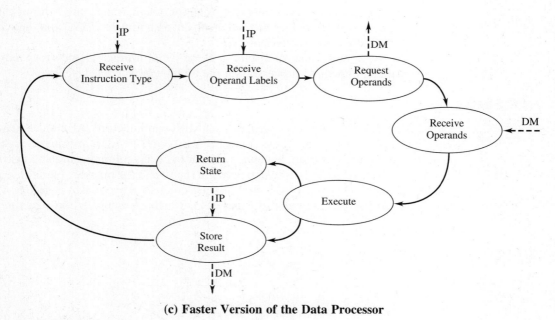

(c) Faster Version of the Data Processor

Figure 2.8 (cont.)

the communications between the functional unit and the other facilities in the model. The communication is synchronous; that is, a token must be present on the state at the beginning and at the end of the communication path for communication to take place and neither token can leave that state until the communication is complete. The state diagram of DP in (b) can be modified to perform two operations (return state, store result) in parallel as shown in (c) in order to enhance the performance of the DP.

Connections between functional units are brought about either by **dynamic** (i.e., interconnections can be altered during the execution as needed) or by **static** (i.e., interconnections cannot be altered) switches. Buses are the simplest and most popular interconnection networks. Other interconnection networks are described in Chapters 5 and 6. Four types of abstract switches can be envisioned to model functional unit interconnections:

1. 1-to-1: A functional unit in one set of functional units is connected to a single unit in another set of functional units. The interconnection may be unidirectional or bidirectional.
2. n-to-n: This is a 1-to-1 connection duplicated n times. That is, the ith unit of one set of functional units connects to the ith unit of another.
3. 1-to-n: One functional unit connects to all the n devices of another set.
4. n-by-n: Each device of one set of functional units can be connected to any device in the other set and vice versa.

The performance of the SISD architecture can be enhanced by the following methods:

a. Optimizing state diagrams such that the token transit time through the diagram is shorter. This method results in an optimized SISD and thus does not yield a new architecture type.
b. Allowing more than one state to be active at a time. This corresponds to utilizing pipelined processors in the architecture.

2.3.2 SIMD

Figure 2.9 shows three top level models for a SIMD architecture. All models have a 1-to-n switch connecting the single control processor (IP) with n arithmetic processors (DPs). In (a) there is a single memory hierarchy (i.e., common data and instruction memory). There is a 1-to-n switch between the IP and the memory hierarchy, and the DP to memory switch is n-to-n. The DPs are connected by an n-by-n switch. This corresponds to the SIMD model of Figure 2.5, which also depicts the structure of

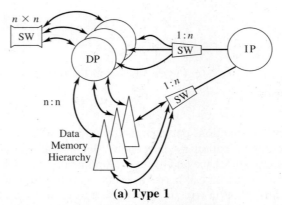

(a) **Type 1**

Figure 2.9   SIMD Models (Skillcorn, 1988) (Reproduced with permission from IEEE.)

2.3 SKILLCORN'S TAXONOMY

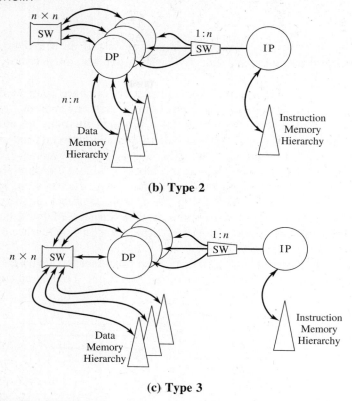

(b) Type 2

(c) Type 3

Figure 2.9 (cont.)

ILLIAC-IV. The DPs in ILLIAC-IV are actually connected by a torus, or mesh, network in which there is no n-by-n physical interconnection. But it is possible to exchange data between all the n DPs by repeated use of the interconnection network, and hence, it is an n-by-n switch. In (b) and (c), separate instruction (IM) and data memory (DM) hierarchies are shown. The IP to IM interconnection is thus 1-to-1.

In (b), the DP interconnections are n-by-n and the DP to DM interconnections are n-to-n. This model depicts the structure of Thinking Machine Corporation's Connection Machine. The Connection Machine uses a hypercube network between the DPs. It is not physically an n-by-n interconnection scheme but allows data exchange between all n DPs by repeated use of the network and hence logically is an n-by-n switch.

In (c), there is no direct connection between DPs and the interconnection between DM and DPs is n-by-n. This model depicts the structure of Burroughs Scientific Processor (BSP). The DP-DM switch BSP is known as a data alignment network because it allows each DP to be connected to its data stream by dynamically changing the switch settings. Note that if the DP-DM switch is n-to-n, as in (a) and (b) above, data has to be moved into appropriate memory elements to allow access from the corresponding DP.

Chapter 5 provides further details on SIMD architectures.

2.3.3 MIMD

Figure 2.10 shows the two common models of an MIMD system: **tightly-coupled (shared memory)** and **loosely-coupled (private, or distributed, memory)** architectures.

In a tightly-coupled system the processors are connected to memories through a dynamic switch. Any processor can access any memory location with the same latency in general. Hence, this is a **uniform memory access (UMA)** architecture. Here, the communication and synchronization between processes running on processors is achieved through shared variables. This corresponds to the MIMD structure of Figure 2.6 except that the memory blocks in Figure 2.6 were not partitioned into DMs and IMs. A memory block can contain instructions, data, or both. The processor running a task is connected to the appropriate block of the memory depending on whether it is fetching instructions or data. Carnegie Mellon University's C.mmp, BBN Butterfly, and Alliant Computer Corporation's FX series are examples of this MIMD structure.

In loosely coupled systems, each processor has its own local (private) memory. Communication between processors is brought about by an explicit request from one

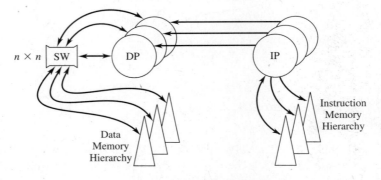

(a) Tightly-Coupled

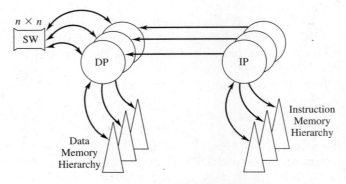

(b) Loosely-Coupled

Figure 2.10 MIMD Models (Skillcorn, 1988) (Reproduced with permission from IEEE.)

2.3 SKILLCORN'S TAXONOMY

processor to another in the form of a message over the interconnection network. These are called **message passing** architectures. Because the memory access time is not uniform across all the processors, these are **nonuniform memory access** (NUMA) architectures. Examples of this type of architecture are Carnegie Mellon University's Cm* and Intel's iPSc.

The advantage of the shared memory structures is the ease of programming due to their common or **shared address space.** The scalability of the architecture is limited by the memory bandwidth and the memory contention problems. The private memory architectures offer better scalability because each processor environment is strictly local so additional processors can be easily added. The nonuniform memory access time presents a problem.

The memory address space in a private memory MIMD can be either private or shared; that is, a **private-address-space** architecture has a distinct address space corresponding to each (local) memory. In a **common-address-space** architecture, on the other hand, the global address space is partitioned among the local memories. This architecture offers the programming ease of the shared memory architectures while retaining the scalability characteristics of message-passing MIMDs. Some examples of this architecture type are the J-machine of MIT and Stanford's DASH. The J-machine has small private memory attached to each of a large number of processors and, yet, has a common address space across the whole machine. The DASH considers local memory as a cache for a large global address space, but the global memory is actually distributed.

Chapter 6 provides further details on MIMD architectures.

2.3.4 Reduction Architectures

Figure 2.11 shows the abstract machine model for a reduction machine, a demand-driven architecture. In a reduction architecture, the computation is organized in the form of a graph such that the root node is an *apply,* the left subtree is the *description of a function,* and the right subtree is a *description of the arguments.* The description could be just the value or a description of how to obtain the value. A *redex* is a subtree in which the function and the argument have already been evaluated. When a redex is executed, the resulting value replaces the redex. In general, *several* redexes would be available for execution starting at the leaves of the tree. Hence, multiple processors can be used to evaluate them concurrently. If no redex is available, then the computa-

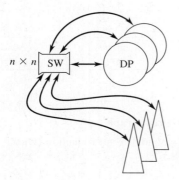

Figure 2.11 Graph Reduction Machine Model (Skillcorn, 1988) (Reproduced with permission from IEEE.)

tion cannot proceed. Because the graph being reduced plays the role of both instructions (in its structure) and data (in its contents), no separate IP is needed and the abstract machine model is that of a tightly coupled MIMD without IPs and IMs.

Reduction architectures employ either a **string** or a **graph** reduction scheme. In string reduction, literals and copies of data values are represented as strings that can be expanded or contracted in a dynamic fashion. In graph reduction, literals and pointers to data values are manipulated. In this scheme, the program is represented as a graph, the memory allocation is dynamic, and the memory locations vacated due to reduction are reclaimed and join the available memory pool.

EXAMPLE 2.4

Figure 2.12(a) shows the graph representation corresponding to the following computation (Duncan 1990):

$$a = (d + e) + (f * g)$$

where $d = 1, e = 3, f = 5,$ and $g = 7.$

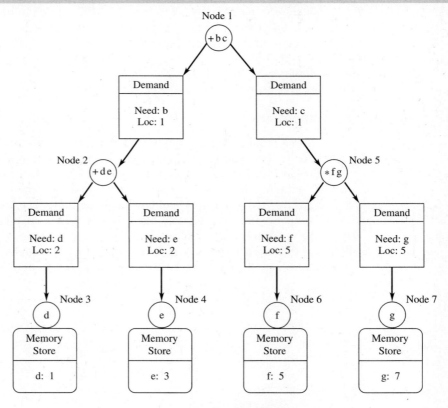

(a) Original Graph

Figure 2.12 Reduction Architecture Demand Token Production (Duncan, 1990) (Reproduced with permission from IEEE.)

2.3 SKILLCORN'S TAXONOMY

> Node 1 creates demands for the execution of nodes 2 and 5. The demands propagate down from these nodes to the leaves of the tree, which propagate results toward their parent nodes 2 and 5. Nodes 2 and 5 are the roots of two redexes. The system state after the execution of these redexes is shown in Figure 2.12(b). The values now propagate to the root node 1 where the value for a is computed.

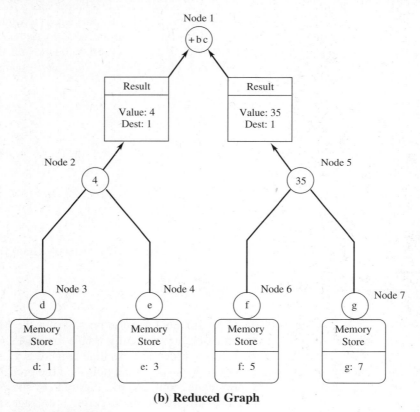

(b) Reduced Graph

Figure 2.12 (cont.)

Some examples of experimental reduction architectures are the reduction machine efforts at Newcastle University, the Cellular Tree Machine of North Carolina State University, and the Applicative Multiprocessing System at the University of Utah.

2.3.5 Dataflow Architectures

Figure 2.11 also represents the abstract machine model for a dataflow machine, which is a data-driven architecture. That is, there is no explicit instruction sequencing mechanism and the computation is guided by data availability and dependencies. The computation model for a dataflow architecture is the directed graph called dataflow graph.

EXAMPLE 2.5

A **dataflow graph** for the computation

$$a = (d + e) + (f * g)$$

is shown in Figure 2.13. Here vertices represent the operators, and the edges show the direction of dataflow. As soon as d and e are available, vertex 1 computes their sum and passes it on to vertex 3. Similarly, vertex 2 computes the product as soon as f and g are available. Vertex 3 performs the addition as soon as its two input operands are available. Several vertices could be active simultaneously, and the activity is completely guided by the availability of data, not by an explicit instruction stream.

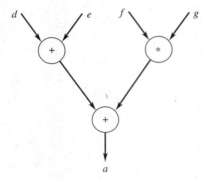

Figure 2.13 Dataflow Graph for $a = (d + e) + (f * g)$

Two types of dataflow architectures are possible. In the Manchester dataflow architecture, all of the data memory is equally visible to all DPs. Thus, the model for this is equivalent to that for the reduction machine (Figure 2.11). In the MIT model (Dennis type), each processor has its own memory and the processors share the data as messages over the interconnection network. Figure 2.14 shows the model for this type. Dataflow architectures are still in the experimental stage, and Chapter 7 provides further details.

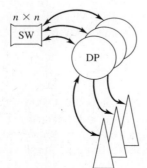

Figure 2.14 Dataflow Model (Dennis Type) (Skillcorn, 1988) (Reproduced with permission from IEEE.)

2.4 DUNCAN'S TAXONOMY

Duncan (1990) defines a parallel architecture as the one that provides an explicit high-level framework for the development of parallel programming solutions by providing multiple processors (simple or complex) that cooperate to solve problems through concurrent execution. With this definition, architecture with low-level parallel mechanisms, such as instruction pipelining, multiple functional units, or separate CPU and I/O processors, are excluded from the class of parallel computers.

This taxonomy classifies parallel architectures into the following classes:

Synchronous architectures
> Vector processors
> SIMD architectures
>> Processor arrays
>> Associative processors
>
> Systolic architectures

MIMD architectures
> Distributed memory (message passing)
> Shared memory

MIMD Paradigm
> MIMD/SIMD
> Dataflow
> Reduction
> Wavefront

The SIMD (processor array), MIMD (distributed and shared memory), dataflow, and reduction classifications were considered previously.

2.4.1 Vector Processors

These architectures are suitable for computations on array-oriented data. They utilize one or more pipelines. Figure 2.15 shows such an architecture. There are n processors (or processing stations) arranged in a pipeline. The data stream (i.e., elements of the array or vector) from the memory enters the pipeline at processor 1 and moves from station to station through processor n, and the resulting data stream enters the memory. The control unit of the machine is shown to have n subunits, one for each processor.

Assuming that a unit of data stays with each station for x seconds, the total processing time per unit of data is (nx) seconds. But once the pipeline is full, there will be an output from the pipeline every x seconds, thereby achieving a high throughput.

Almost all architectures today employ pipelining to various degrees. But vector processor architectures contain ALUs with a high degree of pipelining.

Thus, vector processors are characterized by multiple, pipelined functional units that implement arithmetic and logic operations on both scalar and vector data and can

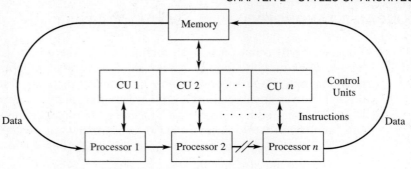

Figure 2.15 Vector Processor Structure

operate concurrently. These architectures provide parallel vector processing by sequentially streaming vector elements through a pipeline of functional units. They can also stream the output results of one pipeline as inputs into another pipeline. This is known as *chaining*.

Figure 2.16 shows the architecture of a **register-based pipeline** similar to the one used by modern vector processors such as Cray-1 and Fujitsu VP-200. **Memory-based** architectures, such as CDC Cyber 205 and Texas Instruments' Advanced Scientific Computer (ASC), use special memory buffers rather than vector registers. Recent multiprocessor architectures such as Cray X-MP and Y-MP are shared memory MIMD architectures with 4 to 16 vector processors. Chapter 3 provides further details on pipeline design, and Chapter 4 describes vector processor architectures further.

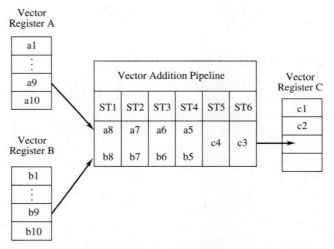

Figure 2.16 Register-to-Register Vector Architecture Operation (Duncan 1990) (Reproduced with permission from IEEE.)

2.4 DUNCAN'S TAXONOMY

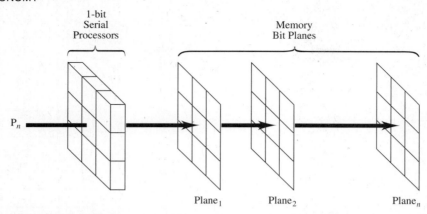

Figure 2.17 Bit-Plane Array Processing (Duncan 1990) (Reproduced with permission from IEEE.)

In the processor array SIMD architecture considered in the previous section, the processors are generally oriented toward operating on word-sized operands that are typically floating-point numbers. One variant of this architecture is the **bit-plane array processing** shown in Figure 2.17, which uses a large number of single bit processors arranged in a symmetrical grid and associated with multiple planes of memory bits that correspond to the dimensions of the processor grid. Here, the processor at location (x, y) of the grid operates on the data at memory bits located at (x, y) on each memory plane.

Examples of this type of architecture are Loral's Massively Parallel Processor and ICL's Distributed Array Processor. Thinking Machine's Connection Machine (models 1 and 2) contains 64K one-bit processors and can be considered to belong to this class.

2.4.2 Associative Processors

An associative processor is an SIMD whose main component is an associative memory (AM). AMs are used in fast search operations where the data pattern being searched for is input into the memory system and the memory provides a list of locations that contain the matching pattern as its output.

Figure 2.18(a) shows the structure and operation of an AM. The data pattern to be searched for is placed in the data register. The mask register designates the portion of the data register that is of interest in the current search. That is, the bit positions in which the mask register contains a 0 do not participate in the search process. Similarly, the word select register is a word mask and allows the selection of all or a subset of words in the memory for comparison. The memory logic compares each memory word with the data register contents (under bit and word masks) and sets the bits of the results register corresponding to those words that match.

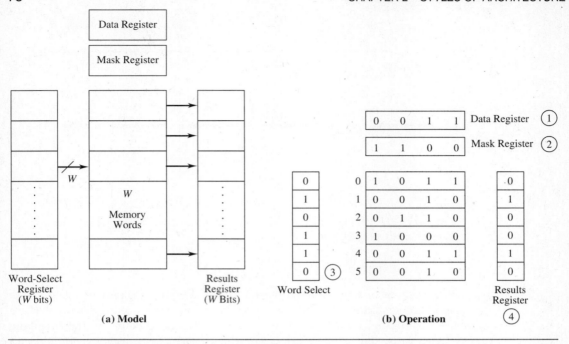

The circled numbers indicate the sequence of operation.
1. The "data" word being searched for is 0011.
2. Most significant 2 bits of "mask" are 1s. Hence, only the corresponding 2 bits of "data" are compared with those of memory words 0 through 5.
3. "Word select" register bit setting indicates that only words 1, 3, and 4 are to be involved in the search process.
4. "Results" register indicates that words 1 and 4 have the needed data.

Note that comparison of data register with memory words is done in parallel. The addresses shown (0 through 5) are for reference only.

Figure 2.18 Associative Memory

EXAMPLE 2.6

In the AM of Figure 2.18(b), there are six 4-bit memory words that contain the data. Only the leftmost two bits of the data register are compared with those of each memory word because only those bits of the mask register are nonzero. Furthermore, only words 1, 3, and 4 participate in the search process because of the word select register settings. Because words 1 and 4 contain the data pattern being searched for, the AM sets corresponding bits of the results register.

2.4 DUNCAN'S TAXONOMY

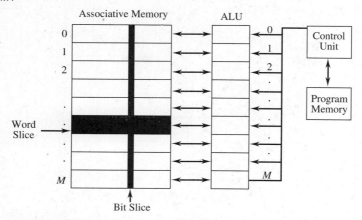

Figure 2.19 Associative Processor

An associative processor (Figure 2.19) is formed by including an arithmetic logic unit at each word of an AM. The associative processor first performs a search through the associative memory for specified data, resulting in the selection of words that contain the matching data as respondents. The ALU corresponding to each respondent is then activated to perform an update. Note that the update may involve the complete word or a selected field (as designated by the mask register). The update is performed in a bit-serial mode if each ALU is a single bit ALU or in a byte- or word-serial mode with an appropriate ALU. The byte- or word-serial modes result in a high hardware cost because one such ALU is required at each associative memory word. Note also that the updating operation can be performed simultaneously on all the respondent memory words. Thus, by using a common control unit to drive the ALUs in a lock-step mode, an SIMD mode of processing is achieved.

Several manufacturers have developed associative processing equipment. However, the cost of associative memories prohibited the wide use of such machines. With the reduction in cost of semiconductor memories, several associative memory systems have become available. These are used as special purpose peripherals attached to any general purpose processor, typically in applications such as signal, voice, and image processing where a fast pattern matching capability is needed. Associative processors are not described further in this book except for the following brief description of the only major commercial associative processor architecture effort.

STARAN, developed by Goodyear Aerospace Corporation, is an associative processor with applications in real-time processing involving a wide variety of sensors, signal processors, displays, and storage devices. Figure 2.20 shows the system structure of a STARAN/645 system at Rome Air Development Center (RADC). STARAN is configured as a peripheral for the host machine (Honeywell 645), the two interfaced with a versatile I/O interface. The function of the sequential controller (DEC PDP-11) is to interface the system peripherals, disk system, and operator to the STARAN.

Figure 2.21 shows the STARAN organization. The memory consists of all the application program equivalents to drive the array controller. The array controller

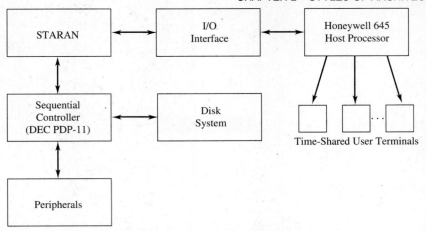

Figure 2.20 STARAN/645 System Structure

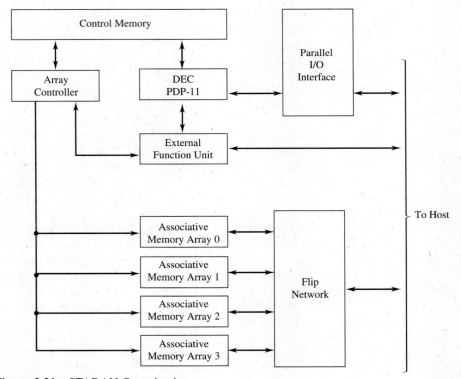

Figure 2.21 STARAN Organization

controls up to 32 modules of 256-by-256-bit associative memory arrays. Each associative memory array is a multidimensional access (MDA) array. The array can be accessed in a bit-slice mode (corresponding bit from each of the 256 words) for input processing or in a word-slice mode (one 256-bit word at a time) for input/output operations. A number of other access modes are allowed.

2.4 DUNCAN'S TAXONOMY

The flip network is an interconnection network that allows the permutations of operands selected from the memory, the ALU registers of the arrays, or the external I/O units, thereby enabling a software reconfiguration of the arrays.

There are three 256-bit registers in each array: the M register contains the write mask for a parallel memory write; the X register along with its logic can perform various logical operations between its own contents and the output of the flip network; the Y register acts as a mask for operations on X register contents.

The first production configuration of STARAN was used in 1972 for on-site tests of air traffic control. Such real-time, massive database-oriented processing is the application for which associative processors are suitable.

2.4.3 Systolic Architectures

Kung (1982) proposed systolic architectures as a means of solving problems of special purpose systems that must often balance intensive computations with demanding I/O bandwidths. Systolic arrays (architectures) are pipelined multiprocessors in which data is pulsed in rhythmic fashion from memory through a network of processors and the results returned to memory (see Figure 2.22). A global clock and explicit timing delays synchronize this pipelined dataflow, which consists of operands obtained from memory and partial results to be used by each processor. The processors are interconnected by regular, local interconnections. During each time interval, these processors execute a short, invariant sequence of instructions.

Systolic arrays address the performance requirements of special purpose systems by achieving significant parallel computation and by avoiding I/O and memory bandwidth bottlenecks. A high degree of parallelism is obtained by pipelining data through multiple processors, typically in two-dimensional fashion. Systolic architectures maximize the computations performed on a datum once it has been obtained from memory or an external device. Hence, once a datum enters the systolic array, it is passed to any processor that needs it without an intervening store to memory.

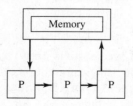

Figure 2.22 A Systolic Architecture (Duncan 1990) (Reproduced with permission from IEEE.)

EXAMPLE 2.7

Figure 2.23 shows how a simple systolic array could calculate the product of two matrices,

$$A = \begin{bmatrix} a & b \\ c & d \end{bmatrix} \text{ and } B = \begin{bmatrix} e & f \\ g & h \end{bmatrix}$$

The zero inputs shown moving through the array are used for synchronization. Each processor begins with an accumulator set to zero and, during each cycle, adds the product of its two inputs to the accumulator. After five cycles the matrix product is complete.

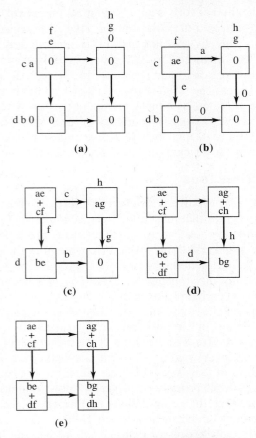

Figure 2.23 Systolic Matrix Multiplication (Duncan 1990) (Reproduced with permission from IEEE.)

A variety of special purpose systems have used systolic arrays for algorithm-specific architectures, particularly for signal processing. In addition, programmable (reconfigurable) systolic architectures, such as Intel's iWarp and Saxpy's Matrix-1, have been constructed. Chapter 5 provides further details.

2.4.4 MIMD/SIMD Architectures

Some experimental architectures constructed during the 1980s implemented a hybrid concept in which selected portions of an MIMD architecture are allowed to be controlled in SIMD fashion. Quite diverse implementation mechanisms were explored for reconfiguring architectures and controlling SIMD execution. Examples of this hybrid architecture are Columbia University's DADO and NON-VON, Purdue University's Partitionable SIMD/MIMD (PASM), and the Texas Reconfigurable Array Computer (TRAC) of the University of Texas. Thinking Machine's CM-5 is a commercial architecture of this type.

The concept can be illustrated using a tree-structured, message-passing computer as the base architecture. The master/slave relation of an SIMD architecture's

2.4 DUNCAN'S TAXONOMY

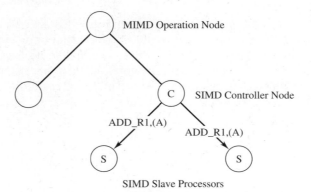

Figure 2.24 MIMD/SIMD Operation (Duncan 1990) (Reproduced with permission from IEEE.)

control and arithmetic processors can be mapped onto the node/descendants relation of a subtree as shown in Figure 2.24. When the root processor node of the subtree operates as a SIMD controller, it transmits instructions to descendent nodes that execute the instructions on a local memory data. This being an MIMD architecture, several such subtrees would be active simultaneously.

The flexibility of these hybrid architectures has made them attractive candidates for areas such as parallel image processing and expert system applications.

2.4.5 Wavefront Array Architectures

Kung (1987) proposed wavefront array concepts to address the same kind of problems as those addressed by systolic arrays (i.e., producing efficient, cost-effective architectures for special purpose systems that balance intensive computations with high I/O bandwidth). Wavefront arrays thus combine systolic data pipelining with an asynchronous dataflow execution paradigm.

Both wavefront and systolic architectures are constructed using modular processors and regular, local interconnection networks. Systolic arrays utilize a global clock and explicit time delays for synchronizing data pipelining while wavefront arrays adopt an asynchronous handshaking as the mechanism for coordinating interprocessor data movement. Thus, when a processor has performed its computations and is ready to pass data to its successor, it informs the successor, sends data when the successor indicates it is ready, and receives an acknowledgment from the successor. The handshaking mechanism makes a computational wavefront pass smoothly through the array where the array processors act as a propagating medium. Thus, the correct sequencing of computations in the wavefront arrays replaces the correct timing of systolic architectures.

EXAMPLE 2.8

The matrix multiplication example of Figure 2.23 is illustrated in Figure 2.25 utilizing a wavefront architecture. The architecture consists of processing elements (PEs) that have a single operand buffer for each input source. Whenever a memory input source is empty and the associated memory contains another operand, that available operand is immediately read. Operands from other PEs are obtained using the asynchronous handshaking protocol. The status of the array after memory input buffers are initially filled is shown in (a). In (b), PE(1, 1) adds the product (ae) to its accumulator and transmits operands a and e to neighboring PEs; thus the first computational wavefront is shown propagating from PE(1, 1) to PE(1, 2) and PE(2, 1). Figure (c) shows the first computational wavefront continuing to propagate, while a second wavefront is initiated by PE(1, 1).

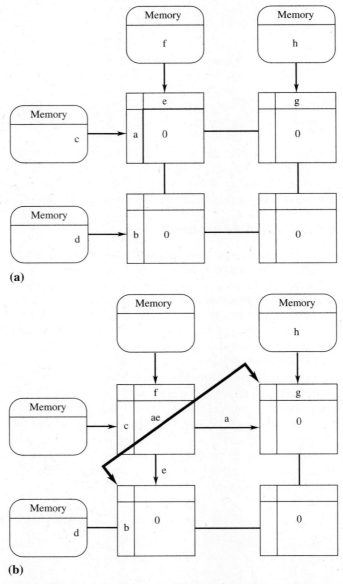

Figure 2.25 Wavefront Array Matrix Multiplication (Duncan 1990) (Reproduced with permission from IEEE.)

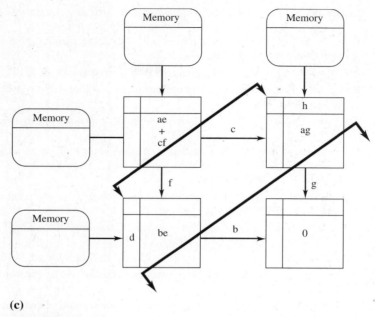

(c)

Figure 2.25 (cont.)

The advantages of wavefront arrays over systolic arrays are greater scalability, simpler programming, and greater fault tolerance. Experimental wavefront arrays have been constructed at Johns Hopkins University, Standard Telecommunications Company, and Royal Signals and Radar Establishment of the United Kingdom.

2.5 SUMMARY

The terminology and basic models of parallel processing were introduced in this chapter. A multitude of architecture classification schemes have been proposed in the literature over the years. The chapter is not an exhaustive survey of architecture taxonomies but uses the most popular taxonomy due to Flynn and two extensions to it. Feng (1972), Handler (1977), and Schwartz (1983) describe several other taxonomies. Further details on the architectures introduced here are given in subsequent chapters of this book.

REFERENCES

Batcher, K. E. 1980. Design of a massively parallel processor. *IEEE Trans. Computers,* Vol. C-29, Sept. 836–844.

Dongara, J. J., ed. 1987. *Experimental parallel computing architectures.* Amsterdam: North-Holland.

Duncan, R. 1990. A survey of parallel computer architectures. *IEEE Computer,* 23(2): 5–16.

Eisenbach, S., ed. 1987. *Functional programming: Languages, tools and architectures.* New York: John Wiley & Sons.

Feng, T. Y. 1972. Some characteristics of associative/parallel processing. Proc. 1972 Sagamore Computing Conf., August, 5–16.

Flynn, M. J. 1966. Very high speed computing systems. Proc. IEEE 54: 1901–1909.

Flynn, M. J. 1972. Some computer organizations and their effectiveness. *IEEE Trans. Computers* C-21 (9): 948–960.

Fountain, T. J. 1987. *Processor arrays: Architectures and applications.* New York: Academic Press.

Gurd, J. and I. Watson. 1980. Data driven systems for high speed parallel computing: Part 1: Structuring software for parallel execution: Part 2: Hardware design. *Computer Design* (June and July): 91–100, 97–106.

Handler, W. 1977. The impact of classification schemes on computer architecture. *Proc. Int'l Conf. on Parallel Processing.* August, 7–15.

Hillis, W. D. 1985. *The connection machine.* Cambridge, Mass: MIT Press.

Hockney, R. W. 1987. Classification and evaluation of parallel computer systems. In *Lecture Notes in Computer Science,* No. 295: 13–25. Berlin: Springer-Verlag.

Hwang, K., ed. 1984. *Tutorial supercomputers: Design and applications.* Los Alamitos, Calif.: Computer Society Press.

Hwang, K. and F. Briggs. 1984. *Computer architectures and parallel processing.* New York: McGraw-Hill.

Kohonen, T. 1987. *Content-addressable memories,* 2nd ed. New York: Springer-Verlag.

Kuck, D. J. 1982. High-speed machines and their compilers. In *Parallel processing systems,* edited by D. Evans. Cambridge: Cambridge University Press.

Kuck, D. J. and R. A. Stokes. 1982. The Burroughs scientific processor. *IEEE Trans. Computers* C-31(5): 363–376.

Kung, H. T. 1982. Why systolic architectures? *IEEE Computer* 15(1): 37–46.

Kung, S.Y. et al. 1987. Wavefront array processors—Concept to implementation. *IEEE Computer* 20(7): 18–33.

Lincoln, N. R. 1978. A safari through the Control Data Star-100 with gun and camera. *Proc. AFIPS NCC,* June.

Lipovski, G. J. and M. Malek. 1987. *Parallel computing: Theory and comparisons.* New York: Wiley and Sons.

Milutinovic, V. M. 1989. *High level language computer architecture.* New York: Computer Science Press.

Myers, G. J. 1982. *Advances in computer architecture.* New York: John Wiley.

Reddi, S. S. and E. A. Feurstel. 1976. A conceptual framework for computer architecture. *ACM Computing Surveys* 8(2) June: 277–300.

Schwartz, J. 1983. A taxonomic table of parallel computers based on 55 designs. New York: Courant Institute.

Siegel, H. J. 1985. *Interconnection networks for large-scale parallel processing: Theory and case studies.* Lexington, Mass.: Lexington Books.

Skillcorn, D. B. 1985. A taxonomy for computer architectures. *IEEE Computer* 21(11): 46–57.

Stolfo, S. J. and D. J. Miranker. 1986. The DADO production system machine. *Journal of Parallel and Distributed Computing* 3(2): 269–296.

Treleaven, P. C., D. R. Brownbridge, and R. P. Hopkins. 1982. Data-driven and demand-driven computer architecture. *ACM Computing Surveys* 14(1): 93–143.

2.5 SUMMARY

Watson, W. J. 1972. The ASC—A highly modular flexible super computer architecture. Proc. AFIPS FJCC, 221–228.

Wolfang, K. G. 1986. Interconnection networks for massively parallel computer systems. In *Lecture Notes in Computer Science,* 272: 321–348. Berlin: Springer-Verlag.

PROBLEMS

2.1. It is said that the Cray series of supercomputers can be classified under all the classes of Flynn's taxonomy. Verify this statement with respect to newer architectures in this series: X-MP/4, Y-MP, and Cray-2.

2.2. Why is the MISD classification of Flynn considered an aberration? Does a pipeline structure fit this classification?

2.3. Develop the two levels of Skillcorn's taxonomy for any single processor system to which you have access.

2.4. Develop the top level models of Skillcorn's taxonomy for a contemporary vector processor, an SIMD, and an MIMD system to which you have access.

2.5. List the characteristics of applications suitable for the following architectures:
  a. SIMD
  b. Shared-memory MIMD
  c. Message-passing MIMD
  d. Dataflow
  e. Associative processors

2.6. How are MIMD systems different from computer networks?

2.7. MIMD systems are generally known as multiprocessor systems. The literature also uses the terms *multiple processor systems* and *multicomputer systems* to describe certain architectures. What is the difference between these architectures?

2.8. What is the machine level program representation in symbolic computers (such as Symbolics 3600, Texas Instruments's Explorer)? How is this representation interpreted? Use manufacturers' manuals to answer this question.

2.9. Myers (1982) classifies language corresponding HLL architectures under Type A and Type B classifications. Investigate the differences between the two.

2.10. Compare and contrast reduction and dataflow architectures.

2.11. Select a parallel processing application with which you are familiar. Investigate the algorithms available, special data structures utilized, architectural concepts used to make those algorithms efficient, and the commercial computer systems used for that application.

2.12. Investigate the scalability characteristics of the parallel architectures listed as examples in this chapter.

2.13. How does an SIMD system handle a conditional branch instruction such as "IF $X = 0$ THEN P ELSE Q," where P and Q are labels of statements in the program? Note that in an SISD either P or Q is executed based on the value of X.

2.14. It is required to compute the sum of 32K 32-bit numbers. Estimate the time required for this computation on:
  a. a 32-bit SISD,
  b. a 16-bit SISD,
  c. an SIMD with 32 32-bit processors,
  d. an SIMD with 16 32-bit processors.

2.15. What is the best way to implement the computation of Problem 2.14 on an MIMD? That is, how do you minimize the overheads involved?

CHAPTER 3

Pipelining

As mentioned earlier, pipelining offers an economical way of realizing parallelism in computer systems. The concept of pipelining is similar to that of an assembly line in an industrial plant wherein the task at hand is subdivided into several subtasks and each subtask is performed by a **stage (segment)** in the pipeline. In this context, the **task** is the processing performed by the conglomeration of all the stages in the pipeline, and the **subtask** is the processing done by a stage. For example, in the car assembly line described earlier, building a car was the task and it was partitioned into four subtasks. The tasks are streamed into the pipeline, and all the stages operate concurrently. At any given time, each stage will be performing a subtask belonging to a different task. If there are N stages in the pipeline, N different tasks will be processed simultaneously, and each task will be at a different stage of processing.

The processing time required to complete a task is not reduced by the pipeline. In fact, it is increased due to the buffering needed between the stages in the pipeline. Because several tasks are processed simultaneously by the pipeline (in an overlapped manner), the task completion rate is higher compared to sequential processing of tasks. That is, the total processing time of a program consisting of several tasks is shorter compared to sequential execution of tasks. As shown earlier, the throughput of an N-stage pipelined processor is nearly N times that of the nonpipelined processor.

The next section provides a model for the pipeline and describes the types of pipelines commonly used. Section 2 describes pipeline control strategies. Section 3 deals with data interlock and other problems in pipeline design, and Section 4 describes dynamic pipelines. Almost all computer systems today employ pipelining

3.1 PIPELINE MODEL

techniques to one degree or another. Section 5 provides a selected set of examples. Chapter 4 describes the architecture of vector processors, which utilize pipeline structures extensively.

3.1 PIPELINE MODEL

Figure 3.1(a) shows a pipeline with k stages ($S_1, S_2, \ldots S_k$) along with a **staging register** at the input of each stage. The input data to any stage is held in the staging register until it is ready to be operated on by that stage. Let t_i denote the processing time and d_i denote the delay introduced by the staging register in stage i. Then, the total processing time T_{pl} for each task through the pipeline is

$$T_{pl} = \sum_{i=1}^{k} (t_i + d_i). \tag{3.1}$$

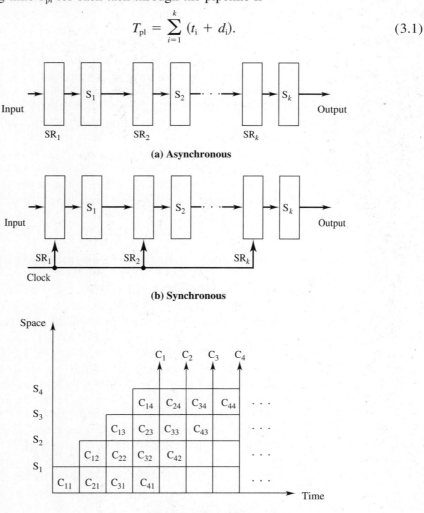

(a) Asynchronous

(b) Synchronous

(c) Space-Time Diagram

Figure 3.1 A k-Stage Pipeline

The second term on the right-hand side of the above equation is the overhead introduced by the pipeline for each task because the time for sequential (i.e., nonpipelined) execution of the task is

$$T_{seq} = \sum_{i=1}^{k} (t_i). \tag{3.2}$$

For this pipeline to operate properly, the data produced by each stage must be input to the staging register of the following stage only after the data in that staging register has been accepted by the stage connected to it. This mode of operation results in an **asynchronous** pipeline. In general, design of asynchronous hardware is tedious. Although if designed properly, it provides a higher speed compared to synchronous designs. Almost all practical pipelines are designed to operate as synchronous pipelines with a clock controlling the data transfer from stage to stage as shown in (b). Obviously, the frequency of the clock is $1/t_{max}$ where, $t_{max} = \text{Max}(t_i + d_i)$, $1 \leq i \leq k$. The clock period is usually called the **pipeline cycle time**. The pipeline cycle time is thus controlled by the slowest stage in the pipeline.

The **space-time diagram** of Figure 3.1(c) shows the taskflow through a four-stage pipeline. Here C_{ij} denotes the jth subtask of the task C_i. Note that C_1 is completed at the end of the fourth cycle by which time the pipeline is full. From then on, one task is completed every cycle.

To attain the maximum throughput, the pipeline cycle must be as small as possible. That is, t_{max} must be minimized. This can be achieved by dividing the computational task into a large number (k) of subtasks, each taking approximately the same computation time (i.e., T_{seq}/k), resulting in a pipeline with k stages and a cycle time

$$t_{cyc} = T_{seq}/k + d \tag{3.3}$$

where for simplicity each staging register is assumed to contribute an equal amount of delay d.

The smaller the value of t_{cyc}, the larger is the processing speed of the pipeline. But small values for t_{cyc} result in a large value for k. As k gets large (i.e., the pipeline gets deeper), the first term on the right-hand side of (3.3) tends to zero and t_{cyc} tends to d. Thus, the pipeline computation rate is bounded by $1/d$. As k increases, the overhead in terms of filling the pipeline at the beginning of the task stream and coordination of dataflow between the stages also increases. Also, each stage in the pipeline potentially accesses the system memory for data and instructions. Because all the k stages are active simultaneously as k becomes large, the memory traffic increases k-fold, thus making the memory system a bottleneck.

Suppose the clock rate of the pipeline is fixed and suppose all stages of a linear pipeline are able to complete their operations in one clock cycle, except stage X, which requires two clock cycles. Because of stage X, the pipeline can produce at most one result every two clock cycles. It is possible to convert the pipeline to produce one result every cycle by dividing stage X. But this requires addition of another latch, thus increasing the total delay. As such, it may be necessary to break the stage X into more than two parts to achieve the desired goal. For pipelines where the maximum clock rate is determined by the slowest stage, it may appear to be possible to speed up the

3.1 PIPELINE MODEL

pipeline arbitrarily by dividing each stage into smaller and smaller parts. However, because the delay of the staging registers is fixed, the pipeline will eventually reach a point where the amount of improvement in speed is negligible and the cost of making such improvements becomes prohibitive.

If N tasks are streamed into the pipeline of Figure 3.1(b), the first k cycles are used to fill the pipeline, at the end of which the first result appears at the output and the remaining $N - 1$ tasks are completed in subsequent $N - 1$ cycles, thus taking a total time of $(k + N - 1)t_{cyc}$. Substituting from equation (3.3), the pipeline processing time becomes $(k + N - 1)(T_{seq}/k + d)$. Thus the staging register delay d contributes an overhead of the order of $(k + N - 1)$. This overhead can only be reduced either by using registers with the smallest possible delay or by limiting the number of stages k in the pipeline to a small number. An ideal design thus strikes a compromise between the number of stages and the pipeline cycle time.

The execution of N tasks in a nonpipelined processor would require $(N \cdot T_{seq})$ time units. The **speedup** S obtained by the pipeline is defined as the ratio of the total processing time of the nonpipelined implementation to that of the pipelined implementation and is given by

$$S = \frac{N \cdot T_{seq}}{(k + N - 1)t_{cyc}}. \tag{3.4}$$

If staging register delay d is ignored, equation (3.4) reduces to the speedup of an ideal pipeline

$$S_{ideal} = (N \cdot k)/(k + N - 1). \tag{3.5}$$

We can include a cost factor into this model (Kogge, 1981) because the parameter of general interest while evaluating different pipeline architectures is the cost per million instructions per second (MIPS) or cost per million floating-point operations per second (MFLOPS). If the hardware cost of the ith stage is c_i and the cost of each staging register is L, the total cost C of the pipeline is given by

$$C = L \cdot k + C_p \tag{3.6}$$

where

$$C_p = \sum_{i=1}^{k} c_i. \tag{3.7}$$

The cost function C increases linearly with the number of stages k.

The composite cost per computation rate is given by $(R \cdot C_p)$. That is,

$$R \cdot C_p = (L \cdot k + C_p)(T_{seq}/k + d) \tag{3.8}$$
$$= L \cdot T_{seq} + L \cdot D \cdot k + C_p \cdot T_{seq}/k + C_p \cdot d.$$

To minimize this,

$$\frac{d}{dk}(R \cdot C_p) = 0. \tag{3.9}$$

That is,

$$L \cdot d - C_p \cdot T_{seq}/k^2 = 0,$$

or
$$k = \sqrt{\frac{C_p \cdot T_{seq}}{L \cdot d}} \qquad (3.10)$$

This provides the condition for the lowest cost per computation.

In practice, making the delays of pipeline stages equal (as assumed above) is a complicated and time-consuming process. It is essential to maximum performance that the stages be close to balanced, but designing circuitry to achieve that requires analyzing a huge number of paths through the circuits and iterating a large number of times over complicated steps. It is done for commercial processors, although it is not easy or cheap to do.

Another problem with pipelines is the overhead in terms of handling exceptions or interrupts. Interrupts can be handled in two ways:

1. the contents of all the stages are saved for an orderly return to that state after the interrupt is serviced or
2. the contents of the pipeline are discarded (except maybe the instruction in the last stage, which is completed before starting the interrupt service), interrupt is serviced, and the pipeline is restarted. Note also that a deep pipeline increases the interrupt handling overhead.

3.1.1 Pipeline Types

It is important to note that the pipeline concept can be applied at various levels. The complete application program can be developed as several modules with each module executing on a pipeline stage; each module could be implemented as a pipeline in which each stage executes a statement or a set of statements within the module; each statement may be executed by a pipeline in which a stage performs one operation in the statement; each operation in a statement can subsequently be executed by a pipelined arithmetic logic unit.

There are two broad types of pipelines: 1) instruction pipelines and 2) arithmetic pipelines. **Instruction pipelines** are used in almost all modern day processors to a varying degree to enhance the speed of the control unit. That is, the control unit is implemented as a pipeline consisting of several stages where each stage is dedicated to perform one phase of the instruction cycle. **Arithmetic pipelines** enhance the throughput of the arithmetic logic units. Further details on these two types of pipelines follow.

INSTRUCTION PIPELINE

Figure 3.2 shows an instruction processing pipeline consisting of six stages. The first stage fetches instructions from the memory, one instruction at a time. At the end of each fetch, this stage also updates the program counter to point to the next instruction in sequence. The decode stage decodes the instruction, the next stage computes the effective address of the operand, followed by a stage that fetches the operand from the memory. The operation called for by the instruction is then performed by the execute stage, and the results are stored in the memory by the next stage.

3.1 PIPELINE MODEL

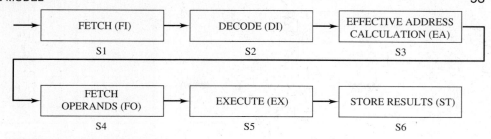

Figure 3.2 An Instruction Pipeline

The operation of this pipeline is depicted by the modified space-time diagram called a **reservation table** shown in Figure 3.3. In a reservation table, each row corresponds to a stage in the pipeline and each column corresponds to a pipeline cycle. An X at the intersection of the ith row and the jth column indicates that stage i would be busy performing a subtask at cycle j, where cycle 1 corresponds to the **initiation** of the task in the pipeline. That is, stage i is *reserved* (and hence not available for any other task) at cycle j. The number of columns in the reservation table for a given task is determined by the sequence in which the subtasks corresponding to that task flow in the pipeline. The reservation table in (b) shows that each stage completes its task in one cycle time, and hence, an instruction cycle requires six cycles to be completed, although one instruction is completed every cycle (once the pipeline is full).

In the above pipeline, the cycle time is determined by the stages requiring memory access because they tend to be slower than the other stages. Assume that a memory access takes $3T$, where T is a time unit, and a stage requiring no memory access executes in T. Then, the above pipeline produces one result every $3T$ (after the first $18T$ during which the pipeline is filled). Compared to this, the sequential execution of each instruction requires $14T$ on asynchronous, and $18T$ on synchronous, control units.

The above pipeline can be rearranged into a 14-stage pipeline shown in Figure 3.4 (Stone, 1987). Here, two delay stages are inserted at each stage requiring a memory access in the original pipeline. This implies that the memory system is reorganized into a 3-stage pipeline. The delay stages provide for the buffering of data to and from the memory. Now the pipeline produces one result every T (ignoring the additional overhead due to staging registers needed between the stages).

The assumption so far has been that the instruction execution is completely sequential in the operation of the above pipeline. As long as that is true, the pipeline

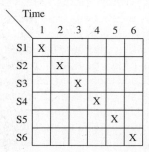

Figure 3.3 Reservation Table

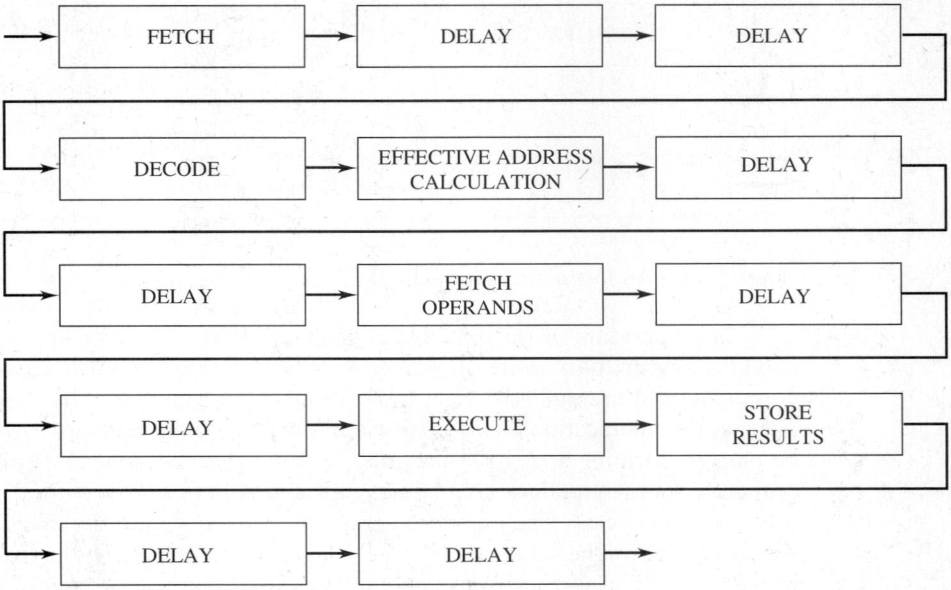

```
→ FETCH → DELAY → DELAY ┐
┌──────────────────────────────────────┘
→ DECODE → EFFECTIVE ADDRESS CALCULATION → DELAY ┐
┌────────────────────────────────────────────────┘
→ DELAY → FETCH OPERANDS → DELAY ┐
┌────────────────────────────────┘
→ DELAY → EXECUTE → STORE RESULTS ┐
┌────────────────────────────────┘
→ DELAY → DELAY →
```

Figure 3.4 Instruction Pipeline with Delays

completes one instruction per cycle. In practice, the program execution is not completely sequential on account of branch instructions. Consider an unconditional branch instruction entering the pipeline of Figure 3.2. The target of the branch is not known until the instruction reaches the address calculate stage 3 (S3). By then, if the pipeline is allowed to function normally, it would have fetched two more instructions following the branch instruction. When the target address is known, the instructions that entered the pipeline after the branch instruction must be discarded and new instructions fetched from the target address of the branch. This pipeline-draining operation results in a degradation of pipeline throughput. A solution would be to freeze the pipeline from fetching further instructions as soon as the branch opcode is decoded (in stage 2 or S2) until the target address is known. This mode of operation prevents some traffic on the memory system but does not increase the pipeline efficiency any, compared to the first method.

When the instruction entering the pipeline is a conditional branch, the target address of the branch will be known only after the evaluation of the condition (in stage 5 or S5). Three modes of pipeline handling are possible for this case. In the first mode the pipeline is frozen from fetching subsequent instructions until the branch target is known, as in the case of the unconditional branch above. In the second mode, the pipeline fetches subsequent instructions normally, ignoring the conditional branch. That is, the pipeline predicts that the branch will not be taken. If indeed the branch is not taken, the pipeline flows normally and hence there is no degradation of performance. If the branch is taken, the pipeline must be drained and restarted at the target address. The second mode is preferred because the pipeline functions normally about 50% of the time on an average. The third mode would be to start fetching the target instruction sequence into a buffer (as soon as the target address is computed in S3) while the nonbranch sequence is being fed into the pipeline. If the branch is not taken, the pipeline continues with its normal operation and the contents of the buffer are ignored. If the branch is taken, the instructions already in the pipeline are discarded (i.e., the pipeline is flushed) and target instructions are fetched from the buffer. The advantage here is that fetching instructions from the buffer is faster than fetching from the memory.

In the last two modes of operation above, all the activity of the pipeline with respect to instructions entering the pipeline following the conditional branch must be marked *temporary* and made permanent only if the branch is not taken.

The above problems introduced into the pipeline by branch instructions are called **control hazards.** Section 3 describes other mechanisms that reduce the effect of control hazards on pipeline performance.

ARITHMETIC PIPELINES

The most popular arithmetic operations utilized to illustrate the operation of arithmetic pipelines in the literature are floating-point addition and multiplication. This section follows that tradition and is heavily influenced by Stone (1987) and Kogge (1981).

FLOATING-POINT ADDITION

Consider the addition of two normalized floating-point numbers:

$$A = (E_a, M_a) \quad \text{and} \quad B = (E_b, M_b)$$

to obtain the sum

$$S = (E_s, M_s)$$

where E and M represent the exponent and mantissa, respectively. The addition follows the steps shown below:

1. Equalize the exponents:

   If $E_a < E_b$, swap A and B; $E_{\text{diff}} = E_a - E_b$.

   Shift M_b right E_{diff} bits.

2. Add mantissas:

   $$M_s = M_a + M_b.$$
   $$E_s = E_a.$$

3. Normalize M_s and adjust E_s to reflect the number of shifts required to normalize.
4. Normalized M_s might have a larger number of bits than can be accommodated by the mantissa field in the representation. If so, round M_s.
5. If rounding causes a mantissa overflow, renormalize M_s and adjust E_s accordingly.

Figure 3.5 shows a five-stage pipeline configuration for the above addition process.

The throughput of the above pipeline can be enhanced by rearranging the computations into a larger number of stages each consuming a smaller amount of time

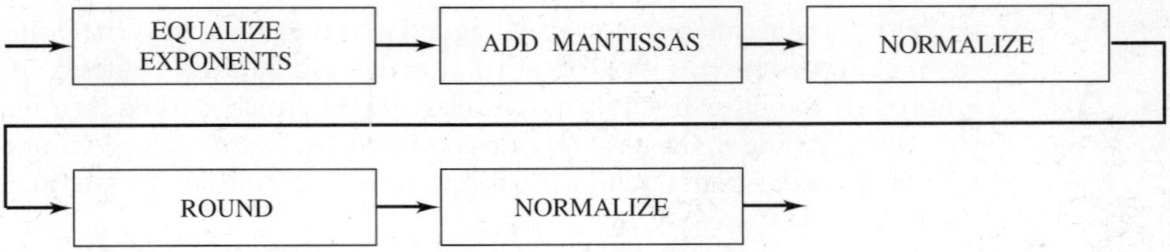

Figure 3.5 Floating-Point Add Pipeline

as shown in Figure 3.6. Here, equalizing exponents is performed using a subtract exponents stage and a shift stage that shifts mantissa appropriately. Similarly, normalizing is split into two stages. This eight-stage pipeline provides a speedup of $8/5 = 1.6$ over the pipeline of Figure 3.5.

In the pipeline of Figure 3.6 we have assumed that the shift stages can perform an arbitrary number of shifts in one cycle. If that is not the case, the shifters have to be used repeatedly. Figure 3.7 shows the rearranged pipeline where the feedback paths indicate the reuse of the corresponding stage.

Pipelines shown in Figures 3.1 through 3.6 are called **linear** pipelines because the tasks flow from stage to stage from the input to the output. The pipeline of Figure 3.7 is **nonlinear** because of the feedback paths it contains.

FLOATING-POINT MULTIPLICATION

Consider the multiplication of the two floating-point numbers $A = (E_a, M_a)$ and $B = (E_b, M_b)$, resulting in the product $P = (E_p, M_p)$. The multiplication follows the pipeline configuration shown in Figure 3.8, and the steps are listed below:

1. Add exponents: $E_p = E_a + E_b$.
2. Multiply mantissas: $M_p = M_a \times M_b$. M_p will be a double-length mantissa.
3. Normalize M_p, and adjust E_p accordingly.

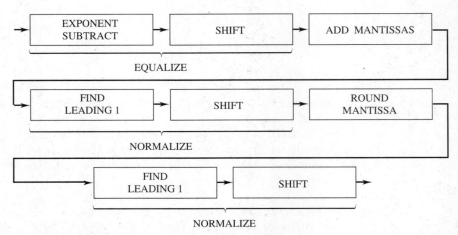

Figure 3.6 Modified Floating-Point Add Pipeline

3.1 PIPELINE MODEL

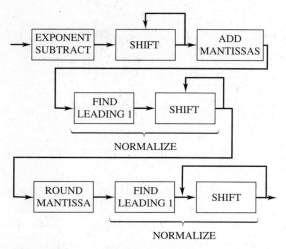

Figure 3.7 Floating-Point Adder with Feedback

4. Convert M_p into single-length mantissa by rounding.
5. If rounding causes a mantissa overflow, renormalize and adjust E_p accordingly.

Stage 2 in the above pipeline would consume the largest amount of time. In Figure 3.9 stage 2 is split into two stages, one performing partial products and the other accumulating them. In fact, the operations of these two stages can be overlapped in the sense that when the accumulate stage is adding, the other stage can be producing the next partial product.

The pipelines shown so far in this section are **unifunction** pipelines because they are designed to perform only one function. Note that the pipelines of Figures 3.7 and 3.9 have several common stages. If a processor is required to perform both addition and multiplication, the two pipelines can be merged into one as shown in Figure 3.10. Obviously, there will be two distinct paths of dataflow in this pipeline, one for addition

Figure 3.8 Floating-Point Multiplication Pipeline

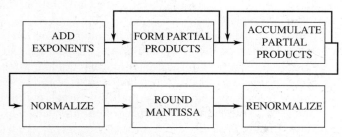

Figure 3.9 Floating-Point Multiplier Pipeline with Feedback Loops

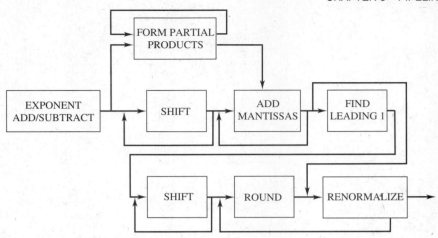

Figure 3.10 Floating-Point Adder/Multiplier

and the other for multiplication. This is a **multifunction** pipeline. A multifunction pipeline can perform more than one operation. The interconnection between the stages of the pipeline changes according to the function it is performing. Obviously, a control input that determines the particular function to be performed on the operand being input is needed for proper operation of the multifunction pipeline.

OTHER PIPELINE TYPES
A brief description of two other popular pipeline classification schemes is provided below.

Handler (1977) classifies pipelines into three classes. The first two classes (instruction pipelines and arithmetic pipelines) are similar to those described above. The third class is that of **processor pipelining.** This class corresponds to a cascade of processors each executing a specific module in the application program. As such, their operation resembles that of linear systolic arrays.

The classification scheme by Ramamoorthy and Li (1977) is based on the (a) functionality, (b) configuration, and (c) mode of operation of the pipeline.

A pipeline can be classified as either unifunctional or multifunctional based on its functionality, as described above. The Cray series of supercomputers have segmented (i.e., pipelined) functional units each dedicated to a single operation (add, divide, multiply, etc.). The Control Data Corporation (CDC) STAR-100 has two multifunction pipelines.

Based on the configuration (i.e., the interconnection pattern between its stages) a pipeline is either **static** or **dynamic.** A static pipeline assumes only one functional configuration at a time, and hence, it is unifunctional until that configuration changes. This type of pipeline is useful when instructions of the same type can be streamed for execution. A static pipeline can be multifunctional, except that its configuration has to change for each function. Such configuration changes are infrequent in static pipelines. That is, typically a long stream of data is processed before the configuration is changed. A dynamic pipeline, on the other hand, allows more frequent changes in its configuration. The configuration might change for each input. Obviously, dynamic pipelines require more elaborate sequencing and control mechanisms compared to static pipelines.

Based on the mode of operation, a pipeline is either a **scalar** or a **vector** pipeline. A scalar pipeline is designed to process a stream of scalar operands. A loop construct normally controls the operation of this type of pipeline, sending the stream of operands from the memory into the pipeline. Vector pipelines, on the other hand, are used in building ALUs for vector processors, machines designed to execute vector instructions efficiently. (See Chapter 4.) Unlike the scalar data stream, the operand stream for a vector pipeline consists of elements of the same vector (array).

The following section details the pipeline control mechanisms that reduce control hazards and enhance pipeline performance.

3.2 Pipeline Control and Performance

For a pipeline to provide the maximum possible throughput, it must be kept full and flowing smoothly. There are two conditions that can affect the smooth flow of a pipeline: 1) the rate of input of data into the pipeline and 2) the data interlocks between the stages of the pipeline when one stage either requires the data produced by the other or has to wait until another stage needing the shared data item completes its operation on that data item. The pipeline control strategy should provide solutions for smooth flow of the pipeline under both of these conditions. The description of data interlock problems is deferred to Section 3. This section provides the details of a control strategy that regulates the data input rate.

EXAMPLE 3.1

Consider the reservation table (RT) of Figure 3.3 for the six stage pipeline of Figure 3.2. This RT implies a strict linear operation of the pipeline. That is, each stage completes its work in one cycle and there are no feedback paths in the pipeline. As such, a new set of operands can be input to the pipeline every cycle, and correspondingly, the pipeline completes one operation per cycle (once it is full).

EXAMPLE 3.2

Consider the nonlinear pipeline shown in Figure 3.11(a). The last two stages in the pipeline are used twice by each operand. That is, stage 3 produces a partial result and passes it on to stage 4. While stage 4 is processing the partial result, stage 3 produces the remaining part of the result and passes it to stage 4. Stage 4 passes the complete result to stage 2. The operation of this pipeline is represented by the RT shown in (b). Because stages 3 and 4 are used in subsequent cycles by the same set of operands, the operand input rate cannot be as fast as one per cycle. The RT can be used to determine the maximum input rate of such pipelines as described next.

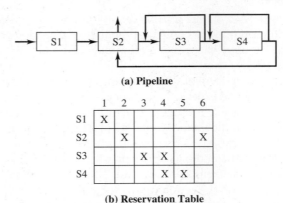

Figure 3.11 A Pipeline with Feedback

The overlapped operation of stages (as in the pipeline of the above example) is primarily due to the nonavailability of appropriate hardware and hence is termed **structural hazard.** For instance, only a single bit shifter may be available and a multiple bit shift capability is required for the task at hand, or a task requires an addition followed by a subtraction and only one ALU is available. One obvious way of avoiding structural hazards is to insert additional hardware into the pipeline. This increases the pipeline complexity and may not be justified especially if the operation requiring additional hardware is infrequent. The following example illustrates the concept of structural hazards with respect to memory requirements.

So far we have concentrated on the operation of pipelines for a single instruction cycle or a single arithmetic operation. The following example illustrates the operation of a pipeline for an instruction sequence (i.e., program).

EXAMPLE 3.3

Consider now the instruction sequence given below to be executed on a processor that utilizes the pipeline of Figure 3.2:

```
LOAD   R1,  MEM1        R1  ←  (MEM1)
LOAD   R2,  MEM2        R2  ←  (MEM2)
MPY    R3,  R1          R3  ←  (R3)×(R1)
ADD    R4,  R2          R4  ←  (R4)+(R2)
```

where R1, R2, R3, and R4 are registers; MEM1 and MEM2 are memory addresses; ( ) denotes *contents of;* and ← indicates a data transfer.

Figure 3.12 depicts the operation of the pipeline. During cycles 1 and 2 only one memory access is needed. In cycle 3 two simultaneous read accesses to memory are needed, one due to CA and the other due to FI. In cycle 4, three read accesses (FO, CA, FI) are needed. In cycles 5 and 6, two read accesses (FI, CA) are needed. Cycles 7, 8, and 9 do not require memory access. Thus, the memory system must accommodate three accesses per cycle for this pipeline to operate properly. If we assume that

3.2 PIPELINE CONTROL AND PERFORMANCE

	\multicolumn{9}{c}{Cycles}
	1	2	3	4	5	6	7	8	9
Load R1, Mem1	FI	DI	CA	FO Read Mem 1	EX Write R1	ST			
Load R2, Mem2		FI	DI	CA	FO Read Mem 2	EX Write R2	ST		
Mpy R3, R1			FI	DI	CA	FO Read R1, R3	EX Write R3	ST	
Add R4, R2				FI	DI	CA	FO Read R2, R4	EX Write R4	ST

Figure 3.12 Pipeline Operation and Resource Requirements

the machine has separate data and instruction caches, then two simultaneous accesses can be handled. This solves the problem in cycles 5 and 6 (assuming that the machine accesses instruction cache during CA). But during cycle 4 two accesses (FI, CA) to data cache would be needed. One way to solve this problem is to *stall* the ADD instruction (i.e., initiate ADD instruction later than cycle 4) until cycle 6 as shown in Figure 3.13. The stalling process results in a degradation of pipeline performance.

Note that the pipeline controller must evaluate the resource requirements of each instruction before the instruction enters the pipeline, so that structural hazards are eliminated. The following section describes one such mechanism.

	\multicolumn{9}{c}{Cycles}
	1	2	3	4	5	6	7	8	9
Load R1, Mem1	FI	DI	CA	FO Read Mem1	EX Write R1	ST			
Load R2, Mem2		FI	DI	CA	FO Read Mem2	EX Write R2	ST		
Mpy R3, R1			FI	DI	CA	FO Read R1, R3	EX Write R3	ST	
Add R4, R2				Stall	Stall	FI	DI	CA	FO Read R2, R4

Figure 3.13 Pipeline Operation with Stalls

3.2.1 Collision Vectors

In what follows, **initiation** refers to the launching of an operation into the pipeline. This corresponds to inputting a new set of data into a static or unifunction pipeline or data and operation designator into a dynamic or multifunction pipeline. The number of cycles that elapse between two initiations is referred to as the **latency.** A **latency sequence** denotes the latencies between successive initiations. A **latency cycle** is a latency sequence that repeats itself. A **collision** occurs if a stage in the pipeline is required to perform more than one task at any time.

The RT shows the busy/nonbusy status of each pipeline stage at a given time slot (cycle) subsequent to initiation of an operation at the first cycle. In order to determine if there will be a collision at any stage at any time if another operation is initiated during the second cycle, a copy of the RT should be superimposed but shifted right one cycle, over the original RT.

EXAMPLE 3.4

Figure 3.14(a) shows such a superimposed RT corresponding to the pipeline of Figure 3.11. Here A designates the reservation of stages due to the first initiation and B designates that due to the second initiation. Because there are two entries in at least one block of the composite RT implying a collision, we cannot initiate an operation in the second cycle.

This superimposition of the RT can be continued to test if an operand input is possible at subsequent times after the first initiation by simply shifting the superimposed copy of the RT by appropriate time slots.

(a) Overlapped Reservation Table   (b) Collision Vector

Figure 3.14 Collision Vector Computation

EXAMPLE 3.5

Figure 3.14(b) shows a **collision vector** (CV) derived by repeated shift and superimposition of RT of Figure 3.11(b) for five time slots following the first input. In this vector the bits are numbered from the right starting with 1. If the ith bit is 1, there will be a collision in the pipeline if an operation is initiated at the ith cycle subsequent to an initiation. If the ith bit is 0, there is no collision. For the above RT, a new initiation is always possible at the sixth cycle after any initiation. Thus, the number of bits in the CV is always one less than the number of columns in the RT. This CV implies that a new operation cannot be initiated either during the first or the fourth cycle after the first initiation.

3.2 PIPELINE CONTROL AND PERFORMANCE

A collision occurs if two operations are initiated with a latency equal to the column distances between two entries on some row of the RT. The set of all possible column distances between pairs of entries in each row of an RT is called the **forbidden set** F of latencies. The CV can thus be derived from F as follows:

$$CV = (v_{n-1}, v_{n-2}, \ldots, v_2, v_1)$$

where
$\quad v_i = 1$ if i is in F,

$\quad v_i = 0$ otherwise,

and n is the number of columns in the RT.

EXAMPLE 3.6

In the RT of Figure 3.11(b), the forbidden set F is $\{1, 4\}$ because the third and fourth rows have pairs of entries that are one column apart and row 2 has entries that are four columns apart. Thus the CV is (01001).

3.2.2 Control

The CV can be utilized to control the initiation of operations in the pipeline.

1. Place the CV in a shift register.
2. If the least significant bit (LSB) of the shift register is 1, do not initiate an operation at that cycle; shift the CV right once, inserting a 0 at the vacant most significant bit (MSB) position.
3. If the LSB of the shift register is 0, initiate a new operation at that cycle; shift the shift register right once inserting a 0 at the vacant MSB. In order to reflect the superimposing status due to the new initiation over the original one, perform a bit-by-bit OR of the original CV with the (shifted) content of the shift register.

The insertion of 0s at the MSB ensures that an operation is guaranteed an initiation within a time no longer than the length of CV after the first initiation.

3.2.3 Performance

Figure 3.15(a) shows the state transitions (indicated by the contents of control shift register) of the four-stage pipeline of Figure 3.11 with the CV (00111). The numbers on the arcs correspond to the cycle number at which the transition takes place, counting from the previous state. Until the pipeline reaches state 4, no operands can be input into the pipeline. After the fourth state (cycle) from the initiation of an operation, another operation can be initiated taking the pipeline back to the original state. If the second operation is not initiated at state 4, the pipeline reaches state 5. Similarly, if the operation is initiated at state 5, the pipeline reaches state 1, otherwise it reaches state 6 after which a new operation can always be initiated.

In the determination of the performance of the pipeline, states 2, 3, and 4 are not important because they correspond to the conditions not allowing an initiation. The

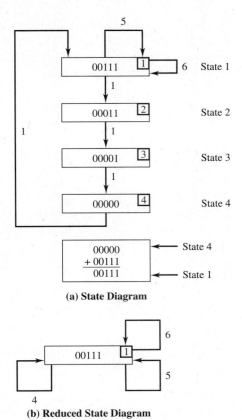

Figure 3.15 State Transitions of the Pipeline in Figure 3.11

state diagram of (a) can thus be simplified to the reduced state diagram shown in (b). Here the transitions corresponding to only the zero bits of CV are shown. The number on the arc between two states is the latency between two initiations represented by those states, and each state is represented by the content of the control shift register after the initiation of the new operation from the previous state. Thus, for this pipeline, the reduced state diagram indicates the three possible initiating conditions. As can be seen, the maximum input rate possible is one every four cycles. We can thus utilize the reduced state diagram to measure the performance of the pipeline. We will illustrate this with another example.

EXAMPLE 3.7

Consider the RT of a four-stage pipeline shown in Figure 3.16(a). The CV for this RT is (101010). The reduced state diagram is shown in (b). State 1 is the initial state at which an operation is initiated. As indicated by the CV, a new operation can be initiated at latencies 1, 3, and 5 (corresponding to the zero bits of CV) while in this state, reaching states 2, 3, and 4, respectively. From each of these new states, possible transitions are indicated in the diagram along with their latencies. Because no new states are reached, the diagram is complete.

3.2 PIPELINE CONTROL AND PERFORMANCE

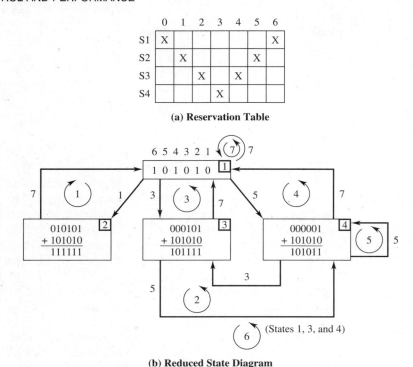

(a) Reservation Table

(b) Reduced State Diagram

Figure 3.16 State Transition Example

Consider the loop (loop 1) formed by states 1 and 2 in the above reduced state diagram. If the pipeline were to follow this loop, it would generate two outputs (once it is full) for every $1 + 7 = 8$ cycles. That is, the number of states traversed by the loop indicates the number of outputs from the pipeline (also, the number of operations that can be initiated) in a time frame obtained by adding the latencies on the arcs forming the loop. That is, the **average latency** for the pipeline traversing this loop is 8/2 or 4. Similarly, loop 2 provides an average latency of 4. The steady state output rate of the pipeline is the reciprocal of the average latency. Thus, this loop provides 0.25 outputs every pipeline cycle. In order for the pipeline to follow the pattern indicated by this loop, the pipeline controller has to bring the pipeline to state 3 from the initial state (state 1) and then initiate operations at 5- and 3-cycle intervals, respectively. The loops in the reduced state diagram are usually termed *cycles*. A *simple cycle* is a closed loop in which each state appears only once per traversal through the cycle. Table 3.1 lists all simple cycles and their average latencies from the above state diagram.

In order to determine the maximum performance possible, all simple cycles in the reduced state diagram need to be evaluated to select the one that provides the largest number of outputs per cycle. The *greedy cycles* in the state diagram are first candidates for such an evaluation. A greedy cycle is a simple cycle in which each latency is the minimal latency from any state in the cycle. Cycles 1 and 2 above are greedy cycles, and the maximum performance of the above pipeline is two operations

TABLE 3.1 AVERAGE LATENCIES

Cycle	Avg. Latency	
1*	4	* Greedy Cycles
2*	4	
3	5	
4	6	
5	5	
6	5	
7	7	

every eight cycles, or 0.25 operations per pipeline cycle. Note that, in general, a greedy cycle need not be the maximum performance cycle.

The bound on the highest possible initiation rate of a pipeline can be obtained by an examination of the reservation table. The row of the reservation table with the maximum number of entries corresponds to the bottleneck in the pipeline and limits the initiation rate. If there are Y marks in this row, the average delay between initiations (i.e., minimum average latency, or MAL) must be Y or greater; and hence, the maximum attainable rate in the pipeline is N/Y where N is the number of stages in the pipeline. Note that the MAL is the smallest average latency that can be achieved by any permissible latency sequence.

In the reservation table of Figure 3.16, the maximum number of entries in any row is 2. Thus, the MAL is 2/6 or 0.33. The above analysis predicts the maximum performance of 0.25, which is lower than the theoretical upper bound of 0.33.

The above observation on MAL is a consequence of the following Lemma by Shar (1972): For any statically configured pipeline executing some RT, the MAL is always greater than or equal to the maximum number of marks in any single row of the RT.

Assume that the initiation rate over a long period of time is r initiations per time unit and the number of marks in the ith row of the RT is N_i. Then the utilization of the ith stage is rN_i. Because the utilization cannot be more than 100%, rN_i must be less than 1 for all i, thus, r cannot be greater than $1/\text{MAX}(N_i)$. Thus, the average latency, being the reciprocal of r thus cannot be greater than $\text{MAX}(N_i)$. This lower bound provides a quick estimate of the maximum performance possible for a given pipeline and the RT.

It is possible to modify an RT to achieve maximum performance by inserting delays. Refer to the book by Kogge (1981) for details.

3.2.4 Multifunction Pipelines

The above control strategy and performance measurement scheme can be extended to multifunction pipelines. In general, a k-function pipeline requires k shift registers in its controller. There will be k RTs each describing the stage allocation pattern for one of the k operations possible. If X and Y designate two operations possible in a multifunction pipeline, V_{XY} denotes a cross-CV corresponding to allowing the operation Y after X has been initiated and V_{XX} denotes the CV corresponding to allowing X after X has been initiated. Thus, there will be a total of k^2 collision vectors, k of which are of the type V_{XX} with the remaining of the type V_{XY}.

3.2 PIPELINE CONTROL AND PERFORMANCE

EXAMPLE 3.8

Consider the RT of Figure 3.17 for a pipeline designed to perform two functions, X and Y. The four CVs are shown in (b). The value of each bit in V_{XX} (1010) and V_{YY} (0110) is determined as before for unifunction pipelines. To determine the cross-CV V_{XY}, the RTs for operations X and Y are overlaid. Bit i of the CV is 1 if in some row of the overlaid RT, an X and a Y appear i columns apart, otherwise it is 0. Thus, $V_{XY} = (1001)$ and $V_{YX} = (0101)$. In (c), the CVs are grouped into two collision matrices where the collision matrix M_X is the collection of CVs corresponding to initiating X after some other operation has been initiated (i.e., X is the second subscript of the CV).

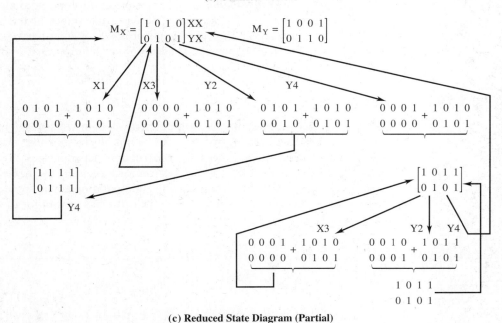

(a) Reservation Tables

(b) Collision Vectors

(c) Reduced State Diagram (Partial)

Figure 3.17 Multifunction Pipeline

The control strategy for the multifunction pipeline is similar to that for the unifunction pipeline. The collision matrix M_X controls the insertion of the operation

X. The controller requires k shift registers. To determine the insertion of operation X at any cycle, M_X is loaded into k control shift registers. Insertion of X after the initiation of operation i is determined by the shift register i (i.e., V_{iX}). If the rightmost bit of shift register i is 0 operation, X is allowed; otherwise it is not allowed to enter the pipeline. All the shift registers are shifted right at each cycle with a 0 entering each shift register at the left. To determine the new state, the shifted matrix is bitwise ORed with the original collision matrix. The reduced state diagram is drawn starting with k initial states, each corresponding to a collision matrix.

Figure 3.17(c) shows the reduced state diagram. Initial state S_X corresponds to M_X and S_Y corresponds to M_Y. There are two components in the marks on each arc leaving a state S_P: the first component designates a row of M_P and the second component designates a zero-bit position of that row. For example, X1 on the arc leaving M_X corresponds to the insertion of X in the first cycle after X has been initiated; Y2 corresponds to the insertion of X two cycles after the initiation of Y, and so forth.

The method for finding the greedy cycles and the maximum performance of multifunction pipelines is complex although it is similar to that for unifunction pipelines.

3.3 OTHER PIPELINE PROBLEMS

In addition to the collision problems in pipelines due to improper initiation rate, data interlocks occur on account of shared data between the stages of the pipeline and conditional branch instructions degrade the performance of an instruction pipeline, as mentioned earlier. These problems and some common solutions are described in this section.

3.3.1 Data Interlocks

An instruction processing pipeline is most efficient when instructions flow through its stages in a smooth manner. In practice, this is not always possible because of the interinstruction dependencies. These interinstruction dependencies are due to the sharing of resources, such as a memory location or a register, by the instructions in the pipeline. In such sharing environments, the computation cannot proceed if one of the stages is operating on the resource while the other has to wait for the completion of that operation.

EXAMPLE 3.9

Consider the following instruction sequence:

```
LOAD  R1, MEM1        R1 ← (MEM1)
LOAD  R2, MEM2        R2 ← (MEM2)
MPY   R1, R2          R1 ← (R2)×(R1)
ADD   R1, R2          R1 ← (R1)+(R2)
```

Figure 3.18 shows the operation of the pipeline of Figure 3.3 for this sequence. Note that, as a result of the second LOAD instruction, R2 is loaded with the data from

3.3 OTHER PIPELINE PROBLEMS

	Cycles								
	1	2	3	4	5	6	7	8	9
Load R1, Mem1	FI	DI	CA Mem1	FO Read Mem1	EX Write R1	ST			
Load R2, Mem2		FI	DI	CA Mem2	FO Read Mem2	EX Write R2	ST		
Mpy R1, R2			FI	DI	CA	FO Read R1, R2	EX Write R1	ST	
Or R2, R2				FI	DI	CA	FO Read R1, R2	EX Write R1	ST

Figure 3.18 Data Hazards

> MEM during cycle 6. But, the MPY instruction reads R2 during cycle 6 also. In general, R2 cannot be guaranteed to contain the proper data until the end of cycle 6, and hence, MPY instruction would operate with erroneous data. Similar **data hazard** occurs in cycle 7. For the results to be correct, we must ensure that R2 and R1 are read in each of these cycles after they have been written into by the previous instruction. One possible solution is to **forward** the data as early as possible to where it is needed in the pipeline. For instance, because the ALU requires contents of R2 in cycle 6, the memory read mechanism can simply forward the data to ALU while it is being written into R2, thus accomplishing the write and read simultaneously. The concept of internal forwarding is described further later in this section.

In general, the following scenarios are possible between instructions *I* and *J* where *J* follows *I* in the program:

1. Instruction *I* produces a result that is required by *J*. Then *J* has to be delayed until *I* produces the result.
2. Both *I* and *J* are required to write into a common memory location or a register, but the order of writing might get reversed due to the operation of the pipeline.
3. *J* writes into a register whose previous contents must be read by *I*. Then *J* must be delayed until the register contents are read by *I*.

If the order of operations is reversed by the pipeline from what was implied by the instruction sequence in the program, then the result will be erroneous. Because an instruction either READs from a resource or WRITEs into it, there are four possible orders of operations by two instructions that are sharing that resource. They are:

1. READ/READ   (READ after READ),
2. READ/WRITE   (READ after WRITE),
3. WRITE/READ   (WRITE after READ), and
4. WRITE/WRITE (WRITE after WRITE).

In each case, the first operation is from the earlier instruction *I* and the second operation is from the later instruction *J*. If the orders are reversed, a **conflict** occurs. That is, a READ/WRITE conflict occurs if the WRITE operation is performed by *J* before the resource has been READ by *I*, and so on.

Reversing the order of READ/READ is not detrimental because data are not changed by either instructions, and hence, it is not considered a conflict. After a WRITE/WRITE conflict, the result in the shared resource is the wrong one for subsequent read operations. If it can be established that there are no READs in between the two WRITEs, the pipeline can allow the WRITE from *J* and disable the WRITE from *I* when it occurs. If the order of READ/WRITE or WRITE/READ is reversed, the instruction reading the data gets an erroneous value. These conflicts must be detected by the pipeline mechanism to make sure that results of instruction execution remain as specified by the program.

There are in general two approaches to resolve conflicts. The first one is to compare the resources required by the instruction entering the pipeline with those of the instructions that are already in the pipeline and stall (i.e., delay the initiation) the entering instruction if a conflict is expected. That is, in the instruction sequence $[I, I+1, \ldots J, J+1, \ldots]$ if a conflict is discovered between the instruction *J* entering the pipeline with instruction *I* in the pipeline, then the execution of instructions $J, J+1, \ldots$ is stopped until *I* passes the conflict point. The second approach is to allow the instructions $J, J+1, \ldots$ to enter the pipeline and handle the conflict resolution at each potential stage where the conflict might occur. That is, suspend only instruction *J* and allow $J+1, J+2, \ldots$ to continue. Of course, suspending *J* and allowing subsequent instructions to continue might result in further conflicts. Thus, a multilevel conflict resolution mechanism may be needed making the pipeline control very complex. The second approach, known as **instruction deferral,** may offer better performance although it requires more complex hardware and independent functional units. Section 4 describes instruction deferral further.

One approach to avoid WRITE/READ conflicts is **data forwarding** in which the instruction that WRITEs the data also forwards a copy of the data to those instructions waiting for it. A generalization of this technique is the concept of **internal forwarding,** which is described next.

INTERNAL FORWARDING

Internal forwarding is a technique to replace unnecessary memory accesses by register-to-register transfers during a sequence of read-operate-write operations on the data in the memory. This results in a higher throughput because slow memory accesses are replaced by faster register-to-register operations. This scheme also resolves some data interlocks between the pipeline stages.

Consider the memory location *M* with which registers R1 and R2 exchange data. There are three possibilities of interest:

3.3 OTHER PIPELINE PROBLEMS

1. **write-read forwarding:** The following sequence of two operations

    M ← (R1)
    R2 ← (M),

    where ← designates a data transfer and ( ) designates the "contents of," can be replaced by

    M ← (R1)
    R2 ← (R1),

    thus saving one memory access.

2. **read-read forwarding:** The following sequence of two operations

    R1 ← (M)
    R2 ← (M)

    can be replaced by

    R1 ← (M)
    R2 ← (R1),

    thus saving one memory access.

3. **write-write forwarding (overwriting):** The following sequence of two operations

    M ← (R1)
    M ← (R2)

    can be replaced by

    M ← (R2),

    thus saving one memory access.

The internal forwarding technique can be applied to a sequence of operations as shown by the following example.

EXAMPLE 3.10

Consider the operation $P = (A \times B) + (C \times D)$ where $P, A, B, C,$ and D are memory operands. This can be performed by the following sequence:

    R1 ← (A)
    R2 ← (R1)×(B)
    R3 ← (C)
    R4 ← (R3)×(D)
    P ← (R4) + (R2)

The dataflow sequence for these operations is shown in Figure 3.19(a). By internal forwarding, the dataflow sequence can be altered to that in (b). Here, A and C are forwarded to the corresponding multiply units eliminating register R1 and R3, respectively. The results from these multiply units are forwarded to the adder eliminating the transfers to R2 and R4.

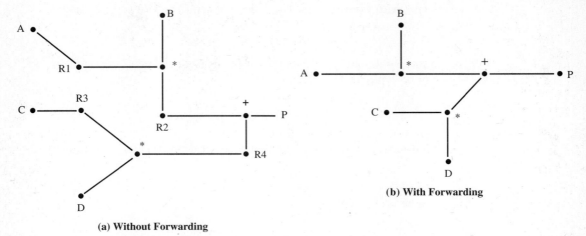

(a) Without Forwarding

(b) With Forwarding

Figure 3.19 Example of Internal Forwarding

In this example, a generalized architecture that allows operations between memory and register operands (as in second and fourth instructions) and register operands (as in the last instruction) was assumed. There are two other possibilities: **load/store** and **memory/memory** architectures. In a load/store architecture, the arithmetic operations are always between two register operands and memory is used for load and store only. In memory/memory architectures, operations can be performed on two memory operands directly. Assessment of the performance of the above instruction sequence on these architectures is left as an exercise.

The internal forwarding technique, as described above, is not restricted to pipelines alone but is applicable to general multiple processor architectures. In particular, internal forwarding in a pipeline is a mechanism to directly supply data produced by one stage to another stage that needs them (i.e., without storing them in and reading them from the memory). Example 3.11 illustrates the technique for a pipeline.

There are other types of data interlocks possible in a pipeline. The following example also illustrates one such interlock and its resolution.

EXAMPLE 3.11

Consider the computation of the sum of the elements of an array A. That is,

$$\text{SUM} = \sum_{i=1}^{n} A_i$$

Figure 3.20(a) shows a pipeline for computing this SUM. It is assumed that the array elements and the SUM are located in memory. Assuming that each stage in the pipeline completes its task in one pipeline cycle time, computation of the first accumulation would be possible. From then on, the fetch sum unit has to wait for two cycles before it can obtain the proper value for the SUM. This data interlock results in the degradation of the throughput of the pipeline to one output every three cycles.

One obvious thing to do is to feed the output of the add unit back to its input as shown in (b). This requires the buffering of the intermediate SUM value in the add

3.3 OTHER PIPELINE PROBLEMS

unit. Once all the elements are accumulated, the value of SUM can be stored into the memory.

If the add unit requires more than one cycle to compute the sum, the above solution again results in the degradation of throughput because the adder becomes the bottleneck.

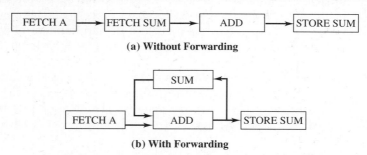

Figure 3.20 Pipeline for Computing Array-Sum

Kogge (1981) provided a solution for such problems by rewriting the summing above as

$$SUM_i = SUM_{i-d} + A_i,$$

where i is the current iteration index, SUM_{i-d} is the intermediate SUM d iterations ago, and d is the number of cycles required by the add unit. Because SUM_{i-d} is available at the ith iteration, this computation can proceed every iteration. But the computation results in d partial sums, each accumulating elements of A, d apart. At the end, these d partial sums should be added to obtain the final SUM. Thus, the pipeline can work efficiently at least during the computation of partial sums.

Thus in the pipeline (a) above if $d = 2$, we will require storing of two partial sums, SUM-1 and SUM-2, obtained one and two cycles ago, respectively, from the current iteration. The buffer holding these partial sums should be arranged as a first-in-first-out buffer so that the fetch sum unit fetches the appropriate value for each iteration.

This type of solution is practical when changing the order of computation does not matter, as in associative and commutative operations such as addition and multiplication. Even in these, changing the order might result in unexpected errors. For instance, in many numerical analysis applications the relative magnitudes of the numbers to be added are arranged to be similar. If the order of addition is changed, this structure would change resulting in a large number added to a small number, thereby altering the error characteristics of the computation.

3.3.2 Conditional Branches

As described earlier in this chapter, conditional branches degrade the performance of an instruction pipeline. The hardware mechanisms described earlier to minimize branch penalty were static in nature in the sense that they did not take into consideration the dynamic behavior of the branch instruction during program execution. Two compiler-based static schemes and two hardware-based dynamic schemes are described below.

BRANCH PREDICTION

The approaches described earlier are in a way branch prediction techniques in the sense that one of them predicted that the branch will be taken and the other predicted that the branch will not be taken. The run time characteristics of the program can also be utilized in predicting the target of the branch. For instance, if the conditional branch corresponds to the end-of-do-loop test in a Fortran program, it is safe to predict that the branch is to the beginning of the loop. This prediction would be correct every time through the loop except for the last iteration. Obviously, such predictions are performed by the compiler that generates appropriate flags to aid prediction during program execution.

In general, the target of the branch is guessed and the execution continues along that path while marking all the results as tentative until the actual target is known. Once the target is known, the tentative results are either made permanent or discarded. Branch prediction is effective as long as the guesses are correct.

DELAYED BRANCHING

The **delayed branching** technique is widely used in the design of microprogrammed control units. Consider the two-stage pipeline for the execution of instructions shown in Figure 3.21(a). The first stage fetches the instruction, and the second executes it. The effective throughput of the pipeline is one instruction per cycle for sequential code. When a conditional branch is encountered, the pipeline operation suffers while the pipeline fetches the target instruction as shown in (b). But if the branch instruction is interpreted as "execute the next instruction and then branch conditionally," then the pipeline can be kept busy while the target instruction is being fetched, as shown in (c). This mode of operation where the pipeline executes one or more instructions following a branch before executing the target of the branch is called delayed branching.

If n instructions enter the pipeline after a branch instruction and before the target is known, then the branch delay slot is of length n as shown below:

```
Branch instruction
successor instruction 1
successor instruction 2
successor instruction 3
     .
     .
successor instruction n
Branch target instruction.
```

The compiler rearranges the program such that the branch instruction is moved n instructions prior to where it normally occurs. That is, the branch slot is filled with instructions that need to be executed prior to branch and the branch executes in a delayed manner. Obviously, the instructions in the branch delay slot should not affect the condition for branch.

The length of the branch slot is the number of pipeline cycles needed to evaluate the branch condition and the target address (after the branch instruction enters the pipeline). The earlier these can be evaluated in the pipeline, the shorter is the branch slot.

3.3 OTHER PIPELINE PROBLEMS

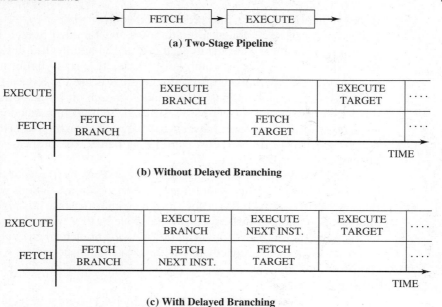

Figure 3.21 Delayed Branching

As can be guessed, this technique is fairly easy to adopt for architectures that offer single-cycle execution of instructions utilizing a two-stage pipeline. In these pipelines, the branch slot can hold only one instruction. As the length of the branch slot increases, it becomes difficult to sequence instructions such that they can be properly executed while the pipeline is resolving a conditional branch.

Modern day RISC architectures adopt pipelines with small numbers (typically two to five) of stages for instruction processing. They utilize delayed branching technique extensively.

The rearrangement of instructions to accommodate delayed branching is done by the compiler and is usually transparent to the programmer. Because the compiled code is dependent on the pipeline architecture, it is not easily portable to other processors. As such, delayed branching is not considered a good architectural feature, especially in aggressive designs that use complex pipeline structures.

All the techniques above are static in nature in the sense that the predictions are made at compile time and are not changed during program execution. The following techniques utilize hardware mechanisms to dynamically predict the branch target. That is, the prediction changes if the branch changes its behavior during program execution.

BRANCH-PREDICTION BUFFER
A branch-prediction buffer is a small memory buffer indexed by the branch instruction address. It contains one bit per instruction that indicates whether the branch was taken or not. The pipeline fetches subsequent instruction based on this prediction bit.

If the prediction is wrong, the prediction bit is inverted. Ideally, the branch prediction buffer must be large enough to contain one bit for each branch instruction in the program, or the bit is attached to each instruction and fetched during the instruction fetch. But that increases the complexity. Typically, a small buffer indexed by several low-order bits of the branch instruction address is used to reduce the complexity. In such cases, more than one instruction maps to each bit in the buffer and, hence, the prediction may not be correct with respect to the branch instruction at hand because some other instruction could have altered the prediction bit. Nevertheless, the prediction is assumed to be correct. Losq (1984) named the branch-prediction buffer a **decode history table.**

The disadvantage with this technique is that by the time the instruction is decoded to detect that it is a conditional branch, other instructions would have entered the pipeline. If the branch is successful, the pipeline needs to be refilled from the target address. To minimize this effect, if the decode history table also contains the target instruction in addition to the information as to the branch taken or not, that instruction can enter the pipeline immediately if the branch is a success.

BRANCH HISTORY

The **branch history** technique (Sussenguth, 1971) uses a branch history table that stores the most probable target address for each branch. This target could well be the target it reached last time during the program execution.

Figure 3.22 shows a typical branch history table. It consists of two entries for each instruction: the instruction address and the corresponding branch address. It is stored in a cache-like memory. As soon as the instruction is fetched, its address is compared with the first field of the table. If there is a match, the corresponding branch address is immediately known. The execution continues with this assumed branch as in branch prediction technique. The branch address field in the table is continually updated as and when the branch targets are resolved.

As can be guessed, the above implementation of the branch history table requires an excessive number of accesses to the table, thereby creating a bottleneck at the cache containing the table.

MULTIPLE INSTRUCTION BUFFERS

Section 1 described the use of multiple instruction buffers to reduce the effect of conditional branching on the performance of the pipeline. The details of a practical architecture utilizing that feature are provided here.

Figure 3.23 shows the structure of the IBM 360/91 instruction processing pipeline where the instruction fetch stage consists of two buffers: the S-buffer is the

Instruction Address	Branch Address

Figure 3.22 A Branch History Table

3.3 OTHER PIPELINE PROBLEMS

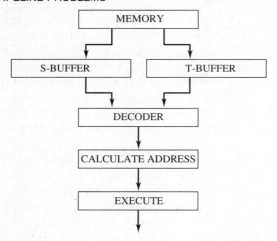

Figure 3.23 Instruction Pipeline with Multiple Instruction Buffers

sequential instruction prefetch buffer and the T-buffer is for the prefetch of target instruction sequence. This stage is followed by the decode and other stages similar to the pipeline in Figure 3.3.

The contents of the S-buffer are invalidated when a branch is successful, and the contents of T-buffer are invalidated when the branch is not successful. The decode unit fetches instructions from the appropriate buffer.

When the decoder issues a request for the next instruction, the S-buffer is looked up (i.e., a single-level, nonsequential search) for sequential instructions or the T-buffer is looked up if a conditional branch has just been successful. If the instruction is available in either buffer, it is brought into the decode stage without any delay. If not, the instruction needs to be fetched from the memory, which will incur a memory access delay.

All nonbranch instructions enter the remaining stages of the pipeline after the decode is complete. For unconditional branch instruction, the instruction at its target address is immediately requested by the decode unit and no further decoding is performed until that instruction arrives from the memory. For conditional branch instruction, the sequential prefetching is suspended while the instruction is traversing the remaining stages of the pipeline. Instructions are prefetched from the target address simultaneously until the branch is resolved. If the branch is successful, further instructions are fetched from the T-buffer. If the branch is not successful, normal fetching from the S-buffer continues.

3.3.3 Interrupts

A complex hardware/software support is needed to handle interrupts on a pipelined processor because many instructions are executed in an overlapped manner and any of those instructions can generate an interrupt. Ideally, if instruction I generates an interrupt, the execution of instructions $I + 1, I + 2, \ldots$ in the pipeline should be postponed until the interrupt is serviced. However, the instructions $I - 1, I - 2, \ldots$

that have already entered the pipeline must be completed before the interrupt service is started. Such an ideal interrupt scheme is known as **precise interrupt** scheme.

Note also that instructions are usually not processed in-order (i.e., the order in which they appear in the program). When delayed branching is used, the instructions in the branch-delay slot are not sequentially related. If an instruction in the branch-delay slot generates the interrupt and the branch is taken, the instructions in the branch-delay slot and the branch-target instruction must be restarted after interrupt is processed. This necessitates multiple program counters because these instructions are not sequentially related.

Several instructions can generate interrupts simultaneously, and these interrupts can be out of order. That is, the interrupt due to instruction I must be handled prior to that due to I + 1. To ensure that, a status vector is attached to each instruction as it traverses the pipeline. The machine state changes implied by the instruction are marked temporary until the last stage. At the last stage if the vector indicates that there has been no interrupt, the machine state is changed. If an interrupt is indicated, an in-order processing of interrupts is performed before state changes are committed.

3.4 DYNAMIC PIPELINES

This chapter has covered static pipelines so far. In these pipelines the interconnections between the stages are fixed. A dynamic pipeline, on the other hand, allows the interconnections between its stages to change (reconfigure) according to the function to be performed. It allows tasks from different RTs to be initiated simultaneously. Consider the multifunction pipeline of Figure 3.10. This pipeline allows both floating-point addition and multiplication operations. But, the interconnection pattern of the stages in the pipeline is decided at the design stage for each operation and does not change as the computations proceed. When an operation is initiated in the pipeline, the controller will reserve the pipeline stages according to the predetermined interconnection pattern for that operation.

For example, the floating-point functional unit of TI-ASC uses four ROM locations to store the interconnection patterns for each of the allowed operations. When an operation is initiated, the controller provides the address of the first location from which the stage interconnections are derived. CDC STAR-100 also allows such reconfiguration in its two static pipeline processors.

The operation of the CDC 6600 and IBM 360/91 CPUs comes close to that of a dynamic pipeline. Each of these CPUs contain multiple functional units. The functional units are not interconnected in a pipeline fashion but communicate with each other either through registers or through a bus. The computation at hand establishes a logical interconnection pattern, which changes as the computation proceeds. The organization of these CPUs allows the implementation of the instruction deferral scheme mentioned earlier.

3.4.1 Instruction Deferral

Instruction deferral is used to resolve the data interlock conflicts in the pipeline. The concept is to process as much of an instruction as possible at the current time and defer the completion until the data conflicts are resolved, thus obtaining a better overall performance than stalling the pipeline completely until data conflicts are resolved.

3.4 DYNAMIC PIPELINES

CDC 6600 Scoreboard (Thornton, 1970)

The processing unit of CDC 6600 shown in Figure 3.24 consists of 16 independent functional units (5 for memory access, 4 for floating-point operations, and 7 for integer operations). The input operands to each functional unit come from a pair of registers, and the output is designated to one of the registers. Thus, three registers are allocated to each functional unit corresponding to each arithmetic instruction. The control unit contains a **scoreboard** that maintains the status of all the registers, the status of functional units, and the register-functional unit associations. It contains an instruction queue called **reservation station.** Instructions first enter into the reservation station. Each arithmetic instruction corresponds to a 3-tuple consisting of two source register and one destination register designations. The load and store instruc-

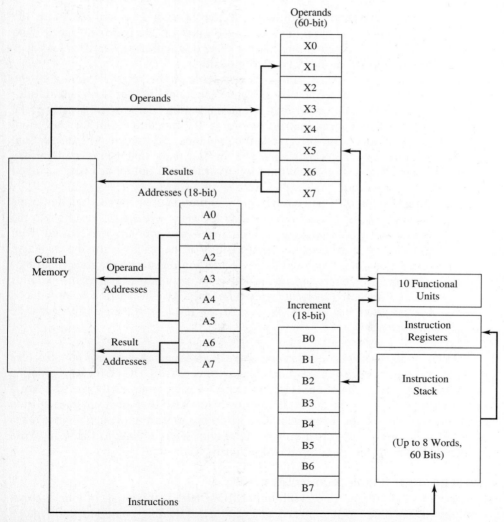

Figure 3.24 Central Processor Operating Registers of CDC 6600 (Courtesy of Control Data Corporation.)

tions consist of a 2-tuple corresponding to the memory address and register designation. The source operands in each instruction have a tag associated with them. The tag provides an indication of the availability of the operand in the register. If the operand is not available, it indicates the functional unit from which the operand is expected.

For each instruction the scoreboard determines whether the instruction can be executed immediately or not based on the analysis of data dependencies. If the instruction cannot execute immediately, it is placed in the reservation station and the scoreboard monitors its operand requirements and decides when all the operands are available. The scoreboard also controls when a functional unit writes its result into the destination register. Thus, the scoreboard resolves all conflicts. The scoreboard activity with respect to each instruction can be summarized in the following steps:

1. If a functional unit is not available, the instruction is stalled. When the functional unit is free, the scoreboard allocates the instruction to it if no other active functional unit has the same destination register. This resolves structural hazards and write/write conflicts.
2. A source operand is said to be available if the register containing the operand is being written by an active functional unit or if no active functional unit is going to write it. When the source operands are available, the scoreboard allocates that instruction to the functional unit for execution. The functional unit then reads the operands and executes the instruction. Write/read conflicts are resolved by this step. Note that the instructions may be allocated to functional units out of order (i.e., not in the order specified in the program).
3. When a functional unit completes the execution of an instruction, it informs the scoreboard. The scoreboard decides when to write the results into the destination register making sure that read/write conflicts are resolved. That is, the scoreboard does not allow writing of the results if there is an active instruction whose operand is the destination register of the functional unit wishing to write its result, if the active instruction has not read its operands yet, or if the corresponding operand of the active instruction was produced by an earlier instruction. Writing of the result is stalled until read/write conflict clears.

Because all functional units can be active at any time, an elaborate bus structure is needed to connect registers and funs. The 16 funs of the CDC 6600 were grouped into four groups with a set of buses (data trunks) for each group. Only one functional unit in each group could be active at any time. Note also that all results are written to the register file and the subsequent instruction has to wait until such a write takes place. That is, there is no forwarding of the results. Thus as long as the write/write conflicts are infrequent, the scoreboard performs well.

IBM 360/91 AND TOMOSULO'S ALGORITHM
Figure 3.25 shows the floating-point unit of IBM 360/91. It consists of four floating-point registers, a floating-point instruction queue, and floating-point adder and multiplier functional units. Unlike CDC 6600, the functional units are pipelined and are

3.4 DYNAMIC PIPELINES

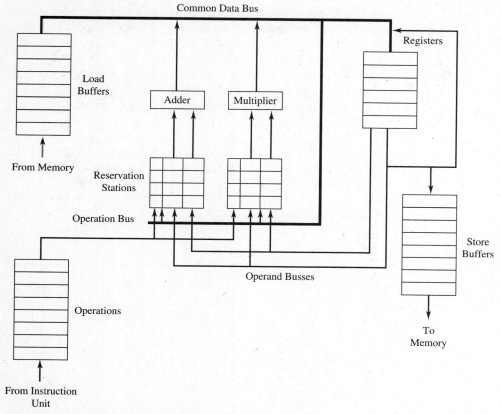

Figure 3.25 IBM 360/91 Floating-Point Unit

capable of starting at most one operation every clock cycle. The reservation stations at each functional unit decide when an instruction can begin execution in that unit, unlike the centralized reservation station of the CDC 6600 scoreboard. The load buffers hold the data from the memory, and the store buffers hold the data destined to memory. The results from functional units are broadcast to all the destinations (reservation stations, registers, and memory buffers) that require them simultaneously over the common data bus (CDB) rather than through registers as in CDC 6600. Instructions obtain their operands from reservation stations rather than from registers, thus overcoming the limitation of a small number of registers.

The following steps constitute Tomosulo's algorithm (1967) for instruction execution:

1. Get the floating-point instruction from the queue and allocate it to an appropriate reservation station if one is available and also send operands from registers (if they are there) to that reservation station. The tag field at the reservation station for each operand indicates whether the operand is available or it contains an indication of which memory buffer it may be in or

which functional unit is producing it. The memory buffers also have a similar tag. If the instruction is a load or store, it is allocated if an empty buffer is available. The instruction stalls if either the memory buffer is not free or reservation station is not available.

2. Execute the instruction if both the operands are available, and send the result to the CDB. If an operand is not available in the reservation station, monitor CDB until that operand is computed by another unit. Write/read conflicts are resolved in this step.

These steps are similar to those used in the scoreboard except that the write/write and read/write conflicts are not specifically checked but eliminated as a by-product of the algorithm.

The following example illustrates instruction deferral and is a simplified version of Tomosulo's algorithm.

EXAMPLE 3.12

Consider the operation $P = A \times B + C \times D$ where $P, A, B, C,$ and D are memory operands. This can be executed by the sequence:

```
1    R1  ←  (A)
2    R2  ←  (B)
3    R2  ←  (R1)×(R2)
4    R3  ←  (C)
5    R4  ←  (D)
6    R4  ←  (R3)×(R4)
7    R4  ←  (R2)+(R4)
8    P   ←  (R4)
```

Figure 3.26 shows the entries in the reservation stations for all the functional units. The tag fields indicate that the value for A is not available in R1 at this time and, hence, operation 1 and, hence, 3, 7, and 8 are deferred until A arrives. Meanwhile, the pipeline can proceed with other operations.

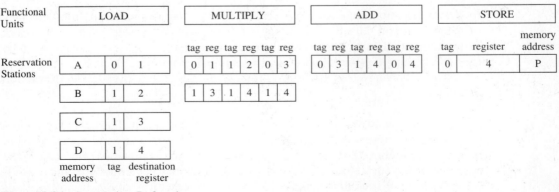

Figure 3.26 Instruction Deferral

The pipeline design techniques, instruction deferral, and forwarding mechanisms described in this chapter reflect the state of the art although first implemented almost 20 years ago. But the inclusion of cache memory into computer systems has contributed to a drastic lowering of time required for memory access. It is now possible to have a large number of registers in the machine structure. With sophisticated compilers now available, it is possible to allocate this large number of registers judiciously thus eliminating a majority of read/write and write/write conflicts.

3.4.2 Performance Evaluation

In static pipelines, because all the initiations are of the same type, it is possible to design an optimal strategy for scheduling the pipeline to provide the maximum processing rate. In dynamic pipelines where several RTs are used for initiation, several equally valid scheduling strategies are possible. Kogge (1981) identifies the following:

a. Maximizing the total number of initiations of any kind in any order per unit time
b. Maximizing the total number of initiations per unit time given that out of this total a percentage must be from each type of RT and no particular order imposed on the sequence
c. Minimizing the total time required to handle a specific sequence of initiation table types

In an instruction processing pipeline of an SISD, the first criterion above corresponds to the maximum number of instructions per second that can be executed in any order; the second criterion imposes an instruction mix (i.e., arithmetic type 40%, branches 10%, and so on); and the third corresponds to the performance of some benchmark program. Thus, the criteria are increasingly restrictive.

Performance measurements of the first type are similar to those applied to static pipelines. The difference is that in computing the average latency of a cycle, the period is divided by the total number of entries in all initiation sets in the arcs making up the cycle. Also, because more than one reservation table may be used for initiations at any time, the lower bound for the average latency cannot be determined simply from the RTs. The following lemma provides the lower bound:

Lemma: The average latency of any cycle for a dynamic pipeline is bounded below by $1/N$, where N is the maximum number of elements in any initiation set.

The second performance measure requires the minimum average latency given a mix of initiations. Thomas and Davidson (1974) extend the solution for the static case to cover this measure. This method assumes that the scheduling algorithm is free to pick any of the RTs to make an initiation. Thus, there is no restriction as to when an RT may be picked or in what order. This assumption reduces the complexity of analysis. The branch-and-bound and linear programming technique used in the analysis computes for a given mix of initiations a collection of simple cycles that provide the MAL. But the analysis does not guarantee that these cycles can be connected. That is, the controller should use additional paths to connect these cycles thus making the control strategy less than optimal.

There is no known solution for the third performance measure except for an exhaustive search process. A schedule that is optimal for one benchmark may not be optimal for another benchmark. Usually variations of greedy strategy are used that at each stage chose from those arcs with appropriate initiation sets the one with the minimum latency.

3.5 EXAMPLE SYSTEMS

A brief description of representative pipelined processors is given in this section. Control Data Corporation's STAR-100 is included for its historic interest. CDC 6600 is included to highlight its pipelined I/O system and to complete the discussion of its CPU, which forms the basis for the Cray vector architecture described in Chapter 4. MIPS Computer Systems's R4000 represents a contemporary architecture.

3.5.1 Control Data Corporation STAR-100

CDC STAR-100, developed in late 1960s, is a pipelined machine and served as the prototype for the Cyber series of machines manufactured by CDC. The structure of STAR-100 is shown in Figure 3.27. The CPU contains two multifunction arithmetic pipelines that can process 64-bit fixed- and floating-point operands and a string processing unit. Pipeline 1 performs addition and multiplication. Pipeline 2 performs addition, multiplication, division, and square-root extraction. It also contains a non-pipelined floating-point division unit. Each pipeline can function as a 64-bit pipeline or as two 32-bit pipelines working in parallel. Hence, there are in effect four 32-bit pipelines. Each of these can produce one floating-point output every 40 ns. Two 128-bit buses supply operands to the CPU from the memory, and one 128-bit bus carries the results back to the memory. There is a fourth 128-bit bus used for instruction fetch and I/O. Each of these buses can transmit 128 bits every 40 ns.

The memory system consists of 32 modules, each with 2K words of 512 bits. The cycle time of the core memory modules is 1.28 μs. The CPU pipelines produce a 128-bit result every 40 ns or a total of 4K bits every 1.28 μs. In order to sustain this rate, the memory has to output two streams of 4K bits and input one stream of 4K bits every cycle. In addition, another stream of 4K bits output is needed for instruction fetch, resulting in a total memory transfer rate of 16 Kbits every cycle. This rate is achieved by each of the 32 modules producing a 512-bit data every cycle.

3.5.2 CDC 6600

The applications envisioned for CDC 6600 introduced in 1964 were large-scale scientific processing and time-sharing of smaller problems. To accommodate large-scale scientific processing, a high-speed, floating-point CPU with multiple functional units was used.

Figure 3.28 shows the structure of the system. Figure 3.24 shows the CPU structure. Details of the CPU operation in terms of computations of the type $Z = A \times B + C \times D$, where Z, A, B, C, and D are memory operands were given earlier in this chapter. The CPU obtains its programs and data from the central memory and can be interrupted by a peripheral processor. There are 24 operating

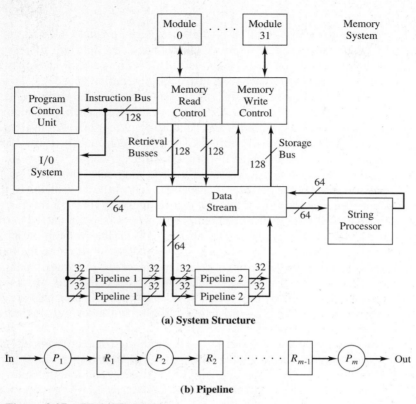

Figure 3.27 CDC STAR-100

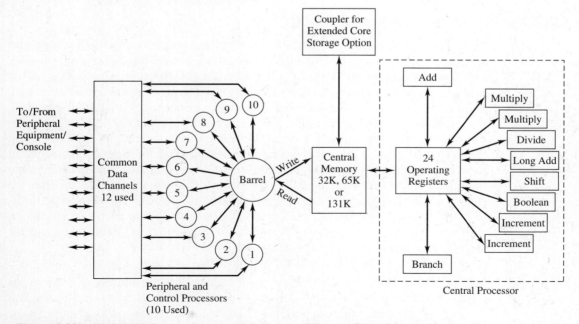

Figure 3.28 CDC 6600 System Structure (Courtesy of Control Data Corporation.)

registers in the CPU: eight 18-bit index registers, eight 18-bit address registers, and eight 60-bit floating-point registers interconnected by data and address paths. Instructions are either 15- or 30-bit long, and there is an instruction stack that can hold up to 32 instructions to enhance the instruction execution speed.

The control unit maintains the scoreboard described earlier. The central memory is organized into 32 interleaved banks of 4K words each. Five memory trunks are provided between the memory and floating-point registers. An instruction calling for an address register implicitly initiates a memory reference on its trunk. An overlapped memory access and arithmetic operation is thus possible.

The I/O subsystem consists of 12 I/O channels controlled by ten peripheral processors. One of the peripheral processors acts as the control unit of the system. The ten peripheral processors access the central memory through the barrel mechanism, which has a 1000-ns cycle. Each peripheral processor is connected to the memory for 100 ns in each barrel cycle. During this 100-ns interval the peripheral processor requests a memory access. The access is complete by the time the barrel visits that peripheral processor in the next cycle. The barrel is a ten-stage pipeline. The request from each peripheral processor enters this pipeline and gets processed in an overlapped manner over the next nine 100-ns intervals. I/O channels are 12-bit bidirectional paths. One 12-bit word can be transferred in or out of the memory every 1000 ns by each channel.

The major characteristics of the CDC 6600 that make it versatile are concurrent operation of the functional units within the CPU, high transfer rates between registers and memory, separation of CPU and I/O activities, and a high bandwidth I/O structure. The Cray series of supercomputers, also designed by Seymour Cray, retain this basic architecture.

3.5.3 MIPS Computer Systems's R4000

MIPS R4000 (Figure 3.29) is a 64-bit RISC architecture with on-chip floating-point unit and cache memory. It has an integer unit and a memory management coprocessor along with the capability to interface a second-level off-chip cache memory. The instruction and data cache are each 8 Kbytes long. The processor characteristics were outlined in Chapter 1. The following paragraphs concentrate on R4000 pipelines.

R4000 is a superpipelined processor. Its pipeline consists of eight stages compared to the usual four- or five- stage pipeline found in contemporary RISC architectures. Typically, a standard (or plain) pipeline has one stage for each function required to process an instruction. A superpipeline, on the other hand, has more than one stage for at least one of the functions. In R4000 the instruction and data cache accesses are spread across three stages with two stages performing look-up and the third performing tag checking. The pipeline runs at 100 MHz. Thus, a new cache access can be started every 10 ns. But the data is available only after 20 ns, and it takes another 10 ns before it is certain that the data is for the correct address.

The eight stages of the R4000 pipeline shown in Figure 3.30 are:

1. **Instruction first (IF):** The branch logic selects the address of the next instruction and sends it to the instruction cache (i-cache) and instruction translation lookaside buffer (i-TLB). This stage fetches instruction from the i-cache.

2. **Instruction second (IS):** This stage completes i-cache fetch and begins i-TLB look-up.
3. **Register fetch (RF):** This stage decodes the instruction fetched, checks for interlock conditions to determine if the instruction needs to be stalled, fetches operands from the register file. I-cache tag is compared with the physical address provided by the i-TLB, to determine whether there was an i-cache hit or miss.

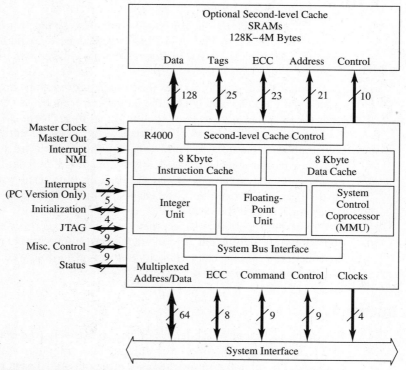

Figure 3.29 Structure of MIPS R4000 Processor (Reprinted with permission from *Microprocessor Report,* October 2, 1991.)

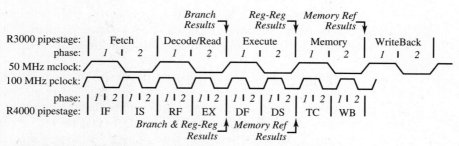

Figure 3.30 MIPS R4000 Pipeline (Reprinted with permission from *Microprocessor Report,* October 2, 1991.)

4. Execute (EX): Begins the instruction execution. The integer unit performs all register-to-register operations, calculates the virtual address for load/store instructions and branch-target virtual addresses for branch instructions.
5. Data fetch first (DF): Begins data fetch, by presenting virtual address to data cache (d-cache) and data TLB (d-TLB).
6. Data fetch second (DS): Completes d-cache fetch and d-TLB look-up. The required data is selected and aligned appropriately from the data delivered by the d-cache.
7. Tag check (TC): This stage compares the tag from d-cache to the physical address provided by d-TLB to determine d-cache hit or miss.
8. Write back (WB): Writes results back to register file.

Note from Figure 3.30 that the branch address must cross three pipeline stages to get from EX to IF, and hence, the latency of branches is three cycles. Similarly, for loads the data has to cross two pipeline stages to get from DS to EX, thus making the load latency to be two cycles. The load is not complete until the end of TC because only then is it possible to know whether there was a hit or miss in d-cache. The pipeline predicts a cache hit statically by passing data from DS to EX. If TC detects a cache miss, the pipeline is frozen such that no valid results are produced by EX. The pipeline remains frozen until the cache miss is resolved and the EX stage completes the operation with the new data.

Although R4000 is superpipelined (with respect to cache accesses), the ALU operations are completed in one stage. This allows the execution of back-to-back dependent operations (such as an add into a register followed immediately by another add that uses that register).

3.6 SUMMARY

Pipelining techniques have been adopted extensively to enhance the performance of serial processing structures. Several pipeline computer systems are commercially available. This chapter covers the basic principles and design methodologies for pipelines. Example systems are described. Almost all the pipeline systems available today utilize static pipelines. A brief introduction to dynamic pipelines, which are more complex to design, is also given in this chapter.

Note that although the throughput of the machine is improved by employing pipeline techniques, the basic cycle time of instructions remain as in nonpipelined implementations. In earlier machines with little or no pipelining, the average clock per instruction (CPI) was 5 to 10. Modern RISC architectures achieved a CPI value close to 1.

Pipelines exploit instruction-level parallelism in the program, whereby instructions that are not dependent on each other are executed in an overlapped manner. If the instruction-level parallelism is sufficient to keep the pipeline flowing full (with independent instruction), we achieve the ideal machine with a CPI of 1.

Three approaches have been tried to improve the performance beyond the ideal CPI case: **superpipelining, superscalar,** and **very long instruction word (VLIW)** architectures (Hennessy and Jouppi, 1991; Stone and Cocke, 1991).

3.6 SUMMARY

A **superpipeline** uses deeper pipelines (recall that MIPS R4000 is called a superpipelined machine) and control mechanisms to keep many stages of the pipeline busy concurrently. Note that as the latency of a stage gets longer, the instruction issue rate will drop and also there is a higher potential for data interlocks.

A **superscalar** machine allows the issue of more than one instruction per clock into the pipeline, thus achieving an instruction rate higher than the clock rate. In these architectures, the hardware evaluates the dependency among instructions and dynamically schedules a packet of independent instruction for issue at each cycle. Intel i860 processor can issue an integer and a floating-point instruction simultaneously.

In a **VLIW** architecture, a machine instruction corresponds to a packet of independent instructions created by the compiler. No dynamic hardware scheduling is used. There are no commercial architectures of this type, although there have been two efforts (Multiflow, Inc. and Cydrome Corporation) to build these machines.

Refer to Jouppi and Wall (1989), Sohi and Vajapeyam (1989), Hennessey and Jouppi (1991), and Stone and Cocke (1991) for a discussion of relative merits of pipeline architectures and current trends.

REFERENCES

Chen, T. C. 1980. Overlap and pipeline processing. In *Introduction to computer architecture,* ed. H. S. Stone. Chicago: Science Research Associates, 427–486.

Handler, W. 1977. The impact of classification schemes on computer architecture, *Proceedings International Conference on Parallel Processing,* 7–15.

Hennessey, J. L., and N. P. Jouppi. 1991. Computer technology and architecture: An evolving interaction. *IEEE Computer* 24(9): 18–29.

Hwang, K., and F. A. Briggs. 1984. *Computer architecture and parallel processing.* New York: McGraw-Hill.

Jouppi, N. P., and D. W. Wall. 1989. Available instruction-level parallelism for superscalar and superpipelined machines. *Proceedings IEEE/ACM Conference on Architectural Support for Programming Languages and Operating Systems.* April, 272–282.

Kogge, P. M. 1981. *The architecture of pipelined computers.* New York: McGraw-Hill.

Losq, J. J., G. S. Rao, and H. E. Sachar. 1984. *Decode history table for conditional branch instructions.* U.S. Patent No. 4,477,872. October.

Patel, J. H., and E. S. Davidson. 1976. Improving the throughput of a pipeline by insertion of delays. *Proceedings of the Third Annual Computer Architecture Symposium.* 159–163.

Ramamoorthy, C. V., and H. F. Li. Pipeline architectures. *ACM Computing Surveys* 9(1): 61–102.

Shar, L. E. 1972. Design and scheduling of statistically configured pipelines. *Digital Systems Lab Report SU-SEL-72-042.* Stanford, Calif.: Stanford University. September.

Shar, L. E. and E. S. Davidson. 1974. A multiminiprocessor system implemented through pipelining. *IEEE Computer* 7(2): 42–51.

Sohi, G. S. and S. Vajapeyam. 1989. Tradeoffs in instruction format design for horizontal architectures. *Proceedings IEEE/ACM Conference on Architectural Support for Programming Languages and Operating Systems.* April, 15–25.

Stone, H. S. 1987. *High performance computer architecture.* Reading, Mass: Addison-Wesley.

Stone, H. S. and J. Cocke. 1991. Computer architectures in the 1990s. *IEEE Computer* 24(9) September, 30–38.

Sussenguth, E. 1971. Instruction sequence control. U.S. Patent No. 3,559,183. January.

Thomas, A. T., and E. S. Davidson. 1978. Scheduling of multiconfigurable pipelines. *Proceedings 12th Annual Allerton Conference Circuits and System Theory*. Champaign-Urbana, 658–669.

PROBLEMS

3.1. Describe the conditions under which an n-stage pipeline is n times faster than a serial machine.

3.2. Design a pipeline ALU that can add two 8-bit integers. Assume that each stage can add two 2-bit integers and employ sufficient number of stages. Show the operation of the pipeline using a reservation table.

3.3. Design a pipeline for multiplying two floating-point numbers represented in IEEE standard format. Assume that addition requires T seconds and multiplication requires $2T$ seconds and shift takes $T/2$ seconds. Use as many stages as needed, and distribute the functions such that each stage approximately consumes the same amount of time.

3.4. Compute the minimum number of pipeline cycles required to multiply 50 floating-point numbers in the pipeline of problem 3.3, assuming that the output from the last stage can be fed back to any of the stages that requires it with the appropriate delay.

3.5. For the following reservation table, derive the collision vector and identify the maximum rate cycle:

	1	2	3	4	5	6	7
S1	X	X		X			
S2		X					X
S3			X				
S4					X		
S5						X	

3.6. For each of the following collision vectors, draw a reduced state diagram and determine the maximum performance possible:
   a. 110010100
   b. 100101
   c. 10101000

3.7. The following reservation tables are for a two-function pipeline:

	1	2	3	4	5	1	2	3	4	5
S1		X		X			Y		Y	
S2				X				Y	Y	
S3	X		X						Y	Y

a. What is the maximum number of initiations possible of any kind in any order?
b. What is the MAL when the order of initiations is XXYY?

3.8. For any computer system you are familiar with, analyze the instruction cycle and split that into a three-stage pipeline in which the stages perform fetch, address compute, and execute functions. What types of problems would you encounter?

3.9. It is required to multiply two $n \times n$ matrices. Design a pipeline with a one-stage adder and a two-stage multiplier where each stage consumes T seconds and compute the execution time for matrix multiplication.

3.10. The following program adds 2 to each element of a vector located starting at memory location V. The index register X contains the number of elements in the vector:

```
LOOP  LDA   V(X)      Load an element into the Accumulator
      ADD   =2        Add 2 to Accumulator
      STA   V(X)      Store it back
      DEX             Decrement Index register
      BNZ   LOOP      Branch back if X is not 0
```

Show the execution characteristics of this code on the pipeline of Figure 3.2. Schedule instructions appropriately to enhance the performance of the pipeline.

3.11. One common mechanism used to enhance pipeline performance while executing loops is called **loop unrolling.** That is, the body of the loop is repeated to form a program with strict sequential instruction stream. Assume that the number of elements in Problem 3.10 is 8.
a. Unroll the loop such that two elements are processed each time through the loop. Determine the performance of the pipeline with appropriate instruction scheduling.
b. Unroll the loop completely (that is, no looping at all). Examine the performance of the pipeline with appropriate scheduling.

3.12. Assume that a CPU uses four cycles (fetch, calculate address, memory read, move the data to the destination register) for a LOAD register instruction; correspondingly four cycles for a STORE instruction, and three cycles (fetch, compute results, move them to the destination register) for other register-to-register instructions. Show the reservation pattern for the following program:

```
LOAD    Z       ACC ← Z
ADD     R1      ACC ← ACC+R1
STORE   Z       Z   ← ACC
SUB     R2      ACC ← ACC−R2
```

where ACC, R1, and R2 are registers, and Z is a memory location. How many cycles are needed to execute this program, assuming maximum instruction overlap?

3.13. Assume that an n-element vector operation takes $s \times n$ cycles on a nonpipelined machine and $f + p \times n$ cycles on a pipelined machine, where f is the pipeline fill time and p is the time taken by stages in the pipeline (in cycles). For what values of n is the pipelined implementation faster?

3.14. In implementing the delayed branch technique, the compiler must determine when an instruction can be moved into the branch delay slot. What conditions are appropriate for the compiler to consider?

3.15. Compare the relative merits of superpipelined and superscalar architectures. To what application environment is each technique suitable? What is an underpipelined architecture?

CHAPTER 4

Vector Processors

Manipulation of arrays or vectors is a common operation in scientific and engineering applications. Typical operations on array-oriented data are:

  a. processing one or more vectors to produce a scalar result (as in computing the sum of all the elements of the vector, finding the maximum or minimum element, etc.);
  b. combining two vectors to produce a third vector (as in addition or multiplication of two arrays element by element);
  c. combining a scalar and a vector resulting in a vector (as in multiplying each element of the vector by a scalar); or
  d. a combination of the above three operations.

Three architectures suitable for the vector processing environment have evolved over the years: pipelined vector processors, parallel array processors, and systolic array architectures.

Pipelined vector processors (or pipelined array processors) utilize one or more pipelined ALUs to achieve high computation throughput. Examples of this type of architecture are: the series of supercomputers from Cray Research, Inc. (Cray-1, Cray-2, Cray X-MP, Cray Y-MP); Cray Computer Corporation (Cray-3, Cray-4); Texas Instruments (ASC); Control Data Corporation (CDC STAR-100 and Cyber series); Fujitsu (VP-200 series), Hitachi (S810 series); Convex Computer Corporation (C1, C2, and C3 series), IBM (3838); and Floating-Point Systems (5000 series). A further distinction can be made between the architectures of this type. All the systems mentioned above except the last two have **integrated CPUs** that perform both scalar- and vector-oriented computations. The last two architectures are known as **attached array processors** because they are used as coprocessors for a scalar-oriented CPU that calls upon these coprocessors when array-oriented computations are required.

Parallel array processors adopt a multiplicity of CPUs that operate on elements of arrays in parallel in an instruction lock-step mode. This is the class of SIMD architectures presented in Chapter 2. These architectures exploit the **data-parallelism** in array-oriented computations.

Systolic array architectures were also introduced in Chapter 2. They are processor array architectures suitable for implementing algorithms constituting a small set of simple operations and allow a highly regular data and control flow. They use extensive pipelining and parallel processing.

This chapter covers pipelined vector processor architectures (more commonly called vector processors), and Chapter 5 provides further details on the other two types.

Vector processors are supercomputers optimized for fast execution of long groups of vectorizable scientific code that operate on large data sets. Because the highest possible computation rate is the main criterion behind building these machines and not the cost optimization (in general), building these machines is often tagged the cost-is-no-object approach to computer architecture. Features that are possible only on these expensive systems eventually trickle down to commodity microprocessors as the hardware technology progresses. As such, these machines could be good indicators of what is to come in future processors.

Vector processors are extensively pipelined architectures designed to operate on array-oriented data. In these processors, the operations on the arrays takes place serially on each element of the array, rather than on all the elements in parallel. The individual elements are streamed into the extensively pipelined CPU to be operated upon. The memory system is also deeply pipelined and interleaved to meet the demand of the pipelined CPU. In addition, the register set of the CPU may be large enough to hold all the elements of one or more vectors. This combination of extensively pipelined CPU and memory, and large register set, provides the high computation throughput achieved by these architectures.

The models for two common vector processor architectures are provided in the next section and are followed by memory design considerations, an important aspect of vector processor design, in Section 2. Section 3 utilizes the Cray series architecture to illustrate the features of practical architectures. Details of two other popular architectures are provided in Section 4. Performance evaluation and programming concepts are covered in Sections 5 and 6, respectively.

4.1 VECTOR PROCESSOR MODELS

The models for two common vector processor architectures are introduced in this section. The following examples illustrate the advantages of vector instruction coding.

EXAMPLE 4.1

Consider element by element the addition of two N-element vectors A and B to create the sum vector C. That is:

$$C_i = A_i + B_i \qquad 1 \leq i \leq N. \tag{4.1}$$

This computation can be implemented on an SISD by the following program:

```
for i = 1, N
    C[i] = A[i] + B[i]
endfor
```

Assuming two machine instructions for loop control and four machine instructions to implement the assignment statement (Read A, Read B, Add, Write C), the execution time of this program is $6 \times N \times T$ where T is the average instruction cycle time of the machine.

Figure 4.1 shows a pipelined implementation of this computation using a four-stage addition pipeline with a cycle time T. Now the program consists of only one instruction:

$$C[i] = A[i] + B[i] \qquad (1 \leq i \leq N).$$

The loop overhead of the SISD program above is thus eliminated, and only one instruction needs to be fetched from the memory. The total execution time is the sum of one instruction fetch and decode time (assumed to be T) and the time to add N pairs of operands using the pipeline.

The performance of a pipelined functional unit is characterized by the **start-up time,** which is the number of clock cycles required prior to the generation of the first result, or simply the depth of the pipeline in clock cycles. After the start-up time the functional unit can deliver one result every clock cycle. Thus, the time to complete an N-element vector operation in a pipeline is:

$$\text{Start-up time} + (N - 1) \times \text{Initiation rate}. \tag{4.2}$$

The **start-up time** in the above pipeline is $4T$, and one operation can be initiated every

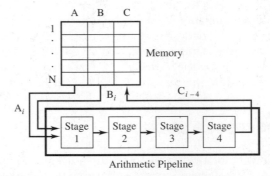

Figure 4.1 Vector Computational Model

cycle. Thus the above vector operation can be completed in $(4 + N - 1) \times T$ cycles. The total execution time thus is:

$$= T + [4 + (N - 1)]T$$
$$= (4 + N)T.$$

Hence, the speedup due to pipelined implementation is:

$$\frac{6NT}{(4 + N)T}. \tag{4.3}$$

This implies a sixfold speedup for large values of N.

Note from (4.2) above that the start-up time adds a considerable overhead for small values of N. For large values of N, the effect of start-up time is negligible and the **completion rate** (i.e., the rate at which the results are produced) tends toward the initiation rate.

The pipelined array processor structure of Figure 4.1 can be generalized to that shown in Figure 4.2 to represent the architecture of contemporary vector processors.

The main memory holds instructions and data. Its organization is a key factor in the performance of the system because vector processors retrieve and store large amounts of data from and to the memory. The memory is usually heavily interleaved to accommodate the fast access requirements of vector data. Note for instance that the pipeline organization in Figure 4.1 requires two read and one write operations from the memory at each cycle. Memory system design should accommodate this access requirement for data fetch and store operations in addition to instruction fetch access requirements.

The scalar processor handles all scalar aspects of processing, such as program control and vector setup, operating system functions, and input/output. It calls upon the vector controller to handle vector computations.

The vector controller decodes vector instructions, computes operand address parameters, initiates the vector memory controller and the arithmetic pipeline operations, and monitors them. At the end of the vector instruction execution, it performs any cleanup and status gathering needed.

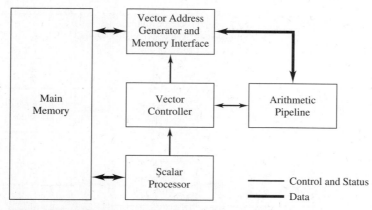

Figure 4.2 Memory-Oriented Vector Processor

The function of the vector address generator and memory interface module is to provide a high speed transfer of data between the arithmetic pipeline and the memory. It receives the operand address parameters from the vector controller and converts them into a series of memory access patterns that access the memory as fast as possible.

The arithmetic pipeline receives the operands from the memory and returns the results to the memory. In practice, there may be more than one arithmetic pipeline in the system. These pipelines could each be dedicated to a single function or may each handle multiple functions.

The above model represents the **memory-oriented** vector processor architecture. CDC STAR-100, described in Chapter 3, belongs to this category.

Figure 4.3 shows the **register-oriented** vector processor architecture commonly used to build modern day supercomputers. In this architecture, scalar and vector data are first brought into a set of registers and the arithmetic pipeline receives the operands from these registers and stores the results into them. Because accessing registers is faster than accessing memory, pipeline throughput would be enhanced compared to the structure of Figure 4.2. Typically, vector operands are transferred between the main memory and the registers in blocks and the arithmetic pipeline accesses these operands from the registers element by element. Thus, the registers serve as buffers between the memory and the pipeline. This buffering also allows the simultaneous operation of the pipeline-register and register-memory interfaces. The Cray, Convex, Hitachi, and Fujitsu machines listed earlier are examples of register-oriented architecture.

The following characteristics of vector processor architectures contribute to their high performance:

1. High-speed memory that allows retrieval and storage of voluminous data.
2. A large number of processor registers with vector registers capable of holding all the elements of vectors of typical length and scalar registers for nonvector data and addresses.
3. Instruction set containing vector-oriented instructions that define operations on the entire vector or vectors.

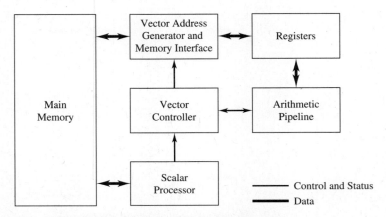

Figure 4.3 Register-Oriented Vector Processor

4. A multiplicity of overlapped processing levels:
   a. Each arithmetic pipeline provides overlapped operations.
   b. If multiple pipelines are employed, they can all be operating in parallel.
   c. The scalar processor overlaps its operations with those of the vector module.
   d. Within the vector module, the vector controller and the vector address generator might be performing their functions in an overlapped manner on different vector instructions.
   e. The memory-register and register-pipeline interfaces operate in an overlapped manner.

The above models also represent the structure of **attached array processors.** The only difference is that in an attached processor architecture, all the functions of the scalar processor are performed by the host computer system. Attached to the host is an array processor that handles all the vector-oriented functions of the structures in Figures 4.2 and 4.3.

As mentioned earlier, memory system performance is an important aspect of vector processor architectures. Memory design considerations are described next. Chapter 5 extends these concepts further.

4.2 MEMORY DESIGN CONSIDERATIONS

Memory **bandwidth** is defined as the average number of words that can be accessed from the memory per second. It depends on the memory system configuration, memory module configuration, and the processor architecture. Memory system configuration is characterized by the number of memory modules, bus width, and address decoding structure (i.e., interleaved, banked, wider-word fetch, etc.). The module characteristics include the size, access time, and cycle time.

Memory bandwidth must match the demand of multiple pipelined processors if the vector processor has to deliver maximum performance.

EXAMPLE 4.2

Consider a vector processor with four 32-bit floating-point processors, each requiring two 32-bit operands every clock cycle and producing one 32-bit result. Assume that one 32-bit instruction is fetched for each arithmetic operation. The memory thus needs to support reading $(2 \times 4 + 1) \times 32 + 32 = 288$ bits and writing $4 \times 32 = 128$ bits every cycle, resulting in a total traffic of 416 bits per cycle. Because each set of operands consists of four 32-bit elements, the bus width to main memory for each access will be $4 \times 32 = 128$ bits. Also, because there are two operand fetches, one instruction fetch, and one result storage every cycle, the main memory should have four 128-bit wide unidirectional buses. If the memory cycle time is 1.28 microseconds (μs) and the processor cycle time is 40 nanoseconds (ns), we would need $1.28 \mu s / 40 ns$, or 32 memory modules, to match the demand rate.

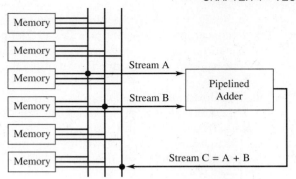

Figure 4.4 Vector Processor with Multiple 3-Port Memory Modules

Commercial vector processors have adopted two mechanisms to meet the above demand requirements: memory systems configured with multiple memory modules allowing simultaneous access and inserting fast (register and/or cache) intermediate memories between the pipelines and the main memory.

Consider the memory structure shown in Figure 4.4. Here the main memory is considered to be composed of multiple modules with each module having three ports corresponding to the three data streams associated with the pipeline. All the streams can be active simultaneously, but only one port of a module can be used at a time.

EXAMPLE 4.3

Consider the vector addition of equation (4.1). Figure 4.5 shows the data structure in a memory system (of the type shown in Figure 4.4) with eight modules. Here all the vectors start in the module 0, thus not permitting us to simultaneously access both the vector elements needed for the operation. We fetch one element at a time and introduce delays (buffers) in the input stream so that the operand fetched first is delayed until the second operand is available at the input to the adder.

```
Module 0 | a0 | b0 | c0 | a8  | b8  | c8  | ...
       1 | a1 | b1 | c1 | a9  | b9  | c9  | ...
       2 | a2 | b2 | c2 | a10 | b10 | c10 | ...
       3 | a3 | b3 | c3 | a11 | b11 | c11 | ...
       4 | a4 | b4 | c4 | a12 | b12 | c12 | ...
       5 | a5 | b5 | c5 | a13 | b13 | c13 | ...
       6 | a6 | b6 | c6 | a14 | b14 | c14 | ...
       7 | a7 | b7 | c7 | a15 | b15 | c15 | ...
```

Figure 4.5 Data Structure for the Computation of $C = A + B$

	0	1	2	3	4	5	6	7	8	9	10
M0	a0	b0				w0			a8	b8	
M1		a1	b1				w1			a9	b9
M2			a2	b2				w2			
M3				a3	b3				w3		
M4					a4	b4				w4	
M5						a5	b5				w5
M6							a6	b6			
M7								a7	b7		
S1			0	1	2	3	4	5			
S2				0	1	2	3	4	5		
S3					0	1	2	3	4	5	

8 mem 1 cycle R/W
3 stage PL, 1 delay on A
No Conflict on Output

Figure 4.6 Reservation Table (3-Stage Adder)

Figure 4.6 shows the reservation table for the addition operation using a three-stage pipelined adder and a memory with eight modules. At time 2, both the operands a0 and b0 are available at the input of the adder, and hence, the result of addition is available at time 5. Because module 0 is free at this time, the result is written into it. From then on, one result is written into the successive modules of the memory every cycle. In this figure the operands fetched are shown by the corresponding element names (a0, a1, b0, b1, etc.); the operation within the pipeline stages is shown by its index value (0, 1, 2, etc.); and the corresponding results are denoted as (w0, w1, etc.). As can be seen, this organization of the memory system and data structure requires the insertion of one delay at the A input of the adder.

EXAMPLE 4.4

Now consider the reservation table of Figure 4.7 for an architecture with a six-module memory, three-stage pipelined adder, and memory access time equivalent to two

	0	1	2	3	4	5	6	7	8	9	10	11	12	13	14
M0	a0	a0	b0	b0			a6	a6	b6	b6	w0	w0			
M1		a1	a1	b1	b1			a7	a7	b7	b7	w1	w1		
M2			a2	a2	b2	b2						w2	w2		
M3				a3	a3	b3	b3						w3	w3	
M4					a4	a4	b4	b4							
M5						a5	a5	b5	b5						
S1						0	1	2	3						
S2							0	1	2	3					
S3								0	1	2	3				

6 mem   3 delays in A
3 stage PL   3 delay on output

Figure 4.7 Reservation Table

processor cycle times. All arrays start in memory module 0 as before. Because each memory access takes two cycles, the first operand from module 0 will be available at the end of clock 1. We can initiate the fetch of the operand b0 from module 0 at this time and the operand will be available at the end of clock 3. In the meantime, we need to buffer the operand a0 for two clock cycles. This is done by introducing delay elements in the input stream A. The result of this operand pair is available at time 7 but cannot be written into module 0 until time 10, because module 0 is busy fetching operands at times 7 through 9. Thus, another three-unit delay is needed at the output of the adder.

Figure 4.8 shows the general structure of the vector processor with delay elements inserted in the input and the output streams. This configuration is similar to the CDC STAR-100 architecture, a memory-oriented vector processor.

It is also possible to enhance the memory bandwidth by structuring the data such that the data elements required at any time are in separate physical modules. For instance, array A in the above example could be stored starting in module 0 and array B starting in module 1. Then both a0 and b0 could be accessed simultaneously. But based on the pipeline characteristics, the results must be stored in a module that is free when they are available. Such storage pattern may not, in general, result in a data structure that allows conflict-free access to the resultant data for subsequent operations.

The above examples illustrate the importance of structuring data in the memory to reduce memory bank conflicts. Chapter 5 discusses this topic further.

Assuming that data is structured in the memory with N banks in an interleaved fashion (i.e., consecutive data elements lay in different physical banks of the memory), one efficient way to fetch N elements is to read all the N banks simultaneously, thus fetching N elements in one cycle. To transfer these N elements simultaneously to the processor, an N-word-wide bus would be needed. One common way to reduce the bus width is to read the memory in a phased manner. That is, the N words are read simultaneously during the first read operation. The data words are transferred to the processor one at a time. As soon as a word is transferred, a read is initiated in the corresponding memory bank. The phased read operation between the banks of the memory is continued until all the data needed are transferred.

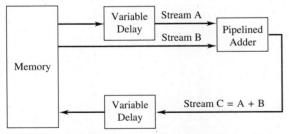

Figure 4.8 Vector Processor with Variable Delays at the Input and Output Data Streams

A common method of further increasing the memory system bandwidth further is to insert high speed intermediate memory between the main memory and the processor pipelines. The intermediate memory can be organized as either a cache or as a set of individually addressable registers. The register organization is preferable because of the overhead imposed by the cache search mechanism. The register organization also allows the accessing of individual elements of a vector directly because each element would lay in an individually addressable register. If the vector data set required for a computation is not stored in the memory properly, memory references would be scattered (i.e., have poor locality), thus making the cache organization inefficient. Also, a vector instruction could reference multiple data elements simultaneously. Searching the cache for multiple elements results in a high overhead.

The Cray series of vector processors described in the next section utilize multiple registers as intermediate memory for data access and cache mechanism for instruction fetching.

4.3 ARCHITECTURE OF THE CRAY SERIES

The Cray-1, a second-generation vector processor from Cray Research, Inc., has been described as the most powerful computer of the late seventies. Benchmark studies show that it is capable of sustaining computational rates of 138 MFLOPS over long periods of time and attaining speeds of up to 250 MFLOPS in short bursts. This performance is about 5 times that of the CDC 7600 or 15 times that of an IBM System/370 Model 168. Thus Cray-1 was uniquely suited to the solution of computationally intensive problems encountered in such fields as weather forecasting, aircraft design, nuclear research, geophysical research, and seismic analysis.

Figure 4.9 shows the structure of the Cray X-MP (successor to Cray-1). A four-processor system (X-MP/4) is shown. The Cray X-MP consists of four sections: multiple Cray-1-like CPUs, the memory system, the I/O system, and the processor interconnection. The following paragraphs provide a brief description of each section.

4.3.1 Memory

The memory system is built out of several sections, each divided into banks. Addressing is interleaved across the sections and within sections across the banks. The total memory capacity can be up to 16 megawords with 64 bits per word. Associated with each memory word, there is an 8-bit field dedicated to single error correction/double error detection (SECDED). The memory system offers a bandwidth of 25 to 100 gigabits per second. It is multiported with each CPU connected to four ports (two for reading, one for writing, and one for independent I/O). Accessing a port ties it up for one clock cycle, and a bank access takes four clock cycles.

Memory contention can occur several ways: a bank conflict occurs when a bank is accessed while it is still processing a previous access; a simultaneous conflict occurs if a bank is referenced simultaneously on independent lines from different CPUs; and a line conflict occurs when two or more of the data paths make a memory request to

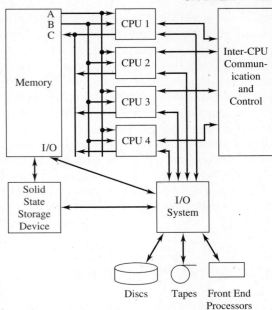

Figure 4.9 Cray X-MP/4 Structure

the same memory section during the same clock cycle. Memory conflict resolution may require wait states to be inserted. Because memory conflict resolution occurs element by element during vector references, it is possible that the arithmetic pipelines being fed by these vector references may experience clock cycles with no input. This can produce a degradation in the arithmetic performance attained by the pipelined functional units. Memory performance is typically degraded by 3% to 7% on average on account of memory contention, and in particularly bad cases by 20% to 33%.

The secondary memory, known as the solid state device (SSD), is used as an exceptionally fast access disk device although it is built out of MOS random access memory ICs. The access time of the SSD is 40 μs, compared to the 16 millisecond (ms) access time of the fastest disk drive from Cray Research, Inc. The SSD is used to store large scale scientific programs that would otherwise exceed main memory capacity and to reduce bottlenecks in I/O-bound applications. The central memory is connected to the SSD through either one or two 1000 Mbyte/second channels. The I/O subsystem is directly connected to the SSD thereby allowing prefetching of large data sets from the disk system to the faster SSD.

4.3.2 Processor Interconnection

The interconnection of the CPUs assumes a coarse-grained multiprocessing environment. Ideally each processor executes a task almost independently, requiring communication with other processors once every few million or billion instructions.

Processor interconnection is comprised of clustered share registers. The processor may access any cluster that has been allocated to it in either user or system monitor mode. A processor in monitor mode has the ability to interrupt any other processor and cause it to go into monitor mode.

4.3.3 Central Processor

Each CPU is composed of low-density ECL logic with 16 gates per chip. Wire lengths are minimized to cut the propagation delay of signals to about 650 picoseconds.

Each CPU is a register-oriented vector processor (Figure 4.10) with various sets of registers that supply arguments to and receive results from several pipelined, independent functional units. There are eight 24-bit address registers (A0 through A7), eight 64-bit scalar registers (S0 through S7), and eight vector registers (V0 through V7). Each vector register can hold up to sixty-four 64-bit elements. The number of elements present in a vector register for a given operation can be contained in a 7-bit vector length register (VL). A 64-bit vector mask register (VM) allows masking of the elements of a vector register prior to an operation. Sixty-four 24-bit address save registers (B0 through B63) and 64 scalar save registers (T0 through T63) are used as buffer storage areas for the address and scalar registers, respectively.

The address registers support an integer add and an integer multiply functional unit. The scalar and vector registers each support integer add, shift, logical, and population count functional units. Three floating-point arithmetic functional units (add, multiply, reciprocal approximation) take their arguments from either the vector or the scalar registers.

The result of the vector operation is either returned to another vector register or may replace one of the operands to the same functional unit (i.e., *written back*) provided there is no recursion.

An 8-bit status register contains such flags as processor number, program status, cluster number, and interrupt and error detection enables. This register can be accessed through an S register.

The exchange address register is an 8-bit register maintained by the operating system. This register is used to point to the current position of the exchange routine in memory. Also, there is a program clock used for accurately measuring duration intervals.

As mentioned earlier, each CPU is provided with four ports to the memory with one port reserved for the input/output subsystem and the other three, labeled *A*, *B*, and *C*, supporting data paths to the registers. All the data paths can be active simultaneously as long as there are no memory access conflicts.

Data transfer between scalar and address registers and the memory occurs directly (i.e., as individual elements into and out of referenced registers). Alternatively, block transfers can occur between the buffer registers and the memory. The transfer between scalar and address registers and the corresponding buffers is done directly. Transfers between the memory and the vector registers are done only directly.

Block transfer instructions are available for loading to and storing from *B* (using port *A*) and *T* (using port *B*) buffer registers. Block stores from the *B* and *T* registers to memory use port *C*. Loads and stores directly to the address and scalar registers use port *C* at a maximum data rate of one word every two clock cycles.

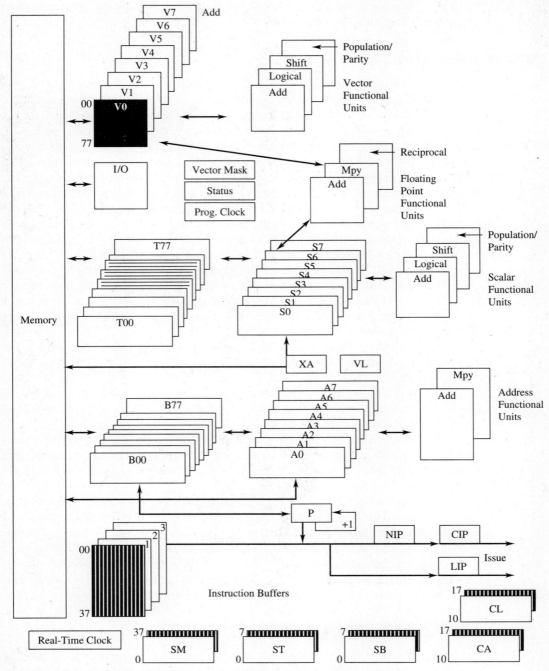

Figure 4.10 Cray X-MP CPU (Courtesy of Cray Research, Inc.)

4.3 ARCHITECTURE OF THE CRAY SERIES

Transfers between the B and T registers and address and scalar registers occur at the rate of one word per clock cycle, and data can be moved between memory and the B and T registers at the same rate of one word per clock cycle. Using the three separate memory ports, data can be moved between common memory and the buffer registers at a combined rate of three words per clock cycle, one word into B and T and one word from one of them.

The functional units are fully segmented (i.e., pipelined), which means that a new set of arguments may enter a unit every clock period (8.5 ns). The segmentation is performed by holding the operands entering the unit and the partial results at the end of every segment until a flag allowing them to proceed is set. The number of segments in a unit determines the start-up time for that unit. Table 4.1 shows the functional unit characteristics.

EXAMPLE 4.5

Consider again the vector addition:

$$C[i] = A[i] + B[i] \quad 1 \leq i \leq N.$$

Assume that N is 64, that A and B are loaded into two vector registers, and that the result vector is stored in another vector register. The unit time for floating-point addition is six clock periods. Including one clock period for transferring data from vector registers to the add unit and one clock period to store the result into another vector register, it would take $(64 \times 8 = 512)$ clock periods to execute this addition in scalar mode.

TABLE 4.1 FUNCTIONAL UNIT CHARACTERISTICS (CRAY X-MP)

Type	Operation	Registers used	Number of bits	Unit time (clock periods)
Address	Integer Add	A	24	2
	Integer Multiply	A	24	4
Scalar	Integer Add	S	64	3
	Shift	S	64	2 or 3
	Logical	S	64	1
	Population	S	64	3 or 4
	Parity, and Leading zero	S & A	64	3 or 4
Vector	Integer Add	V	64	3
	Shift	V & A	64	3 or 4
	Logical	V	64	2
	Second Logical	V	64	3
	Population, and parity	V	64	6
Floating-Point	Add	S or V	64	6
	Multiply	S or V	64	7
	Reciprocal	S or V	64	14
Memory Transfer	Scalar load	S	64	14
	Vector load (64 element)	V	64	17 + 64

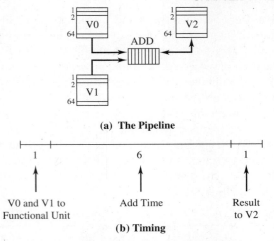

Figure 4.11 Vector Piplining on Cray X-MP

> This vector operation performed in the pipeline mode is shown in Figure 4.11. Here the first element of the result will be stored into the vector register after eight clock periods. Afterward there will be one result every clock period. Therefore the total execution time is $(8 + 63 = 71)$ clock periods.
>
> If $N < 64$, the above execution times would be reduced correspondingly. If $N > 64$, the computation is performed on units of 64 elements at a time. For example, if N is 300, the computation is performed on four sets of 64 elements each, followed by the final set with the remaining 44 elements.

The vector length register contains the number of elements (n) to be operated upon at each computation. If M is the length of vector registers in the machine, the following program can be used to execute the above vector operation for an arbitrary value of N.

```
begin = 1
n = (N mod M)
for i = 0, (N/M)
      for j = begin, begin+n-1
            C[j] = A[j] + B[j]
      endfor
begin = begin + n
n = M
endfor
```

Here, first the (N mod M) elements are operated upon, followed by N/M sets of M elements.

In practice, the vector length will not be known at compile time. The compiler generates the code similar to above, such that the vector operation is performed in sets of length less than or equal to M. This is known as **strip mining.** Strip mining overhead must also be included in start-up time computations of the pipeline.

In order for multiple functional units to be active simultaneously, intermediate results must be stored in the CPU registers. When properly programmed, the Cray architecture can arrange CPU registers such that the results of one functional unit can be input to another independent functional unit. Thus, in addition to the pipelining within the functional units, it is possible to pipeline arithmetic operations between the functional units. This is called **chaining.**

Chaining of vector functional units and their overlapped, concurrent operations are important characteristics of this architecture that bring about a vast speed-up in the execution times. The following example shows a loop where overlapping would occur.

EXAMPLE 4.6

Consider the loop:
```
for J = 1,64
    C(J) = A(J) + B(J)
    D(J) = E(J) * F(J)
endfor
```
Here, the addition and multiplication can be done in parallel because the functional units are totally independent.

The following example illustrates chaining.

EXAMPLE 4.6

```
for J = 1,64
    C(J) = A(J) + B(J)
    D(J) = C(J) * E(J)
endfor
```
Here, the output of add functional unit is an input operand to the multiplication functional unit. With chaining, we do not have to wait for the entire array C to be computed before beginning the multiplication. As soon as $C(1)$ is computed, it can be used by the multiply functional unit concurrently with the computation of $C(2)$. That is, the two functional units form the stages of a pipeline as shown in Figure 4.12.

Assuming that all the operands are in vector registers, this computation, if done without vectorization (i.e., no pipelining or chaining), requires (add: $64 * 8 = 512$ plus multiply: $64 * 9 = 576$) 1088 clock periods. It can be completed in (chain start-up time of 17 plus 63 more computations) 80 clock periods if vectorization (pipelining and chaining) is employed.

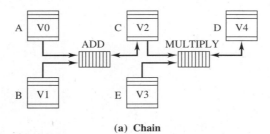

(a) Chain

Figure 4.12 Chaining in Cray X-MP

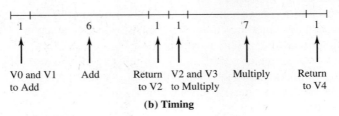

(b) Timing

Figure 4.12 (cont.)

Note that the effect of chaining is to increase the depth of the pipeline and hence the start-up overheads.

If the operands are not already in vector registers, they need to be loaded first and the result needs to be stored into the memory. The two load paths and the path that stores data to memory can be considered functional units in chaining. The start-up time for a load vector instruction is 17 cycles, and thereafter one value per cycle may be fetched. Then any operation using this data may access one value per cycle after 18 cycles. Figure 4.13 shows an example of this. Here, port A is used to read in V0 and port B to read in V1. This occurs in parallel. As soon as each vector register has its first operand, the floating-point add may begin processing, and as soon as the first operand is placed in V2, port C may be used to store it back to memory.

In a chain, a functional unit can only appear once. Two fetches and one store are possible in each chain. This is because Cray systems supply only one of each of the above types of functional units. This demands that, if two floating-point adds are to be executed, they occur sequentially. Because there are two ports for fetching vectors and one port for storing vectors, the user may view the system as having two load functional units and a store functional unit on Cray X-MP. On Cray-1, there is only one memory functional unit.

An operand can only serve as input to one arithmetic functional unit in a chain. An operand can, however, be input to both inputs of a functional unit requiring two operands. This is because a vector register is tied to a functional unit during a vector instruction. When a vector instruction is issued, the functional unit and registers used in the instruction are reserved for the duration of the vector instruction.

Cray Research has coined the term *chime* (chained vector time) to describe the timing of vector operations. A chime is not a specific amount of time, but rather a timing concept representing the number of clock periods required to complete one vector operation. This equates to length of a vector register plus a few clock periods for chaining. For Cray systems, a chime is equal to 64 clock periods plus a few more. Thus, a chime is a measure that allows the user to estimate the speedup available from pipelining, chaining, and overlapping instructions.

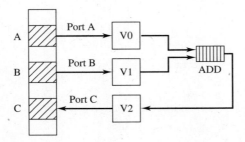

Figure 4.13 Memory and Functional Unit Chaining on Cray X-MP

4.3 ARCHITECTURE OF THE CRAY SERIES

The number of chimes needed to complete a sequence of vector instructions is dependent on several factors. Because there are three memory functional units, two fetches and one store operation may appear in the same chime. A functional unit may be used only once within a chime. An operand may appear as input to only one functional unit in a chime. A store operation may chain onto any previous operation.

EXAMPLE 4.7

Figure 4.14 shows the number of chimes required to perform the following code on Cray X-MP, Cray-1, and the Cray-2 (Levesque and Williamson, 1989) systems:

```
for I = 1 to 64
    A(I) = 3.0 * A(I) + (2.0 + B(I)) * C(I)
endfor
```

The Cray X-MP requires only two chimes while the Cray-1 requires four and the Cray-2, which does not allow chaining, requires six chimes to execute the code. Clock cycles of the Cray-1, the Cray X-MP, and the Cray-2 are 12.5, 8.5, and 4.1 ns, respectively. If a chime is taken to be 64 clock cycles, then the time for each machine to complete the code is:

```
Cray-1:      4 chimes X 64 X 12.5 ns = 3200 ns
Cray X-MP:   2 chimes X 64 X  8.5 ns = 1088 ns
Cray-2:      6 chimes X 64 X  4.1 ns = 1574 ns
```

```
CHIME 1:    A  -> V0                    CHIME 1:    A  -> V0
            B  -> V1                    CHIME 2:    B  -> V1
            2.0 + V1 -> V3                          2.0 + V1 -> V3
            3.0 * V0 -> V4                          3.0 * V0 -> V4

CHIME 2:    C  -> V5                    CHIME 3:    C  -> V5
            V3 * V5 -> V6                           V3 * V5 -> V6
            V4 + V6 -> V7                           V4 + V6 -> V7
            V7 -> A                     CHIME 4:                V7 -> A

        (a) Cray X-MP                                       (b) Cray-1
```

```
CHIME 1:    A  -> V0

CHIME 2:    B  -> V1
            3.0 * V0 -> V4

CHIME 3:    C  -> V5
            2.0 + V1 -> V3

CHIME 4:                V3 * V5 -> V6

CHIME 5:                V4 + V6 -> V7

CHIME 6:                V7 -> A

                (c) Cray-2
```

Figure 4.14 Chime Characteristics

Thus for some instruction sequences, the Cray X-MP with the help of chaining can actually outperform Cray-2, which has a faster clock. Because Cray-2 does allow overlapping, the actual gain of Cray X-MP may not be as large for large array dimensions.

During vector operations, up to 64 target addresses could be generated by one instruction. If a cache were to be used as intermediate memory, the overhead to search for 64 addresses would be prohibitive. Use of individually addressed registers eliminates this overhead. One disadvantage of not using a cache is that the programmer (or compiler) must generate all references to the individual registers. This adds to the complexity of code (or compiler) development.

INSTRUCTION FETCH

Control registers are part of the special purpose register set and are used to control the flow of instructions. Four instruction buffers, each containing 32 words (128 parcels, 16 bits each) are used to hold instructions fetched from memory. Each instruction buffer has its own instruction buffer address register (IBAR). The IBAR serves to indicate which instructions are currently in the buffer. The contents of IBAR are the high order 17 bits of the words in the buffer. The instruction buffer is always loaded on a 32-word boundary. The P register is the 24-bit address of the next parcel to be executed. The current instruction parcel (CIP) contains the instruction waiting to issue, and the next instruction parcel (NIP) contains the next instruction parcel to issue after the parcel in the CIP. Also, there is a last instruction parcel (LIP), which is used to provide the second parcel to a 32-bit instruction without using an extra clock period.

The P register contains the address of the next instruction to be decoded. Each buffer is checked to see if the instruction is located in the buffers. If the address is found, the instruction sequence continues. However, if the address is not found, the instruction must be fetched from memory after the parcels in the CIP and NIP have been issued. The least recently filled buffer is selected to be overwritten so that the current instruction is among the first eight words to be read. The rest of the buffer is then filled in a circular fashion. It takes 3 clock pulses to completely fill the buffer. Any branch to an out-of-buffer address causes a 16-clock pulse delay in processing.

Some buffers are shared between all processors in the system. One of these is a real-time clock. Other registers of this type include a cluster consisting of 48 registers. Each cluster contains 32 (1-bit) semaphore, or synchronization, registers; eight 64-bit ST, or shared-T, registers, and eight 24-bit SB, or shared-B, registers. A system with two processors will contain three clusters while a four-processor system will contain five clusters.

4.3.4 I/O System

The input and output of the X-MP is handled by the input/output subsystem (IOS). The IOS is made of two to four interconnected I/O processors. The IOS receives data from four 100 Mbyte/second channels connected directly to the main memory of the X-MP. Also, four 6-Mbyte/second channels are provided to furnish control between the CPU and the IOS. Each processor has its own local memory and shares a common buffer. The IOS supports a variety of front-end processors and peripherals, such as disk drives and tape drives.

To support the IOS, each CPU has two types of I/O control registers: current address and channel limit. The current address registers point to the current word being transferred. The channel limit registers contain the address of the last word to be transferred.

4.3.5 Other Systems in the Series

Cray Research has continued the enhancement of X-MP architecture to Y-MP and Y-prime series while the enhancement of the Cray-2 line has been taken over by Cray Computer Corporation (headed by Seymour Cray), which is developing Cray-3 and Cray-4 architectures.

Cray Y-MP was introduced in February 1988. It is of the same genre as the Cray X-MP. Cray-3 is a progression of Cray-2 architecture and is the first major system built with gallium arsenide (GaAs) technology. GaAs provides switching speeds at about five times that of silicon semiconductor technology, can handle higher frequencies, generates less noise, is more resistant to radiation, and can operate over a wider temperature range. With its 2-nanosecond clock rate, the Cray-3 is ten times faster and less than half of the size of its predecessor the Cray-2. A brief description of these two architectures is provided below as a representation of the apparent dichotomy of design strategies being employed.

The Y-MP is designed to appear as an X-MP to the user. It extends the X-MP 24-bit addressing scheme to 32 bits, thus allowing an address space of 32 million 64-bit words. It runs on a 6-nanosecond clock and uses 8 processors, thus doubling the processing speed.

The Cray-3 is a 16-processor machine with a 2- to 2.5-nanosecond clock rate. The projected speed is 16 GFLOPS and the projected memory capacity is 512 million words. All this power will be housed in a structure 6 in. deep and 32 in. high.

The Y-prime series utilizes silicon VLSI to improve on Y-MP while the Cray-4, a GaAs machine, would use 64 processors and a 1-nanosecond clock rate to achieve a speed of 128 GFLOPS.

4.4 TWO OTHER ARCHITECTURES

This section provides a brief description of two popular vector processor architectures: the C series of minisupercomputers from Convex Computer Corporation and the 5000 series of attached processors from Floating-Point Systems, Inc. (FPS).

4.4.1 The Convex C Series

The Convex C series is a family of minisupercomputers built out of multiple 64-bit CPUs tightly coupled through a shared memory. The C1 system was announced in 1983; C2, in 1986; and C3, in 1991. In this section a high level description of representative systems is provided as a trace of the evolution of this architecture series. For further details refer to the architecture manuals from Convex Computer Corporation.

Figure 4.15 shows the architecture of C120, a member of the C1 family. It used MSI (medium scale integration) and SSI (small scale integration) level components in

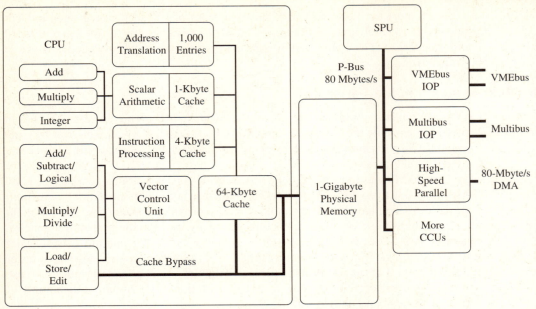

Figure 4.15 Convex C120 System (Courtesy of Convex Computer Corporation.)

TTL (transistor transistor logic) and CMOS (complement metal oxide semiconductor) technologies with the vector function units utilizing CMOS gate arrays.

The memory system is four-way interleaved with a single 80 Mbytes/second port shared by the CPU and the I/O system.

The I/O system is configured around the 80 Mbytes/second P-bus and consists of several channel control units (CCUs) that operate in a block-multiplexed mode. A service processor (SPU), attached to the P-bus and consisting of a Motorola 68000 processor and hard and floppy disk units, can directly access CPU registers.

The main locus of control in the CPU is the address and scalar processor. The vector processor consists of three distinct functional units: add/subtract/logical, multiply/divide, and load/store.

The 30-bit logical addresses are translated into physical addresses using an address translation cache. The CPU also contains a 1-Kbyte data cache, which is accessed while the address is being translated, and a 4-Kbyte instruction cache. The memory access speed is enhanced by the use of a 64-Kbyte data cache (P-cache) into which data are loaded in 32-byte blocks. Most vector operations bypass this cache.

Figure 4.16 shows the structure of the C2 series CPU, built from ECL (emitter coupled logic) and CMOS technologies. The 2-Gbyte memory system is organized as a pair of 32-bit memories (with 7 additional error detection/correction bits) rather than a single 64-bit system. There are five independent paths into the memory system. The CPU and the I/O system can access the memory simultaneously using the five paths through a crossbar network. (Refer to Chapter 6 for details on crossbar networks.) Each memory board has eight independent banks, crossbar hardware, and buffers. Each memory port operates at 200 Mbytes/second.

Figure 4.17 shows the C210-C240 system structure. The I/O system has its own memory port used by a peripheral interface adapter (PIA). Two P-buses are supported

4.4 TWO OTHER ARCHITECTURES

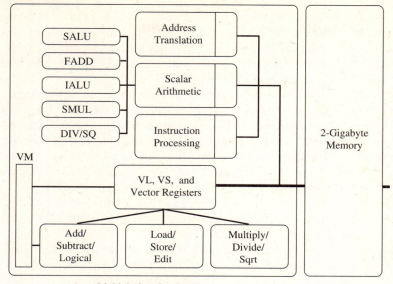

Figure 4.16 Convex C240 System (Courtesy of Convex Computer Corporation.)

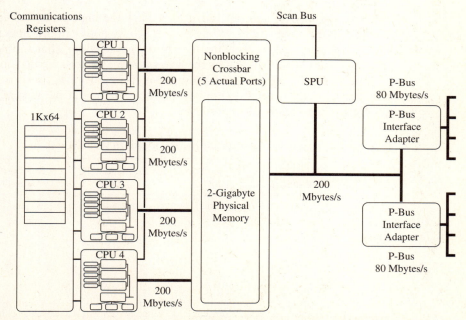

Figure 4.17 Convex C210-C240 System Structure (Courtesy of Convex Computer Corporation.)

by the PIA, allowing the C1 series of CCUs also to be interfaced to the C2 series of systems. The SPU accesses CPU registers through the scan bus.

The functions of the 1000-entry address translation table, 1-Kbyte data cache, and 4-Kbyte instruction cache within the CPU are the same as those in the C1 series. The C2 series does not contain the P-cache.

The CPUs in the system can communicate through the shared memory and through a set of (1 K × 64) communication registers. These registers are partitioned into eight frames of 128 registers each. Each active task utilizes a register frame. The system uses a mechanism called asynchronous self-allocating processors (ASAP) in which the processors automatically allocate themselves to tasks to be performed as they become free. Chapter 7 provides further details on the interaction of multiple CPUs in this system.

The C3 family, introduced in 1991, consists of three lines: the high-end C3800, the departmental C3400, and the economical C3200. Table 4.2 lists the characteristics of this family.

This series of machines use an operating system based on UNIX 4.2 BSD. Convex also provides vectorizing/parallelizing/optimizing compilers for Fortran, C, and Ada languages and for various special application libraries. These machines have been used in large scientific simulation applications such as prediction of wind velocity and severe thunderstorms, and galaxy and atmospheric pollution.

4.4.2 The FPS 5000 Series

As mentioned earlier, an attached array processor is a high-speed computational device attached to a general purpose computer as a host. The host diverts mathematically intensive portions of the code to the array processor (AP), which employs extensive parallelism and pipelining to achieve the high performance necessary for many scientific applications. While the AP is busy number crunching, the host serves interactive users and controls the flow of the application. That is, the scalar aspects of the application are handled by the host while the vector-oriented computations are performed by the AP. Overall throughput is improved because the AP and host activities overlap. A brief description of one commercial AP system, Floating-Point Systems's (FPS) 5000 Series, follows.

TABLE 4.2 CHARACTERISTICS OF CONVEX C3 FAMILY

Line	Technology	Memory (Gbytes)	Performance (peak)	Number of processors
C3800	Gallium Arsenide	4	2 Gflops	1–8
C3400	Gallium Arsenide and Bipolar CMOS	4	800 Mflops	1–8
C3200	ECL and CMOS	2	200 Mflops	1–4

4.4 TWO OTHER ARCHITECTURES

The high performance of the FPS 5000 is achieved primarily through the use of multiple functional units operating in parallel and using pipelining within the individual units. The design also employs multiple memories and multiple data paths between these memories and the arithmetic processors. Based on the configuration, this series of APs provides a computational rate of 8 to 102 MFLOPS. FPS 5000 has been used in medical imaging, signal processing, real-time simulations, seismic processing, and computer graphics applications.

The FPS 5000 consists of the five subsystems (host interface, control processor, system common memory, arithmetic coprocessor, and I/O processors) shown in Figure 4.18, which are interconnected by a control bus and an address/data bus. A brief description of each subsystem follows.

The host interface subsystem is specific for the host computer system used. Host interfaces for Digital Equipment Corporation's VAX and MicroVAX, Gould SEL-32 series, and Concurrent Computer Corporation 3200 series machines are offered by FPS.

The control processor consists of a small amount of local RAM, table memory, three sets of registers, a floating-point adder, a floating-point multiplier, and an integer/addressing unit all coordinated by a control unit. The floating-point adder uses a two-stage pipeline and the floating-point multiplier uses a three-stage pipeline, each providing one result per cycle operating on 38-bit data. The integer/address unit works with 16-bit data and performs both arithmetic and logical operations at one result per cycle. The control processor register set consists of sixty-four 38-bit floating-point registers, sixteen 16-bit integer registers, and a 16 level, 16-bit subroutine return stack. The local RAM contains 64 K, 64-bit words. Table memory uses 38-bit words and consists of 4.5 Kwords of ROM and 8 to 32 Kwords of RAM.

Two floating-point adders and one floating-point multiplier are included in each arithmetic coprocessor, each with a five-stage, one result per cycle pipeline. Each arithmetic coprocessor includes a channel executive unit, which consists of local executive memory, 16 registers, a 24-bit ALU, and a channel code interpreter along with a DMA controller, and can handle a 24-bit external address space.

The arithmetic coprocessor has a 64K, 32-bit word local memory with dual access capability. The table memory has 16 K, 32-bit words. There is also a writeable control store consisting of 4K, 128-bit words of RAM.

Up to three arithmetic coprocessors (working in parallel, and all pipelined to return one result per cycle) can be configured into the system, thus offering a

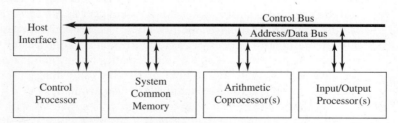

Figure 4.18 The FPS 5000 Series Architecture (Courtesy of Floating-Point Systems, Inc.)

significant speed and accuracy for applications requiring large numbers of calculations. This fact, along with the relatively low cost of the AP, allows near supercomputer performance on a minicomputer budget.

The I/O processors provide a means for connecting external devices, such as analog-to-digital and digital-to-analog converters or other parallel data devices, to the internal I/O and main buses of the AP. They allow communication between APs as long as the IOPs are the same type and transfer data directly to and from the AP system common memory through DMA channels. I/O transfer may be initiated by either the IOP or the AP itself. The peak transfer rate of IOP is about 1 Mword per second. Three different IOPs are offered: the GPIOP, the IOP-16, and the IOP-38. The GPIOP is a fully programmable processor suitable for real-time applications and handles a variety of devices. It consists of two independent interactive processors, a control processor, and a format processor. The control processor handles AP addressing operations and external handshaking while the format processor converts data into recognizable formats. The GPIOP peak transfer rate is 2.9 Mwords per second.

The system common memory is configured with four modules, each containing 256 Kwords. There are several levels in the memory hierarchy. Registers hold both the inputs to and the outputs from all computational units. Just above the registers are several kinds of local memory—local table memory, local data memory, and local program storage. The next level is the system common memory, and the last level is the external memory. The host's memory systems, including secondary storage, can be accessed through the host interface, and the optional IOPs offer access to a number of external devices including hard disks and other APs. This hierarchical memory system allows computations to occur using local storage, which offloads the address/data bus for use by the DMA controllers present in all of the processor units.

Creative use of the I/O processors allows a route for communication with the host without passing through the host interface. Data can be passed through secondary storage media, other APs, or other kinds of devices. Also, the vectored interrupt capability of the GPIOP allows the AP to directly respond to external events. This would also tend to unburden the host and to reduce the need for communication between the host and the AP.

Several software development tools and optimized libraries are available. APEX, the AP executive software, resides on the host and facilitates communication between the host and the AP. Diagnostic software perform testing on the AP internal structure and the host interface. A Fortran 77 language subset, as well as several microcode assemblers, allow the users to write microcode for the control processor and the arithmetic coprocessor. An AP debugger assists in detection and location of AP program errors. Finally, mathematics libraries contain routines specifically written for the control processor and the arithmetic coprocessor. There are over 200 routines available in the standard mathematics library and optional libraries designed for advanced mathematics, signal processing, and image processing. Geophysical, seismic, and simulation applications are also available.

With the emergence of fast microprocessor systems with capabilities to attach several coprocessors, the market for systems of this type is getting smaller. In fact, at this writing, the FPS 5000 series of machines are not being produced, and Floating-Point Systems, Inc. has merged with Cray Research, Inc.

4.5 PERFORMANCE EVALUATION

Levesque and Williamson (1989) provide the following list of major characteristics that affect supercomputer performance:

- Clock speed
- Instruction issue rate
- Size and number of registers
- Memory size
- Number of concurrent paths to memory
- Ability to fetch/store vectors efficiently
- Number of duplicate arithmetic functional units (vector pipelines)
- Whether function calls can be chained together
- Indirect addressing capabilities
- Handling of conditional blocks of code

It is interesting to note that the high performance of all the three vector architectures described in this chapter can be attributed to the following architectural characteristics similar to the above list:

1. Pipelined functional units
2. Multiple functional units operating in parallel
3. Chaining of functional units
4. Large number of programmable registers
5. Block load/store capabilities with buffer registers
6. Multiple CPUs operating in parallel in a coarse-grained parallel mode
5. Instruction buffers

Comparison of vector processor performance is usually done based on **peak** and **sustained** computation rates in terms of MFLOPS. The peak performance rate can only be obtained under the most ideal circumstances, and hence, it does not reflect the true operating environment (Hack, 1986). Thus, the comparison based on sustained rates is more valid. The sustained performance is difficult to determine because it depends on a number of factors:

1. Level of vectorization (i.e., the fraction of the application code that is vectorizable)
2. Average vector length
3. Possibility of vector chaining
4. Overlap of scalar, vector, and memory load/store operations possible
5. Memory contention resolution mechanisms adopted

Consider an application program P. Let T_{scalar} be the time to execute P entirely in scalar (or serial) mode. Let s be the ratio of the speed of the vector unit to that of the scalar unit. Then, the time to execute P entirely in vector mode is T_{scalar}/s. If f is the fraction of P that can be executed on the vector unit, the actual execution time for P in a mixed scalar/vector mode is

$$T_{\text{actual}} = (1 - f)T_{\text{scalar}} + f \cdot T_{\text{scalar}}/s. \tag{4.4}$$

Hence, the speedup is

$$\begin{aligned} S &= T_{\text{scalar}}/T_{\text{actual}} \\ &= \frac{1}{(1 - f) + f/s} \end{aligned} \tag{4.5}$$

This is known as Amdhal's law, attributed to G. M. Amdhal (Lubeck, Moore, and Mendez, 1985).

If f is 1, the speedup equals s, and for $f = 0$, the speedup is 1. A significant increase in speedup is attained only when f is closer to 1. That is, unless a program is heavily vectorized, the slower scalar mode of operation dominates the performance.

It is important to note that the Cray series of machines attacked Amdhal's law by improving the scalar performance alone. In addition to providing an outstanding vector performance, the Cray-1 was also the fastest scalar processor of its time.

Sustained performance of high performance processors is measured by benchmarks that reflect accurately the types of workloads expected on these processors. Refer to Chapter 1 for details on widely known benchmarks.

The peak throughput of representative supercomputers is shown in Table 4.3. In comparison, an Intel 80387–based personal computer with 20MHz clock has a throughput of 0.44 MFLOPS.

Peak and sustained performance characteristics can be estimated based on the execution time of vector loops given in equation (4.2). This equation can be generalized to include other overheads as shown below:

$$\begin{aligned} T_N = T_{\text{memory}} &+ (T_{\text{start-up}} + T_{\text{loop}})\,(N/M + 1) \\ &+ (N - 1)T_{\text{cycle}} \end{aligned} \tag{4.6}$$

Here,

T_N = execution time of a vector loop with N elements;

T_{memory} = time to initialize starting addresses for each vector (a one-time overhead for the loop);

TABLE 4.3 PEAK THROUGHPUT OF REPRESENTATIVE SUPERCOMPUTERS

Processor	Mflops	Cycle Time (ns)
Cray X-MP/4	1100	8.5
Cray-2	1800	4.1
Cyber-205	800	20.0
Hitachi S-810	630	4.5
Fujitsu VP-200	533	15.0
NEC SX-2	1300	6.0

$T_{\text{start-up}}$ = start-up time (including chaining);

T_{loop} = loop management overhead;

$(N/M + 1)$ = strip-mining overhead; and

T_{cycle} = pipeline cycle time (i.e., time to produce one result after the pipeline is full).

The peak performance measure ignores the overhead and, hence, is dependent entirely on T_{cycle}. If the loop contains F floating-point operations, the peak rate in MFLOPS is given by: $(F/T_{\text{cycle}}) \times$ clock rate.

If the MFLOPS rating for a vector of length N is denoted as R_N, the peak rate can be considered the rate for infinitely long vectors (i.e., R_∞), which is given by:

$$R_\infty = \lim_{N \to \infty} \frac{F \times \text{clock rate}}{\text{clock cycles/iteration}} \quad (4.7)$$

The numerator is independent of N, and the denominator corresponds to $\lim_{N \to \infty} (T_N/N)$.

Two other measures of performance commonly used are (Hockney and Jesshope, 1988) $N_{1/2}$ and N_v. $N_{1/2}$ is the vector length needed to achieve $R_\infty/2$. This is representative of the effect of start-up overhead, because, in practice, vectors are not of infinite length. N_v is the length of the vector that makes the vector mode of computation faster than the corresponding computation in scalar mode. This measure takes into account the start-up overhead and also the speed of scalar operations relative to vector operations.

4.6 PROGRAMMING VECTOR PROCESSORS

Vector processors tend to be difficult to program, just as any processor whose processing power comes from its unique hardware configuration. The hardware structures that make vector processors powerful also make the assembler coding difficult. If the machine is difficult to program at the assembler level, writing a compiler to take advantage of the hardware will not be any easier.

Two approaches have been used in providing programming facilities for parallel processors in general and vector processors in particular: development of languages (or extensions to existing languages) that can express the parallelism inherent in the algorithm (Andrews and Olsson, 1993; Decyk, 1993) and development of compilers that recognize the portions of sequential code and *vectorize* them (Banerjee, et. al., 1993; Polychronopoulos, 1988; Kuck, 1978). Both approaches have partially succeeded. In practice, these approaches complement each other rather than exclude each other, because using only one of the two approaches may not result in the most efficient code.

In general, it is not possible to completely vectorize a sequential program. Those portions of the code that are not vectorizable will have to be executed in scalar hardware at a slower rate. Compiler writers in their quest to take advantage of the vector hardware as much as possible have tried to expand the realm of what is vectorizable. By developing new algorithms and approaches, they have been able to take code segments that in the past have been executed in scalar mode and manipulate them so that they can be vectorized. In general, an algorithm that is considered efficient for scalar computation need not be efficient for a vector environment. Modifications are then needed to take advantage of the vector hardware.

EXAMPLE 4.8

Consider the following computation for a scalar processor (Ortega 1988):

```
y = 0
for i = 1 to N
    y = y + x(i) * a(i)
endfor
```

This can be altered for a vector processor as following:

```
0 → r1
a(1) → r2
x(1) → r3
r2 * r3 → r4
r1 = r1 + r4
r1 → main memory (y)
y → r1
a(2) → r2
........
(and so on)
```

Here, r1, r2, and so on are processor registers and → indicates a data transfer. The efficiency of this algorithm could be greatly improved if chaining were allowed by the vector processor and if we were to assume that most register-oriented vector processors allow load operations to occur during arithmetic operations, as shown below:

```
y → r1
a(1) → r2
x(1) → r3
y = y + r2 * r3 by chaining
a(2),x(2) → r1, r2
y = y + x(2) * a(2) by chaining
a(3),x(3) → r1, r2
......
(and so on)
```

This version of the algorithm offers a considerable performance increase over its predecessor. It requires two vector registers, one for a and the other for x. It loads $a(i+1)$ while the multiplication of $x(i)$ and $a(i)$ is being performed, as well as loads $x(i+1)$ during the addition of y to $x(i)a(i)$. It switches back and forth between the vector registers in order to provide the correct values for each operation.

Compilers do not always take advantage of the type of optimizations illustrated above because they do not recognize them. Nevertheless, there are several vectoriza-

4.6 PROGRAMMING VECTOR PROCESSORS

tion techniques adopted by vector processor environments to achieve high performance. Some of these techniques are described below.

Scalar renaming: It is typical for programmers to use a scalar variable repeatedly as shown by the following loop:

EXAMPLE 4.9

```
for i = 1,n
    x = A[i] + B[i]
        .
        .
    Y[i] = 2 * x
        .
        .
    x = C[i]/D[i]
        .
        .
    P = x+2
        .
endfor
```

If the second instance of x is renamed as shown below, the two code segments become data independent, thus allowing a better vectorization.

EXAMPLE 4.10

```
for i = 1,n
    x = A[i] + B[i]
        .
        .
    Y[i] = 2 * x
        .
        .
    xx = C[i]/D[i]
        .
        .
    P = xx+2
        .
endfor
```

Scalar expansion: In the following code segment, x is assigned a value and then used in a subsequent statement.

EXAMPLE 4.11

```
for i = 1,n
    x = A[i] + B[i]
        .
        .
    Y[i] = 2 * x
endfor
```

If the scalar *x* is expanded into a vector as shown below, the two statements can be made independent, thus allowing a better vectorization.

EXAMPLE 4.12

```
for i = 1,n
    x[i] = A[i] + B[i]
        .
        .
    Y[i] = 2 * x[i]
endfor
```

Loop unrolling: For a loop of small vector length it is more efficient to eliminate the loop construct and expand out all iterations of the loop.

EXAMPLE 4.13

The loop:
```
for I = 1 to 3
    x[I] = a[I] + b[I]
endfor
```
is unrolled into the following:
```
x[1] = a[1] + b[1]
x[2] = a[2] + b[2]
x[3] = a[3] + b[3].
```
This eliminates the looping overhead and allows the three computations to be performed independently. (In this case, the computations at each iteration are not dependent on each other. If this is not the case, the computations must be partitioned into non-dependent sets.)

Loop fusion or jamming: Two or more loops that are executed the same number of times using the same indices can be combined into one loop.

4.6 PROGRAMMING VECTOR PROCESSORS

EXAMPLE 4.14

Consider the following code segment:
```
for i = 1, n
    X[i] = Y[i] * Z[i]
endfor
for i = 1, n
    M[i] = P[i] + X[i]
endfor
```
Note that each loop would be equivalent to a vector instruction. X is stored back into the memory by the first instruction and then retrieved by the second. If these loops are fused as shown below, the memory traffic can be reduced:
```
for i = 1, n
    X[i] = Y[i] * Z[i]
    M[i] = P[i] + X[i]
endfor
```
This assumes that there are enough vector registers available in the processor to retain X. If the processor allows chaining, the above loop can be reduced to:
```
for i = 1, n
    M[i] = P[i] + Y[i] * Z[i]
endfor
```

Loop distribution: If the loop body contains dependent (i.e., statements that are data dependent) and nondependent code, a way to minimize the effect of the dependency is to break the loop into two, one containing the dependent code and the other nondependent code.

Force maximum work into inner loop: Because maximizing the vector length increases the speed of execution, the inner loop should always be made the longest. Further, dependency conflicts are avoided by shifting dependencies in an inner loop to an outer loop, if possible.

In addition to the above vectorization techniques, several techniques to optimize the performance of the scalar portions of the code have been devised. Some of these are described below.

Subprogram in-lining: For small subprograms, the overhead of control transfer takes longer than the actual subprogram execution. Calling a subprogram might consume about 10 to 15 clock cycles when no arguments passed, and one argument might nearly double that overhead. In such cases, it is better to move the subprogram code into the calling program.

Eliminate ambiguity using the PARAMETER statement: If the (Fortran) PARAMETER statement is used to define a true constant in every subprogram in which it is used rather than passing it as a call-list parameter or putting it in a common block, the compiler can generate better optimized and unconditionally vectorized code.

Positioning frequently executed scalar conditional blocks first: Code in scalar conditional blocks (if-then-else) is executed in sequential order. Placing the most frequently executed conditional block early in the sequential code will speed up execution time of the code.

Construction of vectorizing compilers and languages for parallel processing has been an active area of research. A complete discussion of these topics is beyond the scope of this book. References listed at the end of this chapter provide further details.

Vector processor manufacturers provide various tools to assist the process of vectorization and multitasking. For instance, the LOOPMARK from Cray Research, Inc. shows which loops were vectorized and which were not. The FLOWTRACE utility measures each routine in the program in terms of time of execution, number of times called, calling routine, routines called, and percentage of overall execution time spent in routine. This information targets areas of code for revision and performance enhancement. Cray also provides a vectorizing Fortran compiler (CFT).

Along with vectorization, multitasking also needs to be optimized. Cray provides a preprocessor for its CFT77 advanced Fortran compiler to aid in partitioning the code for optimal task dispersal.

4.7 SUMMARY

Architectural issues concerned with vector processing schemes are covered in this chapter. These architectures mix pipelining and parallel processing to various degrees. In terms of progression in architecture, attached array processors came first because they are extensions to general purpose hosts. The concept of specialized attached processors (or coprocessors) aiding the host processor is now common even in small microprocessor systems. Vector processors were the second step in the progression of architectures. They integrated the scalar and vector computational tasks into the processor architecture, and the host performed mainly the I/O operations.

Basic models for the two types of vector processor architectures were provided in this chapter. Architectural highlights of three commercial vector processor systems were also listed.

Progress in hardware technology has a tremendous impact on these architectures. For instance, use of gallium arsenide technology in the Cray-3 series of supercomputers has greatly increased the performance from the earlier systems implemented in silicon. As such, the trend has been to make each processor as powerful as possible and to utilize the least number of processors in the architecture. This results in a coarse-grained parallelism and reduces the communication overhead associated with tasks running concurrently on multiple CPUs.

Vector processors belong to the superpipelined architectures category and are suitable for applications that offer a high level of vectorization. These are the applications that call for long vectors. Superscalar architectures, on the other hand, issue multiple instructions per cycle. These are suitable for applications with a high degree of instruction level parallelism.

In general, specialized programming schemes and compilers are needed to efficiently utilize the computational power offered by these architectures. A brief discussion of the programming concepts and vectorization of serial programs is provided in this chapter.

With the advances in hardware technology, it is now possible to build very high-speed pipelined scalar processors. These are usually much cheaper to build and offer performance levels close to those of vector processor architectures, thereby making vector processor architectures obsolete. Indeed, this phenomenon has already occurred with respect to the FPS 5000 series of attached processors.

It is interesting to note that the performance of some modern workstations, notably those with good floating-point hardware (such as IBM RS6000), is approaching the performance of supercomputers, at least in terms of MFLOPS. The major difference between the two, however, is in terms of the memory bandwidth. The workstations with their dynamic RAM main memories cannot compete in memory bandwidth with the high speed, highly interleaved and pipelined memory systems of supercomputers. Thus, the place where the supercomputers really shine is in operating on extremely large data sets and not just in raw FLOPS.

REFERENCES

August, M. C., et. al. 1989. Cray X-MP: The birth of a supercomputer. *IEEE Computer*. January, 45–52.

Andrews, G. R., and R. A. Olsson. 1993. *The SR programming language: concurrency in practice*. Redwood City, Calif.: Benjamin/Cummings.

Banerjee U., R. Eigenmann, A. Nocilau, and D. A. Padua. 1993. Automatic program parallelization. *Proceedings of IEEE* 81(2): 211–243.

Budnik, P., and D. J. Kuck. 1971. The organization and use of parallel memories. *IEEE Transactions on Computers* C-20: 1566–69.

Cheung, T., and J. E. Smith. 1984. An analysis of the Cray X-MP Memory System. *Proceedings IEEE International Conference Parallel Processing*, 499–505.

Convex Computer Corporation. 1988. *Convex C Series*. Publication 080-0010006-001. Richardson, Tex.: Convex Computer Corporation.

Convex Computer Corporation. 1993. Convex's C3 line steps on the GaAs. 1991. *Context* 4(2) Summer. Richardson, Tex.: Convex Computer Corporation.

Cray Research, Inc. 1988. *Cray X-MP and Cray Y-MP computer systems* (training workbook), Egan, MN: Cray Research, Inc.

Decyk, V. K. 1993. How to write (nearly) portable Fortran programs for parallel computers. *Computers in Physics* 7(4), July/August, 418–424.

Ducksbury, P. G. 1986. *Parallel array processing*. New York: Halstead Press.

Floating-Point Systems. 1989. *System Brief: 5000 Series of APs*. Beaverton, Oreg.: Floating-Point Systems.

Floating-Point Systems. 1990. *System Brief: 5800 Series of APs*. Beaverton, Oreg.: Floating-Point Systems.

Hack, J. J. 1986. Peak vs. sustained performance in highly concurrent vector machines. *IEEE Computer* 19(9), September, 11–19.

Hockney, R. W., and C. R. Jesshope. 1988. *Parallel computers 2*. Philadelphia, Penn.: Adam Hilger.

Hwang, K., and F. A. Briggs. 1984. *Computer architecture and parallel processing*. New York, N.Y.: McGraw-Hill.

Johnson, P. M. 1978. An introduction to vector processing. *Computer Design*. February, 89–97.

Jones, T. 1989. Engineering design of the Convex C2. *IEEE Computer* 22(1): 36–44.

Kogge, P. M. 1981. *The architecture of pipelined computers*. New York, N.Y.: McGraw-Hill.

Kuck, D. J. 1978. *The structure of computers and computations*. New York, N.Y.: John Wiley.

Lazou, C. 1988. *Supercomputers and their use*. New York, N.Y.: Oxford University Press.

Levesque, J. M., and J. L. Williamson. 1989. *A guidebook to Fortran on supercomputers*. San Diego, Calif.: Academic Press, Inc.

Lubeck O., J. Moore, and P. Mendez. 1985. A benchmark comparison of three supercomputers: Fujitsu VP-200, Hitachi S810/20 and Cray X-MP/2. *IEEE Computer* 18(12): 10–24.

Ortega, J. M. 1988. *Introduction to parallel and vector solution of linear systems*. New York, N.Y.: Plenum Press.

Patel, J. H., and E. S. Davidson. 1976. Improving the throughput of a pipeline by insertion of delays. *Proceedings of the Third Annual Computer Architecture Symposium*, 159–163.

Polychronopoulos, C. D. 1988. *Parallel programming and compilers*. Boston, Mass: Kluwer Academic Publishers.

Ramamoorthy, C. V., and H. F. Li. 1977. Pipeline architectures. *ACM Computing Surveys* 9(1): 61–102.

Shar, L. E., and E. S. Davidson. 1974. A multiminiprocessor system implemented through pipelining. *IEEE Computer* 7(2): 42–51.

Stone, H. S. 1990. *High-performance computer architecture*. 27. New York, N.Y.: Addison-Wesley Publishing Company.

PROBLEMS

4.1. The following are common operations on matrices: column sum, row sum, transpose, inverse, addition, and multiplication. Examine the algorithm for each operation and develop vectorized procedures for each assuming a vector processor capable of performing vector add, subtract, reciprocal, and multiply operations.

4.2. The following code segment needs to be executed on a vector processor with a five-stage floating-point adder and a six-stage floating-point multiplier:

```
A = B + C
D = s * A
E = D + B
```

where, A, B, C, D, and E are 32 element vectors and s is a scalar. Assume that each stage of the adder and multiplier consumes one cycle, that memory load and store each consume one cycle, and that there are a required number of memory paths. Derive the computation time if chaining is not allowed and if chaining is allowed. Show the timing diagram for each case.

4.3. Solve the above problem assuming that only one path to and from memory is available.

4.4. Assume that the vector processor has vector registers that can hold 64 operands and data can be transferred between these registers in blocks of 64 operands every cycle. Solve Problem 4.2 with these assumptions.

4.5. Modify the following program segments for efficient execution on Cray architecture for $N = 16, 64, 128$:

PROBLEMS

    a.
```
      for I = 1 to N
        for J = 1 to 20
          B(I,J) = K * A(I,J)
        endfor
      endfor
```
    b.
```
      for I = 1 to N
        X(I) = K * X(I)
        Y(I) = Y(I) + X(I-1)
      endfor
```

4.6. For each loop in the above problem, find R_{100} and R_∞ and $N_{1/2}$. Assume $T_{memory} = 10$ cycles and $T_{loop} = 5$ cycles.

4.7. Consider the problem of sorting very large arrays of numbers. Investigate how a vector processor can be used effectively in this task. Select a sorting algorithm, and vectorize it as far as possible.

4.8. Assume that a vector processor has 16 banks of memory organized, as in Figure 4.4, with two-cycle access time. Investigate the best way to represent a 32×32 matrix if the computation requires accessing a) one row at a time, b) one column at a time, and c) either a row or a column at a time.

4.9. Design a memory structure suitable for accessing the matrix in the above problem for a vector processor with vector registers capable of holding 16 elements of data.

4.10. Develop an instruction set for a vector processor that is required to perform common matrix operations. Assume that the processor is a) memory-oriented and b) register-oriented.

4.11. Compare the architecture and performance characteristics of contemporary processor/numeric coprocessor pairs with those of the commercial vector processor architectures described in this chapter.

4.12. Most vector processors use only an instruction cache and no data cache. Justify this architecture.

4.13. Compare the Cray and Convex series of supercomputers with respect to their instruction sets, instruction execution speeds, and policies. What support is provided by the compilers for these machines to make the applications run faster?

4.14. Discuss the special array operations needed on vector processors to enable parallel execution of conditional operations (i.e., vectorizing loops containing branches).

4.15. Assume that a vector processor operates 20 times faster on vector code than scalar code. If only $x\%$ of the program is vectorizable, what is the value of x for the machine to execute the program twice as fast as the scalar processor?

CHAPTER 5

Array Processors

This chapter covers parallel array processors, which are the SIMD class of architectures introduced in Chapter 2. Recall that the major characteristics of these architectures are:

1. A single control processor (CP) issues instructions to multiple arithmetic-logic processing elements (PEs).
2. PEs execute instructions in a lock-step mode. That is, PEs are synchronized at the instruction level and all the PEs execute the same instruction at any time and, hence, the name **synchronous array processors.**
3. Each PE operates on its own data stream. Because multiple PEs are active simultaneously, these architectures are known as **data-parallel** architectures.
4. These are **hardware intensive architectures** in the sense that the degree of parallelism possible depends on the number of PEs available.
5. The PEs are usually interconnected by a data exchange network.

The **associative processor** architectures covered in Chapter 2 also belong to the SIMD classification. Associative processor architectures have not been a commercial success because of their extensive hardware requirements. In addition to the STARAN system described in Chapter 2, Goodyear Aerospace's massively parallel processor (MPP) is the only commercial architecture of this category.

The **systolic architectures** introduced in Chapter 2 are a special type of synchronous array processor architecture. The major characteristics of two commercial systolic architectures are highlighted in this chapter.

The next section revisits the SIMD organization, illustrated in Figure 2.5, as a means of developing a generic model for this class of architectures. The performance of an SIMD architecture is influenced by the data structures used and the memory organization employed. These topics are covered in Section 2. Section 3 introduces interconnection networks and provides details of commonly used topologies in SIMD architectures. Section 4 provides performance evaluation concepts. Section 5 discusses programming considerations. Section 6 describes three SIMD architectures: the ILLIAC-IV, an experimental machine, and two commercial systems—Thinking Machines Corporation's Connection Machine (CM) series and MasPar Corporation's MP series. Section 7 provides the details of two commercial systolic architectures: Intel Corporation's iWARP and Saxpy Computer Corporation's Matrix.

5.1 SIMD ORGANIZATION

The following example compares the operation of an SIMD with that of an SISD system:

EXAMPLE 5.1

Consider element by element the addition of two N-element vectors A and B to create the sum vector C. That is:

$$C[i] = A[i] + B[i] \qquad 1 \le i \le N. \tag{5.1}$$

As noted in Chapter 4, this computation requires N add times plus the loop control overhead on an SISD. Also, the SISD processor has to fetch the instructions corresponding to this program from the memory each time through the loop.

Figure 5.1 shows the SIMD implementation of this computation using N PEs. This is identical to the SIMD model of Figure 2.5 and consists of multiple PEs, one CP, and the memory system. The processor interconnection network of Figure 2.5 is not needed for this computation. The elements of arrays A and B are distributed over N memory blocks, and hence, each PE has access to one pair of operands to be added. Thus, the program for the SIMD consists of one instruction:

C = A + B.

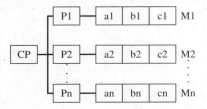

Figure 5.1 SIMD Processing Model

This instruction is equivalent to:

```
C[i] = A[i] + B[i]    (1 ≤ i ≤ N)
```

where i represents the PE that is performing the addition of the ith elements, and the expression in parentheses implies that N PEs are active simultaneously.

The execution time for the above computation is one addition time. No other overhead is needed. But the data need to be structured in N memory blocks to provide for the simultaneous access of the N data elements.

Thus, SIMDs offer an N-fold throughput enhancement over the SISD provided the application exhibits a data-parallelism of degree N. The following sections examine in detail the functional requirements for each component of an SIMD.

5.1.1 Memory

In the SIMD model of Figures 5.1 and 2.5, each PE is connected to its own memory block. (This organization also corresponds to Type 1 of Figure 2.9.) The conglomeration of all the memory blocks forms the system memory. Programs typically occupy parts of several memory blocks. For instance, if the memory addresses are interleaved between the blocks, instructions in a program would spread among all the blocks of the memory. Data are distributed among the memory blocks such that each PE can access the data it operates on. The CP accesses the memory for instruction retrieval, and PEs access the memory for data retrieval and storage. This simultaneous access requirement might result in memory access bottleneck.

One way of minimizing the memory access bottleneck is to include a memory block at the CP in which the instructions reside (resulting in the Type 2 model of Figure 2.9). This organization partitions the system memory into data and program memories. Because the complete memory system is now not available for program storage, the program sizes are restricted by the program memory size.

In both of the above organizations, each PE has its own (i.e., local) memory. This requires that the data be loaded into the memory such that the data elements required for computation by a PE are available in its local memory. Another possible variation is the Type 3 model of Figure 2.9, where the data memories are connected to the PEs with an $(n \times n)$ switch. This switch allows any data memory to be accessed by any PE. That is, the switch is a **data alignment** network. This organization allows a flexible data structuring at the cost of the switch complexity.

As we will see later in this chapter, data structuring is an important consideration in the application of SIMD architectures. In the absence of a data alignment network, additional operations are needed to rearrange data in the memory appropriately (i.e., to facilitate simultaneous access by PEs) as the computation progresses. For example, assume that data is originally organized to provide simultaneous access to the row elements of a matrix. If the subsequent computation requires simultaneous access to column elements, data needs to be reloaded in the memory appropriately before the new computation begins. Several data structuring techniques have been devised over the years to allow various modes of accessing data in SIMDs. Section 3 describes some of these techniques.

5.1.2 Control Processor

The control processor fetches instructions and decodes them. It transfers arithmetic or logic instructions to PEs for execution. That is, the CP generates control signals corresponding to these instructions that are utilized by the PEs. Control instructions are executed by the CP itself. The CP performs all the address computations and might also retrieve some data elements from the memory and **broadcast** them to all the PEs as required. This method of data distribution can be employed when either a PE interconnection network is not available or when broadcasting is more efficient than using the PE interconnection network. The CP is thus equivalent to an SISD processor except that the arithmetic/logic functions are not performed by it.

5.1.3 Arithmetic/Logic Processors

The PEs perform the arithmetic and logical operations on the data. Thus, each PE corresponds to data paths and arithmetic/logic units of an SISD processor capable of responding to control signals from the control unit.

5.1.4 Interconnection Network (IN)

In Type 1 and Type 2 SIMD architectures, the PE to memory interconnection is through an n-to-n switch, and hence, each PE has direct access to the data in its local memory. If the computational algorithm allows each PE to continue processing without needing any data from other PEs (or memory blocks), there is no need for a PE-to-PE interconnection network. In practice, it is not always possible to partition data and computations such that no data exchange between PEs is required. To facilitate such data exchange, an $n \times n$ switch was used to interconnect PEs. In Type 3, there is no PE-to-PE interconnection network because all data exchanges are performed through the $n \times n$ (alignment) switch between the PEs and the memory blocks. That is, instead of moving the data to the PE needing it, the switch settings are altered to connect the PE to the memory that contains the data.

As mentioned earlier, the CP can also retrieve data from memory blocks and distribute them to PEs. If the data exchange is not excessive, this method is efficient enough and a PE interconnection network is not needed. But if the computation requires either a large amount or a complex pattern of data exchange, use of a PE interconnection network would be more efficient.

The interconnection network used with an SIMD is dependent on the data exchange requirements of the computational task at hand. Examples in this section show typical data exchange patterns and corresponding interconnection network requirements. Section 4 provides further details on interconnection networks.

5.1.5 Registers, Instruction Set, Performance Considerations

The unique characteristic of the SIMD architecture is the lock-step instruction execution. This implies that the computational task exhibit a high degree of parallelism (at the instruction level) and that data be structured to allow simultaneous access by the PEs.

EXAMPLE 5.2

Consider the task of computing the column sum of an ($N \times N$) matrix. Figure 5.2 shows the data structure used in an SIMD with N PEs. Each PE has access to one column of the matrix. Thus, the program shown in (b) can be used to perform the column sum computation. The column sum is computed by traversing the loop N times. Thus, the order of computation is N compared to N^2 required on an SISD.

The assembly language equivalent of the program in (b) is shown in (c). In this program, instructions LDA, ADD, and STA are executed simultaneously by all the PEs while the instructions LDX, DEX, BNZ, and HLT are executed by the CP. Thus the instruction set of an SIMD is similar to that of an SISD except that the arithmetic/logic instructions are performed by multiple PEs simultaneously.

M1	M2	M3	···	Mn
a11	a12	a13		a1n
.	.	.		.
.	.	.		.
.	.	.		.
an1				ann
sum1	sum2			sum n
P1	P2	P3	···	PN

```
Sum [i] = 0      (1 < i < N)
For j = 1 to N
    Sum [i] = Sum [i] + A [i][j] (1 < i < N)
end for
```

(a) Data Structure　　　　　　　　　　　　**(b) High-Level Program**

```
        LDA       ZERO           load the accumulator with a 0.
        LDX       N              load index reg. with N.
LOOP    ADD       A-1, 1
        DEX                      Decrement index
        BNZ       LOOP           Add to loop if index=0
        STA       SUM            Store Sum
        HLT                      Halt
ZERO    CONSTANT  0
N       CONSTANT  5              For a 5*5 Matrix
A       CONSTANT  4,2,3,5,6      Column elements
        END
```

(c) Assembly-level Program

Figure 5.2 Matrix Column Addition

A global index register that is manipulated by the CP to access subsequent elements of data in individual memory blocks is assumed in the above example. In practice, each PE will have its own set of (local) index registers in addition to global registers. This allows more flexible data storage and access. Correspondingly, the instruction set will contain two types of index manipulation instructions, one set for the global registers and the other for local registers.

5.1 SIMD ORGANIZATION

EXAMPLE 5.3

Now consider the problem of normalizing each column of an ($N \times N$) matrix with respect to the first element of the column. This can be done in N time units using an SIMD with N PEs, and the data structure is the same as that in Figure 5.2. Because this computation requires a division if the first element of any column is zero, that column should not participate in the normalization process. Because the SIMD works in a lock-step mode, the PEs corresponding to the columns with a zero first element will have to be deactivated during this computation:

To facilitate this type of operation, each PE contains an activity bit as part of its status word. It is set or reset based on the condition within that processor's data stream and controls the activity of the PE during the subsequent cycles.

In addition to the usual instructions that set the condition code bits in the status register, the instruction set of an SIMD contains instructions that allow logical manipulation of the activity bits of all the PEs. These instructions enable manipulation of activity bits to accommodate the activation of appropriate PEs based on complex data conditions.

Conditional branch instructions in the program also utilize the activity bits of PEs as shown by the following example.

EXAMPLE 5.4

Consider the program segment depicted by the flowchart of Figure 5.3. Here, A, B, C, and D represent blocks of instructions. If this program were for an SISD, the processor, after executing A, would have executed either B or C depending on the value of

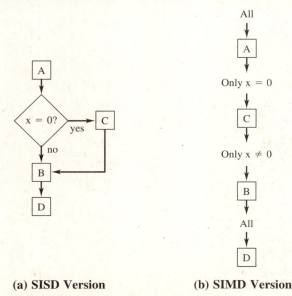

    (a) SISD Version   **(b) SIMD Version**

Figure 5.3 Conditional Branch

174   CHAPTER 5   ARRAY PROCESSORS

X and then would execute D. In an SIMD, some data streams satisfy $X = 0$ and the others satisfy $X \neq 0$. That means that some PEs execute B and the others execute C and that all PEs eventually execute D. To accommodate this computation and to retain the instruction lock-step mode of operation, the branch operation is converted into a sequential operation as shown in (b). Note that all the PEs are not active during the execution of blocks C and B, and hence, the SIMD hardware is not being utilized efficiently. As such, for an SIMD to be efficient, conditional branches should be avoided as much as possible.

Note that the PE interconnection network was not needed in the above applications. The examples in the next section illustrate the need for such a network and provide details of data storage concepts.

5.2 DATA STORAGE TECHNIQUES AND MEMORY ORGANIZATION

As mentioned earlier, the data storage pattern has a significant effect on the performance of SIMDs. The following example introduces the two common data storage formats for matrices.

EXAMPLE 5.5

Consider the **straight storage** format of matrices used in Figure 5.2. It allows accessing all the elements of a row of the matrix simultaneously by the PEs. Thus, while it is suitable for column-oriented operations, it is not possible to access column elements simultaneously. If such an access is needed (for row-oriented operations), the matrix storage needs to be rearranged such that each row is stored in a memory block (as shown in Figure 5.4). This rearrangement is time consuming and, hence, impractical especially for large matrices.

The **skewed storage,** shown in Figure 5.5, solves this problem by allowing simultaneous row and column accesses. Because the matrix is skewed, additional operations are needed to align the data elements. For instance, when accessing rows, note that the elements in the first row are properly aligned. But the second row elements need to be rotated left once after they are loaded into the processor registers. In general, the ith row elements need to be rotated $(i - 1)$ times to the left to align them with the PEs.

Accessing of columns is shown in (b). Note that this requires local index registers. To access the first column, the indexes are set as shown by arrows. To access

M1	M2	M3	$\cdots$	MN
a11	a21			aN1
a12	a22			aN2
a13	a23			:
:	:			
a1N	a2N			aNN

Figure 5.4   Row-Wise Matrix Representation

5.2 DATA STORAGE TECHNIQUES AND MEMORY ORGANIZATION

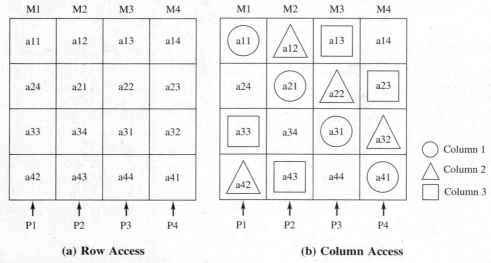

Figure 5.5 Skewed Matrix Representation

> subsequent columns, the indexes are decremented by 1, modulo N. After the elements are loaded into the PE registers, they are aligned by rotating them. The elements of ith column are rotated $(i - 1)$ times left.

The skewed storage thus necessitates a **ring** or **loop** interconnection network between the PEs. This network connects each PE to its right or left neighbor (unidirectional) or both (bidirectional). Correspondingly, the instruction set contains instructions to utilize the functions provided by the PE interconnection network. For instance, in the case of the loop interconnection, instructions of the type SHIFT LEFT and SHIFT RIGHT would be needed. When issued, these instructions shift the data simultaneously between the PEs. The data transfer between the PEs over the interconnection network usually occurs through a set of registers within each PE. The results of computation are normally retained in these registers so that they can be shared with other PEs at register transfer speeds. Figure 5.6 shows a schematic of a unidirectional ring with four PEs.

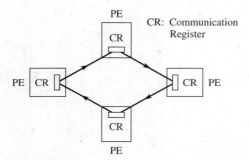

Figure 5.6 Schematic of Ring Interconnection Network with Four PEs

In general, an algorithm that is efficient for an SISD need not be efficient for an SIMD, as illustrated by the following example.

EXAMPLE 5.6

Consider, for instance, the popular matrix multiply algorithm for an SIMD depicted by the program in Figure 5.7(a). Here, to compute the element C[i, j], the ith row elements of A are multiplied element-by-element by the jth column elements of B and the products are accumulated. The algorithm executes in N^3 time.

To implement this algorithm on an SIMD, the first attempt would be to store matrix A by column and B by row so that appropriate row and column can be accessed simultaneously. This allows the generation of the N products simultaneously. But because these products are in N processors, they need to be accumulated sequentially by one processor. Thus, the computation is not going to be efficient.

A slight rearrangement of the algorithm yields a better SIMD computation. The SIMD program shown in (b) assumes that all the three matrices are stored by column in straight storage format in N memory banks. Here k is the processor number. Elements of the ith row are computed one product at a time through the j loop. It takes N iterations of the j loop to complete the computation of the ith row elements of C. This algorithm executes in N^2 time and does not require a sequential mode of operation on the part of PEs.

Note that within the j loop the element A[i, j] is available at the jth processor and is required by all the other processors. This is done by **broadcasting** the content of this value from the jth processor to others. Broadcasting is a common operation in SIMDs and is implemented in one of the two ways mentioned earlier: either the PE

```
for k = 1 to N
    for i = 1 to N
        C[i,k] = 0
        for j = 1 to N
            C[i,k] = C[i,k]+A[i,j]*B[j,k]
        endfor
    endfor
endfor
```
(a) SISD Version

```
for i = 1 to N
  C[i,k] = 0      (1 < k < N)
  for j = 1 to N
    C[i, k] = C[i,k]+A[i,j]*B[j,k]    (1 < k < N)
  endfor
endfor
```
(b) SIMD Version

Figure 5.7 Matrix Multiplication

5.2 DATA STORAGE TECHNIQUES AND MEMORY ORGANIZATION

interconnection network performs the broadcast or the CP reads the value from the jth PE and supplies it to all the PEs. If the ring IN is used, $(N - 1)$ shifts are needed to broadcast the value in any PE. Alternatively, the CP can read the value from the PE and broadcast it in one instruction cycle time.

The remainder of this section concentrates on the memory organization techniques that allow efficient data structuring on SIMDs. As shown above, if a matrix is to be accessed only by rows, we can store the matrix by row in straight storage format. If the columns of a matrix are to be accessed, we can store the matrix by column in straight storage format. These storage formats also allow the accessing of diagonal elements simultaneously. Neither of these techniques is good for an algorithm requiring access to both row and column vectors. The skewed storage format allows such access, but the diagonal elements are not accessible simultaneously in the skewed storage format.

In general, a conflict-free access occurs if in a modular (parallel) memory system with M memory modules, M consecutive accesses to the elements of matrix (vector) are spread over M memory modules. In an interleaved memory system connected to processors through an n-by-n switch, a necessary condition is that the memory access delay be at most equal to M clock periods. If this condition is not satisfied, after M accesses, an access to the first module is made. This module is still busy, because the memory access time is greater than M. This leads to a conflict.

EXAMPLE 5.7

Consider the storage scheme shown below where a dummy column is added to the matrix so that the dummy element in each row provides a cyclical offset to the row. This way no two elements of any row or column are stored in the same module, and thus, the access is conflict free.

M0	M1	M2	M3	← Memory Modules
a00	a01	a02	a03	
	a10	a11	a12	
a13		a20	a21	
a22	a23		a30	
a31	a32	a33		

The address increment required to move from one element to another in vector access is known as *stride*. For the above data structure, the stride for row access is 1, that for column access is 5, and that for diagonal access is 6.

A general rule is that stride s for an access to a vector (matrix) stored in modular memory should be relatively prime to m, the number of memory modules. That is,

$$\text{GCD}(s, m) = 1 \tag{5.2}$$

for m successive accesses to be spread across m modules. Here, GCD denotes the greatest common divisor. Thus, the access of diagonal elements in the above example is not conflict free, because the stride is 6. Budnick and Kuck (1971) suggested using memory with a prime number of modules. The reasoning behind this suggestion was that if M is prime, then

$$\text{GCD}(s, m) = 1 \tag{5.3}$$

for all $s < m$. This gives a wide range of choices for the stride that satisfies the condition for conflict-free access.

This concept was used in the design of the Burroughs Scientific Processor (BSP), which had 17 memory modules and 16 processors. The block diagram of the BSP is as shown in Figure 5.8. Alignment networks were used to twist the data to the required position once accessed from the memory or before storing into memory.

EXAMPLE 5.8

The following example shows the vector access in computers with a prime number of memory modules:

Here m is 5 and a (4×4) matrix with two dummy columns is shown.

```
M0       M1       M2       M3       M4    ← Memory Modules
-----------------------------------------
a00      a01      a02      a03
-----------------------------------------
         a10      a11      a12      a13
-----------------------------------------
                  a20      a21      a22
-----------------------------------------
a23                        a30      a31
-----------------------------------------
a32      a33
-----------------------------------------
```

Stride for row access = 1
Stride for column access = 6
Diagonal access with stride = 7

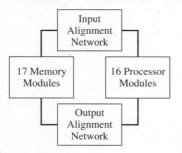

Figure 5.8 Burroughs Scientific Processor

5.2 DATA STORAGE TECHNIQUES AND MEMORY ORGANIZATION

```
      M0      M1      M2      M3      M4
      ----------------------------------------
      a00     a01     a02     a03
      ----------------------------------------
              a10     a11     a12     a13
      ----------------------------------------
                      a20     a21     a22
      ----------------------------------------
      a23                     a30     a31
      ----------------------------------------
      a32     a33
      ----------------------------------------
      a00     a33     a11             a22      READ
      a00     a11     a22     a33              ALIGN
```

The following are some problems with BSP and other architectures using a prime number of memory modules:

1. Delay due to input and output alignment networks.
2. Addressing is complex when M is not a power of 2.
3. Because each access has to be from the main memory, buffering of data is not possible, and hence results in a large delay in terms of data access.

The skewed storage scheme characteristics can be generalized. The skewed storage of Figure 5.5 is usually denoted as (1, 1) skewed storage because the stride in both dimensions of the matrix is 1.

Let k be the array dimension and m the number of memory modules. The stride in i^{th} dimension is si. For a two-dimensional array in general with a $(s1, s2)$-skewing scheme, the columns will be said to be $s1$-ordered, the rows $s2$-ordered, and the main diagonal $(s1 + s2)$-ordered.

Let a d-ordered n vector (mod m) denote a vector of n elements, the ith element of which is stored in memory module $(di + c)$ (mod m), where c is an arbitrary constant. Then a sufficient condition for a conflict-free access to such a vector is (Budnick and Kuck, 1971; Kuck, 1977):

$$m \geq n \times \text{GCD}(d, m) \tag{5.4}$$

EXAMPLE 5.9

If a two-dimensional array is stored in $(s1, s2)$ order in m memory modules to obey the above rule, we can access without conflict: any $s1$-ordered n-element column because $m > n \times \text{GCD}(s1, m)$; any $s2$-ordered n-element row because $m > n \times \text{GCD}(s2, m)$; and the $(s1 + s2)$-ordered main diagonal because $m > n \times \text{GCD}(s1 + s2, m)$.

Note that it must be possible to index into each of the memory modules independently in order to exploit skewing schemes effectively.

5.3 INTERCONNECTION NETWORKS (FENG, 1978)

PEs and memory blocks in an SIMD architecture are interconnected by either an n-to-n or an n-by-n switch as shown above. Also, an n-by-n switch between the PEs is needed in general to allow fast exchange of data as the computation proceeds. From here on, the term *interconnection network (IN)* will be used to refer to the interconnection hardware rather than the term *switch*. The term *switch* is more generally used to refer to a component of an IN (as discussed later in this section).

As mentioned earlier, the PE-to-PE interconnection network for an SIMD depends on the dataflow requirements of the application. In fact, depending on the application, most of the computation can be accomplished by the interconnection network itself if the network is chosen appropriately, thus reducing the complexity of PEs drastically.

Several INs have been proposed and built over the last few years. This section introduces the terminology and performance measures associated with INs and describes common INs as applied to SIMD systems. Chapter 6 extends this description to MIMD architectures.

5.3.1 Terminology and Performance Measures

An IN consists of several **nodes** interconnected by **links**. A node, in general, is either a PE or a memory block or a complete computer system consisting of PEs, memory blocks, and I/O devices. A link is the hardware interconnect between two nodes. The IN facilitates the transmission of **messages** (data or control information) between processes residing in nodes. The two functional entities that form the interconnection structure are **paths** and **switches.** A path is the medium by which a message is transmitted between two nodes and is comprised of one or more links and switches. The link just transmits the message and does not alter it in any way. A switch, on the other hand, may alter the message (i.e., change the destination address) or route it to one of the number of alternative paths available.

A path can be unidirectional point-to-point, bidirectional point-to-point, or bidirectional and visit more than two nodes. The first two types are classified as **dedicated** paths, and the last type is the **shared** path.

Two message transfer strategies are used—**direct** and **indirect.** In the direct strategy, there will be no intervening switching elements between communicating nodes. In the indirect strategy, there will be one or more switching elements between the nodes. If an indirect transfer strategy is chosen, either a **centralized** or a **decentralized** transfer control strategy can be adopted. In a central strategy, all switching is done by a single entity (called the switch controller). In a decentralized strategy, on the other hand, the switch control is distributed among a number of switching elements.

For instance, in a ring network there is a path from each node to every other node. The path to the neighboring node from any node is of length 1, while the path

5.3 INTERCONNECTION NETWORKS (FENG, 1978)

between nonneighboring nodes is of length equal to the number of links that need to be traversed (i.e., number of hops needed) to transmit messages between those nodes. If a decentralized control strategy is used, each intermediate node in the path serves as a switch that decodes the destination address and transmits the message not addressed to it to the next node. In the examples provided earlier in this chapter, the CP is the controller of the ring and issues multiple shift instructions depending on the distance (see below) between the source and destination nodes.

In general, an IN should be able to connect all the nodes in the system to one another, transfer maximum number of messages per second reliably, and offer minimum cost. Various performance measures have been used to evaluate INs. They are described below.

1. **Connectivity** (or **degree** of the node) is the number of nodes that are immediate neighbors of a node (i.e., the number of nodes that can be reached from the node in one hop).

   For instance, in a unidirectional ring each node is of degree 1 because it is connected to only one neighboring node. In a bidirectional ring, each node is of degree 2.

2. **Bandwidth** is the total number of messages the network can deliver in unit time. A message is simply a bit pattern of certain length consisting of data and/or control information.

3. **Latency** is a measure of the overhead involved in transmitting a message over the network from the source node to the destination node. It can be defined as the time required to transmit a zero-length message.

4. **Average distance,** where the distance between two nodes is the number of links in the shortest path between those nodes in the network, is given by:

$$d_{avg} = \frac{\sum_{d=1}^{r} d \cdot N_d}{N - 1} \tag{5.5}$$

   where N_d is the number of nodes at distance d apart; r is the **diameter** (i.e., the maximum of the minimum distance between all pairs of nodes) of the network; and N is the total number of nodes. It is desirable to have a low average distance. A network with low average distance would result in nodes of higher degree (i.e., larger number of communication ports from each node), which may be expensive to implement. Thus, a normalized average distance can be defined as:

$$d_{avg(normal)} = d_{avg} \times P \tag{5.6}$$

   where P is the number of communication ports per node.

5. **Hardware complexity** of the network is proportional to the total number of links and switches in the network. As such, it is desirable to minimize the number of these elements.

6. **Cost** is usually measured as the network hardware cost as a fraction of the total system hardware cost. The incremental hardware cost (i.e., **cost modularity**) in terms of how much additional hardware and redesign is needed to expand the network to include additional nodes is also important.

7. **Place modularity** is a measure of expandability in terms of how easily the network structure can be expanded by utilizing additional modules.
8. **Regularity** means there is a regular structure to the network, and the same pattern can be repeated to form a larger network. This property is especially useful in the implementation of the network using VLSI circuits.
9. **Reliability and fault tolerance** is a measure of the redundancy in the network to allow the communication to continue in case of the failure of one or more links.
10. **Additional functionality** is a measure of other functions (such as computations, message combining, arbitration, etc.) offered by the network in addition to the standard message transmission function.

A complete IN (i.e., an *n*-by-*n* network in which there is a link from each node to every other node—see Figure 5.12) is the ideal network because it satisfies the minimum latency, minimum average distance, maximum bandwidth, and simple routing criteria. But the complexity of this network becomes prohibitively large as the number of nodes increases. Expandability also comes at a high cost. As such, the complete interconnection scheme is not used in networks with a large number of nodes. There are other topologies that provide a better cost-to-performance ratio.

The following design choices were used by Feng (1978) to classify INs (see Figure 5.9):

1. Switching mode
2. Control strategy
3. Topology
4. Mode of operation

Switching modes and control strategies were defined earlier in this section. The IN topologies used in computer systems today have been adopted from the multitude of topologies used in telephone switching networks over the years. These topologies can be classified as either **regular** or **irregular.** Irregular topologies are usually a result of the interconnection of existing isolated systems to allow communication between them. INs used in tightly coupled multiple-processor systems tend to be regular in the sense that a definite pattern exists in the topology.

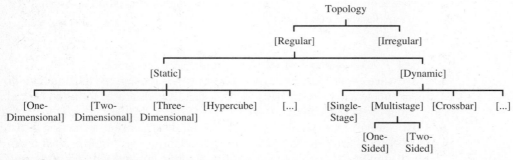

Figure 5.9 Feng's Taxonomy (Feng, 1978)

The topologies can be further classified as either **static** or **dynamic.** In a **static** topology, the links between two nodes are passive, dedicated paths. They cannot be changed to establish a direct connection to other nodes. The interconnections are usually derived based on a complete analysis of the communication patterns of the application. The topology does not change as the computation progresses. In **dynamic** topologies, the interconnection pattern changes as the computation progresses. This changing pattern is brought about by setting the network's active elements (i.e., switches).

The mode of operation of a network can be **synchronous, asynchronous,** or **combined** as dictated by the data manipulation characteristics of the application. The ring network used in the examples earlier in this chapter is an example of a synchronous network. In these networks, communication paths are established and message transfer occurs synchronously. In asynchronous networks, connection requests are issued dynamically as the transmission of the message progresses. That means that the message flow in an asynchronous network is less orderly compared to that in a synchronous network. A combined network exhibits both modes of operation.

5.3.2 Routing Protocols

Routing is the mechanism that establishes the path between two nodes for transmission of messages. It should be as simple as possible and should not result in a high overhead. It should preferably be dependent on the state of each node rather than the state of the whole network. Three basic routing protocols (or switching mechanisms) have been adopted over the years: **circuit switching, packet switching,** and **wormhole switching.**

In **circuit switching,** a path is first established between the source and the destination nodes. This path is dedicated for the transmission of the complete message. That is, there is a dedicated hardware path between the two nodes that cannot be utilized for any other message until the transmission is complete. This mode is ideal when large messages are to be transmitted.

In **packet switching,** the message is broken into small units called **packets.** Each packet has a destination address that is used to route the packet to the destination through the network nodes in a **store and forward** manner. That is, a packet travels from the source to the destination, one link at a time. At each (intermediate) node, the packet is usually stored, or buffered. It is then forwarded to the appropriate link based on its destination address. Thus, each packet might follow a different route to the destination and the packets may arrive at the destination in any order. The packets are reassembled at the destination to form the complete message. Packet switching is efficient for short messages and more frequent transmissions. It increases the hardware complexity of the switches because of the buffering requirements.

The packet switching mode is analogous to the working of the postal system in which each letter is a packet. Unlike messages in an IN, the letters from a source to a destination follow the same route and they arrive at the destination usually in the same order they are sent. The circuit switching mode is analogous to the telephone network in which a dedicated path is first established and maintained throughout the conversation. The underlying hardware in the telephone network uses packet switching, but what the user sees is a (virtual) dedicated connection.

The **wormhole switching** (or **cut-through routing**) is a combination of the above two methods. Here a message is broken into small units (called **flow control digits** or **flits**) as in packet switching. But all flits follow the same route to the destination, unlike packets. Because the leading flit sets the switches in the path and the others follow, the store and forward buffering overhead is reduced.

Routing mechanisms can be either **static** (or **deterministic**) or **dynamic** (or **adaptive**). Static schemes determine a unique path for the message from the source to the destination, based solely on the topology. Because they do not take into consideration the state of the network, there is the potential of uneven usage of the network resources and congestion. Dynamic routing, on the other hand, utilizes the state of the network in determining the path for a message and hence can avoid congestion by routing messages around the heavily used links or nodes.

The routing is realized by setting switching elements in the network appropriately. As mentioned earlier, the switch setting (or control) function can either be managed by a **centralized controller** or can be **distributed** to each switching element. Further detail on routing mechanisms is provided in the following sections along with the description of various topologies.

5.3.3 Static Topologies (Feng, 1978)

Figures 5.10 through 5.13 show some of the many static topologies that have been proposed and that represent a wide range of connectivity. The simplest among these is the linear array in which the first and last nodes are each connected to one neighboring node and each interior node is connected to two neighboring nodes. The most complex is the complete IN in which each node is connected to every other node. A brief description of each of these topologies follows.

LINEAR ARRAY AND RING (LOOP)

In the one-dimensional mesh or linear array in Figure 5.10(a), each node is connected to its neighboring node and each interior node is connected to two of its neighboring nodes while the boundary nodes are connected to only one neighbor. The links can either be unidirectional or bidirectional.

A ring or loop network is formed by connecting the two boundary nodes of the linear array as shown in Figure 5.10(b). In this structure, each node is connected to two neighboring nodes. The loop can either be unidirectional or bidirectional. In a

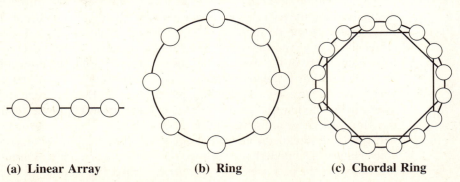

(a) Linear Array (b) Ring (c) Chordal Ring

Figure 5.10 One-Dimensional Networks

unidirectional loop, each node has a source neighbor and a destination neighbor. The node receives messages only from the source and sends messages only to the destination neighbor. Messages circulate around the loop from the source with intermediate nodes acting as buffers to the destination. Messages can be of fixed or variable length, and the loop can be designed such that either one or multiple messages can be circulating simultaneously.

The logical complexity of the loop network is low. Each node should be capable of originating a message destined for a single destination, recognize a message destined for itself, and relay messages not destined for itself. Addition of a node to the network requires only one additional link, and flow of messages is not significantly affected by this additional link. The fault tolerance of the loop is low. The failure of one link in a unidirectional loop causes the communication to stop (at least between the nodes connected by that link). If the loop is bidirectional, the failure of one link does not break the loop. Two link failures partition the loop into two disconnected parts. Loops with redundant paths have been designed to provide the fault tolerance. The chordal ring in Figure 5.10(c) in which the degree of each node is 3 is an example. The bandwidth of the loop can be a bottleneck as the communication requirements increase. It is also possible that one node can saturate the entire bandwidth of the loop.

Loop networks evolved from the data communication environments in which geographically dispersed nodes were connected for file transfers and resource sharing. They have used bit-serial data links as the communication paths.

Note that when a loop network is used to interconnect PEs in an SIMD system the message transfer between PEs is simultaneous because the PEs work in a lock-step mode. The transfer is typically controlled by the CP through SHIFT or ROTATE instructions issued once (for transfer between neighboring PEs) or multiple times (for transfers between remote PEs). The links typically carry data in parallel, rather than in bit-serial fashion.

TWO-DIMENSIONAL MESH

A popular IN is the 2-dimensional mesh (**nearest neighbor**)**,** used by ILLIAC IV, Goodyear Massively Parallel Processor (MPP), ICL Distributed Array Processor (DAP), and IBM Wire Routing Machine (WRM). Figure 5.11(a) shows a two-dimensional mesh. Here, the nodes are arranged in a two-dimensional matrix form and each node is connected to four of its neighbors (north, south, east, and west).

The connectivity of boundary nodes depends on the application. The WRM uses a pure mesh in which boundary nodes have degree 3 and corners have degree 2. In the mesh network of ILLIAC-IV the bottom node in a column is connected to the top node in the same column and the rightmost node in a row is connected to the leftmost node in the next row. This network is called a **torus**.

The cost of a two-dimensional network is proportional to N, the number of nodes. The network latency is $\sqrt{N}$. The message transmission delay depends on the distance of the destination node to the source, and hence, there is a wide range of delays. The maximum delay increases with N.

A higher-dimensional mesh can be constructed analogous to the one- and two-dimensional meshes above. A k-dimensional mesh is constructed by arranging its N nodes in the form of a k-dimensional array and connecting each node to its (2^k) neighbors by dedicated, bidirectional links. The diameter of such a network is $\sqrt[k]{N}$.

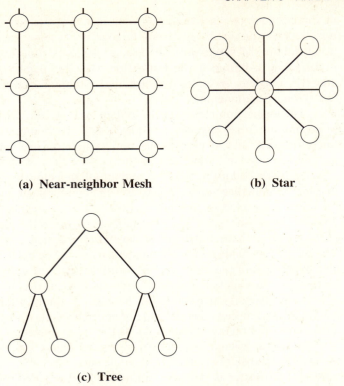

(a) Near-neighbor Mesh   (b) Star

(c) Tree

Figure 5.11 Two-Dimensional Networks

The routing algorithm commonly employed in mesh networks follows a traversal of one dimension at a time. For instance, in a four-dimensional mesh, to find a path from the node labeled (a, b, c, d) to the node labeled (p, q, r, s), we first traverse the first dimension to the node (p, b, c, d), then the next dimension to (p, q, c, d), then the third dimension to (p, q, r, d), and finally the remaining dimension to (p, q, r, s).

It is not possible to add a single node to the structure in general. The number of nodes and the additional hardware needed depends on the mesh dimensions. As such, the cost and place modularities are poor. Because of the regular structure, the routing is simpler. The fault tolerance can be high because the failure of a node or a link can be compensated by other nodes and other alternative paths possible.

STAR

In the star interconnection scheme shown in Figure 5.11(b), each node is connected to a central switch through a bidirectional link. The switch forms the apparent source and destination for all messages. The switch maintains the physical state of the system and routes messages appropriately.

The routing algorithm is trivial. The source node directs the message to the central switch, which in turn directs it to the appropriate destination on one of the dedicated links. Thus, if either of the nodes involved in message transmission is the central switch, the message path is just the link connecting them. If not, the path consists of two links.

5.3 INTERCONNECTION NETWORKS (FENG, 1978)

The cost and place modularity of this scheme are good with respect to PEs but poor with respect to the switch. The major problems are the switch bottleneck and the catastrophic effect on the system in the case of the switch failure. Each additional node added to the system requires a bidirectional link to the switch and the extension of switch facilities to accommodate the new node.

Note that the central switch basically interconnects the nodes in the network. That is, the interconnection hardware is centralized at the switch, which often allows centralized instead of distributed control over routing. The interconnection structure within the switch could be of any topology.

BINARY TREES

In binary tree networks, as shown in Figure 5.11(c), each interior node has a degree 3 (two children and one parent), leaves have a degree 1 (parent), and the root has a degree 2 (two children).

A simple routing algorithm can be used in tree networks. In order to reach node Y from node X, ascend the tree from X until an ancestor of Y is reached and then descend to Y. To find the shortest path, first find the ancestor of Y at the lowest level in the tree while ascending from X and then decide whether to follow the right or left link while descending toward Y.

The nodes of the tree are typically numbered consecutively, starting with the root node at 1. The node numbers of the left and right children of node z are $2z$ and $2z + 1$, respectively. Further, the node numbers at level i (with the root level being 1) will be i bits long. Thus, the numbers for the left and right children of a node can be obtained by appending a 0 (left child) or a 1 (right child) to the parent's number. In order to find a path from node X and to node Y with this numbering scheme, first extract the longest common bit pattern from the numbers of X and Y. This is the node number of their common ancestor A. The difference in the lengths of numbers of X and A is the number of levels to be ascended up from X. In order to reach Y from A, first remove the common (most significant) bits in numbers A and Y. Then descend based on the remaining bits of Y, going left on 0 and right on 1 until all the bits are exhausted (Almasi and Gottlieb, 1989).

For a tree network with N nodes, the latency is $\log_2 N$, the cost is proportional to N, and the degree of nodes is 3 and is independent of N.

COMPLETE INTERCONNECTION

Figure 5.12 shows the complete IN in which each node is connected to every other node with a dedicated path. Thus, in a network with N nodes, all nodes are of degree $N - 1$ and there are $N(N - 1)/2$ links. Because all nodes are connected, the minimal length path between any two nodes is simply the link connecting them.

Routing algorithm is trivial. The source node selects the path to the destination node among the $(N - 1)$ alternative paths available, and all nodes must be equipped to receive messages on a multiplicity of paths.

This network has a poor cost modularity, because the addition of a node to an N node network requires N extra links and all nodes must be equipped with additional ports to receive the message from the new node. Thus, the complexity of the network grows rapidly as the number of nodes increase. Hence, complete INs are used in environments where only a small number of nodes (4 to 16) are interconnected. The place modularity is also poor for the same reasons the cost modularity is poor.

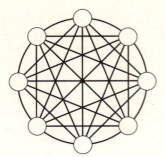

Figure 5.12 Completely Connected Network

This network provides a high bandwidth, and its fault tolerance characteristics are good. Failure of a link does not make the network inoperable, because alternative paths are readily available (although the routing scheme gets more complex).

HYPERCUBE

The hypercube is a multidimensional near-neighbor network. A k-dimensional hypercube (or a k-cube) contains 2^k nodes, each of degree k. The label for each node is a binary number with k bits. The labels of neighboring nodes differ in only one bit position.

Figure 5.13 shows the hypercubes for various values of k. A 0-cube has only one node. A 1-cube connects two nodes labeled 0 and 1. A 2-cube connects four nodes labeled 00, 01, 10, and 11. Each node is of degree 2, and the labels of neighboring nodes differ in only one bit position. A 3-cube has eight nodes with labels ranging from 000 through 111 (or decimal 0 through 7). Node (000), for example, is connected directly to nodes (001), (010), and (100), and the message transmission between these neighboring nodes requires only one hop. To transmit a message from node (000) to node (011), two routes are possible: 000 to 001 to 011 and 000 to 010 to 011. Both routes require two hops. Note that the source and destination labels differ in two bits, implying the need for two hops. To generate these routes a simple strategy is used. First, the message is at 000. The label 000 is compared with the destination address 011. Because they differ in bit positions 2 and 3, the message is routed to one of the corresponding neighboring nodes, 010 or 001. If the message is at 010, this label is again compared with 011. Note the difference in position 3, which implies that it be forwarded to 011. A similar process is used to route from 001 to 011.

Thus, the routing algorithm for the hypercube is simple. For a k-dimensional hypercube, the routing algorithm uses at most k steps. During step i the messages are routed to the adjacent node in dimension i if the ith bit of X is 1; otherwise, the messages remain where they are.

Hypercube networks reduce network latency by increasing the degree of each node (i.e., connecting each of the N nodes to $\log_2 N$ neighbors). The cost is of the order of $N \log_2 N$ and the latency is $\log_2 N$.

Several commercial architectures using the hypercube topology (from Intel Corporation, nCUBE Corporation, and Thinking Machine Corporation) are now available. One major disadvantage of the hypercube topology is that the number of nodes should always be a power of two. Thus, the number of nodes needs to double every time a single node is added to the network.

5.3 INTERCONNECTION NETWORKS (FENG, 1978)

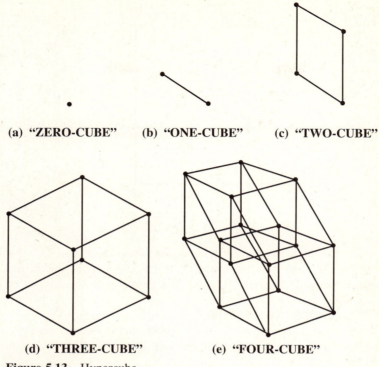

Figure 5.13 Hypercube

5.3.4 Dynamic Topologies (Almasi and Gottlieb, 1989)

A parallel computer system with static interconnection topology can be expected to do well on applications that can be partitioned into processes with predictable communication patterns consisting mostly of exchanges among neighboring processing elements. Some examples of such application domains are the analysis of events in space, vision, image processing, weather modeling, and VLSI design. If the application does not exhibit such predictable communication patterns, machines with static topologies become inefficient because the message transmission between nonneighboring nodes results in excessive transmission delays. Hence, computer systems using static INs tend to be more special purpose compared to those using dynamic INs. Both SIMD and MIMD architectures have used static topologies.

Several dynamic INs have been proposed and built over the last few years with a wide range of performance/cost characteristics. They can be classified under the following categories:

1. Bus networks
2. Crossbar networks
3. Switching networks

BUS NETWORKS
Bus networks are simple to build. Several standard bus configurations have evolved with data path widths as high as 64 bits. A bus network provides the least cost among

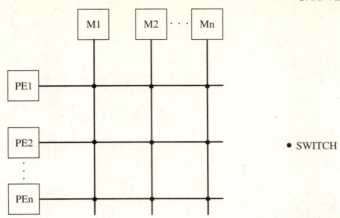

Figure 5.14 N × N Crossbar

the three types of dynamic networks and also has the lowest performance. Bus networks are not suitable for PE interconnection in an SIMD system. Chapter 6 provides further details on bus networks in the context of MIMD architectures.

CROSSBAR NETWORKS

A crossbar network is the highest performance, highest cost alternative among the three dynamic network types. It allows any PE to be connected to any other nonbusy PE at any time.

Figure 5.14 shows an $N \times N$ crossbar, connecting N PEs to N memory elements. The number of PEs and memory elements need not be equal, although both are usually powers of 2. The number of memory elements is usually a small multiple of the number of PEs. There are N^2 crosspoints in the crossbar, one at each row-column intersection. If the PEs produce a 16-bit address and work with 16-bit data units, each crosspoint in the crossbar corresponds to the intersection of 32 lines plus some control lines. Assuming 4 control lines to build a 16×16 crossbar, we would need at least ($16 \times 16 \times 36$) switching devices. To add one more PE to the crossbar, only one extra row of crosspoints is needed. Thus, although the wire cost grows as the number of processors N, the switch cost grows as N^2, which is the major disadvantage of this network.

In the crossbar network of Figure 5.14, any PE can be connected to any memory and each of the N PEs can be connected simultaneously to a distinct memory. In order to establish a connection between a PE and a memory block, the switch settings at only one crosspoint need to be changed. Because there is only one set of switches in any path, the crossbar offers uniform latency. If two PEs try to access the same memory, then there is a contention and one of them needs to wait. Such contention problems can be minimized by memory organizations discussed in Section 5.2.

The operation of the MIMD requires that the processor-memory interconnections be changed in a dynamic fashion. With high speed switching needed for such operation, high frequency capacitive and inductive effects result in noise problems that dominate crossbar design. Because of the noise problems and high cost, large crossbar networks are not practical.

The complete connectivity offered by crossbars may not be needed always. Depending on the application, a sparse crossbar network in which only certain cross-

5.3 INTERCONNECTION NETWORKS (FENG, 1978)

points have switches may be sufficient as long as it satisfies the bandwidth and connectivity requirements.

The above description uses memory blocks as one set of nodes connected to a set of PEs. In general, each node could be either a PE, a memory block, or a complete computer system with PE, memory, and I/O components.

In an SIMD architecture using crossbar IN for PEs, the switch settings are changed according to the connectivity requirements of the application at hand. This is done by either the CP or a dedicated switch controller. Alternatively, a decentralized control strategy can be used where the switches at each crosspoint forward the message toward the destination node.

SWITCHING NETWORKS

Single-stage and multistage switching networks offer a cost-to-performance compromise between the two extremes of bus and crossbar networks. A majority of switching networks proposed are based on an interconnection scheme known as perfect shuffle. The following paragraphs illustrate the single stage and multistage network concepts as applied to SIMD architectures through the perfect shuffle IN. The discussion of other switching networks is deferred to Chapter 6.

PERFECT SHUFFLE (STONE, 1971)

This network derives its name from its property of rearranging the data elements in the order of the perfect shuffle of a deck of cards. That is, the card deck is cut exactly in half and the two halves are merged such that the cards in similar position in each half are brought adjacent to each other.

EXAMPLE 5.10

Figure 5.15 shows the shuffle network for eight PEs. Two sets of PEs are shown here for clarity. Actually, there are only eight PEs. The shuffle network first partitions the

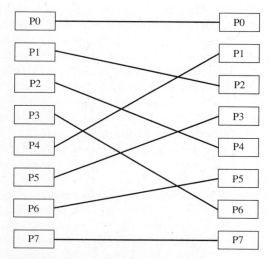

Figure 5.15 Perfect Shuffle Network

PEs into two groups (the first containing 0, 1, 2, and 3 and the second containing 4, 5, 6, and 7). The two groups are then merged such that 0 is adjacent to 4, 1 to 5, 2 to 6, and 3 to 7.

The interconnection algorithm can also be derived from a cyclic shift of the addresses of PEs. Let the total number of PEs be $N = 2^n$. Then, each PE has an n-bit address in the range 0 to $(2^n - 1)$. To determine the destination of a PE after a shuffle, the n-bit address of the PE is shifted left once cyclically.

The shuffle shown in Figure 5.15 is thus derived as follows:

PE	Source	Destination	PE
0	000	000	0
1	001	010	2
2	010	100	4
3	011	110	6
4	100	001	1
5	101	011	3
6	110	101	5
7	111	111	7

This transformation can be described by:

$$\text{Shuffle}(i) = 2i \quad \text{if } i < N/2$$
$$= 2i - N + 1 \quad \text{if } i \geq N/2 \quad (5.7)$$

The shuffle network of Figure 5.15 is a **single stage** network. If an operation requires multiple shuffles to complete, the network is used multiple times. That is, the data **recirculate** through the network. Figure 5.16 shows a **multistage** shuffle network for eight PEs in which each stage corresponds to one shuffle. That is, the data inserted into the first stage ripple through the multiple stages rather than recirculating through a single stage. In general, multistage network implementations provide faster computations at the expense of increased hardware compared to single stage network implementations. The following example illustrates this further.

In the network of Figure 5.16, the first shuffle makes the vector elements that were originally $2^{(n-1)}$ distance apart adjacent to each other; the next shuffle brings the elements originally $2^{(n-2)}$ distance apart adjacent to each other, and so on. In general, the ith shuffle brings the elements that were $2^{(n-i)}$ distance apart adjacent to each other. In addition to the shuffle network, if the PEs are connected such that adjacent PEs can exchange data, the combined network can be used efficiently in several computations.

Figure 5.17 shows a network of eight PEs. In addition to the perfect shuffle, adjacent PEs are connected through a function block capable of performing several operations on the data from the PEs connected to it. Several possible functions are shown in (b). The add function returns the sum of the two data values to the top PE.

5.3 INTERCONNECTION NETWORKS (FENG, 1978)

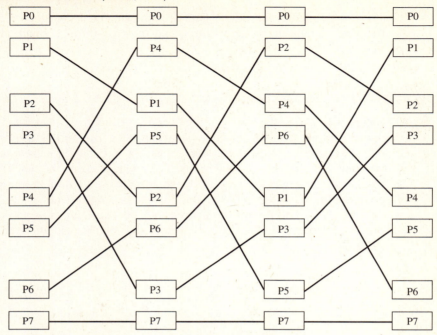

Figure 5.16 Movement of Data in a Perfect Shuffle Network

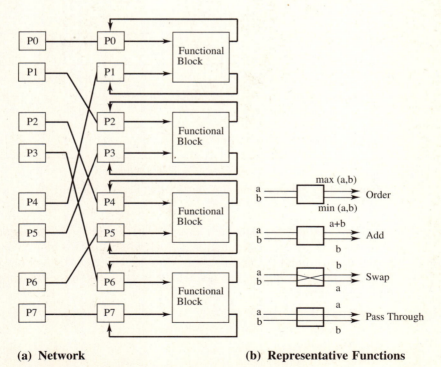

(a) Network **(b) Representative Functions**

Figure 5.17 Processors Connected by Perfect Shuffle

The order function rearranges data in increasing or decreasing order. The exchange function exchanges the data values, and the pass-through function retains them as they are.

EXAMPLE 5.11

Figure 5.18 shows the utility of the network of Figure 5.17 in the accumulation of N data values in the PEs. Each stage in the network shuffles the data and adds the neighboring elements with the sum appearing on the upper output of the SUM block. All four SUM blocks are required in the first stage. Only the first and the third SUM blocks are needed in the second stage and only the first one in the last stage for this computation. If each shuffle and add consumes T time units, this addition requires only $\log_2 N \times T$ time units compared to $N \times T$ time units required by a sequential process. Also note the CP will have to issue only one instruction (ADD) to perform this addition.

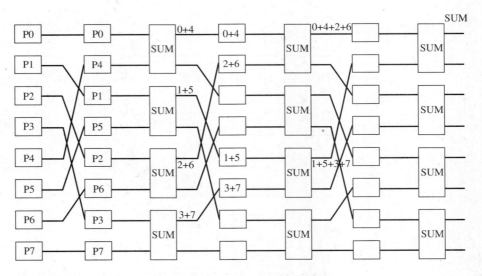

Figure 5.18 Accumulation of N Items Using Perfect Shuffle

The addition of N elements can also be accomplished by the single stage network of Figure 5.17, where each functional block will be a SUM block. Now the data have to circulate through the network $\log_2 N$ times. Thus the CP will have to execute the following program rather than a single instruction (as in the implementation with a multistage network):

```
for i = 1 to log₂ N
     shuffle
     add
endfor
```

5.4 PERFORMANCE EVALUATION AND SCALABILITY

Assuming T time units for shuffle and add as before, the single stage network implementation requires an execution time of: $T \times \log_2 N$ + fetch/decode time for instructions in the loop body each time through the loop plus the loop control overhead.

EXAMPLE 5.12

Figure 5.19 shows the sorting of N data values using the shuffle-operate network above. Here the operate function corresponds to the functional block rearranging the data elements in adjacent PEs in increasing order (if required). Again, sorting requires order of $\log_2 N$ time.

Processor	Data	Shuffle	Operate	Shuffle	Operate	Shuffle	Operate
0	5	5	5	5	9	9	9
1	6	3	3	9	5	7	7
2	9	6	6	3	3	5	6
3	4	2	2	1	1	6	5
4	3	9	9	6	7	3	4
5	2	1	1	7	6	4	3
6	1	4	7	2	4	1	2
7	7	7	4	4	2	2	1

Cycle 1　　　Cycle 2　　　Cycle 3

Figure 5.19 Sorting Using Perfect Shuffle

For the above sort operation, it is required that the original data be **bitonic**. A vector data is bitonic if 1) the vector elements increase monotonically and then decrease monotonically (with either the increasing or decreasing portions allowed to be empty) or 2) a cyclic shift of the vector elements satisfies the property 1.

There are several switching networks based on the perfect shuffle concept. For further details on INs refer to Chapter 6, the review article by Feng (1981), and books by Hillis (1981), Siegel (1985), and Johnson and Durham (1986).

5.4 PERFORMANCE EVALUATION AND SCALABILITY

If the algorithm and data partitioning allow a degree of parallelism N, an SIMD with N processors can execute the algorithm in a single time unit, that is, O(1). This is an enhancement of execution speed by N-fold (i.e., the speedup is N), because the execution time of the same algorithm on an SISD would be of the O(N). If the SIMD has only p PEs where $p < N$, the data are partitioned into N/p segments and the PEs operate simultaneously on the p elements of each segment. The computation then would be of the O(N/p), and hence, the speedup is p.

The speedup S provided by a parallel computer system is usually defined as:

$$S = \frac{\text{sequential execution time}}{\text{parallel execution time}} \tag{5.8}$$

In general, there can be more than one sequential algorithm to solve a given problem. On an SISD, it is natural to use the fastest among the available algorithms. It is possible that either the fastest algorithm is not known or, if known, may be difficult to implement on the given SISD system. Then we would use the fastest among the known implementable algorithms. The numerator of the above equation corresponds to the running (or execution) time of such an algorithm.

All the sequential algorithms available to solve a problem may not be equally suitable for parallel implementation. In particular, the best sequential algorithm may not be the one that is most parallelizable. Thus, the denominator of the above equation is the running time of the most efficient parallel algorithm for the given architecture.

Theoretically, the maximum speedup possible with a p processor system is p. It is possible to obtain a speedup greater than p (i.e., a **superlinear** speedup) if either a nonoptimal sequential algorithm has been used in the computation of sequential run time or some hardware characteristic results in excessive execution time for the sequential algorithm. Consider, for instance, an application to compute the sum of a large set (N) of numbers. If the complete data set does not fit into the main memory of the SISD, the overall computation time would be increased because some of the data has to be retrieved from the secondary memory. When the same algorithm is implemented on an SIMD with p processors, the data are partitioned into p sets of N/p units each. Each of these sets may be small enough to fit in the main memory. Thus, the overall execution time would be less than N/p, resulting in a speedup of greater than p.

EXAMPLE 5.13

Consider the problem of accumulating N numbers. The execution time on an SISD is of the O(N). On an SIMD with N processors and a ring interconnection network between the processors, the execution consists of ($N - 1$) communication steps and ($N - 1$) additions, resulting in a total time (assuming communication and addition each take 1 time unit) of $2(N - 1)$ or O($2N$). Thus, the speedup is 0.5.

If the processors in the SIMD are interconnected by a perfect shuffle network (as in Figure 5.18), the execution consists of $\log_2 N$ shifts and $\log_2 N$ additions, resulting in a total time of $2\log_2 N$ or O($\log_2 N$). Hence, the speedup is of the O($N/\log_2 N$).

Ideally, an SIMD system with p processors should deliver a speedup of p. This is not possible in practice, because all the processors in the system cannot be kept busy performing useful computations all the time on account of the characteristics of the algorithms. The timing diagram of Figure 5.20 illustrates the operation of a typical

5.4 PERFORMANCE EVALUATION AND SCALABILITY

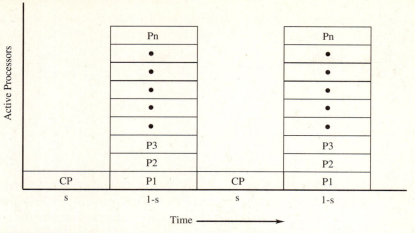

Figure 5.20 Computation Cycle in an Array Processor

SIMD system. Here the horizontal axis represents time and the processor activity is plotted on the vertical axis. For a short period of time, only the control processor is busy initializing variables, fetching and decoding instructions to be sent to the arithmetic processors, and performing other serial computations. Following this serial period, the arithmetic processors perform the computation in parallel. This mode of operation repeats with each parallel segment preceded by a serial segment. The **efficiency** is a measure of the fraction of time that the processors are busy. In Figure 5.20, the fraction of time spent in serial code is s. That is, only one processor is busy during this time. The fraction of time spent in parallel code is $(1 - s)$ when all the p processors are busy. If the number of processors is p, the efficiency E is given by:

$$E = s/p + (1 - s)$$
$$= 1 - s(1 - 1/p) \tag{5.9}$$

As p increases, the efficiency tends to $(1 - s)$, the serial code execution time remains s, but the parallel code execution time shortens (assuming that the degree of parallelism offered by the algorithms is at least p). Thus, the serial code dictates the efficiency. In an ideal system, s is 0, and hence, E is 1. In practice, E is between 0 and 1 depending on the degree to which the processors are utilized.

EXAMPLE 5.14

The efficiency of accumulating N numbers on an N-processor SIMD with perfect shuffle network is of the order of $(1/\log_2 N)$.

If we normalize the computation times such that the serial execution time in Figure 5.20 is one unit and if the code that can be run in parallel takes N time units on a single processor system, the parallel execution time shrinks to N/p when run on a p processor system. Then s is the ratio of serial time to total execution time:

$$s = \frac{1}{1 + N/p}$$

$$= \frac{p}{p + N}. \qquad (5.10)$$

For large values of p, s tends to 1, and hence, the efficiency approaches 0 because the parallelizable portions of code take a vanishingly small fraction of time while the serial code occupying only one processor makes the remaining processors idle.

The efficiency is also defined as the ratio of speedup to the number of processors in the parallel system. Thus,

$$E = \frac{S}{p}. \qquad (5.11)$$

The cost of solving a problem on a parallel architecture is defined as the sum of the time that each of the p processors is busy solving that problem. The cost is thus the product of the parallel run time and the number of processors p (i.e., **processor-time product**). A parallel architecture is said to be **cost optimal** if the cost of solving a problem on that architecture is proportional to the execution time of the fastest algorithm for solving that problem on a single processor system.

The **scalability** of a parallel system is a measure of its ability to increase speedup as the number of processors increases. A parallel system is **scalable** if its efficiency can be maintained at a fixed value by increasing the number of processors as the **problem size** increases. Here the problem size is defined as the total number of operations required to solve the problem. For instance, the problem size of computing the sum of an array of N elements is N; the problem size of adding two $N \times N$ matrices is N^2; and that of multiplying two $N \times N$ matrices is N^3.

In general, the SIMD systems are inherently scalable because the processor and interconnection hardware can simply be replicated as the problem size increases.

It is ideal to execute an algorithm with a degree of parallelism N on an SIMD with N processors, thus obtaining the maximum possible speedup. As the problem size increases, the hardware complexity and cost usually dictate that the number of processors not be arbitrarily increased. Then the parallel system is **scaled down** in terms of the number of processors. That is, an algorithm designed to run on an N processor system (i.e., N **virtual processors**) is mapped to run on p **physical processors,** where $N > p$. Thus, each of the p physical processors emulates N/p virtual processors. In general, there will be multiple mappings of virtual to physical processors. For the computation to be efficient, the mapping should be such that it minimizes the communication time between the virtual processors by mapping them to near-neighbor physical processors as far as possible.

EXAMPLE 5.15

The problem of accumulating N numbers can be solved in two methods on an SIMD with p processors and a perfect shuffle interconnection network. Here $p < N$ and we assume that N/p is less than or equal to p. In the first method, each block of p numbers are accumulated in $O(\log_2 p)$. Because there are N/p such blocks, the execution time is $O(N/p \times \log_2 p)$. The resulting N/p partial sums are then accumulated in $O(\log_2 p)$. Thus, the total run time is $O(N/p \times \log_2 p + \log_2 p)$. In the second method, each of the p blocks of N/p numbers is allocated to a processor. The run time for computing the partial sums is then $O(N/p)$. These partial sums are accumulated using the perfect shuffle network in $O(\log_2 p)$. Thus, the total run time is $O(N/p + \log_2 p)$. The second method offers a better run time than the first.

If N/p is greater than p, then further portioning of the computations to fit the p processor structure is needed. Computation of run time for this case is left as an exercise.

The performance of an SIMD thus depends not only on the algorithm employed but also on the data partitioning techniques and the interconnection structure used.

In addition to the above theoretical performance measures, the comparison of high-performance computers is usually done based on their peak computation rates in terms of MFLOPS and MIPS. This mode of comparison does not reflect the true operating environment because the peak performance rate of an array processor can only be obtained under ideal circumstances. Of much greater validity are the sustained performance rates. Sustained performance is usually measured by benchmarks that reflect accurately the types of workloads expected on these processors. Chapter 1 provides the details of several widely known benchmarks.

5.5 PROGRAMMING SIMDs

As shown earlier in this chapter, the instruction set of an SIMD system is similar to that of an SISD except that the arithmetic/logic instructions are executed by all the PEs simultaneously and the control instructions are executed by the CP. The SIMD instruction set contains additional instructions for IN operations, manipulating local and global registers, and setting activity bits based on data conditions. Programming SIMDs at the assembly language level is very similar to that with SISDs.

A high-level programming language for SIMD systems should allow architecture independent programming. For instance, the programmer programs assuming an appropriate number of virtual processors based on the problem size rather than the actual number of (physical) processors in the system. The compiler then maps the virtual processors to physical processors and generates the code for communication between the processors. Thus, the compiler complexity will be higher than that for traditional SISD compilers. The language should also allow the explicit representation of the data parallelism.

Popular high-level programming languages such as Fortran, C, and LISP have been extended to allow data-parallel programming on SIMDs. Sections 6 and 7 provide further details on these language extensions. There are also compilers that translate serial programs into data parallel object codes.

An algorithm that is efficient for SISD implementation may not be efficient for an SIMD as illustrated by the matrix multiplication algorithm of Section 3. Thus, the major challenge in programming SIMDs is in devising an efficient algorithm and corresponding data partitioning such that all the PEs in the system are kept busy throughout the execution of the application. This also requires minimizing conditional branch operations in the algorithm.

The data exchange characteristics of the algorithm dictate the type of IN needed. If the desired type of IN is not available, routing strategies that minimize the number of hops needed to transmit data between nonneighboring PEs will have to be devised.

5.6 EXAMPLE SYSTEMS

This section provides brief descriptions of the hardware, software, and application characteristics of three SIMD systems. The ILLIAC-IV has been the most famous experimental SIMD architecture and is selected for its historical interest. MasPar Corporation's MP series is oriented toward massive data-parallel number crunching applications. Thinking Machine Corporation's Connection Machine series, originally envisioned for data-parallel symbolic computations, now also allows numeric applications.

5.6.1 ILLIAC-IV

The ILLIAC-IV project was started in 1966 at the University of Illinois. The objective was to build a parallel machine capable of executing 10^9 instructions per second. To achieve this speed, a system with 256 processors controlled by a control processor was envisioned. The set of processors was divided into four quadrants of 64 processors each, each quadrant to be controlled by one control unit. Only one quadrant was built, and it achieved a speed of 2×10^8 instructions per second.

Figure 5.21 shows the system structure. The system is controlled by a Burroughs B-6500 processor. This machine compiles the ILLIAC-IV programs, schedules array programs, controls array configurations, and manages the disk file transfers and peripherals. The disk file unit acts as the backup memory for the system.

Figure 5.22 shows the configuration of a quadrant. The control unit (CU) provides the control signals for all processing elements ($PE_0 - PE_{63}$), which work in an instruction lock-step mode. The CU executes all program control instructions and transfers processing instructions to PEs. The CU and the PE array execute in parallel. In addition, the CU generates and broadcasts the addresses of operands that are common to all PEs, receives the status signals from PEs, from the internal I/O operations, and from the B-6500, and performs the appropriate control functions.

Each PE has four 64-bit registers (accumulator, operand register, data routing register, and general storage register); an arithmetic-logic unit; a 16-bit local index

5.6 EXAMPLE SYSTEMS

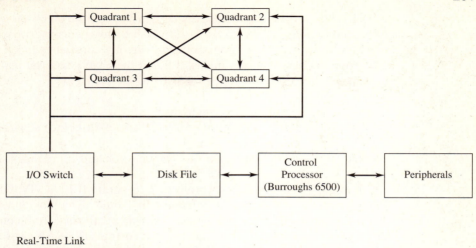

Figure 5.21 ILLIAC-IV Structure

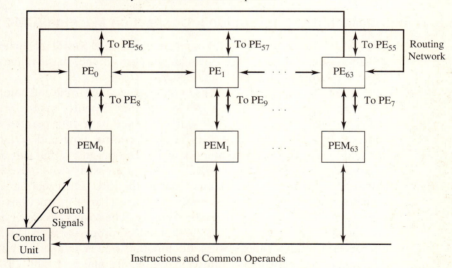

Note: PE_i is connected to PE_{i+1}, PE_{i-1}, PE_{i+8}, and PE_{i-8}; $0 \leq i \leq 63$.

Figure 5.22 A Quadrant of ILLIAC-IV

register; and an 8-bit mode register that stores the processor status and provides the PE enable-disable information. Each processing element memory (PEM) block consists of a 250 nanosecond cycle time memory with 2K, 64-bit words.

The PE-to-PE routing network connects each PE to four of its neighbors. The PE array is arranged as an 8 × 8 torus. Interprocessor data communication of arbitrary distances is accomplished by a sequence of routings over the routing network.

The processing array is basically designed to operate on 64-bit operands. But it can be configured to perform as a 128, 32-bit subprocessor array or a 512, 8-bit subprocessor array. The subprocessor arrays are not completely independent because of the common index register in each PE and the 64-bit data routing path.

The applications envisioned for ILLIAC-IV were:

1. manipulation of large matrices,
2. computations of solutions for large sets of difference equations for weather prediction purposes, and
3. fast data correlation for fast-response, phased-array radar systems.

Two high-level languages were used to program ILLIAC-IV: CFD (a Fortran-like language) oriented toward computational fluid dynamics and GLYPNIR, an ALGOL-like language. A compiler that extracts parallelism from conventional Fortran programs and converts them into parallel Fortran (IVTRAN) was also developed. There was no operating system. Being an experimental machine, the ILLIAC-IV did not offer either a software library or any software development tools, thereby making it difficult to program. The ILLIAC-IV is now located at the NASA Ames Center and is not operational.

5.6.2 Thinking Machines Corporation's Connection Machine (CM-2)

The CM-2, introduced in 1987, is a massively parallel SIMD machine configured with up to 64K single bit processors, providing a performance in the range of 2.5 GFLOPS. Table 5.1 summarizes its characteristics.

The CM-2 hardware consists of from one to four front-end computers, a parallel processing unit (PPU), and an I/O system that supports mass storage and graphic display devices (Figure 5.23). It can be viewed as a data-parallel extension to the conventional front-end computers because control flow and serial operations are handled by the front-end computers while the operations that can be run efficiently in parallel are executed on the PPU. A 4×4 crossbar switch (Nexus) connects the front-end computers to the four sections of the PPU. Each section is controlled by a sequencer that decodes the assembly language (Paris) instructions and generates a series of microinstructions for each processor. The sequencers are implemented using Advanced Micro Devices' 2901/2910 bit-sliced processor with 16K, 96-bit words of microcode memory. Interprocessor communication is handled by either a hypercube interconnection network or a faster multidimensional grid that allows processors to simultaneously transmit data in regular patterns.

PROCESSOR

The processors are implemented using four different chip types: the processor chip, the memory chip, and two floating-point accelerator chips. The processor chip (Figure 5.24) contains the ALU, flag registers, NEWS interface, router interface, and I/O interface for 16 processors. The 16 processors are connected by a 4×4 mesh allowing processors to communicate with their North, East, West, and South (NEWS) neighbors. The 64K bits of bit-addressable memory are implemented using commercial RAM chips. The first of the floating-point chips contains an interface that passes

5.6 EXAMPLE SYSTEMS

TABLE 5.1 CONNECTION MACHINE CHARACTERISTICS

General	
Processors	65,536
Memory	512 Mbytes
Memory bandwidth	300 Gbits/s
Input/Output Channels	
Number of channels	8
Capacity per I/O controller	40 Mbytes/s
Total I/O controller transfer rate	300 Mbytes/s
Capacity per framebuffer	1 Gbits/s
Typical Application Performance (Fixed Point)	
General computing	2500 MIPS
Terrain mapping	1000 MIPS
Document search	6000 MIPS
Interprocessor Communication	
Regular pattern of 32-bit messages	250 million/s
Random pattern 32-bit messages	80 million/s
Sort 64K 32-bit keys	30 million/s
Variable Precision Fixed Point	
64-bit integer add	1500 MIPS
16-bit integer add	3300 MIPS
64-bit move	2000 MIPS
16-bit move	3800 MIPS
Double Precision Floating Point	
4K × 4K matrix multiply benchmark	2500 MIPS
Dot product	5000 MIPS
Single Precision Floating Point	
Addition	4000 MFLOPS
Subtraction	4000 MFLOPS
Multiplication	4000 MFLOPS
Division	1500 MFLOPS
Peak performance	32 GFLOPS

the data on to the second chip, which is the floating-point execution unit. These two chips are required for every 32 processors when floating-point acceleration is needed. Thus, each section of the PPU contains 1024 custom processor chips, 512 floating-point interface chips, 512 floating-point execution chips, and 128 megabytes of RAM.

The 16 flag registers include 8 bits for general purpose use and 8 bits that have functions predefined by the hardware. Special purpose flags include the NEWS flag that can be written to directly from the ALU of one of the adjacent processing elements, two flags for message router data movement and handshaking, a memory parity flag, a flag for daisy-chaining processing elements, a zero flag for reading or for operations that do not need to write to a flag, and two flags used primarily for diagnostics.

The CM-2 processor cell executes only one simple, but powerful, instruction that produces outputs based on a memory/flag lookup table. Figure 5.25 shows a processing cell for CM-1; however, the basic structure is the same for CM-2 (with memory increased from 4K to 64K). The ALU executes this instruction by taking three 1-bit inputs and producing two 1-bit outputs. Two of the inputs are taken from

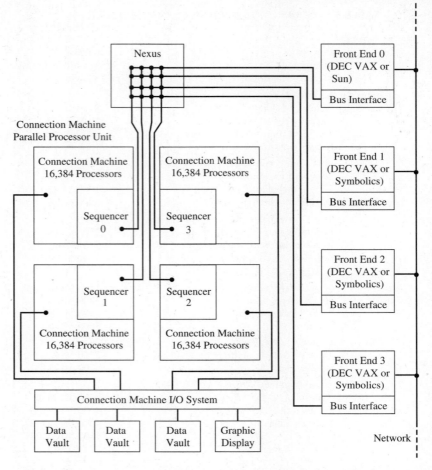

Figure 5.23 Architecture of CM-2 (Courtesy of Thinking Machines Corporation.)

that processor's memory, and the third bit is taken from one of the flag bits. The outputs are then calculated from 1 of 256 possible functions found in the memory/flag lookup table using two 8-bit control bytes provided by the sequencer. One output bit is written back into the memory, and the other is written to one of the flag bits for subsequent processing. All processors receive the same instruction from the sequencer; however, individual processors may be masked off using a flag bit that controls processor activation.

The ALU cycle is broken up into subcycles. On each cycle the data processors can execute one low-level instruction (called a nanoinstruction) from the sequencer and the memories can perform one read or write operation. For instance, the basic ALU cycle for a two-operand integer add consists of three nanoinstructions:

```
LOADA: read memory operand A, read flag operand, latch one
       truth table,
LOADB: read memory operand B, read condition flag,
       latch other truth table, and
STORE: store memory operand A, store result flag.
```

5.6 EXAMPLE SYSTEMS

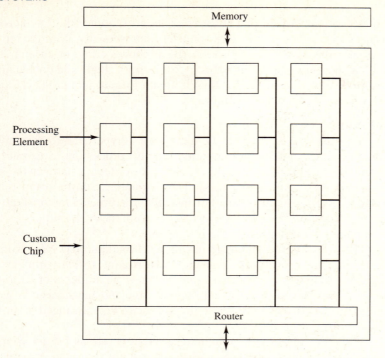

Figure 5.24 Connection Machine Custom Chip (Courtesy of Thinking Machines Corporation.)

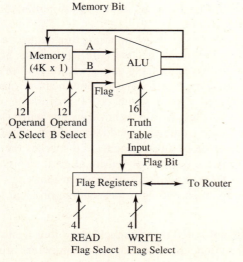

Figure 5.25 Connection Machine Processing Element (Model CM-1) (Courtesy of Thinking Machines Corporation.)

Arithmetic is performed in a bit serial fashion. At about a half a microsecond per bit plus overhead, a 32-bit add takes about 21 microseconds. With the maximum of 64K processors all computing in parallel, this produces a rate of around 2500 MIPS.

The floating-point accelerator performs both single and double precision operations on data in IEEE standard floating-point format, increasing the rate of floating-point operations by more than a factor of 20.

HYPERCUBE

The processors are linked by a 12-dimensional hypercube router network. Message passing occurs in a data parallel mode (i.e., all processors can simultaneously send data into the local memories of other processors or fetch data from the local memories of other processors into their own). The communication hardware supports certain message-combining operations. For instance, the processors to which multiple messages are sent receive the bitwise logical OR from the ALU output of all the messages, or the numerically largest, or the integer sum.

The simplest mode of communication is broadcasting a value from the front-end system to all the processing elements (PEs). A context flag within each PE controls which PEs receive the broadcast value. When large amounts of data must be loaded into the Communication Machine memory, the I/O mechanism is generally faster. Regular, grid-based communication is used with data arranged in an n-dimensional grid or torus.

The following parallel communications operations permit elements of parallel variables to be rearranged and combined into parallel variables of different geometries:

1. Reduce & Broadcast—applies an operator (such as SUM) across the elements of a parallel variable.
2. Grid (NEWS)—shifts the elements of a parallel variable by a fixed amount along each dimension of the variable.
3. General (Send, Get)—sends or gets values from arbitrary processor locations to processors. Provision is made for simultaneous access and combining of colliding data.
4. Scan—applies a binary associative operator to a sequence of processors. Cumulative results are returned in a new parallel variable. Scans implement parallel prefix operations over a set of data elements and form an important new class of parallel computation and communication operations. Scans may also be performed over a sequence of processors partitioned into disjoint sets. This provides the algorithm designer with a mechanism for simultaneously processing data arranged into multiple, variable length sets.
5. Spread—takes one or more data elements and spreads them throughout a processor set. In the case of an n-dimensional grid, a spread may be used to copy an $n - 1$ subspace along a single dimension.
6. Sort—sorts elements in ascending or descending order of key.

NEXUS

The Nexus is a 4 $\times$ 4 crosspoint switch that connects up to four front-end computers to up to four sequencers. The connections to front-end computers are through high-speed, 32-bit, parallel, asynchronous data paths while the connections to sequencers are 32-bit synchronous paths. The CM can be configured as up to four sections under front-end control using the Nexus. These sections can be for different users or purposes. Any front-end can be connected to any section or valid combination of sections. For instance, in a CM-2 system with 32K processors (i.e., four 8K processor sections) and four front-ends, all four sections can be ganged to be controlled by any one front-end; two 8K sections can be assigned to each of the two front-ends while the other two sections are ganged to provide 16K processors to a third front-end; and the fourth front-end is used for purposes not related to the PPU.

ROUTER

The routing network is used to transmit data from one processor chip to the other. Messages travel from one router node to another until they reach the chip containing the destination processor. Suppose a processor j on chip i wants to communicate with processor l on chip k. It first sends the message to the router on its own chip. This router forwards the message to the router on chip k, which in turn delivers the message to the appropriate memory location for processor l. The routing algorithm used by the router moves messages across each of the 12 dimensions of the hypercube in sequence. If there are no conflicts, a message will reach its destination within one cycle of this sequence, because any vertex of the cube can be reached from any other by traversing no more than 12 edges. The router allows every processor to send a message to any other processor with all messages being sent and delivered at the same time. The messages may be of any length. The throughput of the router depends on the message length and on the pattern of accesses.

The entities that operate on data in parallel within the CM are the physical processors. However, each physical processor can simulate any number of conceptual processing entities called virtual processors. This simulation is transparent to the user. The router logic supports the virtual processor concept. When a message is to be delivered by a router node, it is placed not only within the correct physical processor, but in the correct region of memory for the virtual processor originally specified as the message's destination.

NEWS GRID

The CM-1 NEWS grid is a two-dimensional mesh that allows nearest-neighbor communication. In the CM-2, the two-dimensional grid was replaced by a more general n-dimensional grid. This allows nearest-neighbor grid communication of multiple dimensions. Possible grid configurations for 64K processors are: 256×256, 1024×64, 8×8192, $64 \times 32 \times 32$, $16 \times 16 \times 16 \times 16$, and $8 \times 8 \times 4 \times 8 \times 8 \times 4$. The NEWS grid allows processors to pass data according to a regular rectangular pattern. The advantage of this mechanism over the router is that the overhead of explicitly specifying destination addresses is eliminated.

INPUT/OUTPUT SYSTEM

Each 8K-processor section is connected to one of the eight I/O channels (Figure 5.26). Each I/O channel may be connected to either a high resolution graphics display framebuffer module or an I/O controller. I/O transfers are initiated by the front-end computers through Paris instructions to the sequencers, which cause direct, parallel transfers between the I/O devices and the data processors.

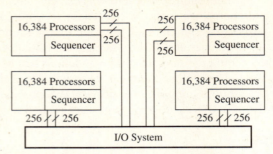

Figure 5.26 Connection Machine I/O System (Courtesy of Thinking Machines Corporation.)

Each I/O channel consists of 256 data bits and is switched through sequencer control among two 4K banks of processors (i.e., 256 chips × 16 processors = 4K processors and 256 parallel bits of data). Data is passed along the channels (see Figure 5.27) to the I/O controllers with parity checked for each byte and is stored in one of 512, 288-bit buffers (32 parity bits + 256 data bits). When the buffers are full, the I/O controller signals that it is ready to send data to a data vault.

Each I/O controller is connected to one or more data vaults via an 80-bit bus. Data vaults combine high reliability with rapid transfer rates for large blocks of data.

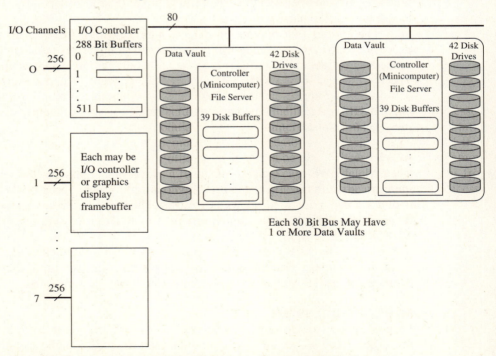

Figure 5.27 Connection Machine Data Vault (Courtesy of Thinking Machines Corporation.)

With a capacity of 10 Gbytes each, eight data vaults operating in parallel can achieve transfer rates of 40 Mbytes/s. Data vaults consist of 39 individual disk drives and 3 spare drives in case of failures. The 64 data bits received from the I/O controller are split into two 32-bit words and 7 error correcting code (ECC) bits are added to each. The 39 bits are stored in 39 disk buffers, which are eventually written to individual drives. The ECC permits 100% recovery of data if one drive fails.

As an alternative to the I/O controller, a high resolution graphics display framebuffer module may be connected to one of the eight I/O channels. This module supports a high-speed, real-time, tightly coupled graphical display, utilizing a 1,280 × 1,024-pixel framebuffer module with 24-bit color and four overlays.

SOFTWARE

System software is based upon the operating system or environment of the front-end computers with minimal software extensions. Thus, users can program using familiar languages and program constructs with all development tools provided by the front-end. The flow of control, including storage and execution of the program and all interaction with the user and/or programmer, is handled entirely by the front-end. In addition to the assembly language Paris (parallel instruction set), the high-level languages used for programming the CM are *LISP, CM-LISP, and C*. These are data parallel dialects of Common LISP and C, respectively.

PARIS

Paris includes operations such as integer arithmetic, floating-point arithmetic, interprocessor communication, vector summation, matrix multiplication, and sorting. The front-end sends Paris instructions to the PPU. The program control structures are not part of the Paris instruction set because they are handled by the front-end computer.

The Paris user interface consists of a set of functions, subroutines, and global variables. The functions and subroutines direct the actions of the CM processors, and the variables allow the user program to find out such information about the CM system as the number of processors available and the amount of memory per processor.

Consider the following C code:

```
while (CM_f_gt_constant(z, 1.0, 23, 8),
       CM_global_logior(CM_test_flag, 1)) {
  CM_f_divide_constant_2(z, 2.0, 23, 8);
}
```

It repeatedly causes every processor whose floating-point z field is greater than 1.0 to be divided by 2; the loop is terminated when no processor has a z value greater than 1. Here the functions whose names begin with "CM_" are Paris operations. CM_f_gt_constant causes every processor to compare a field to a common, broadcast constant storing a bit reflecting the result in its *test* flag. CM_f_divide_constant similarly causes every processor to divide a floating-point field by a common constant; and CM_global_logior takes a bit field (test flag) from every processor and returns to the front-end the result of a many-way bitwise inclusive-OR operation. The while construct is not part of the Paris language.

*LISP

The *LISP is an extension of Common LISP for programming the CM in a data-parallel style. The parallel primitives of *LISP support the CM model. That is, each processor executes a subset of Common LISP with a single thread of control residing on the front-end. The language supports all of the standard Common LISP data types in addition to a parallel data type called pvar (parallel variable).

The Common LISP feature of run time type checking is retained, and hence *LISP also requires no declarations. The standard functions for reading or writing the contents of a variable (pref and pref-grid) in combination with the macro set f are used to store data from the front-end into a pvar of a processor. The assignment operator (*set) stores the value of a pvar expression into the destination pvar. Each of the following parallel functions accept a scalar and return a pvar that contains the scalar in all active processors:

```
mod!!    ash!!    round!!    integerp!!
max!!    min!!    if!!       eql!!
ldb!!    dpb!!    byte!!     numberp!!
```

C*

C* is an extension of C designed to support data-parallel programming. It features a new data type based on classes in C++, a synchronous execution model, and some extensions to C syntax. Pointers are used for interprocessor communication. A synchronous computation model is assumed by C*, where all instructions are issued from the front-end. It allows different processors of CM to have different memory layouts, because they may hold different kinds of data. A structure type called domain allows the specification of the memory layout. Accordingly, the C* code is divided into serial and parallel portions. The code that belongs to a domain is parallel and is executed by many data processors while the serial code is executed by the front-end.

The data is divided into scalar and parallel portions, described by the keywords *mono* and *poly*, respectively. Mono data resides in the memory of the front-end while the poly data resides in the memory of the data processors. There are no new operators for parallel computation. At compile time, distinction is made between the two types of data and scalar operators are extended (through overloading) to operate on parallel data.

There is one new statement type in C*—the selection statement. This is used to activate multiple processors. The C* compiler parses the C* source code, performs type and dataflow analysis, and translates parallel code into a series of function calls that invoke CM Paris operations.

APPLICATIONS

Paris presents the user with an abstract machine architecture much like the physical CM hardware but with two important extensions: a much richer instruction set and the virtual processor abstraction. It provides a set of parallel primitives ranging from simple arithmetic and logical operations to high-level, APL-like reduction (parallel prefix) operations, sorting, and communications. The virtual processor mechanism supported at the Paris level is transparent to the user. When the system is initialized, the number of processors required by the application is specified. If this number

5.6 EXAMPLE SYSTEMS

exceeds the available physical processors, the local memory of each processor splits into as many regions as necessary with the processors automatically time sliced among the regions.

The CM has been used in the following application areas:

1. Document retrieval from large databases, analysis of English text, and memory-based reasoning
2. Circuit simulation and optimization of cell placement
3. Object recognition and image processing
4. Computer-generated graphics for animation and scientific visualization
5. Neural net simulation, conceptual clustering, classifier systems, and genetic algorithms
6. Modeling geological strata using reverse time migration techniques
7. Protein sequence matching
8. N-body interactions, such as modeling defect movement in crystals under stress and modeling galaxy collisions
9. Fluid flow modeling, cellular autonoma, and Navier-Stokes–based simulation

A brief description of document retrieval application on the CM follows. Locating information in natural language documents contained in large databases is an important problem. Two general methods of accessing such databases are: free text search and keyword search. Free text search systems allow the user to search the text of the documents for arbitrary combinations of words, whereas keyword systems require that indexers read all the documents in a database and assign them keywords from a controlled vocabulary. In the latter system, the user searches for information or documents using some combination of keywords from this controlled vocabulary.

The CM employs the relevance search technique in which the user provides a list of keywords or a question. These words are broadcast to all the processors along with the numerical weights associated with each word. Each processor notes whether each word occurs in its article; if so, a corresponding numerical score, based on a weighting scheme, is incremented. The weight assigned to a word is inversely proportional to its frequency in the database. This weighting mechanism ensures that uncommon words have higher influence than the common words. When all the words have been compared, the articles with the largest scores are retrieved and presented to the user. The user can browse through the documents returned and find one or more documents of interest.

In the document database, one article is stored per processor in a compressed form (called content kernel). The source document is stored in the front-end. Each word of the content kernel is represented as a bit vector and stored in the form of a table called a kernel. This coding method, called surrogate encoding, maps each word into n different bits by using n hash functions. On each keyword, the processor applies the n hash functions to calculate the hash number. This number is then compared with each entry of the kernel, and if a match occurs, the score of that article is incremented. The articles with highest scores are then retrieved.

5.6.3 MasPar Corporation's MP Series

The MasPar MP-1 is a data parallel SIMD system with the basic configuration consisting of the data parallel unit (DPU) and a host workstation (DEC VAX station 3520). The DPU consists of from 1,024 to 16,384 processing elements (PEs). The maximum performance ranges up to 26,000 MIPS and 1,300 MFLOPS. The peak I/O bandwidth to the external host for a fully configured system is 200 Mbytes per second. If the multistage global router is interfaced with application specific hardware, then I/O rates of up to 1.3 gigabytes per second may be supported. The programming environment is UNIX-based and fully supports network system access. Many programming languages are available on the host workstation, which may call functions on the DPU that are developed using MasPar Fortran (MPF) or MasPar Programming Language (MPL). An image processing toolset is available and includes optimized codes for performing image data operations on the MP-1 DPU as well as display features on the host workstation.

HARDWARE ARCHITECTURE

The MP-1 DPU consists of a PE array and an array control unit (ACU). The ACU fetches and decodes instructions, computes address and scalar data values, and issues control signals to the PE array. It is a 14 MIPS scalar RISC processor with most instructions executing in one 80 ns clock cycle.

The PE array (Figure 5.28) is configurable from 1 to 16 identical processor boards. Each processor board has 64 PE clusters (PECs) of 16 PEs per cluster. Each processor board thus contains 1024 processor elements.

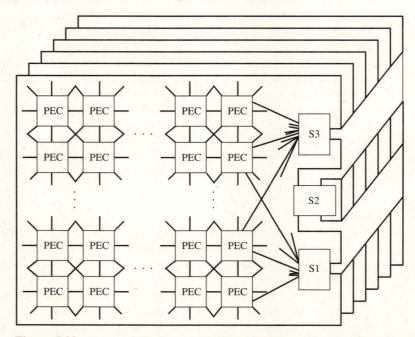

Figure 5.28 Array of PE Clusters (MP-1) (Courtesy of MasPar Corporation.)

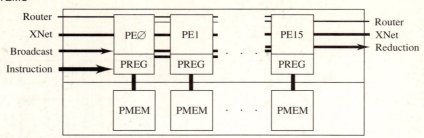

Figure 5.29 PE Cluster (MP-1) (Courtesy of MasPar Corporation.)

Each PEC (Figure 5.29) is composed of 16 PEs and 16 processor memories (PMEM). Each PE has a large register set (PREG). Load and store instructions move data between PREG and PMEM. The 16 PEs in a cluster share an access port to the multistage crossbar router.

The ACU issues the same control signals to all PEs, but the operation of each PE is locally enabled by the E-bit in its flag unit. During floating-point operations, some microsteps are data dependent, so the PEs locally disable themselves as needed by the exponent and mantissa units.

The MP-1 instruction set supports 32 bits of PE number and 32 bits of memory address per PE. It focuses on conventional operand sizes of 8, 16, 32, and 64 bits, and hence, PEs with smaller or larger ALU widths can be implemented without changing the programmers instruction model.

Each PE provides floating-point operations on 32- and 64-bit IEEE or VAX format operands and integer operations on 1-, 8-, 16-, 32-, and 64-bit operands. The PE floating-point/integer hardware has a 64-bit mantissa unit, a 16-bit exponent unit, a 4-bit ALU unit, and a flags unit. These units perform floating-point, integer, and Boolean computations. Most data movements within each PE occur on the internal 4-bit nibble bus and the bit bus (Figure 5.30).

Each PE has forty 32-bit registers available to the programmer and eight 32-bit registers that are used internally to implement the instruction set. The registers are bit and byte addressable.

Processor memory (PMEM) is implemented with 1-Mbit DRAMs that are arranged in the cluster so that each PE has 16 Kbytes of data memory. A processor board has 16 Mbytes of memory, and a 16-board system has 256 Mbytes of memory. The PMEM can be directly or indirectly addressed. Up to 32 load/store instructions can be queued and executed while the PE computations proceed. Using fast page mode DRAMs, a 16K PE system delivers memory bandwidth of over 12 gigabytes per second.

The X-net interconnect directly connects each PE with its eight nearest neighbors in a two-dimensional mesh. Each PE has four connections at its diagonal corners, forming an X pattern. A tristate node at each X intersection permits connections with any of eight neighbors using only four wires per PE.

Figure 5.28 shows the X-net connections between PE clusters. The PE chip has two clusters of 4-by-4 PEs and uses 24 pins for X-net connections. The cluster, chip, and board boundaries are not visible, and the connections at the PE array edges are wrapped around to form a torus. The torus facilitates several important matrix algorithms and can emulate a one-dimensional ring with two X-net steps.

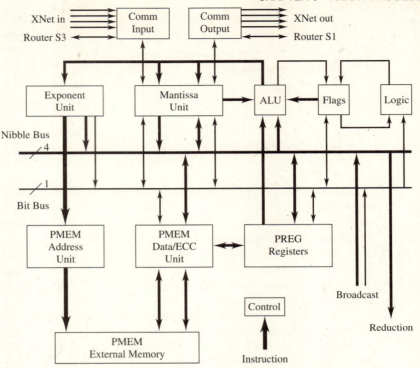

Figure 5.30 MP-1 Processor-Memory Interconnection (Courtesy of MasPar Corporation.)

All PEs have the same direction controls. For instance, every PE sends an operand to the north and simultaneously receives an operand from the south. The X-net uses a bit-serial transmission. The PEs use the shift capability of the mantissa unit to generate and accumulate bit-serial messages. Inactive PEs can serve as pipeline stages to expedite long distance communications jumps through several PEs.

The multistage crossbar interconnection network provides global communications between all the PEs and forms the basis for the MP-1 I/O system. The MP-1 network uses three router stages, shown as S1, S2, and S3 in Figure 5.28, to implement the function of a 1024 × 1024 crossbar switch. Each cluster of 16 PEs shares an originating port connected to router stage S1 and a target port connected to router stage S3. Connections are established from an originating PE through stages S1, S2, and S3 and then in the target PE. A 16K PE system has 1024 PE clusters.

Originating PEs compute the address of the target PE and transmit it to the router S1 port. Each router stage selects a connection to the next stage based on the target PE address. Once established, the connection is bidirectional and can move data between the originating and target PEs. The target PE returns an acknowledge message.

The multistage crossbar is well matched to the SIMD architecture because all communications paths are of equal length, and therefore, all communications arrive at their targets simultaneously. The router chip connects 64 input ports to 64 output ports by partially decoding the target PE addresses.

The array control unit can broadcast data to all the PEs. Similarly, the enabled PEs can simultaneously return data to the ACU through the global OR tree with bits from each PE ORed together at a rate of one result every clock cycle.

The I/O system consists of dedicated I/O RAM buffers arranged 16 Mbytes per board for a total of 256 Mbytes RAM in a 16K PE system. An equal number of I/O boards and PE boards are required. The I/O RAM is accessed by the PEs through the multistage global router. The external host workstation interface is the MasPar I/O Channel (MPIOC). This channel has a 64-bit data bus with a 200 Mbyte/second transfer rate. A parallel disk array is available to provide a sustained disk transfer rate of 9 Mbytes/sec with peak transfer rates up to 14.5 Mbytes/sec. This disk system interfaces directly to an MPIOC.

PROGRAMMING ENVIRONMENT

The MasPar programming environment (MPPE) is a comprehensive set of development tools and provides a single context for software development integrating myriad steps into a fluid, graphical process. Built on the X-Window standard, it can be used from any networked terminal or workstation that supports this protocol.

The programming environment allows a range of languages to be used on the host; however, the DPU must be accessed from these languages from vendor-supplied libraries or user-developed code using the MasPar Fortran (MPF) or MasPar Programming Language (MPL). When code is developed using MPF the compiler automatically generates appropriate code streams for the MP-1's multiple functional units from a single source program. Code developed with MPL is callable as subroutines from standard UNIX languages, such as C. MPL's interface library routines facilitate this process by handling communications between the UNIX subsystem and the DPU.

MPF is based on the Fortran 90 standard. Its extensions integrate arrays of any size directly into the language and provide control structures essential to data-parallel programming. There are five significant additions in MPF:

1. Arrays as first-class language elements. Instead of using iterative DO loops to program operations on arrays, statements may be constructed as simple array equations.
2. Array sectioning. A section of an array may be specified with a triplet notation: a start index, a bound, and a stride. The array is then used as an operand in an array computation.
3. Vector-valued subscripts. An array may be constructed from arbitrary permutations of another array using vector-valued subscripts. As such, an array of pointers is used as the index to an array of data to provide an arbitrary ordering operation. This feature is important in resolving data dependent operations in the PE array.
4. WHERE/ELSEWHERE/ENDWHERE statements. The MPF's WHERE statement permits operations to be performed based on the values of specific elements in the arrays.
5. Fortran 90 intrinsics. The MPF set of intrinsic functions provides MP-1 optimized algorithms for matrix and array operations.

MPL is based on C and is minimally extended with new keywords, statements, and library functions that operate on parallel data. Unlike MPF, MPL fully exposes the architecture and behavior of the MP-1's functional units and only generates code for the DPU. MPL uses the programming model: "One C program running on all PEs." The primary extensions include:

1. The plural declaration. An MPL plural declaration causes parallel data to be allocated in such a way that parallel execution can take place.
2. Processor selection by conditional expressions. Selecting which PEs are to be active for a set of commands is critical, and MPL's conditional statements provide for enabling or disabling the PEs.
3. Differentiated data structures. While the same plural data definitions apply to all PEs, MPL supplies techniques that let different PEs use their data space differently.
4. Communications syntax. Two primitives are included—X-net for accessing X-net communications and router for accessing router communications.
5. Additions to standard library functions to support parallel data operations.

The MPPE provides a consistent set of tools for developing parallel data applications. Utilizing the X-Window's interface, the developer may maintain several interactive sessions on a workstation including source code editing, compilation, linking, and interactive debugging. All the tools work from the same knowledge base so changes made with one tool are known immediately to the others. The tools are continuously available, thus reducing the time expended switching tools, which in turn reduces development time. The debugger provides on-demand debugging, enabling the developer to stop a program at any time, use the debugger, and then continue without having to restart from the beginning of the program. The debugger also allows the ability to debug optimized code because it accesses the same knowledge base as the compiler. Graphical displays of data or PE utilization are provided with the Animator Toolset.

APPLICATIONS

The important characteristics of the MP-1 include: distributed and isolated local processor memory for high-memory bandwidth; local memory indirect addressing, which provides indexed data access for optimizing PE loads; and massive parallel data communications between processors via the X-net and global router connections. Some applications for which solutions are implemented on the MP-1 are outlined below.

MAXIMUM ENTROPY METHOD APPLIED TO DEBLURRING IMAGES

The maximum entropy method draws inferences from incomplete information, and as a procedure, it can be used for including an unknown probability distribution given only partial data. Images in this study are approximately 106 pixels. The modified Newton method for the solution involves inversion of a matrix of order $(106)^2$. Because the data set is so large, a modified successive approximation approach is performed instead of the matrix inversion to make the computation tractable. Weighting factors are iterated at each point in a 2D array until convergence has reached the specified limit or is diverging. The MP-1 utilizes local processor indirect memory addressing to index subsequent data points after reaching convergence on the previous data point. Thus, each PE in the array is loaded with several data points to increase processor utilization for an unknown distribution of convergence rates for the data points.

MANDELBROT SET

The Mandelbrot Set is a set of numbers for which the computation of $z = z^2 + c$ is performed where c is a point in the complex plane. Computation of each point in this solution is terminated when $z > 2$ or the maximum iteration count is reached.

Typically, load balancing is applied to MIMD architectures. However, in the case of the MP-1 with indirect local memory addressing, skewing sets of data points distributed across the PE array is an effective means of load balancing. It is shown that skewing the data set when loading the PE array provides the best cost-to-performance ratio in distributing the data elements. The main advantage of skewing the data set is the relatively uniform distribution of data points across the PE array where the maximum iteration count is reached, thereby reducing the number of idle PEs as the computation progresses.

The following pseudo code is representative of this implementation.

```
done ← FALSE;
count ← 0;
while NOT(done)
        forall processors with INDEX ⇐ 1000
                perform computation on datum X[INDEX]
                ITERS ← ITERS + 1;
                FORALL converged OR (ITERS > Maxiterations) THEN
                        Set processor converged;
                     IF (count MOD 11 = 0)  THEN      /* if new load interval*/
                        forall converged processors
                                INDEX ← INDEX + 1;
                                ITERS ← 0;
                                reset processor converged;
                count ← count + 1;
        if (global_convergence) done = TRUE;
```

LARGE FAST FOURIER TRANSFORMS (FFT)

In general the complexity of the FFT is of the order $N \log_2 N$. The typical algorithm first sorts the data in bit-reversed order of the values. The data are then operated upon $\log_2 N$ times in a loop that successively computes transforms of length $2, 4, 8, \ldots, N$, where the necessary subtransforms for the current loop were computed in the previous loop. The final result is the transformed data. The MP-1 X-net communication provides an efficient means for the lower to higher order transforms as each stage of the FFT is completed. As each stage progresses, data from a processor of distance $N/2$, $N/4, N/8, \ldots, 1$ are required for the subsequent stage. These communication patterns are regular and can be efficiently performed using nearest neighbor communications. Thus, the time to perform an N-point FFT on an MP-1 with at least N processors is $O(\log_2 N)$.

MP-2

MasPar Computer Corporation has recently announced the MP-2 series, with a performance rating five times that of MP-1. This series is offered in five configurations containing from 1K to 16K processors. The system is built using chips containing thirty-two 32-bit RISC processors. Each chip delivers 133 MIPS and 12.3 MFLOPS and has a communication bandwidth of 40 Mbytes/second.

5.7 SYSTOLIC ARRAYS

As described in Chapter 2, a systolic array is a special purpose planar array of simple processors that feature a regular, near-neighbor interconnection network. Two general purpose systolic architectures are described in this section: Intel Corporation's iWARP, which can also operate in an MIMD mode, and Saxpy Computer Corporation's Matrix-1, which is an SIMD. Refer to Johnson et al. (1993) for a comparison of recent systolic architectures.

5.7.1 Intel Corporation's iWarp (Intel, 1991)

The iWarp is a distributed parallel computing system developed jointly by Carnegie Mellon University (CMU) and Intel Corporation. This system evolved from the WARP machine, a programmable systolic array developed at CMU and General Electric. The building block of an iWarp system is the iWarp cell, built out of a single chip iWarp processor connected to the local memory. Parallel systems are built by linking together iWarp cells. The iWarp processor integrates both high speed computation and communication capability in a single component. It employs instruction level parallelism to allow simultaneous operation of multiple functional units and can simultaneously communicate with a number of iWarp processors at high speeds. Further, its communication mechanisms support different programming models, including the tightly coupled computing mode of systolic arrays and the message-passing style of MIMD machines (described in Chapter 6).

The two common intercell communication patterns found in parallel distributed systems are memory communication and systolic communication. In conventional message-passing, messages are delivered from the local memory of the sending cell to that of the receiving cell. That is, a message is first built in the local memory of the sending cell and then delivered to that of the receiving cell. Only when the full message is available in the local memory of the receiving cell is it ready to be operated upon by its program. Thus, both the sending and the receiving cells perform memory communication.

In memory communication, the program running on the cell is insulated from communication aspects. In the case of the sending cell, once it builds the message in its local memory, delivering it over the network is handled independently by some network software. In the case of a receiving cell, the program is not involved in receiving the message, and will operate on the message only after the entire message has been delivered to the local memory by the network software. Thus, in memory communication the communication is decoupled from computation. While the message is being delivered and buffered through memory, the program at the sending and the receiving cell can operate autonomously on its local data.

An iWarp cell is said to perform systolic communication if the program has direct fine grain access to the head or tail of the message queue as the message is being sent or received; it is said to perform memory communication otherwise. That is, in a systolic algorithm, an array of cells perform computations on long data streams flowing through the array. All data sent along each directed connection in a systolic array can be viewed as belonging to one message. However, instead of waiting until all the data in the message have arrived, each cell operates on the data items within a message as they arrive individually. Similarly, each cell sends out computed results individually as they are generated. The advantages of systolic communication over memory communication are:

1. Fine grain communication: The program at the sending cell can send out data items individually as soon as they are produced; similarly the program at the receiving cell can use data items individually as soon as they are received. This allows programs to communicate and synchronize with each other at word level rather than message level granularity.
2. Reduced access to local memory: Incoming and outgoing data need not be buffered in the cell's local memory unless it is required by the computation. Since memory access is typically a bottleneck in the cell's performance, the reduced access to local memory may translate into increased computation performance.
3. Increased instruction level parallelism: At each cell, systolic inputs and outputs provide additional parallel sources of operands for instructions. These operands can help keep the multiple functional units busy and increase instruction level parallelism.
4. Reduced size of local memory: Avoiding buffering data in the local memory also reduces the memory size requirement for some applications.

SYSTEM ARCHITECTURE

An iWarp system shown in Figure 5.31 is made up of an array of iWarp cells connected by physical communication pathways. Each iWarp cell consists of an iWarp component and the local memory. The iWarp component contains independent communication and computation agents. These agents are closely coupled and independently controlled to allow overlapped communication and computation and to provide greater efficiency for random communication. Nonadjacent cells in the array communicate without disturbing the computation on intermediate cells.

Tasks can be distributed to meet the needs of application scenarios. The routing and logical connection mechanism of cells provides the capability of reconfiguring the array for fault tolerance and degradation. Suspect cells or dead cells can be bypassed.

Each iWarp cell supports four full duplex I/O channels. Each I/O channel is labeled with a unique name: XLeft (XL), XRight (XR), YUp (YU), or YDown (YD).

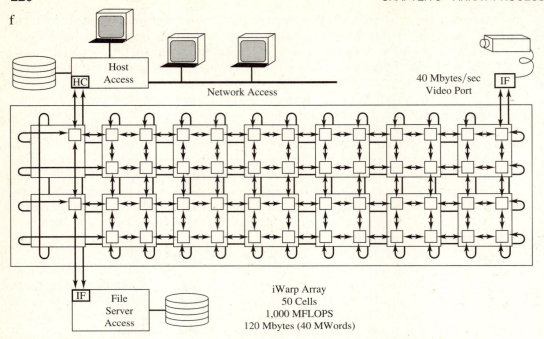

Figure 5.31 iWarp System Configuration Concept (Courtesy of Intel Corporation.)

Each channel input or output link has a sustained performance of 40 Mbytes/sec. This configuration gives a combined input data bandwidth of 160 Mbytes/sec and an output bandwidth of 160 Mbytes/sec per iWarp cell. The computation agent can use half of this bandwidth, 80 Mbytes for input and 80 Mbytes for output. The I/O data capacity of the local memory is 160 Mbytes/s. Each cell has a peak performance of 20 MFLOPS for 32-bit single precision and 10 MFLOPS for 64-bit double precision arithmetic. The iWarp component contains 650,000 transistors on a 550 mil square die and is packaged in a pin-grid array with 271 pins.

THE IWARP COMPONENT

The iWarp component shown in Figure 5.32 is the basic building block of the iWarp system. Each iWarp component is a complete computer that includes I/O interfaces to connect many devices in a large array of processors. The component architecture is divided into a computation agent and a communication agent, both of which function independently.

THE COMPUTATION AGENT

The computation agent (Figure 5.33) consists of the following functional units:

> Register file unit: The 15-port register file routes data between functional units. It is a general purpose, multiported shared RAM containing 128 32-bit locations. The access is by bytes, half-words, words, or double

5.7 SYSTOLIC ARRAYS

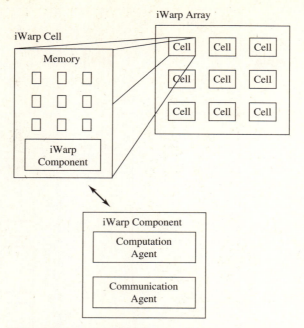

Figure 5.32 iWarp Cell Architecture (Courtesy of Intel Corporation.)

words, depending on the instruction used. The register file consists of nine standard ports: three ports to the integer logic unit, three to the floating-point adder, and three to the floating-point multiplier.

Local memory unit: The local memory unit provides the interface between the iWarp component and its local memory. The local memory contains both data and instructions, so the local memory unit provides a direct interface to both the instruction cache in the program store unit and the register file unit. Local memory contains two separate buses to maximize performance: a 24-bit address bus and a 64-bit data bus.

Program store unit: The program store unit fetches instructions from local memory, stores them in an instruction cache, and provides them to the instruction sequencing unit. The program store unit contains a 1-Kbyte instruction cache, which is fully associative, and an 8-Kbyte instruction ROM.

Instruction sequencing unit: The instruction sequencing unit receives instructions from the program store unit and controls the flow of program execution by decoding all instructions.

Integer logic unit: The integer logic unit is a 32-bit processor generating addresses for data access to local memory. The integer logic unit runs at 20 MIPS. The integer logic unit accesses two operands, performs a computa-

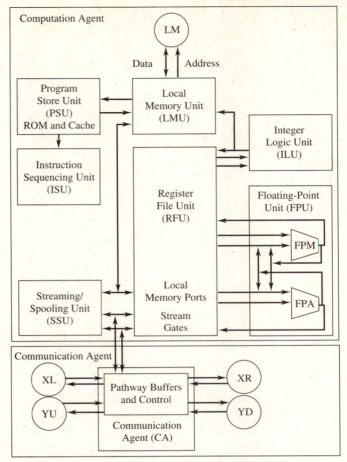

Figure 5.33 iWarp Component Architecture Block Diagram (Courtesy of Intel Corporation.)

tion, and writes the result back into the register file unit. The long instruction word architecture of the iWarp processor allows the integer logic unit to operate in parallel with the floating-point unit.

Floating-point unit: The floating-point unit contains a nonpipelined adder and a multiplier, which run on a two-clock instruction cycle, each producing a result every 100 nanoseconds. In this time, the adder and multiplier can each access two operands from the register file unit, perform a computation, and write the result back to the register file unit.

Streaming/spooling unit: The streaming/spooling unit is a DMA controller that spools data from the communication agent to memory and streams data from memory to the computation units through the stream gates of the register file unit. If the processor receives a message while it is busy, the streaming/spooling unit can direct the data into a preassigned buffer in memory, holding it until the processor is available.

5.7 SYSTOLIC ARRAYS

COMMUNICATION AGENT

The communication agent provides communication between cells in an iWarp array by controlling the transfer of data over the physical links between cells. Each cell in an iWarp array connects to its neighbors through four physical links. (See Figure 5.33.) Each of the physical links has two unidirectional buses, one to transmit data and the other to receive data. Data is transmitted between the cells in units called messages. Bits 0 through 19 of the header contain the destination address for the message, and bits 20 through 23 contain control information.

As described earlier, the functional units work together to perform the following communication/computation functions:

Express messages: The physical pathway hardware for the cell automatically passes the message on to an adjacent cell. Routing information provided at the message level supports corner-turning (i.e., a message from an X pathway is transferred to a Y pathway). Figure 5.34(a) illustrates the communication through express messages.

Systolic computation: The computation agent takes data directly from the pathway. The results are sent back on the pathway to another processor in the array as illustrated in Figure 5.34(b).

Spooling and streaming: A variation in the systolic computation that supports buffering messages in memory is as shown in Figure 5.34(c). If the computation engine is busy and a systolic message is received, the spooler can perform a DMA transfer of the data directly into a preassigned buffer in the memory. The buffer holds the message until the processor is available to respond. The data is then streamed out of the memory and presented to the processor by the streamer as if it had been received over the communication pathway.

Memory-to-memory message passing: In this case, the received message automatically goes to memory to be used by the processor at a later time, and the messages sent from the memory are spooled out as shown in Figure 5.34(d).

LOGICAL PATHWAYS

The logical pathways between iWarp cells are time multiplexed onto physical pathways. Several logical pathways share the same physical pathway and avoid deadlock and minimize data starvation problems for unbalanced tasks. Basically, logical pathways can be viewed as a 20×20 crossbar. The system allocates logical pathways to physical pathways under software control.

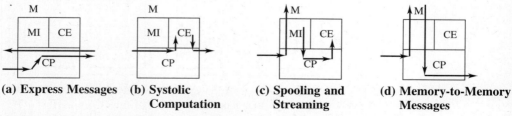

(a) Express Messages (b) Systolic Computation (c) Spooling and Streaming (d) Memory-to-Memory Messages

Figure 5.34 iWarp Communication Modes (Courtesy of Intel Corporation.)

A quad cell board contains four iWarp components and four banks of local memory. The single board array is a quad cell board designed to allow the installation of an iWarp in the card cage of a Sun workstation. When combined with a Sun interface board, the single board array forms a complete iWarp array. Local memory on the quad cell board can be expanded with the memory expansion module, which contains up to two banks of additional memory.

SOFTWARE ENVIRONMENT

The iWarp software environment supports high-performance computation in signal and image processing and scientific applications. It is composed of a program development environment that resides on the host workstation and execution support that resides on the iWarp array. Parallel user code is executed on the array of iWarp cells while the sequential code can either run on the host or on a single iWarp cell. Figure 5.35 illustrates the relationship between iWarp's software and hardware architectures.

The host environment includes program development software and the software that supports communication between the host and the iWarp array. The host software grants access to the iWarp array and maintains the connection between a user's system and the iWarp system after access is granted. The program development environment is supported on Sun workstations using SunOs. Figure 5.36 illustrates the structure of the host environment, which provides UNIX-based program development tools such as cross compilers, assembler, linker, debugger, and diagnostics.

The iWarp C and Fortran compilers are highly optimizing compilers that generate object code for individual cells. They pack multiple operations into each wide instruction word allowing the iWarp functional units to execute those operations simultaneously. The C compiler is an industry standard with iWarp-specific extensions that provide access to the systolic pathway. The Fortran compiler accepts the

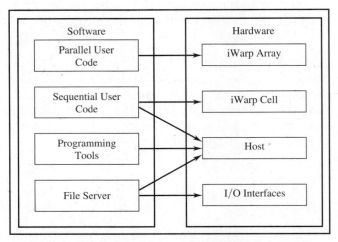

Figure 5.35 Relationship Between iWarp Software and Hardware Architecture (Courtesy of Intel Corporation.)

5.7 SYSTOLIC ARRAYS

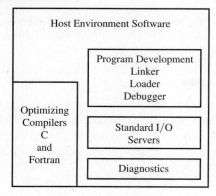

Figure 5.36 iWarp Host Environment (Courtesy of Intel Corporation.)

Fortran 77 source with VMS and iWarp-specific extensions. The iWarp extensions for C and Fortran support are systolic communication (send and receive primitives), iWarp condition code checking, assembly code in-lining capability and pragma support for in-lining specification.

These compilers employ a variety of optimizations to fully use the multiple functional units of iWarp cells. Two of these optimizations are software pipelining and local code compaction. These code scheduling techniques allow the compilers to generate code with multiple operations in the same machine instruction.

With software pipelining, an iteration of a loop in the source program can be initiated before preceding iterations are completed. This technique exploits the repetitive nature of loops to generate efficient code for processors with multiple functional units. At any time, multiple iterations are simultaneously in different stages of the computation. The steady state of this pipeline constitutes the loop body of the object code. The following example shows the source code and the pseudoassembler output that illustrates software pipelining of a simple loop:

```
DO I = 1, 10
    A(I) = A(I)*C
ENDDO
```

Register R1 contains the iteration count minus 2, register R2 contains the constant C, and registers R3 and R4 contain intermediate results.

```
{ ld a1, r3                                                          }
{ fmul r2, r3, r4;     ld a2,r3                                      }
loop r1
el {    st r4,   ai-2;   fmul r2, r3, r4;     ld ai, r3              }
   {                     st r4, an-1          fmul r2, r3, r4        }
   {                                          st r4, an              }
```

Here three iterations of the loop are computed simultaneously. The *steady state* of the loop is shown on the line beginning with el (for..end loop). On the ith iteration, the load of $A(I)$ is performed in parallel with the multiplication of $A(I-1)$ and C, and the result is stored into $A(I-2)$.

Code compaction can be performed when there are enough source level operations to make the optimization worthwhile. The following example shows a sequence of operations typical of complex arithmetic:

```
REAL = (TEMP! * WREAL) _ (TEMP * WIMAG)
IMAG = (TEMP! * WIMAG) _ (TEMP@ * WREAL)
```

There are six operations. With compaction, two of the operations can be overlapped, resulting in four instructions actually being used. Loading and storing of values can also be overlapped. Some additional optimizations include: redundant instruction elimination, flow of control optimizations, algebraic simplification, peephole optimization, and function-preserving transformations.

APPLY: FOR IMAGE PROCESSING APPLICATIONS

Apply is a special purpose, high-level language for image processing applications that frees the programmer from having to perform low-level interprocess communication. It provides for the pixel generation of the output image; allows a local operation to be represented easier than with a serial language like C; and has special functions for borders, image expansion, and reduction. It is designed for writing two-dimensional local operator algorithms and generates parallel code that runs on an array of iWarp cells of any size.

In Apply, the data objects are scalars and two-dimensional arrays of scalars having various types (byte, integer, real, double). Conventional expression syntax is used to specify computations on these data objects. Apply procedures are called from Fortran or C language main programs in much the same way as other procedures are called. On the calling side, arguments to the Apply procedures are declared according to syntax and semantics of the Fortran or C languages. Image data from the calling program is transferred to the array of computational cells on which the Apply routine is executed, and the results are returned to the calling program. This data transfer is transparent to the Apply programmer.

Apply functions are not complete programs but procedures that must be called from a C main program. These calls are no different than a call to any other C function, except for the performance gain due to parallel execution. A master-slave computation model is utilized. All flow of control for the sequential part of the program is contained in the C language main program, which runs on the master processor. Apply-generated functions run in parallel on a group of slave processors under the direction of the master processor. The master directs the slave program to invoke certain code sections for storage management, data movement, computation, and so on.

Apply facilitates the data decomposition style of computation. The Apply compiler distributes image data by rows with each processor receiving a contiguous set of data from the input image. Input data partitions are overlapped so computations can be performed within the specified window. Each slave cell performs the computation on its set of data and produces a corresponding part of the result. The Apply compiler determines which data belong to which processors and how many loop iterations each processor is to perform. The first data partition is accepted by a slave processor, which begins its part of the computation at the same time as it forwards the remaining data

5.7 SYSTOLIC ARRAYS

to the rest of the slave processors. Input image data enter from the upper left of the processor array as a single high-speed data stream and results leave at the lower right.

APPLICATIONS

The iWarp system has been used in a broad range of high performance image and signal processing applications. Figure 5.37 shows the application of iWarp for matrix multiplication. Here matrices A and B are multiplied to form the matrix C. The familiar dot product method is used in which the dot product of each row of A with each column of B is performed, requiring n^3 multiply-accumulate operations. Consider a linear array of n iWarp cells across which the n columns of matrix B are distributed so that each cell has a column of B. Because each row of matrix A is applied against each column of B, we pass each row of matrix A down the array and perform the corresponding dot product operation as elements flow past the cells. Thus, each cell j performs the computation $a(i, k) * b(k, j) + c(i, j)$, as each $a(i, k)$ value flows through the array. The first result, $c(1, 1)$, is complete and can flow out of the array when the dot product between $a(1, n)$ and $b(1, n)$ has completed in cell 1. Other results of matrix C are completed in turn as the rows of A proceed through the iWarp array.

5.7.2 Saxpy Matrix-1

This description of Matrix-1 is adapted from Fousler and Schreiber (1987). The key architectural features are the Matrix-1's use of a large global memory; the use of Fortran as the programming language; the emphasis on block algorithms; and the provision in the hardware of double-buffered, software-managed local memory for the systolic array to support block algorithms.

ARCHITECTURE

The principal components of the Matrix-1 are illustrated in Figure 5.38. They are:

1. The system controller, a general-purpose computer that executes the application program and allocates Matrix-1 resources

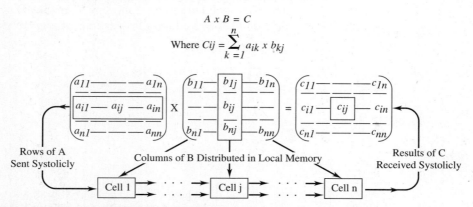

Figure 5.37 Matrix Multiply Example (Courtesy of Intel Corporation.)

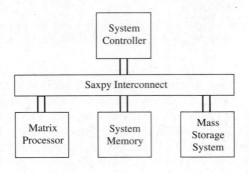

Figure 5.38 Block Diagram of the Matrix-1 System (Fousler and Schreifer, 1987) (Reproduced with permission from IEEE.)

2. The matrix processor, a linear array of up to 32 pipelined, floating-point processors that have systolic and global interconnections
3. The system memory, which stores all data arrays for use by the matrix processor
4. The mass storage system, an I/O interface that provides access to high-speed data-storage peripherals
5. The Saxpy interconnect, a combined control and data bus that links the other four units of the Matrix-1

The system controller is a Digital Equipment Corporation VAX. It can compile and link the application program. Its main function is to execute the application program, sending control information across the remainder of the hardware. Data are stored in the system memory, and the matrix processor performs practically all floating-point computations; the system controller's job is to coordinate resources.

The matrix processor subsystem (Figure 5.39) has three principal components: the matrix processor (the programmable array); the matrix processor interface (the data path between the processor array and the Saxpy interconnect); and the matrix control processor (a fast integer processor that decodes commands received over the Saxpy interconnect from the system controller and then controls the interface and processor array in order to perform the desired computation).

The matrix processor (Figure 5.40) is an array of 8, 16, 24, or 32 vector processors; these are called computational zones. It is an SIMD architecture; all zones receive the same control and address instructions at a given clock cycle. The

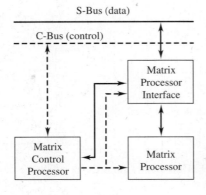

Figure 5.39 The Matrix Processor Unit Subsystem (Fousler and Schreiber, 1987) (Reproduced with permission from IEEE.)

5.7 SYSTOLIC ARRAYS

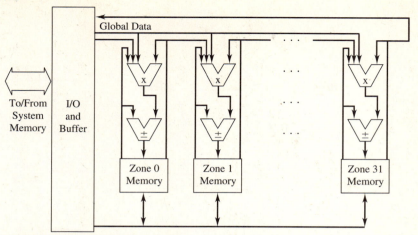

Figure 5.40 The Matrix Processor Zone Architecture (Fousler and Schreiber, 1987) (Reproduced with permission from IEEE.)

matrix processor can function in systolic mode (in which data are transferred linearly across the zones) or in block mode (in which all zones operate independently and use local data). Both operational modes can be used within a single subroutine.

Each zone has a pipelined, 32-bit floating-point multiplier; a pipelined, 32-bit floating adder with logic capabilities (its ALU); and a 4K-word local memory. These components operate on a 64-nanosecond clock. The multiplier and adder are cascaded. Lookup tables are provided for use in reciprocal and square root calculations. Because each of the zones may begin a multiplication and an ALU operation with every clock cycle, the peak computing rate of the matrix processor is 64 floating-point operations per clock, or an average of one per nanosecond, for a total of 1000 MFLOPS. The instruction set of the matrix processor zone includes a large variety of vector operations.

Although the matrix processor is an SIMD architecture and thus all the zones nominally execute the same operations in parallel, two of its mechanisms allow the programmer more freedom. First, any subset of the zones may be disabled by setting the bits of a program-controlled mask. This permits single vector computation and calculations on a subset of the zones. Second, the zone memories allow indirect addressing in which elements of one vector are used as pointers into another vector. *Scatter* and *gather* vector operations are implemented with this indirect-addressing hardware and operate at half speed (i.e., one word every two cycles).

Within the matrix processor there are three types of data interconnections, all of which are one word wide and operate at the clock speed of the matrix processor. First, the systolic data path connects each zone to its right neighbor; the last zone can connect to the systolic output buffer (which is the global buffer) or, in a circular fashion, to the first zone. Second, the global buffer is the source for a broadcast data path connected to all the zones. Third, the local memory of each zone has several connections, both to the zone's processing elements and to the matrix processor interface.

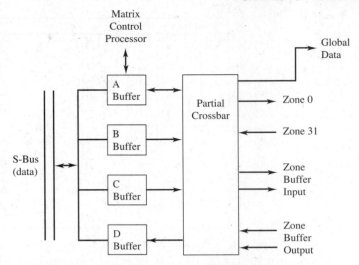

Figure 5.41 The Matrix Processor Interface (Fousler and Schreiber, 1987) (Reproduced with permission from IEEE.)

The matrix processor interface (Figure 5.41) mediates between the system data bus and the internal buses of the matrix processor. Four buffers are used to hold blocks of data that are in transit between the system memory and the matrix processor. The buffers are two-sided and can concurrently carry on transfers with the matrix processor zone memories. Furthermore, the buffers support bidirectional transfers by allowing a read and write operation in a single clock cycle. The local memories of the zones are also bidirectional, two-sided, and can support data transfers involving the matrix processor interface concurrently with computational reads and writes. Thus, the matrix processor interface can mediate bidirectional transfers between system memory and the matrix processor in parallel with the occurrence of full-speed computation. The matrix processor interface buffers are connected through a partial crossbar switch to the internal buses of the matrix processor and its interface. In transferring data, the interface buffers allow random access, which, among other things, permits the programmer to transpose arrays *on-the-fly* as they are transited between the system memory and the matrix processor. Such a facility allows full-speed access to certain arrangements of noncontiguous system memory locations.

The matrix control processor executes computational subroutines to control the flow of data between system memory and the matrix processor and to issue the computational instructions to the zones. For example, to multiply two matrices, the matrix control processor decomposes large data arrays into arrays of 32×32 blocks, issues commands to the matrix processor interface that instruct it to move blocks as necessary from system memory to the matrix processor and back, and issues vector-command sequences to the matrix processor that instruct it to perform operations on the 32×32 blocks. Data transfer and computational commands are interleaved so as to overlap operations for maximum efficiency; the resulting concurrent execution allows the matrix processor to compute at full speed without waiting for data.

In programming the matrix control processor, one views the individual zones as vector computers. The machine instruction set is based on a set of vector operations replicated across all zones. The pipelining and the various registers and multiplexers in the matrix processor zone are not seen by the programmer, nor are they directly controlled by a matrix control processor program. Control of these elements is achieved by instruction-decode hardware and microcode in the matrix processor.

The application programmer at the system controller level need not be aware of the implementation details of the computational subroutines. The internal details of the matrix processor and the matrix control processor are hidden from the application level; each subroutine implements a mathematical operation (for example, fast Fourier transform or matrix multiply) on an entire system memory array.

The floating-point data processed by the Matrix-1 reside in the system memory, which ranges in size from 16M to 128M words. The Matrix-1's ability to store large data sets in main memory can reduce significantly the amount of intermediate data transfer to auxiliary storage devices. Moreover, the Matrix-1 allows only a single job to use the system memory and matrix processor at a given time, so that every job is guaranteed to have all the available memory. Performance is therefore predictable and is not reduced by the cost of swapping or the other overheads incurred in sharing memory. All application and system programs reside in the system controller's memory and, therefore, do not consume space in the system memory.

The system memory is not virtually addressable, and hence, no address translation is needed. Programs exceeding the 128M-word limit must implement their own off-line memory management. General experience in large-scale scientific computing indicates that hardware paging strategies deserve improvement and that users obtain high performance by managing large data sets themselves.

Memory cycle time is 100 namoseconds. A wide word consisting of eight adjacent 32-bit words is read or written in each cycle. Successive accesses to consecutive wide word locations can occur at the rate of one per cycle. Thus, the memory bandwidth is 80M words per second when one is accessing large contiguous blocks of data. Reduced bandwidth performance is characteristic of several modes of nonsequential access, including the random wide word access and single word access modes. The memory includes single error correction and double error detection on pairs of 32-bit words.

The mass storage system (Figure 5.42) supports two types of I/O activity. It makes possible direct memory access transfers between disk files and system memory. Disk files may be striped across several drives to increase transfer rates up to the limit of 3M words per second. The second type of I/O activity implements staged transfers between external memory and peripherals without using the Saxpy interconnect. Each type of data transfer may be carried out in parallel with computations and their attendant data movement.

The Matrix-1 and iWarp are the first commercial general purpose systolic computers. Both have a general purpose host, a global memory, and a linear array of processors with local memory. Unlike Matrix-1, iWarp is an MIMD and the iWarp array allows two-way systolic dataflow. It has neither a global data path nor global I/O paths.

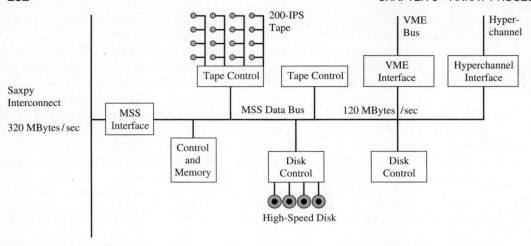

Figure 5.42 Mass Storage System (Fousler and Schreiber, 1987) (Reproduced with permission from IEEE.)

These machines use different programming models. The iWarp prograf mming language W2 generates code for the whole system (host, interface unit, and array). It is the programmer's responsibility to determine which computations are performed by which cells and the movement of data between the cells and between the cells and the memory. In Matrix-1, the programmer decides what is done in the host and what is done in the array. The Fortran compiler for the array code performs the optimizations.

5.8 SUMMARY

Architectural issues concerned with parallel array processor or SIMD schemes are covered in this chapter. These architectures are suitable for computational environments that exhibit a high degree of data parallelism. They can be considered a special subset of MIMD architectures that offer the least amount of overhead.

This chapter also provides a description of hardware and software characteristics of two commercial SIMD systems (Thinking Machine Corporation's Connection Machine and MasPar Corporation's MP series), an experimental SIMD (ILLIAC-IV), and two commercial systolic systems (Intel's iWARP and Saxpy Matrix-1).

In general, an efficient algorithm for an SISD system is not efficient on an SIMD. New algorithms and correspondingly specialized programming languages are needed to efficiently utilize the computational power offered by SIMD architectures. Data structuring and memory organization also contribute heavily to the efficiency of SIMD systems.

The processor interconnection network is a major component of an SIMD. These networks are tailored to the application at hand and hence make the architecture specialized to the application. Common interconnection networks were introduced in this chapter. Chapter 6 extends this description as applied to MIMD architectures.

It is interesting to note the tremendous architectural diversity among the SIMDs. Massively parallel SIMD architectures, such as the Connection Machine, employ hundreds or thousands of simple processors, while moderately parallel machines, such as the Matrix-1, use fewer (up to 32) processing elements. While the IBM GF-11 is an SIMD intended for a specific application, Matrix-1 and Connection Machine are general purpose computers. The Connection Machine features a distributed memory and a near-hypercube interconnection network; the GF-11 has a multistage network connecting its processors to its memory modules; the Matrix-1 has a shared memory connected by a high-bandwidth bus to the ring-connected, linear processor array; and the iWarp uses a two-dimensional torus network.

REFERENCES

Agrawal, D. P., K. V. Janakiram, and G. C. Pathak. 1986. Evaluating the performance of multicomputer configurations. *IEEE Computer* 19(5) (May): 23–37

Almasi, G. S. and A. Gottlieb. 1989. *Highly parallel computing.* Redwood City, Calif.: Benjamin Cummings.

Anderson, G. A., and E. D. Jensen. 1975. Computer interconnection structures: Taxonomy, characteristics, and examples. *ACM Computing Surveys* 7(4): 197–213.

Baxter, B., and B. Greer. 1991. *Apply: A parallel compiler for image-processing applications.* Beaverton, OR: Intel Corporation.

Bernhardt, M., and P. Wiley. 1991. Background information on iWarp: Real-time super computing for advanced signal and image processing. Beaverton, OR: Intel Supercomputer Systems Division.

Bhuyan, L. N., and D. P. Agrawal. 1984. Generalized hypercube and hyperbus structures for a computer network. *IEEE Transactions on Computers* C-33(1) pp. 426–439.

Bonavito, N. L. 1990. Maximum entropy method applied to deblurring images on a MasPar MP-1 computer. McLean, Va: *Applied Imagery Pattern Recognition Workshop.*

Borkar, S., et al. 1988. iWarp: An integrated solution to high-speed parallel computing. *Proceedings Supercomputing Conference.* Orlando, Fa.

Budnik P., and D. J. Kuck. 1971. The organization and use of parallel memories. *IEEE Trans. Computer* C-20: 1566–9.

Chen, P-Y., D. H. Lowrie, and P-C. Yew. 1981. Interconnection networks using shuffles. *IEEE Computer* 14(12) December: 55–64.

Cox, G. 1991. An architectural view of high performance signal and image processing. *Proceedings Supercomputing USA/Pacific.*

Ducksbury, P. G. 1986. Parallel array processing. New York: Halstead Press.

Feng, T-Y. 1981. A survey of interconnection networks. *IEEE Computer* 14 (December): 12–27.

Fousler, D. E. and R. Schreiber. 1987. The Saxpy Matrix-1: A general-purpose systolic computer. *IEEE Computer* 20(7): 35–43.

Hillis, W. D. 1985. *The Connection Machine.* Cambridge, Mass.: MIT.

Hillis, W. D. and G. L. Steele. 1985. *The Connection Machine LISP Manual.* Cambridge, MA: Thinking Machines Corporation.

Hillis, W. D. 1987. The Connection Machine. *Scientific American* (June).

Hockney, R. W., and C. R. Jesshope. 1988. *Parallel computers 2.* Philadelphia, Penn.: Adam Hilger.

Hord, R. M. 1983. *The ILLIAC-IV: The first supercomputer.* Rockville, Md.: Computer Science Press.

Hord, R. M. 1990. *Parallel supercomputing in SIMD architectures.* Reading, MA: CRC Press.

Hwang, K. and D. Degroot. 1989. *Parallel processing in supercomputers—artificial intelligence.* McGraw Hill.

Intel Corporation. 1991. *Introduction to iWarp.* Beaverton, OR: Intel Corporation.

Johnson, K. T., A. R. Hurson, and B. Shirazi. 1993. General-purpose systolic arrays. *IEEE Computer* 26(11): 20–31.

Kahle, B. A. and W. D. Hillis. 1989. The Connection Machine Model CM-1 architecture. *IEEE Transactions on Systems, Man, and Cybernetics* 19(4) pp. 246–252.

Kuck, D. J. 1989. *The structure of computers and computations* Vol. 1. New York: John Wiley & Sons.

Kumar, V. K. P. 1991. *Parallel architectures and algorithms for image understanding.* Boston, MA: Academic Press, Inc.

Lawrie, D. H. 1975. Access and alignment of data in an array processor. *IEEE Transactions on Computers* 24(12): 1145–1155.

Lipvoski, J. G., and M. Malek. 1987. *Parallel computing: Theory and comparisons.* New York: John Wiley & Sons.

MasPar Computer Corporation. 1990. Large fast fourier transforms. Application Note 005.0990. Sunnyvale, Calif.: MasPar Computer Corporation.

MasPar Computer Corporation. 1990. MasPar data-parallel programming languages. Sunnyvale, Calif.: MasPar Computer Corporation.

MasPar Computer Corporation. 1990. MasPar 1200 Series Computer System. Sunnyvale, Calif.: MasPar Computer Corporation.

MasPar Computer Corporation. 1990. MasPar parallel disk array. Sunnyvale, Calif.: MasPar Computer Corporation.

MasPar Computer Corporation. 1990. MP-1 family data-parallel computers. Sunnyvale, Calif.: MasPar Computer Corporation.

MasPar Computer Corporation. 1990. MP-1 MasPar programming environment. Sunnyvale, Calif.: MasPar Computer Corporation.

MasPar Computer Corporation. 1990. Indirect addressing and load balancing for faster solutions to Mandelbrot set on SIMD architectures. Application Note AN101, Sunnyvale, Calif.: MasPar Computer Corporation.

Masson, G. M., G. C. Gingher, and S. Nakamura. 1979. A sampler of circuit switching network. *IEEE Computer* 12(6) 32–48.

Nickols, J. R. 1990. The design of the MasPar MP-1: A cost effective massively parallel computer. *Proceedings of IEEE Compcon.* Spring. Los Alamitos, Calif.

Reddaway, S. F. 1973. DAP—A distributed array processor. *First Annual IEEE/ACM Symposium on Computer Architecture.*

Shiva, S. G. 1991. *Computer design & architecture.* Glenview, IL: HarperCollins.

Siegel, H. J. 1985. *Interconnection networks for large scale parallel processing.* Lexington, Mass: Lexington Books.

Stone, H. S. 1971. Parallel processing with the perfect shuffle. *IEEE Transactions on Computers* C-20 (February): 153–161.

Stone, H. S. 1971. Parallel processing with the perfect shuffle. *IEEE Transactions on Computers* C-20(3) 153–161.

Stone, H. S. 1990. *High-performance computer architecture.* New York: Addison-Wesley.

Ziff-Davis Publishing Co. 1992. *Data sources report.* Boston, MA: Ziff-Davis Publishing Co.

PROBLEMS

5.1. The following are common operations on matrices: column sum, row sum, transpose, inverse, addition, and multiplication. Examine the algorithm for each operation, and develop vectorized procedures for each assuming a vector processor capable of performing vector add, subtract, reciprocal, and multiply operations.

5.2. Assume $N \times N$ matrix for each operation in the above problem. Develop procedures suitable for an SIMD with N processing elements. Specify how the matrices are represented in the N memory blocks of the SIMD.

5.3. Solve Problem 5.2 for an SIMD with M processing elements where $M < N$ and N is not a multiple of M.

5.4. Develop procedures and data structures for the matrix operations in Problem 5.1 for execution on one quadrant of the ILLIAC-IV.

5.5. Consider the 8×8 mesh of ILLIAC-IV. An application requires that each PE update its content by the average of values in its four neighboring PEs. Write an assembly language program to run this computation for five iterations assuming:
  a. Each PE computes the new value based on current contents of the neighbors and then updates its value.
  b. The update is performed one row at a time starting from the top row of PEs.

5.6. Develop the architectural facilities needed if the procedures in the above problem need to run until a convergence condition is satisfied (the new value is different from the old value by a small ϵ in all the PEs, for instance).

5.7. Consider an 8×8 crossbar that interconnects eight PEs. Show the active crosspoints needed in this crossbar if only the following interconnections are needed:
  a. a unidirectional ring;
  b. a bidirectional ring (i.e., one dimensional nearest neighbor);
  c. two-dimensional nearest-neighbor (as in ILLIAC-IV);
  d. three-dimensional hypercube; and
  e. shuffle exchange.

5.8. Consider the nearest-neighbor mesh interconnection of the ILLIAC-IV with 64 PEs (PE_0 through PE_{63}), organized as an 8×8 array. PE_i is connected to PE_{i+1}, PE_{i-1}, PE_{i+8}, and PE_{i-8}. Determine the minimum number of routing steps needed to send data from PE_i to PE_j where $j = (i + k) \bmod 64$ and $0 \leq k \leq 63$, $0 \leq i \leq 63$.

5.9 A plus-minus-2i IN connects each PE_j ($0 \leq j \leq N - 1$) of an N processor system to all PE_{k+} and PE_{k-}, where $k+ = (j + 2i) \bmod N$ and $k- = (j - 2i) \bmod N$; and $0 \leq i \leq n$, $n = \log_2 N$.
  a. Show the structure of the network for $N = 8$.
  b. What is the maximum number of routing steps needed to transfer data from PE_i to PE_j where i and j are arbitrary integers and $0 \leq j \leq N - 1$, $0 \leq i \leq N - 1$?
  c. Show the single and multistage implementations.

5.10. It is required to broadcast a data value in one PE to all the other PEs in an SIMD system with N PEs. Determine the number of steps needed if the network is each of the following types:
   a. single-stage shuffle exchange
   b. hypercube

5.11. What is the maximum number of hops needed to route a single data item on a) a 64×64 processor array and b) a 4096-node hypercube?

5.12. Show that an n-cube has the same topology as an $n \times n$ array with toroidal edge connections.

5.13. List the desired characteristics of a compiler that performs parallelization of the sequential code for an SIMD.

5.14. Estimate the time needed to perform the multiplication of two $(N \times N)$ matrices on an $(N \times N)$ systolic array.

5.15. Trace the evolution of the Connection Machine series (CM-1, CM-2, and CM-5) in terms of architectural characteristics and intended applications.

CHAPTER 6

Multiprocessor Systems

The most important characteristic of the multiprocessor systems discussed in this chapter is that all the processors function independently. That is, unlike the SIMD systems in which all the processors execute the same instruction at any given time, each processor in a multiprocessor system can be executing a different instruction at any time. For this reason, Flynn classified these systems as multiple instruction stream multiple data stream (MIMD) computers.

As mentioned earlier, the need for parallel execution arises because the device technology limits the speed of execution of any single processor. SIMD systems increased the performance and the speed manifold simply because of data parallelism. But, such parallel processing improves performance only in a limited case of applications which can be organized into a series of repetitive operations on uniformly structured data. Because a number of applications cannot be represented in this manner, SIMD systems are not a panacea. This led to the evolution of a more general form, the MIMD architectures in which each processing element has its own arithmetic/logic unit (ALU) and control unit and, if necessary, its own memory and input/output (I/O) devices. Thus each processing element is a computer system in itself, capable of performing a processing task totally independent of other processing elements. The processing elements are interconnected in some manner to allow exchange of data and programs and to synchronize their activities.

The major advantages of MIMD systems are:

1. **Reliability:** If any processor fails, its workload can be taken over by another processor thus incorporating graceful degradation and better fault tolerance in the system.
2. **High performance:** Consider an ideal scenario where all the N processors are working on some useful computation. At times of such peak performance, the processing speed of an MIMD is N times that of a single processor system. However, such peak performance is difficult to achieve on account of the overhead involved with MIMD operation. The overhead is due to:
    1. communication between processors,
    2. synchronization of the work of one processor with that of another processor,
    3. waste of processor time if any processor runs out of tasks to do, and
    4. processor scheduling (i.e., allocation of tasks to the processors).

A **task** is an entity to which a processor is assigned. That is, a task is a program, a function, or a procedure in execution on a given processor. **Process** is simply another word for a task. A processor or a processing element is a hardware resource on which tasks are executed. A processor executes several tasks, one after another. The sequence of tasks performed in succession by a given processor forms a **thread.** Thus, the path of execution of a processor through a number of tasks is called a thread. Multiprocessors provide for the simultaneous presence of a number of threads of execution in an application.

EXAMPLE 6.1

Consider Figure 6.1 in which each block represents a task and each task has a unique number. As required by the application, task 2 can be executed only after task 1 is completed and task 3 can be executed only after task 1 and task 2 are both completed. Thus, the line through tasks 1, 2, and 3 forms a thread (A) of execution. Two other

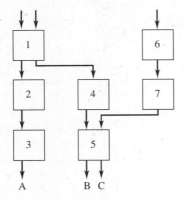

Figure 6.1 Threads of Execution

threads (B and C) are also shown. These threads limit the execution of tasks to a specific serial manner. Although task 2 has to follow task 1 and task 3 has to follow task 2, note that task 4 can be executed in parallel with task 2 or task 3. Similarly, task 6 can be executed simultaneously with task 1, and so on. Suppose the MIMD has three processors and if each task takes the same amount of time to execute, the seven tasks shown in the figure can be executed in the following manner.

Time slot	Processor 1	Processor 2	Processor 3
1	Task 1	Task 6	
2	Task 2	Task 4	Task 7
3	Task 3		Task 5

Initially, Because there are only two tasks that can be executed in parallel, they are arbitrarily allocated to processors 1 and 2 and processor 3 sits idle. At the end of the first time slot, each of the three processors gets a task from the three different threads. Thus, tasks 2, 4, and 7 are executed in parallel. Finally, tasks 3 and 5 are again executed in parallel with one of the processors sitting idle due to the lack of tasks at that instant.

Figure 6.1 implies that the application at hand is partitioned into seven tasks and exhibits a **degree of parallelism** of 3 because at the most three tasks can be executed simultaneously. It is assumed that there is no interaction between the tasks in this figure. In practice, tasks communicate with each other because each task depends on the results produced by other tasks. Refer to Figures 1.6, 1.7, and 1.8 for an illustration of the data dependencies between tasks. Obviously, the communication between tasks is reduced to zero if all the tasks are combined into a single task and run on a single processor (i.e., SISD mode).

The **R-to-C ratio,** where R is the length of the run time of the task and C is the communication overhead produced by that task, signifies **task granularity.** This ratio is a measure of how much overhead is produced per unit of computation. A high R-to-C ratio implies that the communication overhead is insignificant compared to computation time while a low R-to-C ratio implies that the communication overhead dominates computation time and, hence, a poorer performance.

High R-to-C ratios imply **coarse grain** parallelism while low R-to-C ratios result in **fine grain** parallelism. The general tendency to obtain maximum performance is to resort to the finest possible granularity, thus providing for the highest degree of parallelism. However, care should be taken to see that this maximum parallelism does not lead to maximum overhead. Thus, a trade-off is required to reach an optimum level of granularity.

This chapter describes the architectural concepts, programming considerations, and applications of MIMD systems. The next section provides models for the two common MIMD organizations. Section 2 describes the memory organization and the cache coherence problem. Section 3 extends the description of interconnection networks from Chapter 5 to MIMD architectures. Operating system considerations for multiprocessors are the theme of Section 4. Programming considerations are discussed in Section 5. Section 6 presents performance evaluation techniques, and Section 7 provides a brief description of five commercial multiprocessor systems.

6.1 MIMD ORGANIZATION

As mentioned earlier, in an MIMD system each processing element works independently. Processor 1 is said to be working independently of processors 2, 3, . . . N at any instant if, and only if, the task being executed by processor 1 has no interactions with the tasks executed by processors 2, 3, . . . N and vice versa at the same instant. However, the results from the tasks executed on processor X now may be needed by processor Y sometime in the future. In order to make this possible, each processor must be capable of communicating the results of the task it performs to other processors that require those results. This is done by sending the results directly to a requesting process or storing them in a shared memory area (i.e., a memory to which each processor has equal and easy access). These communication models have resulted in two popular MIMD organizations (presented in Chapter 2). These are:

1. shared memory, or tightly coupled architecture, and
2. message passing, or loosely coupled architecture.

6.1.1 Shared Memory Architecture

Figure 6.2(a) shows the structure of a shared memory MIMD. Here any processor i can access any memory module j through the interconnection network. Computation results are stored in the memory by the processor that executed that task. If these results are required by any other task, they can be easily accessed from the memory. Note that each processor is a full-fledged SISD capable of fetching instructions from the memory and executing them on the data retrieved from the memory. No processor has a local memory of its own. This is called a **tightly coupled** architecture because the processors are interconnected such that the interchange of data between them through the shared memory is quite rapid. This is the main advantage of this architecture. Also, the memory access time is the same for all the processors, and hence, the name **uniform memory architecture** (UMA).

If the processors in the system are nonhomogeneous, data transformations will be needed during exchange. For instance, if the system consists of both 16-bit and 32-bit processors and the shared memory consists of 32-bit words, each memory word must be converted into two words for the use of 16-bit processors and vice versa. This is an overhead.

Another problem is the memory contention, which occurs whenever two or more processors try to access the same shared memory block. Because a memory

6.1 MIMD ORGANIZATION

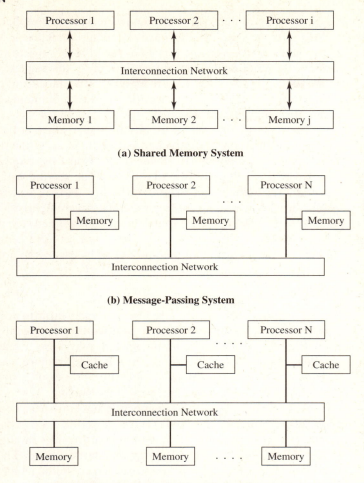

Figure 6.2 MIMD Structures

block can be accessed only by one processor at a time, all the other processors requesting access to that memory block must wait until the first processor is through using it. Also, if two processors simultaneously request access to the same memory block, one processor should be given preference over the other. Memory organization concepts are discussed in Section 2.

6.1.2 Message-Passing Architecture

This is the other extreme where there is no shared memory at all in the system. Each processor has a (local) memory block attached to it. The conglomeration of all local memories is the total memory that the system possesses. Figure 6.2(b) shows a block diagram of this configuration, also known as **loosely coupled** or **distributed memory** MIMD system. If data exchange is required between two processors in this configuration, the requesting processor *I* sends a message to processor *J* in whose local memory the required data are stored. In reply to this request the processor *J* (as soon it can) reads the requested data from its local memory and passes it on to processor *I* through the interconnection network. Thus, the communication between processors occurs through message passing.

The requested processor usually finishes its task at hand and then accesses its memory for the requested data and passes them on to the interconnection network. The interconnection network routes them toward the requesting processor. All this time the requesting processor sits idle waiting for the data, thus incurring a large overhead. The memory access time varies between the processors; hence, these architectures are known as **nonuniform memory architectures** (NUMA). Thus, a tightly coupled MIMD offers more rapid data interchange between processors than a loosely coupled MIMD while the memory contention problem is not present in a message-passing system because only one processor has access to a memory block.

6.1.3 Other Models

Shared memory architectures are also known as **multiprocessor** systems while message-passing architectures are called **multicomputer** systems. These architectures are two extremes. MIMD systems in practice may have a reasonable mix of the two architectures as shown in Figure 6.2(c). In this structure, each processor operates in its local environment as far as possible. Interprocessor communication can be either through the shared memory or by message passing.

Several variations of this memory architecture have been used. For instance, the Data Diffusion Machine (DDM) (Hagersten, 1992) uses a cache only memory architecture (COMA) in which all system memory resides in large caches attached to the processors in order to reduce latency and network load. The IBM Research Parallel Processor (RP3) consists of 512 nodes, each containing 4 megabytes of memory. The interconnection of nodes is such that the 512 memory modules can be used as one global shared memory or purely as local memories with a message-passing mode of communication or a combination of both.

MIMD systems can also be conceptually modeled as either **private-address-space** or **shared-address-space** machines. Both address-space models can be implemented on shared memory and message-passing architectures. Private memory, shared-address-space machines are NUMA architectures that offer scalability benefits of message-passing architectures with the programming advantages of shared-memory architectures. An example of this type is the J-machine from MIT, which has a small private memory attached to each of a large number of nodes but has a common address space across the whole system. The DASH machine from Stanford considers local memory a cache for the large global address space, but the global memory is actually distributed. In general, the actual configuration of an MIMD system depends on the application characteristics for which the system has been designed.

6.2 MEMORY ORGANIZATION

Two parameters of interest in MIMD memory system design are **bandwidth** and **latency.** For an MIMD system to be efficient, memory bandwidth must be high enough to provide for simultaneous operation of all the processors. When memory modules are shared, the memory contention must be minimized. Also, the latency (the time elapsed between a processor's request for data from the memory and its receipt) must be minimized. This section examines memory organization techniques that reduce these problems to a minimum and tolerable level.

Memory latency is reduced by increasing the memory bandwidth, which in turn is accomplished by one or both of the following mechanisms:

1. By building the memory system with multiple independent memory modules, thus providing for concurrent accesses of the modules. **Banked, interleaved,** and a combination of the two addressing architectures have been used in such systems. A recent trend is to use multiport memory modules in the design to achieve concurrent access.
2. By reducing the memory access and cycle times utilizing memory devices from the highest speed technology available. This is usually accompanied by high price. An alternative is to use cache memories in the design.

In order to understand the first method, consider an MIMD system with N processors and a shared memory unit. In the worst case, all but one processor may be waiting to get access to the memory and not doing any useful computation, because only one processor can access the memory at a given time. This causes a bottleneck in the overall performance of the system. A solution to this problem is to organize memory such that more than one simultaneous access to the memory is possible.

EXAMPLE 6.2

Figure 6.3(a) shows an MIMD structure in which N memory modules are connected to N processors through a crossbar interconnection network. All the N memory modules can be accessed simultaneously by N different processors through the crossbar. In order to make the best possible use of such a design, all instructions to be executed by one processor are kept in one memory module. Thus, a given processor accesses a given memory block for as long a time as possible and the concurrency of memory accesses can be maintained longer. This mode of operation requires the banked memory architecture. If an interleaved memory architecture is used, consecutive addresses lie in different memory modules. Thus, the instructions corresponding to a task would be spread over several memory modules. If two tasks require the same code segment, it is possible to allow simultaneous access to the code segment as long as one task starts slightly (at least one instruction cycle time) earlier than the other. Thus, processors accessing the code march one behind the other spreading the memory access to different modules and minimizing contention.

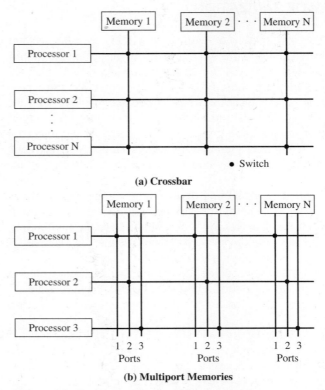

Figure 6.3 Processor-Memory Interconnection

Figure 6.3(b) shows the use of multiport memories. Here each memory module is a three-port memory device. All three ports can be active simultaneously, reading and writing data to and from the memory block. The only restriction is that only one port can write data into a memory location. If two or more ports try to access the same location for writing, only the highest priority port will succeed. Thus, multiport memories have contention resolution logic built into them and provide for concurrent access at the expense of complex hardware. Large multiport memories are still expensive because of their hardware complexity.

The architecture of Figure 6.2(c) depicts the second method for increasing memory bandwidth. Here the cache memory is a high-speed buffer memory that is placed in proximity to the processor (i.e., local memory). Anytime the processor wants to access something from the memory, it first checks its cache memory. If the required data is found there (i.e., a cache hit), it need not access the main (shared) memory, which is usually 4 to 20 times slower. The success of this strategy depends on how well the application can be partitioned such that a processor accesses its private memory for as long as possible (i.e., high cache hit ratio) and rarely accesses the shared memory. This also requires that the interprocessor communication be minimized.

6.2.1 Cache Coherence

Consider the multiprocessor system of Figure 6.2(c) in which each processor has a local (private) memory. The local memory can be viewed as a cache. As the computation proceeds, each processor updates its cache. But updates to a private cache are not visible to other processors. Thus, if one processor updates its cache entry corresponding to a shared data item, the other caches containing that data item will not be updated, and hence, the corresponding processors operate with stale data. This problem wherein the value of a data item is not consistent throughout the memory system is known as **cache incoherency.** Hardware and software schemes should then be applied to ensure that all processors see the most recent value of the data item all the time. This process makes the caches coherent.

Two popular mechanisms for updating cache entries are **write-through** and **write-back.** In write-through, a processor updating the cache also simultaneously updates the corresponding entry in the main memory. In write-back, an updated cache-block is written back to the main memory just before that block is replaced in the cache.

The write-back mechanism clearly does not solve the problem of cache incoherency in a multiprocessor system. Write-through keeps the data coherent in a single processor environment. But consider a multiprocessor system in which processors 1 and 2 both load block A from the main memory into their caches. Suppose processor 1 makes some changes to this block in its cache and writes-through to the main memory. Processor 2 will still see stale data in its cache because it was not updated. Two possible solutions are: (1) Update all caches that contain the shared data when the write-through takes place. Such a write-through will create an enormous overhead on the memory system. (2) Invalidate the corresponding entry in other processor caches when a write-through occurs. This forces the other processors to copy the updated data into their caches when needed later.

Several cache coherency schemes have evolved over the years:

1. The least complex scheme for achieving cache coherency is not to use private caches. In Figure 6.4, the cache is associated with the shared memory system rather than with each processor. Any memory write by a processor will update the common cache (if it is present in the cache) and will be seen by other processors. This is a simple solution but has the major disad-

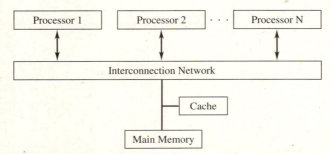

Figure 6.4 System with Only One Cache Associated with the Main (Shared) Memory

vantage of high cache contention because all the processors require access to the common cache.

2. Another simple solution is to stay with the private cache architecture of Figure 6.4, but to cache only nonshared data items. Shared data items are tagged as noncached and stored only in the common memory. The advantage of this method is that each processor now has its own private cache for nonshared data, thus providing a higher bandwidth. One disadvantage of this scheme is that the programmer and/or compiler has to tag data items as cached or noncached. It is preferable to have cache coherency schemes that are transparent to the user. Furthermore, more access to shared items could result in high contention.

3. **Cache flushing** is a modification of the previous scheme in which the shared data are allowed to be cached only when it is known that only one processor will be accessing the data. After the shared data in the cache are accessed and the processor is through using them, it issues a flush-cache instruction that causes all the modified data in the cache to be written back to the main memory and the corresponding cache locations to be invalidated. This scheme has the advantage of allowing shared areas to be cached, but it has the disadvantage of the extra time consumption for the flush-cache instruction. It also requires program code modification to flush the cache.

4. The above coherency schemes either eliminate private caches, limit what may be cached, or require programmer's intervention. A caching scheme that avoids these problems is **bus watching** or **bus snooping.** Bus-snooping schemes incorporate hardware that monitors the shared bus for data LOAD and STORE into each processor's cache controller as shown in Figure 6.5. The snoopy cache controller controls the status of data contained within its cache based on the LOAD and STORE seen on the bus.

If the caches in this architecture are write-through, then every STORE to cache is written through simultaneously to the main memory. In this case, the snoopy controller sees all STOREs and takes actions based on them. Typically, if a STORE is made to a locally cached block and the block is also cached in one or more remote caches, the snoopy controllers in

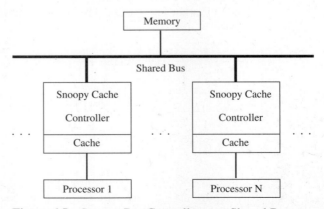

Figure 6.5 Snoopy Bus Controller on a Shared Bus

remote caches will either update or invalidate the blocks in their caches. The choice of updating or invalidating remote caches will have its effect on the performance. The primary difference is the time involved to update cache entries versus merely changing the status of a remotely cached block. Second, as the number of processors increases, the shared bus may become saturated. Note that for every STORE main memory must be accessed and for every STORE hit additional bus overhead is generated. LOADs are performed with no additional overhead.

5. A solution more appropriate for bus organized multiprocessor systems has been proposed by Goodman (1983). In this scheme, an invalidate request is broadcast only when a block is written in cache for the first time. The updated block is simultaneously written through to the main memory. Only if a block in cache is written to more than once, is it necessary to write it back before replacing it. Thus, the first STORE causes a write-through to the main memory and it also invalidates the remotely cached copies of that data. Subsequent STOREs do not get written to the main memory, and because all other cache copies are marked invalid, copies to other caches are not required. When any processor executes a LOAD for this data, the cache controller locates the unit (main memory or cache) that has a valid copy of the data. If the data is in a block marked dirty, then the cache supplies the data and writes the block to the memory. This technique is called **write-once.**

In a write-back cache scheme, because a modified cache block is loaded to the main memory only when that block is to be replaced, the bandwidth on the shared bus is conserved. Thus, this scheme is generally faster than write-through. But this added throughput is at the cost of a more complex bus-watching mechanism. In addition to the cache controller watching a bus, it must also maintain ownership information for each cached block, allowing only one copy of the cached block at a time to be writable. This type of protocol is called an **ownership protocol.**

An ownership protocol works, in general, as follows. Each block of data has one owner. If main memory or a cache owns a block, all other copies of that block are read-only (RO). When a processor needs to write to an RO block, a broadcast to the main memory and all caches is made in an attempt to find any modified copies. If a modified copy exists in another cache, it is written to main memory, copied to the cache requesting read-write privileges, and then the privileges are granted to the requesting cache.

This section has addressed the most primitive cache coherency schemes. Cache coherence has been an active area of research and has resulted in several other schemes. Refer to Gallant (1991); Agarwal et al, (1988); and Eggers (1989) for further details.

6.3 INTERCONNECTION NETWORKS (FENG, 1981)

The interconnection network is an important component of an MIMD system. The ease and speed of processor-to-processor and processor-to-memory communication is dependent on the interconnection network design. A system can use either a static or a dynamic network, the choice depending on the dataflow and program characteristics of the application. The design, structure, advantages, and disadvantages of a number of interconnection networks were described in Chapter 5. This section extends that description to MIMD systems.

In a shared memory MIMD system, the data exchange between the processors is through the shared memory. Hence an efficient memory-to-processor interconnection network is a must. This network interconnects the *nodes* in the system, where a node is either a processor or a memory block. A processor-to-processor interconnection network is also present in these systems. This network (more commonly called a synchronization network) provides for one processor to interrupt the other to inform that the shared data are available in the memory.

In a message-passing MIMD system, the interconnection network provides for the efficient transmission of messages between the nodes. Here a *node* is typically a complete computer system consisting of a processor, memory, and I/O devices.

The most common interconnection structures used in MIMD systems are:

1. bus,
2. loop or ring,
3. mesh,
4. hypercube,
5. crossbar, and
6. multistage switching networks.

The following table lists representative MIMD systems and their interconnection networks.

Interconnection network	Example systems
Bus	Carnegie Mellon University Cm* Sequent Symmetry and Balance
Crossbar	Alliant FX/8
Multistage	Carnegie Mellon University C. mmp BBN Butterfly IBM GF-11 and RP3
Hypercube	Intel iPSC nCUBE systems
Three-Dimensional Torus	Cray Research Inc. T3D
Tree	Columbia University DADO and NON-VON Thinking Machines' CM-5

Details of loop, mesh, hypercube, and crossbar networks were provided in Chapter 5 as applied to SIMD systems. These networks are also used in MIMD system design, except that the communication occurs in an asynchronous manner, rather than in the synchronous communication mode of SIMD systems. The rest of this section highlights the characteristics of these networks as applied to MIMD systems and covers bus and multistage switching networks in detail.

6.3 INTERCONNECTION NETWORKS (FENG, 1981)

6.3.1 Bus Network

Bus networks are simple to build and provide the least cost among the three types of dynamic networks discussed in Chapter 5. They also offer the lowest performance. The bandwidth of the bus is defined as the product of its clock frequency and the width of the data path. The bus bandwidth must be large enough to accomodate the communication needs of all the nodes connected to it. Because the bandwidth available on the network for each node decreases as the number of nodes in the network increases, bus networks are suitable for interconnecting a small number of nodes.

The bus bandwidth can be increased by increasing the clock frequency. But technological advances that make higher bus clock rates possible also provide faster processors. Hence, the ratio of processor speed to bus bandwidth is likely to remain the same, thus limiting the number of processors that can be connected to a single bus structure.

The length of the bus also affects the bus bandwidth because the physical parameters, such as capacitance, inductance, and signal degradation, are proportional to the length of wires. Also, the capacitive and inductive effects grow with the bus frequency, thus limiting the bandwidth.

Figure 6.6 shows a shared memory MIMD system. The global memory is connected to a bus to which several nodes are connected. Each node consists of a processor, its local memory, cache, and I/O devices. In the absence of cache and local memories, all nodes try to access the shared memory through the single bus. For such a structure to provide maximum performance, both the shared bus and the shared memory should have high enough bandwidths. These bottlenecks can be reduced if the application is partitioned such that a majority of memory references by a processor are to its local memory and cache blocks, thus reducing the traffic on the common (shared) bus and the shared memory. Of course, the presence of multiple caches in the system brings in the problem of cache coherency.

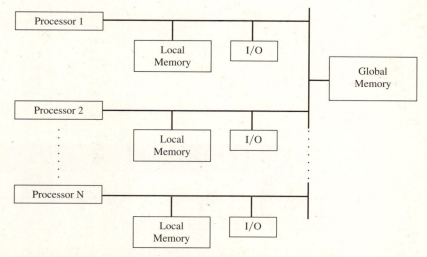

Figure 6.6 Shared-Memory, Shared-Bus MIMD Architecture

If we use a multiport memory system for the shared memory, then a multiple bus interconnection structure, as shown in Figure 6.3(b), can be used with each port of the memory connected to a bus. This structure reduces the number of processors on each bus.

Another alternative is a **bus window** scheme shown in Figure 6.7(a). Here a set of processors is connected to a bus with a switch (i.e., a bus window) and all such buses are connected to form the overall system. The message transmission characteristics are identical to those of a global bus, except that multiple bus segments are available. Messages can be retransmitted over the paths on which they were received or on other paths.

Figure 6.7(b) shows a **fat tree** network that is gaining popularity. Here communication links are fatter (i.e., have higher bandwidth) when they interconnect more nodes. Note that in practice, applications are partitioned such that the processes in the same cluster communicate with each other more often than with those in other clusters. As such, the links near the root of the tree must be thinner compared to the ones near the leaves. Thinking Machines Corporation's CM-5 uses the fat tree interconnection network.

Several standard bus configurations (Multibus, VME Bus, etc.) have evolved over the years. They offer support (in terms of data, address, and control signals) for multiprocessor system design.

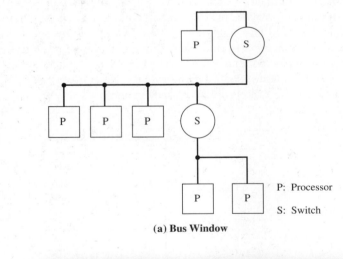

(a) Bus Window

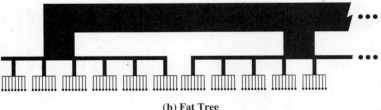

(b) Fat Tree

Figure 6.7 Interconnection Structures

6.3.2 Loop or Ring Network

The ring network is suitable for message-passing MIMD systems. The nodes are interconnected by a ring as in Figure 5.10(b) with a point-to-point interconnection between the nodes. The ring could be either unidirectional or bidirectional. In order to transmit a message, the sender places the message on the ring. Each node in turn examines the message header and buffers the message if it is the designated destination. The message eventually reaches the sender, which removes it from the ring.

One popular protocol used in rings is the **token ring** (IEEE 802.5) standard. A token (which is a unique bit pattern) circulates over the ring. When a node wants to transmit a message, it accepts the token (i.e., prevents it from moving to the next node) and places its message on the ring. Once the message is accepted by the receiver and reaches the sender, the sender removes the message and places the token on the ring. Thus, a node can be a transmitter only when it has the token.

Because the interconnections in the ring are point-to-point, the physical parameters can be controlled more readily, unlike bus interconnections especially when very high bandwidths are needed.

One disadvantage of the token ring is that each node adds a 1-bit delay to the message transmission. Thus, the delay increases as the number of nodes in the system increases. If the network is viewed as a pipeline with a long delay, the bandwidth of the network can be effectively utilized. To accommodate this mode of operation, the nodes usually overlap their computations with the message transmission.

One other way to increase the transmission rate is to provide for the transmission of a new message as soon as the current message is received by the destination node, rather than waiting until the message reaches the sender where it is removed.

6.3.3 Mesh Network

Mesh networks are ideal for applications with high near-neighbor interactions. If the application requires a large number of global interactions, the efficiency of the computation goes down because the global communications require multiple hops through the network. One way to improve the performance is to augment the mesh network with another global network. MasPar architectures (discussed in Chapter 5) and Intel iPSC architectures utilize such global interconnects.

6.3.4 Hypercube Network

One advantage of the hypercube network is that routing is straightforward and the network provides multiple paths for message transmission from each node. Also, the network can be partitioned into hypercubes of lower dimensions; hence, multiple applications utilizing smaller networks can be simultaneously implemented. For instance, a 4-dimensional hypercube with 16 processing nodes can be used as two 3-dimensional hypercubes, four 2-dimensional hypercubes, and so on.

One disadvantage of the hypercube is its scalability because the number of nodes must be increased by powers of two. That is, to increase the number of nodes from 32 to 33, the network needs to be expanded from a 5-dimensional to a 6-dimensional network consisting of 64 nodes. In fact, the Intel Touchstone project has switched over to mesh networks from hypercubes due to this scalability issue.

6.3.5 Crossbar Network

The crossbar network (Figure 5.14) offers multiple simultaneous communications with the least amount of contention but at a high hardware complexity. The number of memory blocks in the system is at least equal to the number of processors. Each processor-to-memory path has just one crosspoint delay.

The hardware complexity and the cost of the crossbar are proportional to the number of crosspoints. Because there are N^2 crosspoints in an $(N \times N)$ crossbar, the crossbar becomes expensive for large values of N.

6.3.6 Multistage Networks

Multistage switching networks offer a cost/performance compromise between the two extremes of bus and crossbar networks. A large number of multistage networks have been proposed over the past few years. Some examples are the Omega, Baseline, Banyan, and Benes networks. These networks differ in their topology, operating mode, control strategy, and type of switches used. They are capable of connecting any source (input) node to any destination (output) node, but they differ in the number of different N-to-N interconnection patterns they can achieve. Here, N is the number of nodes in the system.

These networks are typically composed of 2-input, 2-output switches (as shown in Figure 6.8) arranged in $\log_2 N$ stages. Thus, the cost of the network is of the order of $N \log_2 N$ compared to N^2 of the crossbar. Communication paths between nodes in these networks are of equal length (i.e., $\log_2 N$). In general, the latency is thus $\log_2 N$ times that of a crossbar. In practice, large crossbars have longer cycle times compared to those of the small switches used in multistage networks.

The majority of multistage networks are based on the perfect shuffle interconnection scheme described in Chapter 5. Two popular networks in this class are the Omega and Benes networks.

OMEGA NETWORK (ALMASI AND GOTTLIEB, 1989)
The Omega network is the simplest of the multistage networks. An N-input, N-output Omega interconnection topology is shown in Figure 6.9. It consists of $\log_2 N$ stages. The perfect shuffle interconnection is used between the stages. Each stage contains $N/2$ 2-input, 2-output switches. These switches can perform the four functions shown in Figure 6.8.

The network employs the packet switching mode of communication where each packet is composed of data and the destination address. The address is read at each switch, and the packet is forwarded to the next switch until it arrives at the destination node. The routing algorithm follows a simple scheme. Starting from the source, each switch examines the leading bit of the destination address and removes that bit. If the bit is 1, then the message exits the switch from the lower port, otherwise from the upper port.

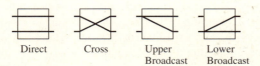

Figure 6.8 2×2 Crossbar

6.3 INTERCONNECTION NETWORKS (FENG, 1981)

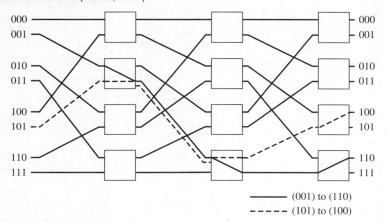

Figure 6.9 Omega Network

Figure 6.9 shows an example in which the message is sent from node (001) to node (110). Because the first bit of the destination address is 1, the switch in the first stage routes the packet to its lower port. Similarly, the switch in the second stage also routes it to its lower port because the second bit of the address is also 1. The switch in the third stage routes it to its upper port because the third bit of the address is 0. The path is shown as a solid line in the figure.

The above routing algorithm implies a distributed control strategy because the control function is distributed among the switches. An alternative control strategy would be a centralized control in which the controller sends control signals to each switch based on the routing required. It may operate either on a stage-by-stage basis starting from the first to the last, or it may reset the whole network each time depending on the communication requirements.

Figure 6.9 also shows (in dotted lines) the path from node (101) to node (100). Note that the link between stages 1 and 2 is common to both the paths shown in the figure. Thus, if nodes (001) and (101) send their packets simultaneously to the corresponding destination nodes, one of the packets is blocked until the common link is free. Hence, this network is called a *blocking* network.

Note that there is only one unique path in this network from each input node to an output node. This is a disadvantage because the message transmission gets blocked even if one link in the path is part of the path for another transmission in progress. One way to reduce the delays due to blocking is to provide buffers in switching elements so that the packets can be retained locally until the blocked links are free. The switches can also be designed to combine messages bound for the same destination. Recall that a crossbar is a nonblocking network, but it is much more expensive than an Omega network.

BENES NETWORK (ALMASI AND GOTTLIEB, 1989)

Unlike the Omega network, which has a single unique path between a source and a destination node, a Benes network provides multiple paths between the source and the destination nodes. Figure 6.10 shows the 8 × 8 Benes network. Note that the number of stages has increased to five and each stage contains four 2-input, 2-output switches.

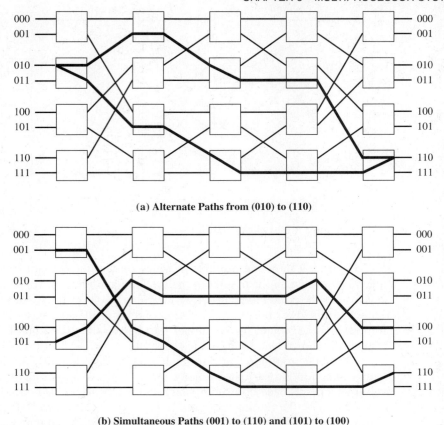

Figure 6.10 8 × 8 Benes Network

The paths available for packet transmission from node (010) to node (110) are shown in (a). The two blocking connections in the Omega network of Figure 6.9 can be made simultaneously in this network as shown in (b).

The routing algorithm for the Benes network is not as simple as that for the Omega network. Each path needs to be determined independently before the transmission begins. When multiple simultaneous transmissions are required, the network can achieve most of the permutations if all the connections required are known before the routing computation begins. If all the desired connections are not known at the beginning, the network rearranges some routings made earlier to accommodate new requests. Hence, it is called a *rearrangeble* network.

The Benes network offers the advantages of reduced blocking and increased bandwidth over the Omega network, but it requires more complex hardware and increases the network latency because of the increased number of stages. It is suitable for circuit-switched environments because the routing computations take a considerable amount of time. A Benes network is used by the IBM GF-11 to interconnect 576 processors. Each switch in this network is a 24 × 24 crossbar.

The progress in hardware technology has resulted in the availability of fast processors and memory devices, two components of an MIMD system. Standard bus systems, such as Multibus and VME Bus, allow the implementation of bus-based MIMD systems as mentioned earlier. Although hardware modules to implement other interconnection structures (loop, crossbar, etc.) are now appearing off-the-shelf, the design and implementation of an appropriate interconnection structure is still the crucial and expensive part of the MIMD design.

6.4 OPERATING SYSTEM CONSIDERATIONS

In an MIMD system, several processors are active simultaneously. Each active processor is associated with one or more memory blocks depending on data and program characteristics. The I/O devices are either dedicated to individual processors or are shared by all the processors. The overall working of the system is coordinated by a multiprocessor operating system whose functions are similar to those of an SISD operating system, except for a much higher complexity. The major functions of the multiprocessor operating system are:

1. Keeping track of the status of all the resources (processors, memories, switches, and I/O devices) at all times.
2. Assigning tasks to processors in a justifiable manner (i.e., to maximize processor utilization).
3. Spawning or creating new processes such that they can be executed in parallel or independent of each other.
4. Collecting their individual results when all the spawned processes are completed, and passing them to other processes as required.

EXAMPLE 6.3

Consider, for example, the element-by-element addition of two vectors A and B to create vector C. That is,

$$c_i = a_i + b_i \quad \text{for } i = 1 \text{ to } n. \tag{6.1}$$

It is clear that the computation consists of n additions that can be executed independently of each other. Thus, an MIMD with n processors can do this computation in one addition time. If the number of processors m is less than n, the first m tasks are allocated to the available processors and the remaining tasks are held in a queue. When a processor completes the execution of the task allocated to it, a new task (from the queue) is allocated to it. This mode of operation continues until all the tasks are completed, as represented by the following algorithm:

1. /* Spawn n − 1 processes each with a distinct process identification number k. Each spawned process starts at 'label' */
```
for k = 1 to n − 1
FORK label(k);
```

2. /*The process that executed FORK is assigned k = n. This is the only process that reaches here, the other spawned processes jump directly to 'label' */

   `k = n;`

3. /* add k^{th} element of each vector; n different processes perform this operation, not necessarily in parallel */

   `label: c[k] = a[k] + b[k];`

4. /* terminate the n processes created by FORK; only 1 process continues after this point */

   `JOIN n;`

The new aspects of this algorithm are the FORK and JOIN constructs. They are two of the typical commands to any multiprocessing operating system used to create and synchronize tasks (processes). The FORK command requests the operating system to create a new process with a distinct process identification number (k in this example). The program segment corresponding to the new process starts at the statement marked *label*.

Note that initially the entire algorithm above constitutes one process. It is first allocated to one of the free processors in the system. This processor through the execution of the FORK-loop (step 1) requests the operating system to create $(n-1)$ tasks after which it continues with step 2. Thus, after the execution of step 2, there are n processes in all waiting to be executed. The process with $k = n$ continues on the processor that is already active (i.e., the processor that spawned the other processes). The remaining $n-1$ processes created by the operating system enter a process queue. The processes waiting in the queue are allocated processors as processors become available.

In this example, the kth process adds k^{th} elements of A and B creating the kth element of C. The program segment corresponding to each process ends with the JOIN statement. The JOIN command can be viewed as the inverse of the FORK command. It has a counter associated with it that starts off at 0. A processor executing the JOIN increments the counter by 1 and compares it to n. If the value of the counter is not equal to n, the processor cannot execute any further, and hence it terminates the process and returns to the available pool of processors for subsequent allocation of tasks. If the value of the counter is n, the process, unlike the others that were terminated, continues execution beyond the JOIN command. Thus, JOIN ensures that the n processes spawned earlier have been completed before proceeding further in the program.

Several aspects of the above algorithm are worth noting.

1. This algorithm does not use the number of processors m as a parameter. As such, it works on MIMD systems with any number of processors. The overall execution time depends on the number of processors available.

6.4 OPERATING SYSTEM CONSIDERATIONS

2. Operating system functions of creating and queuing tasks, allocating them to processors, and so on are done by another processor (or a process) that is not visible in the above discussion.
3. The procedure for creating processes requires $O(N)$ time. This time can be reduced to $O(\log_2 N)$ by a more complex algorithm that makes each new process perform fork, thus executing more than one fork simultaneously.
4. Step 1 of the algorithm was executed only $n-1$ times, thus the nth process was not specifically created by a FORK but was given to the processor that was active already. Alternatively, the FORK loop could have been executed n times. Then the processor executing the loop must have been deallocated and brought to the pool of available processors. A new process then could have been allocated to it. Thus, the above procedure eliminates the overhead of deallocation and allocation of one process to a processor. Typically, creation and allocation of tasks results in a considerable overhead requiring execution of about 50 to 500 instructions.
5. Each process in this example performs an addition and hence is equivalent to three instructions (Load A, Add B, Store C). Thus, the process creation and allocation overhead mentioned above is of the order of 10 to 100 times the useful work performed by the process. As such, the above computation would be more efficient on an SISD rather than an MIMD. But the example serves the purpose of illustrating the operation of an MIMD system.

EXAMPLE 6.4

As another example, the implementation of matrix multiplication algorithm on MIMD is shown below.

```
/* Input: 2 N X N matrices A and B */
/* Output: Product matrix C */
        for k = 1 to n - 1    /*spawn n - 1 processes    */
          FORK label(k);
        endfor;
        k = n;    /*the nth process    */
/* n different processes with distinct process ID numbers
reach this point */
label:   for i = 1 to n
         c[i, k] = 0;
         for j = 1 to n
            c[i, k] = c[i, k] + a[i, j] * b[j, k];
         endfor;
         endfor;
         JOIN n; /* terminate the N processes and gather
                            results    */
```

Fig. 6.11 shows how this algorithm is executed on an MIMD. Here matrices A and B are assumed to be of the order 5×5 and the MIMD has 4 processors. The task is first allocated to processor 2, which executes the FORK loop to spawn other

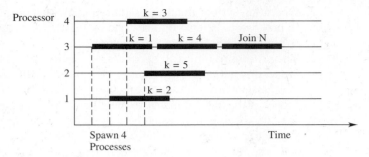

Figure 6.11 Execution-Time Characteristics

processes, while other processors are idle. The first process (corresponding to $k = 1$) is allocated to processor 3; the second ($k = 2$), to processor 1; and the third ($k = 3$), to processor 4. After spawning the fourth process ($k = 4$), processor 2 continues to execute the process $k = 5$ while process $k = 4$ is placed in the queue. Processor 3 completes the task ($k = 1$) first allocated to it. Because the other processes have not reached the JOIN yet, processor 3 cannot continue and hence joins the available processor pool. Process $k = 4$ waiting in the queue is then allocated to it. Meanwhile processors 1, 2, and 4 complete their tasks and execute the JOIN. Processor 3 is the last to execute JOIN (i.e., when the JOIN counter reaches 5) and thus continues execution beyond the JOIN instruction.

Again it is assumed that the operating system functions are performed by a fifth processor not visible in the above description. Further details on fork and join constructs are provided later in this chapter.

In the above example, a task consists of the code segment starting at label and ending at JOIN. For this task to execute independently of other tasks, the data required by it (matrix A and the kth column of matrix B) should be available for its exclusive use. That means, the code segment should be duplicated for each task and a corresponding number of copies of matrix A should be made. This duplication increases the memory requirements tremendously and hence is impractical for large values of n. One solution would be to organize the memory in an interleaved fashion and let all the tasks share the single copy of the code segment and data segment corresponding to the A matrix although in a delayed manner (i.e., each task is started slightly later than the previous one so that the memory references are distributed to several physical memory modules). Of course, this does not guarantee a contention-free operation always although it minimizes the memory contention.

6.4.1 Synchronization Mechanisms

There is no explicit interprocess communication in the above example. In practice, the various processes in the multiprocessor system need to communicate with each other. Because the processes executing on various processors are independent of each other and the relative speeds of execution of these processes cannot be easily estimated, a well-defined synchronization between processes is needed for the communication

6.4 OPERATING SYSTEM CONSIDERATIONS

(and hence the results of computation) to be correct. That is, processes in an MIMD operate in a **cooperative** manner and a **sequence control** mechanism is needed to ensure the ordering of operations. Processes also **compete** with each other to gain **access** to shared data items (and other resources). An **access control** mechanism is needed to maintain orderly access. This section describes the most primitive synchronization techniques used for access and sequence control.

EXAMPLE 6.5

Consider two processes, $P1$ and $P2$, to be executed on two different processors. Let S be a shared variable (location) in the memory. The sequence of instructions in the two processes is as follows:

```
P1:  1. MOV Reg1,[S]    /* The first operand is the
                           destination */
     2. INC Reg1        /* Increment Reg1 */
     3. MOV [S],Reg1

P2:  1'. MOV Reg2,[S]
     2'. ADD Reg2,#2    /* Add 2 to Reg2 */
     3'. MOV [S],Reg2
```

The only thing we can be sure of as far as the order of execution of these instructions is concerned is that instruction $2(2')$ is executed after instruction $1(1')$ and instruction $3(3')$ is executed after instructions $1(1')$ and $2(2')$. Thus, the following three cases for the actual order of execution are possible:

1. 1 2 3 1'2'3' or 1'2'3'1 2 3 : location S finally has the value 3 in it. (Assuming $S = 0$, initially.)
2. 1 1'2 2'3 3' : location S finally has value 2 in it.
3. 1 1'2'2 3'3 : location S finally has value 1 in it.

The desired answer is attained only in the first case and that is possible only when process $P1$ is executed in its entirety before process $P2$ or vice versa. That is, $P1$ and $P2$ need to execute in a **mutually exclusive** manner. The segments of code that are to be executed in a mutually exclusive manner are called **critical sections.** Thus, in $P1$ and $P2$ of this example, the critical section is the complete code corresponding to each process.

EXAMPLE 6.6

As another example consider the code shown in Figure 6.12 to compute the sum of all the elements of an n-element array A. Here, each of the n processes spawned by the fork loop adds an element of A to the shared variable SUM. Obviously, only one process should be updating SUM at a given time. Imagine that process 1 reads the value of SUM and has not yet stored the updated value. Meanwhile if process 2 reads SUM and updates are done by process 1 followed by process 2, the resulting SUM would be erroneous. To obtain the correct value of SUM, we should make sure that,

```
            SUM = 0;
            for k = 1 to n - 1     /*spawn n - 1 processes    */
                FORK label (k);
            end for;
            k = n;                  /*the nth process          */
            /*n different processes with distinct process id
                       numbers reach this point                */
   label: LOCK (flag);
          SUM = SUM + A(k);
          UNLOCK (flag);
          JOIN n;    /*terminate the N process and gather
                              results   /*
```

Figure 6.12 Synchronization Using LOCK/UNLOCK

once process 1 reads SUM, no other process can access SUM until process 1 writes the updated value. This is the mutual exclusion of processes. The mutual exclusion is accomplished by LOCK and UNLOCK constructs. This pair of constructs has a flag associated with it. When a process executes LOCK, it checks the value of the flag. If the flag is ON, it implies that some other process has accessed SUM; hence, the process waits until the flag is OFF. If the flag is not ON, the process sets it ON and gains access to SUM, updates it, and then executes the UNLOCK, which clears the flag. Thus, the LOCK/UNLOCK brings about the synchronization of the processes.

Note that during the LOCK operation, the functions of fetching the flag, checking its value, and updating it must all be done in an **indivisible** manner. That is, no other process should have access to the flag until these operations are complete. Such indivisible operation is brought about by a hardware primitive known as TEST_AND_SET.

TEST_AND_SET
The use of the TEST_AND_SET primitive is shown in Figure 6.13. Here K is a shared memory variable that can have a value of either 0 or 1. If it is 0, the TEST_AND_SET returns a 0 and sets K to 1. The process enters its critical section. If K is 1, TEST_AND_SET returns 1, thus locking the process from entering the critical section. When the process is through executing its critical section, it resets K to 0, thus allowing a waiting process access into its critical section.

Note that in Figure 6.13 the critical section is not part of the while loop. The range of the while loop is a single statement (terminated by ";"). The while loop makes the process wait until K goes to 0, to enter the critical section. There are two modes of implementing the wait: busy waiting (or spin lock) and task switching. In the first mode, the process stays active and repeatedly checks the value of K until it is zero. Thus, if several processes are busy waiting, they keep the corresponding processors busy but no useful work gets done. In the second mode, the blocked process is enqueued and the processor is switched to a new task. Although this mode allows better utilization of processors, the task-switching overhead is usually high unless special hardware support is provided.

6.4 OPERATING SYSTEM CONSIDERATIONS

```
P1: while not (TEST_AND_SET(k));
```
    critical section of P1;
```
    k = 0;
P2: While not (TEST_AND_SET(k));
```
    critical section of P2;
```
    k = 0;
/*      The body of TEST_AND_SET procedure */
        TEST_AND_SET
        {
            temp = k;
            k = 1;
            return (temp);
        }
```

Figure 6.13 Use of TEST_AND_SET

Note that several processes could be performing the test-and-set operation simultaneously, thus competing to access the shared resource K. Hence, the process of examining K and setting it must be indivisible in the sense that K cannot be accessed by any other process until the test and set is completed once. TEST_AND_SET is usually an instruction in the instruction set of the processor and is the minimal hardware support needed to build other high-level synchronization primitives.

The TEST_AND_SET effectively **serializes** the two processes so that they execute in a mutually exclusive manner. Once a process is in the critical section, other processes are **blocked** from entering it by the TEST_AND_SET. Thus, the mutual exclusion is brought about by **serializing** the execution of processes and hence affecting the parallelism. Also the blocked processes incur overhead due to busy waiting or task switching.

SEMAPHORES

Dijkstra (1965) introduced the concept of semaphores and defined two high-level synchronization primitives P and V based on the **semaphore** variable S. They are defined below.

P(S) or WAIT(S)
If $S = 0$, the process invoking P is delayed until $S > 0$.
If $S > 0$, $S = S - 1$ and the process invoking P enters the critical section.

V(S) or SIGNAL(S)
$$S = S + 1$$

S is initialized to 1. The testing and decrementing of S in P(S) is indivisible as is the incrementing of S in V(S). Figure 6.14 shows the use of P and V to synchronize processes $P1$ and $P2$ of Figure 6.13.

```
P1: P(S);
    ┌─────────────────┐
    │critical section;│
    └─────────────────┘
    V(S);
P2: P(S);
    ┌─────────────────┐
    │critical section;│
    └─────────────────┘
    V(S);
```

Figure 6.14 Synchronization Using P and V

S is a binary variable in the implementation of P and V above. If S is an integer variable, it is called a counting semaphore. If it is initialized to M, then M processes can be in the critical section at any time.

BARRIER SYNCHRONIZATION

Consider the following subprogram running on an MIMD in a parallel manner:

```
for i = 1 to n
{
    step A[i];
    step B[i];
    step C[i];
}
```

Here *step* refers to a computation that generates the value for the corresponding variable. This subprogram is divided say into n processes with each independent process taking care of what would be one iteration of the for loop in a sequential environment. On account of the nature of MIMD performance, nothing can be predicted about the order of these steps on various processors. The only thing we are sure of is that, for a given value of i (i.e., for a given process), the steps will be in the order A followed by B followed by C. Thus, A[1], A[2], B[1], C[1], B[2], C[2] and A[2], B[2], C[2], A[1], B[1], C[1] are both valid sequences.

Suppose the algorithm requires that the results from steps A and B of all iterations are needed in step C of the iterations. This is possible if, and only if, all the processes execute their steps A and B before any process starts its step C. This is ensured by the inclusion of a barrier command after step B in the algorithm as shown below:

```
for i=1 to n
{
    step A[i];
    step B[i];
    BARRIER;
    step C[i];
}
```

Note that in this method of synchronization, the processes must wait for the slowest process to reach the barrier before continuing. Thus, if the slowest process executes much longer than the others, most of the processors are tied up busy waiting. Also if the number of processes busy waiting is greater than the number of processors available, a **deadlock** occurs. A deadlock occurs when there exists a cycle of precedence such that A is waiting for B, B is waiting for C, and so on, with the last element in the cycle waiting for A. None of the processes can continue to execute unless the deadlock is broken by aborting one or more of them.

FETCH_AND_ADD

FETCH_AND_ADD is similar to TEST_AND_SET in its implementation but is a **nonblocking** synchronization primitive. That is, it allows the operation of several processes in the critical section in a parallel, yet nonconflicting, manner. FETCH_AND_ADD is shown below:

```
FETCH_AND_ADD(S, T)
    {  Temp = S;
       S = S + T;
    }
        Return Temp;
```

Two parameters are passed to FETCH_AND_ADD: S, the shared variable, and T, an integer. If S is initialized to 0 and two processes $P1$ and $P2$ make a call to FETCH_AND_ADD at roughly the same time, the one reaching the FETCH_AND_ADD first receives the original value of S and the second one receives $(S + T)$. The two processes can execute independently further although the updating of S is effectively serialized. In general, the FETCH_AND_ADD gives each contending process a unique number and allows them to execute simultaneously unlike the TEST_AND_SET, which serializes the contending processes.

As another example, the instruction FETCH_AND_ADD (SUM, INCREMENT) provides for the addition of INCREMENT to SUM by several processes simultaneously and results in the correct value of the SUM without the use of LOCK/UNLOCK.

FETCH_AND_ADD is useful for cases in which the same variable is accessed by several contending processes. FETCH_AND_ADD on different variables is done sequentially if those variables reside in the same memory. The implementation cost of FETCH_AND_ADD is high. As such, it is limited to environments in which updates become a bottleneck because tens of processes are contending for access to the shared variable. If only one process requests access to the shared variable at a time, TEST_AND_SET is more economical.

Note that the processes in a message-passing MIMD are automatically synchronized because a message cannot be received before it is sent. Message-processing protocols deal with the problems of missing or overwritten messages and sharing of resources.

This section has described the most primitive synchronizing mechanisms. Refer to Dinning (1989) and Graunke (1990) for further details.

6.4.2 Heavy- and Lightweight Processes

Consider the UNIX operating system in which a new process is created by forking an existing process. When a fork is executed, the running program is interrupted (and usually swapped to disk) and two copies of the program are swapped back into the memory. These two copies are identical in all aspects except that the programmer uses their process ID to determine which process code is executing at that time. A process consists of program code, data, page tables, and file descriptors. The address space of a process consists of three segments: code, data, and stack. Processes do not share addresses and hence are mutually independent. An attempt by one process to access any segment of the other process is trapped as a fatal error. Creation of tasks of this type results in a high overhead; hence, these processes are called **heavyweight** processes. This mode of operation is good when the tasks are heterogeneous and is usually called **multitasking**.

In parallel programming environments, the tasks tend to be homogeneous. They share data segments between them, and the high overhead of task creation is not desirable. For these reasons, extensions to UNIX have created the concept of **lightweight** processes, and this mode of operation is termed **microtasking**.

For example, the Sequent Computer Corporation uses DYNIX, an extension to UNIX on their Balance series of multiprocessors. A process in DYNIX consists of the code, data, and stack segments as in UNIX. In addition, a shared data segment is also created. Subsequent microtasks spawned by the task copy all but the shared data segment into their address spaces. Thus, only one copy of shared data segment exists among all the worker tasks.

This model of execution requires high-level-language primitives to declare data elements as shared or private, and two types of synchronization mechanisms are needed, one for microtasking and the other for multitasking. Some of the DYNIX primitives are listed below:

m_fork: Execute a subprogram in parallel

m_set_procs: Set the number of processes to be created by a subsequent m_fork.

m_kill_procs: Kill child processes.

m_lock, m_unlock: lock and unlock variables of the type slock_t (microtasking).

m_sync: Wait for all microtasks to arrive at the barrier.

m_single: Make the child processes to spin until the parent process has executed the code following m_single call and calls the m_multi.

m_multi: Resume all worker microtasks in parallel.

s_init_lock, s_lock, s_unlock: Initialize, lock and unlock, lock variables of the type slock_t (multitasking).

s_init_barrier: Initialize the barrier.

s_wait_barrier: Wait for all multitasks to arrive.

The following code segment from Kallstrom and Thakkar (1988) illustrates the use of the above primitives. It creates one supervisor and $(n - 1)$ workers where each worker's task is the function work().

6.4 OPERATING SYSTEM CONSIDERATIONS

```
shared int x;
shared struct y_struct {
    int state;
    slock_t lp;         /*primitive lock*/
    } y
/* Supervisor */
main() {
    s_init_lock (&y.lp);      /*initialize lock*/
    m_set_procs(n);           /*initialize n_1 workers*/
    m_fork(work);
    m_kill_procs();           /*done*/
    }
/* Workers */
work() {
    /* Microtask locking */
    m_lock();                 /* Mutual exclusive access to
                                 x */
    x++;
    printf ("Worker");
    m_unlock();               /* End of critical section */
    /* A barrier */
    m_single();               /* Workers wait here */
    printf ("Supervisor")     /* Only Supervisor does this */
    m_multi();                /* Workers resume */
    /* Multitask lock */
    s_lock(&y.lp);            /* lock the struct y */
    y.state = o;
    printf ("Structure");
    s_unlock(&y.lp):          /* Unlock */
}
```

Refer to DYNIX manuals for further details.

6.4.3 Scheduling

Recall that a parallel program is a collection of tasks. These tasks may run serially or in parallel. An **optimal schedule** determines the allocation of tasks to processors of the MIMD system and the execution order of the tasks so as to achieve the shortest execution time. The scheduling problem in general is NP-complete. But several constrained models have evolved over the years, and currently this problem is an active area of research in parallel computing.

Scheduling techniques can be classified into two groups: static and dynamic. In **static** scheduling, each task is allocated to a particular processor based on the analysis of the precedence constraints imposed by the tasks at hand. Each time the task is executed, it is allocated to that predetermined processor. Obviously, this method does not take into consideration the nondeterministic nature of tasks brought about by conditional branches and loops in the program. The target of the conditional branch and the upper bounds of the loops are not known until the program execution begins. Thus, static scheduling will not be optimal.

In **dynamic** scheduling, tasks are allocated to processors based on the execution characteristics. Usually some **load balancing** heuristic is employed in determining optimal allocation. Because the scheduler has only the knowledge of local information about the program at any time, finding the global optimum is difficult. Another disadvantage is the increased overhead because the schedule has to be determined while the tasks are running.

Refer to Adam (1974), Bashir (1983), and El-Rewini (1990) for further details.

6.5 PROGRAMMING

The basic idea behind parallel processing is that a job is divided up and parceled out to multiple processors to form a cooperative effort. This chapter has so far concentrated on how the hardware and operating system software incorporate facilities for parallelism. These facilities can be exploited in full only if there exist techniques for specifying to the hardware what is to be executed in parallel in a given job.

Parallelism refers to the simultaneous execution of tasks, task steps, programs, routines, subroutines, loops, or statements. Five levels of parallelism can be identified:

1. Parallelism at the level of independent tasks and programs—totally different programs run on different processors at any time.
2. Parallelism at the level of task steps and related parts of a program—different parts of the same program are made to execute on different processors.
3. Parallelism at the level of routines and subroutines—a number of different subroutines (programs or functions) of a given program are made to execute on different processors in a parallel manner.
4. Parallel execution of loops—given a loop construct in a program, the iterations of this loop may be executed in parallel on different processors.
5. Parallel execution of statements and instructions—individual statements forming a program are parceled out to different processors to be executed in parallel.

Note that the higher the level, the finer the granularity of the software process. As pointed out by Ghezzi (1985), a parallel program must have the ability to:

1. define the set of subtasks to be executed in parallel (at any of the above five levels);
2. start and stop the execution of subtasks; and
3. coordinate and specify the interaction between subtasks while they are executing.

A sequential program (i.e., a program for an SISD) has four main constructs. For each of these constructs, a corresponding parallel construct can be identified as shown in the following:

6.5 PROGRAMMING

1. Sequential one-line statements are executed one after the other. The corresponding parallel construct is the **parbegin/parend** that brackets a set of statements for concurrent execution as in Concurrent Pascal and Algol 68. The statements occurring between parbegin and parend will not be necessarily executed in the order in which they appear in the program; instead they will be distributed over a number of processors that will execute them independently. Eventually all the results will be collected and passed on to the statement following the parend construct. An example showing the function of the parbegin/parend construct is provided later in this section.
2. In order to make the logical order of execution different from the physical order of the statements in a sequential program, goto (unconditional) and if_then_else (conditional) constructs are used. The analog of these constructs for parallel programs is the **fork/join** pair of statements discussed earlier. An example of a language that uses a variant of fork/join is PL/1.
3. The simple looping construct (for, do) in case of sequential programs is comparable to the **doall** construct for parallel programs, which is used to designate a block of nearly identical statements to be executed in parallel. In the best case, if there are N iterations in a loop, all these N iterations will be allocated to N different processors and executed simultaneously, thus attaining an N-fold speedup.

EXAMPLE 6.7

Consider again the problem of performing the element-by-element addition of two linear arrays, $A[1..N]$ and $B[1..N]$. A for-loop solution for this problem is as follows:

```
for i = 1 to N do
    sum[i] := A[i] + B[i];
endfor
```

This solution is satisfactory for a purely sequential environment. Running this on an MIMD system requires that the N summing tasks are parceled out to as many processors as possible and performed in parallel. This intention is explicitly indicated in the following program segment:

```
forall i = 1 to N do
    sum[i] := A[i] + B[i];
```

The keyword **forall** implies that the N processes are created and distributed among the processors, which execute them in parallel. Considering the best case, N processors get these N processes at a time when all of them are free. Obviously, all the processes will be executed together and the total time taken will be equal to the time taken for one iteration of the sequential for loop, yielding a speedup of N.

4. In sequential programs, subprograms (procedures or functions) can be called more than once by the main module and other modules. Correspondingly, processes, tasks, procedures, and so on can be declared for parallel execution (as in Concurrent Pascal and Ada).

Partitioning an application into subtasks for parallel execution on an MIMD is not trivial. There are efforts to devise compilers that recognize the parallelism in a sequential program and partition it for a particular MIMD architecture although such partitioning is not yet completely automatic and requires the interaction of the application designer with the compiler. There are also efforts to design languages that allow explicit specification of parallel tasks in the application (Perrott, 1987 and Babb, 1988).

It is possible to extend existing sequential languages to accommodate MIMD programming. The additional constructs needed for programming shared-address-space MIMD systems are: the primitives for mutual exclusion and synchronization (described in the previous section); the primitives for creating processes; and the primitives to allocate shared variables. For programming message-passing MIMD systems, the constructs needed are the messages SEND and RECEIVE. The rest of this section provides further details on these parallel program constructs.

6.5.1 Fork and Join

The code segment in Figure 6.15 generalizes the fork/join construct. Here A through F each represent a set of sequential statements in the code. The whole code segment in the figure is the only process to begin with. The first fork instruction, FORK c, spawns a new process, which starts execution from the statement labeled c while the original process continues into B. Similarly, FORK e and FORK f spawn two more new processes.

Each time a process encounters the JOIN m, g instruction, it decrements m by 1 and jumps to label g if m is zero after the decrement operation; the process cannot continue if m is nonzero. The two processes that do this are C and D. After both these

```
    m = 2
    n = 3
    A
    FORK c
    B
    FORK e
    FORK f
    D
    JOIN m,g; /* join 2 processes and goto label g */
g:G
    JOIN n, h; /* join 3 processes and goto label h */
h:H
    quit;
c:C
    JOIN m, g;
e:E
    JOIN n, h;
f:f
    JOIN n, h;
```

Figure 6.15 Generalized Fork/Join Construct

processes execute the JOIN m, g, the value of m reaches zero (because it is initialized to 2), thus joining the two processes to form a single process G. Note that the order in which the JOIN statement is executed does not matter and, in general, cannot be predicted. The first process executing the JOIN is terminated (because all the processes controlled by m have not completed yet), and the second process executing the JOIN continues to G.

Similarly, the three processes D, E, and F will each encounter the JOIN n, h instruction. Each one of these three processes will decrement the counter n (which is initialized to 3) once when it executes the JOIN instruction. Finally, the process that reduces the counter n to zero will continue to H.

It is entirely up to the programmer to ensure that JOIN works in harmony with FORK. As the example shows, JOIN can be used to join processes formed by any FORK. Because FORK can appear in loops and conditional statements, an arbitrary number of parallel processes can be created. Because JOIN can be used to join any of these processes to each other, a powerful mechanism for starting and stopping parallel activities is provided by the fork/join construct. A disadvantage is that there is a high potential that the resulting code may be unstructured, error-prone, and tough to understand.

6.5.2 Parbegin/Parend

The parbegin/parend construct is less powerful but more structured compared to fork/join. It is less powerful because it can only represent properly nested process flow graphs. That is, what parbegins must parend. An example follows:

EXAMPLE 6.8

```
A
parbegin
    C
    begin
        B
        parbegin
            D
            E
            F
        parend
        G
    end
parend
H
```

This code consists of three modules to be executed sequentially: A, the module delimited by (outer) parbegin . . parend, and H. The second module consists of two sequential code modules: C and the module delimited by begin . . end. The latter module, in turn, consists of three modules: B, the module delimited by (inner) parbegin . . . . parend, and G.

> During the execution of this code, processes D, E, and F are assigned to different processors and are executed independently. The parend statement makes sure all the processes that were started separately after the matching parbegin are completed before the next statement G begins. It is the same case with the outer parbegin/parend pair, which ensures that processes C and G end before H is executed.

The significant thing about the parbegin/parend construct is that it identifies candidates for parallel execution so that the compiler can retain this simultaneity in the code. It does not force parallel execution. The degree of parallelism at run time is dependent on the availability of processors at that time.

6.5.3 Doall

Doall and constructs such as forall, pardo, and doacross are like parbegin except that the statements eligible for parallel execution are in a loop. Thus, the statements to be executed simultaneously are identified by an index rather than by writing them out explicitly as is the case with parbegin/parend. Moreover, the number of statements between parbegin and parend is a predetermined, static quantity while the number of loop iterations in case of a doall loop may be computed during run time and is thus a dynamic quantity.

6.5.4 Shared Variables

In shared-address programming, two types of variables are used: **shared** and **private** (or **local**). Typical declaration constructs are:

```
shared float x;
private float z;
```

6.5.5 Send/Receive

The typical format for the SEND construct is:

```
SEND (dest, type, length, flag, message)
```

where dest is the destination node address, type is the type of message, length is the message length, flag is a control parameter indicating the mode of message transmittal, and message is the actual message. There are two modes of message transmittal commonly used: **blocked** and **unblocked.** In the blocked mode, the sender is blocked until either the message received by the destination or a response is received. In the unblocked mode, the sender dispatches the message and continues its processing activity.

The typical format for the RECEIVE construct is:

```
RECEIVE(source, type, length, flag, buf)
```

where source is the identity of the processor from which the message is received, type refers to one of several types of messages that can be received, length is the message length, flag is the blocking/nonblocking mode indicator, and buf is the memory buffer address where the message needs to be stored for further processing.

6.6 PERFORMANCE EVALUATION AND SCALABILITY

As mentioned earlier, the granularity plays an important role in determining the performance of an MIMD system. In a coarse-grained application, the task size is large and thus the run time quantum (R) is quite large compared to the communication overhead (C). That is, the task in itself accomplishes a lot and not much communication is required between the various processes executing on different processors. Thus, the coarse-grained parallelism is characterized by a high R-to-C ratio. On the other hand, a large number of small-sized tasks running on many processors require frequent and maybe long sessions of processor-to-processor communication. Such fine grain parallelism is characterized by a low R-to-C ratio.

The definitions of Section 5.4 for the speedup, the efficiency, and the cost of parallel computer architectures apply to MIMD systems also and are illustrated by the following examples.

EXAMPLE 6.9

Consider again the problem of accumulating N numbers. The execution time on an SISD is of the $O(N)$. On an MIMD with N processors and a ring interconnection network between the processors, the execution requires $(N - 1)$ time units for communication and $(N - 1)$ time units for addition. Thus, the total time required is $2(N - 1)$ or $O(2N)$, and hence, the speedup is 0.5.

If the processors in the MIMD are interconnected by a hypercube network, this computation requires $\log_2 N$ communication steps and $\log_2 N$ additions, resulting in a total run time of $2\log_2 N$. Hence,

$$\text{Speedup } S = N/(2\log_2 N) \text{ or } O(N/\log_2 N)$$
$$\text{Efficiency } E = 1/(2\log_2 N) \text{ or } O(1/\log_2 N), \text{ and}$$
$$\text{Cost} = N \times 2\log_2 N \text{ or } O(N\log_2 N).$$

EXAMPLE 6.10

The problem of accumulating N numbers can be solved in two methods on an MIMD with p processors and a hypercube interconnection network. Here $p < N$ and we assume that N/p is less than or equal to p. In the first method, the p numbers in each block are accumulated in $(2\log_2 p)$. Because there are N/p such blocks, the execution time is $(2N/p \log_2 p)$. The resulting N/p partial sums are then accumulated in $(2\log_2 p)$. Thus, the total run time is $(2N/p \log_2 p + 2\log_2 p)$. In the second method, each of the p blocks of N/p numbers is allocated to a processor. The run time for computing the partial sums is then $O(N/p)$. These partial sums are accumulated using the perfect shuffle network in $(2\log_2 p)$. Thus the total run time is $(N/p + 2\log_2 p)$. The second method offers a better run time than the first.

If N/p is then greater than p in the first method above, further portioning of the computations to fit the p processor structure is needed. Computation of run time for this case is left as an exercise. The run time characteristics for the second method would be the same as above for this case also.

6.6.1 Scalability

As defined earlier, the **scalability** of a parallel system is a measure of its ability to increase speedup as the number of processors increases. A parallel system is **scalable** if its efficiency can be maintained at a fixed value by increasing the number of processors as the **problem size** increases.

As the number of processors in an MIMD system increases, it should be possible to solve larger problems. For a given problem size, the efficiency of the system should be maximized while minimizing the run time. In general, it is possible to increase the number of processors and solve a larger problem (i.e., scale up the problem size). Depending on the problem domain and the parallel system architecture, a variety of constraints may be applicable. In **time-constrained scaling** (Gustafson, 1992), the problem size is scaled up with the increasing number of processors while keeping the run time constant. In **memory-constrained scaling** (Sun and Ni, 1993), an attempt is made to solve the largest problem that can fit in the memory.

Let T_s be the (best possible) run time of a problem on a single processor system, and let T_p be the corresponding (best possible) run time on an MIMD system with p processors. Then the overhead cost T_o is given by:

$$T_o = T_p p - T_s. \tag{6.2}$$

This overhead in MIMD systems is due to the interprocessor communication, load imbalance, and extra computations required due to algorithms used, and so forth. The overhead is also a function of the problem size and the number of processors. From this equation, the parallel run time is:

$$T_p = (T_o + T_s)/p, \tag{6.3}$$

and hence the speedup S is:

$$\begin{aligned}S &= T_s/T_p \\ &= T_s p/(T_o + T_s).\end{aligned} \tag{6.4}$$

The efficiency E is:

$$\begin{aligned}E &= S/p \\ &= T_s/(T_s + T_o) \\ &= 1/(1 + T_o/T_s).\end{aligned} \tag{6.5}$$

As p increases, T_o increases, and if the problem size is kept constant, T_s remains a constant. From equation (6.5), E then decreases. If the problem size is increased while keeping p constant, T_s increases, T_o grows at a smaller rate than the problem size (if the system is scalable), and hence E increases. Thus, E can be maintained at a fixed value for scalable systems by increasing problem size as p increases.

The rate at which the problem size has to grow as p is increased to maintain a fixed E is a characteristic of the application and the system architecture. The system is said to be **highly scalable** if the problem size needs to grow only linearly, as p grows, to maintain a fixed efficiency.

From equation (6.5),
$$T_o/T_s = (1 - E)/E.$$
Hence,
$$T_s = ET_o/(1 - E).$$
For a given value of E, $E/(1 - E)$ is a constant K. Then
$$T_s = KT_o. \tag{6.6}$$

Because T_o is a function of p, the problem size determined by T_s above is also a function of p. Equation (6.6) is called the **isoefficiency function** (Gupta and Kumar, 1993) of the MIMD system. A small isoefficiency function indicates that small increments in problem size are sufficient to maintain efficiency when p is increased. A large isoefficiency function represents a poorly scalable system. If the parallel system is not scalable, the isoefficiency function does not exist.

Several other scalability criteria have been proposed over the years. Refer to Kumar and Gupta (1991); Carmona and Rice (1991); Marinescu and Rice (1991); and Tang and Li (1990) for further details.

6.6.2 Performance Models

Several performance models have been proposed over the years for evaluating MIMD systems. All these models are based on several assumptions that simplify the model. As such, none of the models may be a true representative of a practical MIMD system. Nonetheless, these models are helpful in understanding how MIMD systems behave and how their efficiency can be affected by various parameters. We now briefly describe three models introduced by Indurkhya, Stone, and XiCheng (Indurkhya et al., 1986).

THE BASIC MODEL

Consider a job that has been divided into M tasks that has to execute as efficiently as possible on a multiprocessor with N processors. The assumptions associated with this model are:

1. Each task is equal in size and takes R time units to be executed on a processor.
2. If two tasks on different processors wish to communicate with each other, they do so at a cost of C time units. This is the communication overhead. However, if the two tasks are on the same processor (obviously executed one after the other), the overhead for their communication is zero.

Suppose K_i tasks are assigned to the ith processor in the machine. Here i varies between 1 and N, and K_i varies from 0 to M. Also assume that each processor is free before these tasks are distributed so that all the processors start executing at the same time. In this scenario, the processor that gets the maximum number of tasks will take the longest to finish its run time quantum. In fact, this will be the total run time of the job. Thus, the total run time of the job is $R(\max(K_i))$.

Here K_i tasks on the ith processor need to communicate with the rest of the $(M - K_i)$ tasks on the other processors. Only two tasks can communicate at the same time, and each such communication introduces an overhead of C time units. The total communication time for this job is:

$$(C/2) \sum_{i=1}^{N} (K_i(M - K_i)). \tag{6.7}$$

The total execution time (ET) for this job is thus

$$ET = R(\max(K_i)) + (C/2) \sum_{i=1}^{N} (K_i(M - K_i)) \tag{6.8}$$

Now consider the following scenarios. First, all the tasks are assigned to a single processor. In this case, which is equivalent to a SISD, the first term of equation (6.8) becomes RM because all the M tasks will be executed serially by a single processor. The second term will be zero because all the tasks are executed on a single processor. Thus,

$$ET = RM. \tag{6.9}$$

In the second scenario, we assume that all the tasks are distributed equally among all the processors. Thus, each processor gets M/N tasks, and hence $K_i = M/N$ for all i. Substituting this in equation (6.8):

$$ET = R(M/N) + CM^2/2 - CM^2/2N. \tag{6.10}$$

If we equate the results from equations (6.9) and (6.10), we get a point where the performance of an MIMD with equal task distribution among all the processors is the same as that of an SISD in which a single processor performs all the tasks. This threshold is represented by:

$$R/C = M/2. \tag{6.11}$$

Thus, if the task granularity is above the threshold $M/2$, then an equal distribution of tasks on MIMD systems is the best solution; but if it is below the threshold, then executing the job on a SISD is most efficient, irrespective of the number of processors in the MIMD. This proves that the communication overhead should be kept within a certain limit in order to make parallel execution on an MIMD more beneficial than serial execution on an SISD.

The ratio of the right-hand sides of equations (6.9) and (6.10) gives the so-called speedup of an MIMD as compared to an SISD. Thus,

$$\text{speedup} = RM/(RM/N + CM^2/2 - CM^2/2N). \tag{6.12}$$

6.6 PERFORMANCE EVALUATION AND SCALABILITY

From this equation, it is clear that if N (the number of processors) is large, speedup is a constant R/CM for a given granularity and a given number of tasks. Thus, as N increases, the speedup reaches a saturation. In other words, simply increasing the number of processors to improve the performance of an MIMD is not an intelligent step because after a certain stage the speedup stops increasing while the cost keeps rising.

MODEL WITH LINEAR COMMUNICATION OVERHEAD

In the previous model we considered a case in which each task undergoes a unique communication with each task on other processors. This results in quadratic communication overhead. However, if we assume that each task has to communicate with all other tasks but the information contents are the same for all the other tasks, the communication overhead becomes linear with respect to N because the given task does not have to uniquely call the other tasks one by one. With this model, the cost of an assignment of a job with M tasks to an MIMD with N processors is

$$ET = R(\max(K_i)) + CN. \tag{6.13}$$

Considering an equal distribution of tasks among all the processors, this equation can be written as

$$ET = RM/N + CN. \tag{6.14}$$

Thus, we see that as N increases the second term increases linearly with N while the first decreases with N. Thus, as N initially increases, the execution time decreases until it reaches a minima after which the addition of a processor to the system has a degradable effect rather than a beneficial one. From equation (6.9) the execution time decrease with the addition of a new processor is:

$$\begin{aligned} ET \text{ decrease} &= RM/N + CN - RM/N+1 - C(N+1) \\ &= RM/N(N+1) - C. \end{aligned} \tag{6.15}$$

At the point of minima discussed above, the performance of the system is the best. That is, the right-hand side of the equation (6.10) is zero at such a point. Hence,

$$R/C = N(N + 1)/M,$$

and hence,

$$N \approx \sqrt{(MR/C)}. \tag{6.16}$$

Thus, with this model, the magnitude of parallelism is only the square root of what was anticipated.

MODEL WITH OVERLAPPED COMMUNICATION

In all the models discussed so far, we have considered useful computation and communication overhead as two entities that are exclusive of each other (i.e., they cannot be performed concurrently). This need not be the case in practice. In this model, we assume that the communication time fully overlaps with the useful computation being performed by the other processors.

With this model, the total execution time (ET) will be the greater of the two terms that represent the run time and the communication overhead, respectively. Again with K_i tasks having been allocated to the ith processor, the total run time for this set up will be

$$R1 = R(\max(K_i)).$$

The total overhead due to communication will be, as in the first model,

$$C1 = C/2 \sum_{i=1}^{N}(K_i(M - K_i)).$$

Then

$$ET = \text{Max}(R1, C1). \qquad (6.17)$$

For full utilization of a fully overlapped model, it is desirable that $R1 = C1$. That is, the communication overhead requires the same amount of time as the useful computation. If this is also combined with the condition of equal task distribution among all the processors, we get

$$R1 = RM/N \quad \text{and} \quad C1 = CM^2/2(1 - 1/N)$$

and equating them we get

$$R/C = NM/2, \qquad (6.18)$$

or

$$N = 2R/CM.$$

This equation shows that it is advisable to decrease N as the parallelism (i.e., M) increases. Also because $C1$ grows M times faster than $R1$, it is really important to keep it less than $R1$. If $C1$ is greater than $R1$, the overall execution time becomes solely dependent on the communication overhead.

STOCHASTIC MODEL

In practice all tasks are not of equal length. Then the objective is to scatter all the tasks on the processors such that all the processors are busy for equal periods of time. In the previous models, this objective was fulfilled by assigning an equal number of tasks to all the processors. In the stochastic model, it is clear that equal distribution (numberwise) of tasks will not lead to equal processing times for all the processors. If the workload is uneven, that is an unequal number of tasks are to be assigned to different processors, it may be possible to assign tasks to processors in such a way that overhead is greatly reduced. As is clear from equation (6.8), the communication overhead increases if the distribution of tasks is made more uniform over all the processors. In other words, the more uneven the distribution, the less the communication costs. Moreover, having unequal size tasks favors unequal distribution of tasks so that the average busy time of each processor remains roughly the same.

In summary, the running time of a program diminishes as the number of processors increase, but the overhead cost tends to shoot up with an increasing number of processors. The rate of increase of overhead cost may be much faster than the rate of decrease of the run time. Task granularity also plays a crucial part in determining the efficiency of a given model.

Several other analytical techniques have been used in performance evaluation. The major shortcoming of these techniques is that they do not fully represent the operating scenario of the system, because each technique makes several simplifying assumptions to manage the complexity of the model. Use of benchmarks is considered a more practical method for performance evaluation.

Chapter 1 provides details of representative benchmarks. In 1985, the National Institute for Standards and Technology (NIST) held a workshop on techniques for performance evaluation of parallel architectures, and it has also published a list of benchmarks to include: Linpack, Whetstones, Dhrystones, NAS Kernel, Lawrence Livermore Loops, Fermi, JRR, and Mendez. Levitan (1987) has proposed a suite of synthetic benchmarks for evaluation of interconnection structures. The PERFECT and SLALOM benchmarks are more recent ones. Because the amount of parallelism varies among benchmarks, each benchmark will provide a different performance rating for the same architecture. Also because the ability of an architecture to utilize the parallelism in the benchmark varies, the rating provided by a given benchmark varies across the architectures.

6.7 EXAMPLE SYSTEMS

This section provides a brief description of five commercially available multiprocessor systems: Alliant Computer Systems Corporation's FX series, a shared memory system; Intel Corporation's iPSC and INMOS Limited's Transputer, two message-passing architectures; Thinking Machine Corporation's CM-5, a hybrid SIMD/MIMD system; and Cray Research, Inc.'s T3D, a distributed memory, shared address space MIMD system.

6.7.1 Alliant FX Series

The Alliant FX series consists of a line of systems classified as minisupercomputers, designed for scientific and visualization applications. The application of the FX line ranges from departmental computer servers through mainframe and supercomputer levels. The FX architecture has been designed around the idea that parallelism is the best means by which to attain near supercomputer performance at a reasonable cost. Alliant's architecture is flexible and scalable, and it supports parallel processing at several different levels.

The FX line is flexible in that it supports a wide variety of hardware and software configurations to implement parallel processing, vectorized processing, visualization, and networking. Optional special purpose controllers (such as graphics processors, direct memory access devices, etc.) are available to implement specialized functions more efficiently.

The scalability is brought about by providing for the addition of processors incrementally to an initial configuration without changing any application code. This system growth path allows for a minimal initial cost with the capability of meeting growing demand on the system.

Parallel processing is supported at the instruction level, the loop level, and the task level (Figure 6.16). Instruction level parallelism is implemented through pipeline techniques in the functional units of computational elements (CEs) and the vectorization capabilities of the CEs. Loop level parallelism is attained through grouping the CEs in a dynamic fashion to break up a loop into a variable number of pieces, each of which is executed on an individual processor. Alliant has focused much of its system design around this level of parallelism. The system uses a concurrency control bus to control this level of parallelism and to handle data dependencies that are inherent in program loops. When a loop that has the proper characteristics to allow for multiprocessing is executed, the system is able to identify and use any idle processors through the concurrency control bus. This process can be accomplished in approximately 12 clock cycles. The combination of this fast transition from serial execution to multiprocessing and the dynamic allocation of a variable number of processors at the loop level is one of the exceptional features of this architecture. Task level parallelism is implemented by allowing different job streams to run on different CEs and interactive processors (IP). The CEs are dedicated to doing most of the computational work of a program, including all of the floating-point operations. The IPs perform all the I/O services; most of the operating system functions, such as file system maintenance; and the user interface.

The general structure of the Alliant FX is shown in Figure 6.17. Because it is a shared memory system, the physical memory of the system occupies the central position in the figure. All the memory modules communicate with the outer world through the use of the memory bus. As mentioned earlier, there are two types of processors: CEs and IPs. These processors communicate to the memory through caches via a crossbar network. There are two types of caches in the system (one for each type of processor)—computational processor caches (CPCs) corresponding to the CEs and interactive processor caches (IPCs) corresponding to the IPs.

At the low end of the series is the FX/4, which is built around a maximum of 4 CEs, 1 CPC, up to 6 IPs, up to 2 IPCs, and 128 MB physical memory and which runs 47.2 MFLOPS (64-bit). The FX/40 is one step up in performance from the FX/4. This system is basically the same except that the CEs are replaced with advanced computational elements (ACEs) that provide substantially higher performance. The FX/40 is rated at 94.4 MFLOPS. The FX/8, next in line, offers up to 8 CEs, a

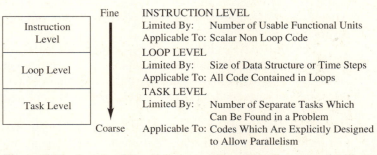

Figure 6.16 Levels of Parallelism on Alliant FX (Courtesy of Alliant Computer Systems Corporation.)

6.7 EXAMPLE SYSTEMS

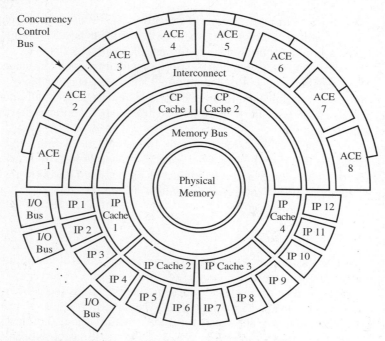

Figure 6.17 Alliant FX System (Courtesy of Alliant Computer Systems Corporation.)

maximum of 2 CPCs, up to 12 IPs, 4 IPCs, and up to 256 MB of physical memory. This configuration can deliver 94.4 MFLOPS peak performance. The FX/80, which has basically the same configuration as the FX/8, except that the CEs are replaced by ACEs, is rated at 188.8 MFLOPS. Two FX/80s can be clustered together to form an FX/82 cluster. This configuration supports shared peripherals and can attain a peak performance rate of 377.6 MFLOPS. The fastest machine in the series is the FX/2800. This system differs from the other systems in that it uses Intel i860 processors as super computational elements (SCEs), as well as for super interactive processors (SIPs). Also the cache configuration has been changed so that all processors use the same cache, and cache capacity is increased to 4MB. Even though there are several differences between the new system and the old systems, the means by which the FX series implements parallelism at all levels has been retained along with the memory system architecture. The FX/2800 can support 14 SCEs and 14 SIPs, which are divided into processor modules of 2 SCEs and 2 SIPs. It has a peak 64-bit performance of 1.12 GFLOPS.

PARALLELISM

The bulk of the computational workload is handled by the CEs, which are fully functional, independent, 64-bit general purpose, microprogrammed computers. Each CE has dedicated hardware to support pipelined instruction execution, pipelined vector processing, pipelined floating-point operations, and concurrent processing control. The instruction pipelining hardware can simultaneously execute up to five instructions in different stages of execution. For vector processing, each CE has eight 32-element vector registers, where an element can be a 32-bit integer or a 32- or 64-bit floating-point number. CEs run in parallel with the IPs.

Instruction level parallelism is exploited by each CE using a five-stage instruction pipeline and multiple functional units. Instruction fetch, address calculations, memory references, integer calculations, and floating-point addition and multiplication can all execute in parallel because each function is performed by a separate hardware unit.

Loop level parallelism occurs frequently in scientific and engineering applications. In this system, loop level parallelism is achieved by distributing loop iterations across a CE-complex for simultaneous execution. The following is an example of how Alliant achieves loop level parallelism. Given the loop:

```
DO I = 0,20
    Loop code
END DO
```

the FX/Fortran compiler inserts concurrency control instructions into the generated assembly code. Initially, code execution is serial. Concurrency begins when the active CE transmits a concurrency start instruction across the concurrency control bus. At this point, each participating CE is given a loop iteration to execute. At the end of a loop iteration, a concurrency repeat instruction is issued to the CE so that it can begin processing another iteration. When all the iterations have been performed, one of the CEs continues serially and the others become idle.

When a CE is detached from a CE-complex, it behaves as a separate processor and is treated as a separate entity by the operating system. In this way, individual tasks can be allocated to dedicated CEs, thereby increasing total system throughput at the individual task level.

MEMORY MANAGEMENT

The hierarchical memory subsystem implemented through different caches that buffer data between the processors and main memory supports the memory bandwidth required (Figure 6.18). This design allows the systems to use more conventional, inexpensive memory, and to still supply the processors with required bandwidth. Cache coherency is maintained throughout the memory system by hardware built into the different caches. This hardware passively listens to the address bus, and if it contains a reference to a block of code that has been requested from memory, it will send its copy to the requesting device (Figure 6.19).

The main memory is comprised of four-way interleaved 32-MB modules that can supply the memory bus with 188 MB/second for read access and 150 MB/second for write access. The memory bus consists of two 72-bit wide data paths, a 28-bit address bus, and a control bus. Data is always transferred in blocks of four 8-byte words with alternating words using alternating data paths. This wide word memory access is implemented by the fact that only the caches and special purpose I/O devices directly access main memory (Figure 6.20).

The Alliant systems use a segmented virtual memory scheme to address memory. The system uses a 4-KB memory page and has a virtual address limit of $2^{32} - 1$.

6.7 EXAMPLE SYSTEMS

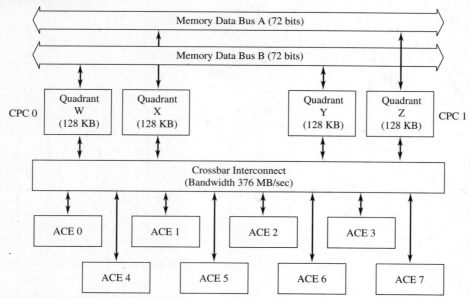

Figure 6.18 Alliant FX Interconnection Structure (Courtesy of Alliant Computer Systems Corporation.)

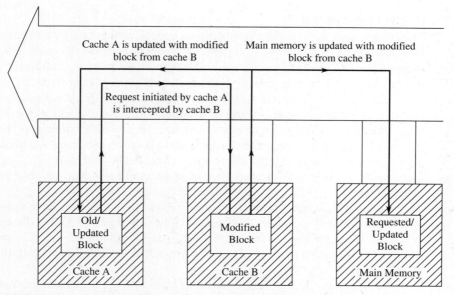

Figure 6.19 Cache Coherency Mechanism on Alliant FX (Courtesy of Alliant Computer Systems Corporation.)

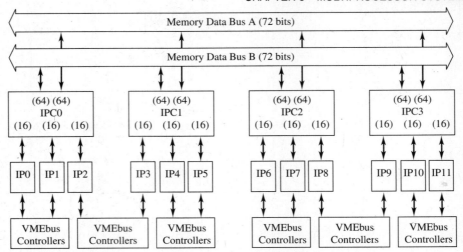

Figure 6.20 Alliant Memory Bus and I/O (Courtesy of Alliant Computer Systems Corporation.)

INPUT/OUTPUT

These systems are capable of supporting a variety of peripherals including disk and tape systems, terminals, and printers as well as local and wide area networking. The input/output is achieved through either an IP configuration or through a high speed port (HSP). Both the IP configuration and the HSP utilize the direct memory access (DMA) methods of I/O.

OPERATING SYSTEM

This series uses the Concentrix operating system, which is an extended version of Berkeley UNIX. Concentrix is capable of multiple computing resource scheduling, mapped file I/O, demand-paged copy-on-write virtual memory, multiprocessing and multitasking, shared user memory, and real-time support (Figure 6.21).

The Concentrix operating system runs symmetrically on all processors; each resource executes a common image of the operating system. A global locking scheme is provided to coordinate processor access to critical code regions and shared data. The coherency logic in the caches ensures that all processors have a common view of global memory. The symmetric approach is what allows Concentrix to schedule all the processors for simultaneous execution and automatically load-balance jobs across processors.

Concentrix schedules interactive user utilities and operating system tasks for processing on the IPs. Smaller computation jobs are scheduled for the detached ACEs. When not being utilized, detached ACEs are used to offload the IPs. Compute-intensive jobs that require parallel processing are scheduled for the computational complexes.

As shown in Figure 6.22, Concentrix transparently schedules job A to run in a parallel on a complex of four ACEs, smaller serial jobs on detached ACEs, and job C for explicit parallel tasking.

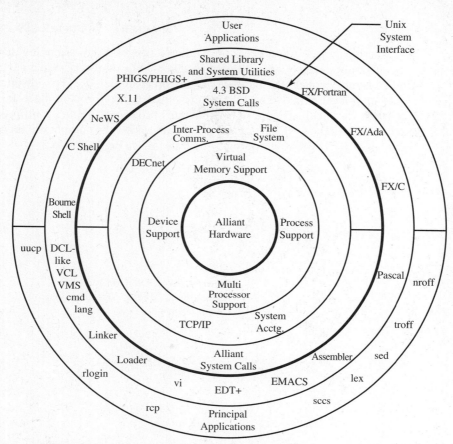

Figure 6.21 Concentrix Operating System (Courtesy of Alliant Computer Systems Corporation.)

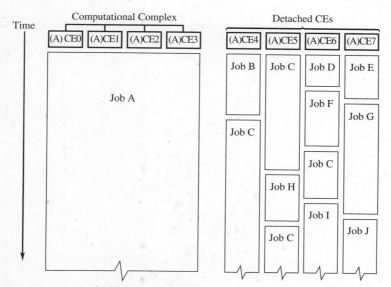

Figure 6.22 Parallel Task Execution on Alliant FX (Courtesy of Alliant Computer Systems Corporation.)

Macrotasking is the process of dividing a program into segments that are then executed simultaneously on multiple processors. The multiprocessing capabilities of Alliant systems provide the opportunity for programmers to take advantage of this form of high-level parallelism. Concentrix supports two forms of macrotasking. The Unix fork system call (Figure 6.23) generates processes that are multiprocessed on detached ACEs. The CNCALL, concurrent call, allows the computational complex to execute each iteration of a loop on a separate ACE (Figure 6.24).

```
INTEGER PID, FORK
  :
DO I = 1, 4
   PID = FORK( )
   IF (PID .EQ. 0) THEN
      CALL TASK (I)
      STOP
   END IF
END DO
```

Figure 6.23 FORK on Alliant FX (Courtesy of Alliant Computer Systems Corporation.)

```
      Program Macrotask

      Parameter (N_TASK = 4)

      CALL INPUT_DATA

CVD$ CNCALL
      DO 10 ITASK=1, N_TASK
         IF (ITASK .EQ. 1) THEN
            CALL TASK1
         ELSEIF (ITASK .EQ. 2) THEN
            CALL TASK2
         ELSEIF (ITASK .EQ. 3) THEN
            CALL TASK3
         ELSEIF (ITASK .EQ. 4) THEN
            CALL TASK4
         ELSE
            STOP
         ENDIF
 10   CONTINUE
      CALL OUTPUT_DATA
      END
```

Figure 6.24 CNCALL on Alliant FX (Courtesy of Alliant Computer Systems Corporation.)

6.7 EXAMPLE SYSTEMS

APPLICATIONS

Because of the high throughput of the Alliant series due to the parallel and vector capabilities, it is often used in simulation coupled with visualization. Visualization is a techology that combines high-performance computing with graphics and animation. Graphics often require intensive matrix and linear computations, and the Alliant is well suited for this task and allows users to view complex data as images rather than as a series of numbers. The Alliant is often networked with other systems such as a Cray, VAX clusters, Workstations, and PCs. This allows each system to perform at its highest level to accomplish a variety of scientific and engineering applications.

One of the most interesting applications of the Alliant FX series machines is the Cedar project at the Center for Super-computing Research and Development at the University of Illinois at Urbana-Champaign. The purpose of the project is to "demonstrate that parallel processing can deliver good performance over a wide range of applications." The design of a supercomputer often limits the types of problems with which it can maintain good performance. For example, the highest-performance processors, such as Cray's systems, have peak performances in the hundreds of MFLOPS but require dense array operations with regular memory addressing to approach their peak performance. Applications that require irregular addressing, therefore, show decreased performance. Using low-performance processors (less than 2 MFLOPS) is no solution to this problem, on account of the sheer number of processors necessary to get the required performance and the complexity of coordinating the processors. A system based on midperformance processors (10–100MFLOPS) would require fewer processors and therefore less coordination. Cedar is such a system.

Cedar (Figure 6.25) consists of several FX/80s (processor clusters) connected to a global memory by a two-level crossbar. The connection is achieved by replacing one of the CP caches in each system with an interface to the crossbar. The global memory contains one module for each individual processor, and each module consists of two interleaved banks and a synchronization processor.

Altogether this system adds another level of parallelism on top of those available in the FX/80. This is intercluster parallelism. Because the communication and synchronization costs at this level are much higher than within a cluster, intercluster communication should be minimized. Therefore the first step in designing an algorithm for Cedar is to decompose the task in a way that minimizes intercluster communication. Then within each cluster, the designer can take advantage of the conventional levels of parallelism available in the FX/80s.

Note that although the FX architecture was well received, the Alliant Computer Systems Corporation ceased its operations in 1992.

6.7.2 Intel iPSC Series

The Intel iPSC series is a family of successive generation parallel computers developed for research and industry use. The first commercial system, the iPSC/1, introduced in 1985, was superseded by the iPSC/2 in 1987 and the iPSC/860 in 1990.

The basic concept behind the iPSC architecture is the idea of concurrent processing, and the hypercube network is used as a means by which concurrency is

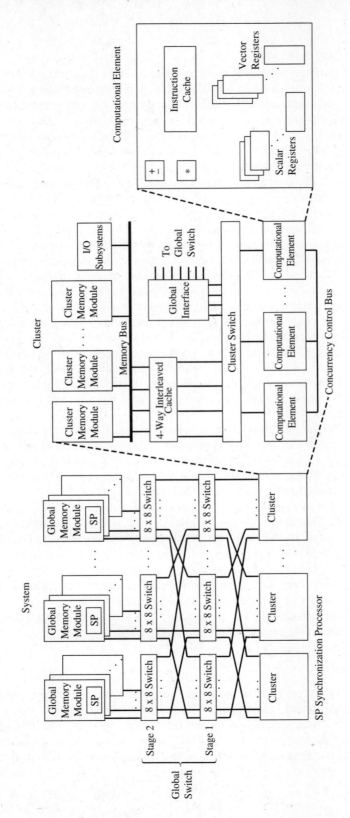

Figure 6.25 Cedar Project

6.7 EXAMPLE SYSTEMS

achieved with efficiency. The iPSC makes use of the hypercube topology in the following way:

1. The computing unit placed at each node consists of a self-contained processor/memory pair.
2. The hypercube interconnect network becomes a message-passing system through which node processors communicate with each other.

The computational element of the iPSC system is the *cube*, which is the hypercube interconnection of processing nodes. A second functional element, the *cube manager*, was added to provide overall control of the cube and to act as a conduit for input and output to the cube.

The iPSC/1 consisted of a cube and a cube manager. The nodes in the cube were built around Intel 80286/80287 processors with 512 Kbytes of memory. Research has shown that a major problem area in distributed memory systems lies in the inefficiency of internodal communications and the iPSC/1 is no exception. The iPSC/1 uses a *store-and-forward* message-passing scheme, which by its nature requires processor/memory resource utilization at each node along the path of the message. For messages of any distance (i.e., passing through multiple nodes), performance of the overall system becomes bogged down in communication processing overhead.

Problem solving on the iPSC begins by first mapping the problem at hand to the set of nodes available in the particular iPSC. This means that the overall problem must be segmented into separate processes, each of which is then assigned to a unique computing node. This segmentation can occur in a time domain or in a process domain. Timewise segmentation is easier to conceptualize because it is inherent in problems dealing with natural phenomena. Once the different software segments are ready, they are loaded into the respective processors by the cube manager, which then initializes the system. Upon initialization, the computation units begin executing independently and simultaneously, sending and receiving internodal messages as needed to perform the various tasks required at the different nodes. The cube manager remains active by sending global commands to the nodes, sending messages, receiving intermediate status, and processing results from individual nodes as they continue executing.

The iPSC/2 is similar to the iPSC/1 in that it contains the cube and the cube manager functional units. The nodes, however, are built around the 80386/80387 processors and 4 Mbytes of memory expandable to 16 Mbytes. In addition to the increased computing power gained by employing the 80386/80387 processors, the iPSC/2 includes system features that reduce two major difficulties encountered in the use of the iPSC/1. First, the problem of inefficient internodal communication is largely solved by a new message-passing scheme referred to by Intel as direct connect communication. With this new scheme, a direct connect module (DCM) is included at each node operating separately from the existing processor/memory unit. Unlike the store-and-forward scheme of the iPSC/1, the direct connect network (DCN) dynamically creates a routing path from node *A* to node *Z* as needed, releasing the links in the path upon completion of the message transmission. With DCMs in place at each node, transmission of a message adds little processing overhead and no storage overhead to intermediate nodes on the routing path. With minimal interaction between the DCM and the processor/memory unit especially at intermediate nodes, node-to-node message passing has little impact on the computing performance of the nodes. This greatly aids the program developer who can concentrate on an efficient mapping of the problem at hand to the set of nodes in the cube, rather than worry about the avoidance of large path distances. In fact, the DCN allows the programmer to view the cube as a completely connected graph so that the path length from one node to any other node is the same.

The latest in the iPSC series, the iPSC/860, is similar to the iPSC/2 but because each node contains Intel's i860 RISC processor, system performance ratings far surpass existing supercomputers. This is because the i860 microprocessor is essentially a supercomputer on a chip, capable of delivering 80 MFLOPS with a price/performance rating a fraction of that of the Cray series of machines. For comparison, the cost of an i860 microprocessor system is about $1000 while the cost of the Cray type of supercomputers delivering from 100 to 1200 MFLOPS ranges from about $2.5 million to $20 million. As another comparison, it is estimated that a single i860 node will perform the computing equivalent of 16 iPSC/2 nodes and will perform with the computing power of an entire IBM 3090/VF—a supercomputer with vectorizer. With such a magnitude of computing power at each node, the iPSC/860 has an outstanding peak performance rating ranging from 480 MFLOPS to 7.6 GFLOPS depending on system configuration. The migration of applications from the iPSC/2 system to the iPSC/860 will be eased because the i860 RISC processor is compatible with the i386 processor at the source code level.

Figure 6.26 shows the structure of the iPSC/2 system. As mentioned earlier, each node of iPSC/2 contains the 32-bit Intel 80386 microprocessor and 80387 floating-point coprocessor, one megabyte of memory and a direct-connect routing module for high-speed message passing within the system's hypercube communication network. In addition to the seven full duplex communication channels used to connect up to 128 hypercube nodes, each routing module provides an eighth channel for high-speed external communication to mass storage, graphics, and other peripherals.

The cube manager functions for the iPSC/2 are contained in the system resource manager (SRM). The SRM is an Intel 310 supermini host computer that provides systemwide control and also provides a user entry point to the cube.

For high-speed transfer of large blocks of data within a node and between nodes via the hypercube network, each node contains a multichannel direct memory access (DMA) controller. One channel is dedicated to inbound messages and another to outbound. Two other channels with a total DMA bandwidth of 10.7 Mbytes per second are available to software.

For further functional extensions, each node is equipped with a standard, high speed iLBX interface. On the backplane, each pair of odd/even slots is connected by the iLBX-II bus. In this way, the odd-numbered slots may be occupied by various node expansion boards including the VX vector processor and SX scalar extension. Transfers across the local bus interface average 10 Mbytes per second.

The scalar performance of the 80387 arithmetic coprocessor is approximately equal with the SX scalar extension module, based upon the Weitek 1167 floating-point

6.7 EXAMPLE SYSTEMS

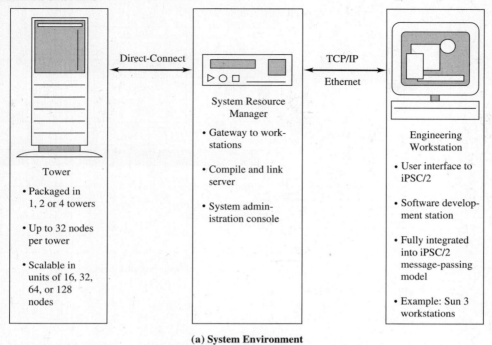

(a) System Environment

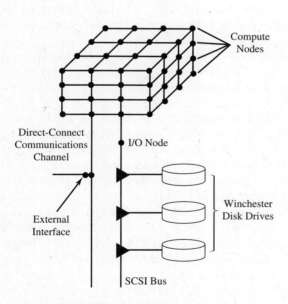

(b) System Overview

Figure 6.26 Intel iPSC/2 System (Courtesy of Intel Scientific Computers.)

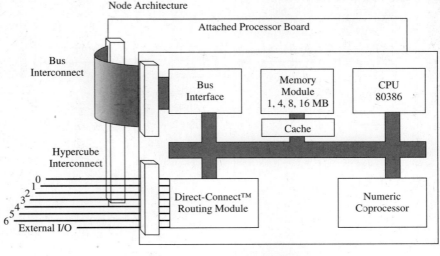

(c) **Node Architecture**

Figure 6.26 (continued)

unit. The module is appropriate for scalar intensive computations as well as for computations with short vectors.

The vector extension combines the benefits of high-level parallelism through concurrent computing with the low-level parallelism of vector processing. Performance multiplies when applications have both vector computation and a high degree of concurrency through problem decomposition.

Each VX vector-extended node obtains peak performance that exceeds 6 MFLOPS double precision and 20 MFLOPS single precision. A variety of complex functions are supported by efficient short-vector functions, implemented with pipelines and high-speed random access memory.

The DCM handles the communication between nodes on the hypercube. A major weakness of the original iPSC, the iPSC/1, was in the message routing. The iPSC/1 used store-and-forward message passing in which the overhead of messages for intermediate nodes tended to increase start-up times and degrade performance. The incremental cost of sending a message to a distant node in the network was so great that programmers spent a great deal of time trying to maximize near-neighbor communication or locality wherever possible. Store-and-forward messaging also consumed node CPU cycles for relaying messages to other nodes when they could have been more profitably applied to the application in the node. Because a single node could only relay one message at a time, the message throughput was far less than what the network could theoretically provide.

The direct connect module for routing was introduced in the iPSC/2. The direct connect module (DCM) is a communication processor that is totally separate from the node processor. Each node in the iPSC/2 system has its own DCM. Each DCM supervises eight full duplex serial communication channels with performance of 2.8 megabytes per second and per channel in each direction. Up to eight messages may be simultaneously routed over these channels, which can connect up to 128 hypercube nodes. Use of the direct connect technology and the NX/2 operating system allows the iPSC/2 to perform as if each node were directly connected to all the other nodes. As a result, nearest-neighbor mapping is no longer a concern.

Hardware communication circuits between communicating nodes are created dynamically with direct connect routing. The DCM is a hardware message router that automatically routes messages without interrupting the processing going on in intermediate nodes. The only time a node processor is involved with a message is at the source or the final destination of that message. When node A wants to send a message to node B wherever it is in the network, the network builds a communication circuit between A and B dynamically and then transmits the complete message. At the end of the transmission, the circuit is released for use in other communications. The intermediate node processors, along with their memory and associated coprocessors, are completely separate from the message that traveled through their respective direct connect modules.

Direct connect communication is fast and efficient. The time to build an end-to-end circuit is short—just a few microseconds per node in the path. Once the path is built, messages move between sender and receiver at the full hardware speed of 2.8 megabytes per second. This is true whether the nodes are near neighbors or at opposite corners of the hypercube. A circuit is released a link at a time as the end of the message moves through each node along the path. Other circuits waiting to be formed automatically grab the free links as they become available.

All of the necessary hardware for building the circuits and moving the data are contained in the node's DCM. A single DCM can handle up to eight simultaneous communications at one time, all at full hardware speed. Each DCM contains eight routing units along with the one kilobyte inbound and outbound FIFO (first-in, first-out) buffers, serializer and deserializer, and multiple arbitration units. The routers are connected in a partial crossbar configuration to enable all eight to be operating.

Once the node's operating system NX/2 (node executive) moves a message from its local memory to the outbound buffer, the hardware takes over. The front of the message contains destination address information that is used to form the circuit. The correct router on each DCM at each node in the path is automatically selected until the destination node is reached. Once the circuit is complete, a hardware signal is sent and data starts to flow at full speed. As the last bits of the message pass through each router, the router releases its portion of the circuit and makes itself available to other message traffic. When the message is received at the destination, hardware verifies the check-sum on the message and causes an interrupt if there is an error. The message is deposited in the destination inbound buffer and is then moved to the node's local memory.

The iPSC/2 router is composed of eight independent routing elements—one for each of the eight incoming channels, which are numbered 0 through 7. The node interface consists of two unidirectional parallel channels, the node source and node sink. Each routing element can route messages from its incoming channel to one or more outgoing channels as defined by the n-cube routing algorithm. The eighth-channel routing element is a special case whose routing does not operate like channels 0 through 6. It acts as a repeater for remote node source and sink channels, which provide a gateway into and out of the network for remote devices.

The NX/2 presents flexible message-passing services to the application. It can automatically route and deliver messages to any process. It is a multitasking operating system that is designed to ensure reliable, optimal communications via the direct connect routing system. It provides the program's interface to the direct connect communication network. The communication interface is consistent whether communicating with other processes in the same node, to remote nodes, or to the SRM.

Communication on the iPSC/2 hypercube is asynchronous because there is no rendezvous or synchronization between the processors at the moment of message passing. When the destination processor is not yet expecting a message at the time of its arrival, it is buffered by the node operating system. Each message can be given a label that specifies its type. The type gives an indication of the contents of the message. The receiver can select a message by specifying the type of message he or she wants to receive. The receiver can also suppress this selection, which indicates that it will accept any type of message.

The communication primitives exist in a blocking (synchronous) or nonblocking (asynchronous) version. In the blocking version, the sending or receiving process is halted until the message has been sent or received. For a send operation, the buffer that contained the message is then free for further use. For a receive operation, the message is then available in the buffer specified by the programmer. In the nonblocking version, the program merely informs the operating system that a message should be sent or received. The processor proceeds with computations while the communication processor handles the message request. The communications buffer should not be accessed or reused until the process is informed by the operating system that the communication is complete. Some basic communication primitives are as follows:

Blocking

```
csend(type,buf,len,node,pid)   : Send a message and wait
                                 for completion
crecv(type,buf,len)            : Receive a message and wait
                                 for completion
```

Non-blocking

```
isend(type,buf,len,node,pid)   : Send a message
irecv(type,buf,len)            : Receive a message
msgdone(id)                    : Determine whether
                                 communication
                                 has completed
msgwait(id)                    : Wait until completion of
                                 communication operation
```

Figure 6.27 compares a sequential program for matrix multiplication to that on the iPSC system.

NX/2 supports multiple tasks per node in private address spaces, dynamic memory management, and UNIX-compatible file I/O. All NX/2 services are available to all iPSC/2 system programming languages in the form of language-specific interface libraries. NX/2's message-passing facilities are also available from computers and workstations connected to the iPSC/2 system.

6.7 EXAMPLE SYSTEMS

Sequential vs. Parallel Matrix Multiply	

program mxm
dimension a(n, n), b(n, n), c(n, n)
 	
do 30 i = 1,n
 	
do 20 j = 1,n
  c(i, j) = 0.
  do 10 k = 1,n
    c(i, j) = c(i, j) + (a(i, k) * b(k,j))
10 continue
 	
20 continue
30 continue
 	
end
	program mxm
	dimension a(m, n), b(m, n), c(m, n)
	indx = me * m + 1
	do 40 iter = 1, numnodes()
	call csend (indx, b, 4*n*m, nextnode, mpid)
	do 30 i = 1,m
	jc = indx
	  do 20 j = 1,m
	    c(i, jc) = 0.
	    do 10 k = 1,n
	      c(i, jc) = c(i, jc) + (a(i,k) * b(k,j))
	10 continue
	  jc = jc + 1
	20 continue
	30 continue
	call crecv (−1, b, 4*m*n)
	indx = infotype()
	40 continue
	end

Figure 6.27 Matrix Multiplication on iPSC (Courtesy of Intel Scientific Computers.)

A problem in the past, not just with the iPSC but with other concurrent systems as well, has been the lack of program development facilities. The iPSC/2 system eases this problem through its interface to user workstations either local or remote. Additionally, a collection of software development tools in the concurrent workbench has been developed by Intel that provides a number of computer program development aids.

PERFORMANCE

The iPSC/2 delivers the performance of conventional supercomputers. A single processing node can be configured with performance comparable to a supermini, and the system itself can be expanded in size to achieve a much higher overall performance. System processing speed peaks at over 500 million instructions per second (MIPS) and 1.2 billion floating-point operations per second. A comparison of price shows the iPSC/2 family at a cost less than $10K/MFLOP.

Figure 6.28 compares latency and bandwidth for node-to-node communication for three different communication performance tests. Ring of Nodes sends and receives messages in a ring of nodes used to measure unidirectional communication between near neighbors. This test program usually displays a system's best message-passing performance because the receives are always pending. The 1-Hop Two Node Echo program is used to measure unidirectional communication between near neighbors. In this measurement, receives are not pending. The 5-Hop Two Node Echo program is the same as the 1-Hop Two Node Echo program except that a node five hops away is echoing the message. It is a good basic test of multihop communication performance.

The jump in latency and drop in bandwidth at the 100-byte to 104-byte transition is due to the changeover from short message to long message protocol in NX/2.

Latency (ms)			
Message Length in Bytes	Ring of Nodes	1-Hop Two-Node Echo	5-Hop Two-Node Echo
0	0.49	0.55	0.55
8	0.54	0.55	0.61
64	0.55	0.56	0.62
100	0.56	0.57	0.63
104	1.00	1.01	1.14
1024	1.38	1.34	1.48
8192	3.93	3.92	4.05
16384	6.87	6.87	7.00

Bandwidth (KB/s)			
Message Length in Bytes	Ring of Nodes	1-Hop Two-Node Echo	5-Hop Two-Node Echo
0	0.00	0.00	0.00
8	14.68	14.54	13.11
64	115.32	114.38	103.22
100	178.57	175.44	158.73
104	96.65	102.97	91.23
1024	765.90	764.18	691.89
8192	2084.49	2089.80	2022.71
16384	2383.13	2384.86	2340.57

Figure 6.28 Message Latency and Band Width (iPSC 2) (Courtesy of Intel Scientific Computers.)

The additional hops in the 5-Hop Two Node Echo program appear to each cost about 10 microseconds. The hardware design predicts between 3 and 12 microseconds depending on traffic conditions.

Figure 6.29 shows the characteristics of iPSC/860 systems. As impressive as the performance capability of the iPSC/860 is, far greater strides in supercomputing are expected from two projects at Intel Scientific Computing. Currently, Intel is under contract to produce a Touchstone computer that will deliver 150 GFLOPS. The complexity of this system is on the order of thousands of nodes, and the system will operate at 100 times the performance of today's fastest machines. Even more impressive is the second government-sponsored project known as TERAOPS, the goal of which is to build a computer that can operate at 1000 times the speed of today's fastest computers, roughly 1 trillion instructions per second. In addition to the advanced architectures, a significant part of the research involved in these projects is aimed at the development of sophisticated, encompassing software development and user interface environments capable of allowing many multiple users access to the supersystems of the future. The goal is to provide a *seamless* environment for many users, each at a local workstation such that each user views the supercomputer as just another computing machine requiring input and producing output, much like the conventional sequential machines of today.

APPLICATIONS

The iPSC system has been used in applications such as modeling complex structures that include aircraft flowfields for advanced fighter design, mapping earth's substrata for oil exploration, and three-dimensional capacitance simulation for modeling VLSI circuit design.

6.7 EXAMPLE SYSTEMS

	iPSC 860 System Specifications				
Number of CPUs	8	16	32	64	128
Peak Performance (GFLOPS)					
Double Precision	.48	.96	1.9	3.8	7.6
Single Precision	.64	1.3	2.6	5.1	10
Memory Capacity (MBytes)					
Standard	64	128	256	512	1,204
Maximum	12	1,024	2,048	4,096	8,192
Storage (GBytes)					
Standard	.65	1.3	1.9	4.5	9.1
Maximum	9.1	20	40	82	165
Internal Network (MBytes/sec.) (Bisection Bandwidth)	22.4	44.8	89.6	179.2	358.4
External I/O					
Available Channels	7	15	31	63	127
Maximum I/O (MBytes/sec.)	19.6	42.0	86.8	176.4	355.6
Physical Size (feet)					
Width	1.8	1.8	3.6	3.6	5.3
Height 5.0, Depth 2.1					
Operating Temperature (°C)	10-30	10-30	10-30	10-30	10-30

Figure 6.29 Intel iPSC 860 Characteristics (Courtesy of Intel Scientific Computers.)

At Northrop Corporation, the iPSC is used to simulate a wind tunnel and corresponding computational fluid dynamics (CFD) applications. It allows the engineer to perform parametric studies of varying aircraft configurations more quickly and cheaply than through extensive wind tunnel testing.

At Exxon, the iPSC system is used in seismic simulation. Because the structure of the earth's substrata in a region cannot be determined with absolute accuracy, indirect means are required. Seismic simulation involves using an iPSC system to combine information from a variety of sources, such as geological data on the prehistoric formation of the region, characteristics of the strata derived from previous wells, gravitational measurements, and low resolution images compiled from seismic soundings. From these sources, the iPSC system produces a composite picture, which is then compared with field data for accuracy.

A recent application of the iPSC/860 is at the Oakridge National Laboratory for the exploration of the behavior of exotic alloys and many peculiar properties of materials (Stapleton, 1990). In this application, a 15,000-line Fortran program, running at 50 MFLOPS on a Cray-2, was ported to a 128-processor iPSC/860. Some of the algorithms were redesigned to take advantage of the inherent parallelism in the application, and the new version ran at 660 MFLOPS. After some of the routines were converted to assembly language, the code achieved a rate of 1.8 GFLOPS.

6.7.3 INMOS Limited Transputer

The transputer family of high performance microprocessors are produced by INMOS Limited in the U.K. The most significant feature of a transputer is the ability to perform multitasking in hardware with submicrosecond switching. A *process* is the basic software building block for a transputer. Processes can reside in the same transputer or on different transputers. In either case, the communication between processes is provided by the hardware. The language Occam provides a framework for designing concurrent systems using transputers. A program running in a transputer is equivalent to an Occam process, and a network of transputers corresponds to an Occam program. Transputers can be programmed in most high-level languages. Occam is used as a harness to link modules written in other languages.

INTERNAL ARCHITECTURE

Internally, a transputer consists of a memory, a processor, a communication system, an external memory interface (enabling additional local memory to be used), and other application-specific interfaces connected via a 32-bit bus. Figure 6.30 shows the general structure.

The processor contains three registers (A, B, and C) used for integer and address arithmetic. They also form a hardware stack. Similarly, in transputers with a floating-point unit (FPU), there is a three-register floating-point evaluation stack (AF, BF, and CF registers). In addition, there are four pointer registers (Fptr0, Fptr1, Bptr0, Bptr1) and two timer registers (Time0 and Time1). There are two single-bit flags to represent errors (Error and HaltonError). The workspace pointer register points to an area of store where local variables are stored, the instruction pointer register points to the next instruction to be executed, and the operand register is used in the formation of instruction operands.

The first in the transputer family is T414. It is a 32-bit processor with 2 Kbyte on-chip RAM and four interprocessor links. It is capable of addressing up to 4 Gbytes

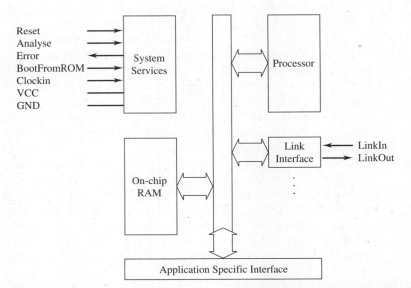

Figure 6.30 Transputer Architecture (Courtesy of SGS-Thomson Microelectronics Ltd., formerly INMOS Ltd.)

6.7 EXAMPLE SYSTEMS

of external memory using multiplexed address and data lines and is rated at 10 MIPS. The other members of the family are:

T212: 16-bit processor, 2 Kbyte RAM, 64K address range, with separate address and data buses.

M212: A T212 with two of the four links replaced by built-in disc controller circuitry.

T800: A T414 with an FPU, additional instructions, improved links, and 4 Kbyte RAM.

T222: A T212 with 4 Kbyte RAM.

T801: A T800 with separate address and data buses for faster memory access.

T425 and T805: Upgraded versions of T414 and T800 with additional instructions to facilitate single stepping and other debugging aids.

Figure 6.31 shows the details of the T800.

COMMUNICATION
A link between two transputers is implemented by connecting a link interface of one to a link interface of the other by two one-directional signal lines along which data is transmitted serially. These two signal lines provide two Occam channels, one in each

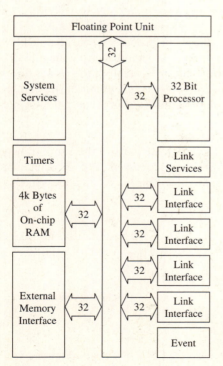

Figure 6.31 INMOS T800 Architecture (Courtesy of SGS-Thomson Microelectronics Ltd., formerly INMOS Ltd.)

direction. The communication protocol supports byte transmission (i.e., each message is transmitted as a sequence of bytes), requiring only the presence of a single byte buffer in the receiving transputer to ensure that no information is lost. The link protocol is shown in Figure 6.32.

A channel between two processes executing on the same transputer is implemented by a single word (channel word) in the memory. A channel between processes executing on different transputers is implemented by using point-to-point links. When a pair of processes communicate with each other, one of the processes outputs a message to the channel and the other inputs the message from the same channel. Thus, the communication is synchronous and unbuffered. The communication can only take place when both the processes are ready. Whichever process reaches the input or the output statement first must wait until the other process is ready. Once both processes are ready, the inputting and outputting can proceed. This form of communication is equivalent to handshaking in other hardware systems and provides the necessary level of process synchronization.

After transmitting each data byte, the sender waits until an acknowledge is received, indicating that the receiver has received the data and is ready to accept another data packet. The sending link reschedules the sending process only after the acknowledge for the final byte of the message has been received. Because the communication is point-to-point, the channel needs no process queue and because it is synchronous, there is no message queue. Also there is no requirement for a message buffer.

The processor provides a number of operations to support message passing, the most important being *input message* and *output message* instructions. These instructions use the address of the channel to determine whether the channel is internal or external (i.e., soft or hard), allowing for a process to be completely written and compiled without the knowledge of where its channels are connected.

A process performs an input or output by loading the evaluation stack with a pointer to a message, the address of a channel, and a count of the number of bytes to be transferred, and then executing an input message or an output message instruction.

INTERNAL CHANNEL COMMUNICATION

Here the processes that intend to communicate exist in the same transputer and the channel word is shared between the two processes. The channel word holds the identity of a process or holds a special value *Empty*. When a message is passed using

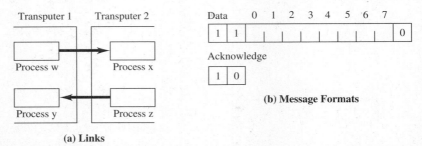

Figure 6.32 Link Protocol (Courtesy of SGS-Thomson Microelectronics Ltd., formerly INMOS Ltd.)

6.7 EXAMPLE SYSTEMS

the channel, the identity of the first process to become ready is stored in the channel word and the processor starts to execute the next process from the scheduling list. When the second process to use the channel becomes ready, the message is copied, the waiting process is added to the scheduling list, and the channel is reset to its initial state. It does not matter whether the inputting or the outputting process becomes ready first.

When a process attempts to communicate, it examines the contents of the channel word. If the value is empty indicating that the other process is not ready, it stores its process descriptor in the channel word and deschedules. When the other process is ready, it examines the contents of the channel word and finds a valid process descriptor. It then infers that the other process is ready, transfers the block of bytes, and restarts the other process.

Note that all this is implemented in the microcode of the transputer. At the machine code level, a process just executes an instruction requesting that the data be read or written to a channel.

Figure 6.33(a) shows a process P, which is about to execute an output instruction on an empty channel C. The evaluation stack holds a pointer to a message, the address of a channel C, and a count of the number of bytes in the message. After executing the output instruction, channel C holds the address of the workspace of P, and the address of the message to be transferred is stored in the workspace of P, as shown in (b). P is descheduled, and the processor starts to execute the next process from the scheduling

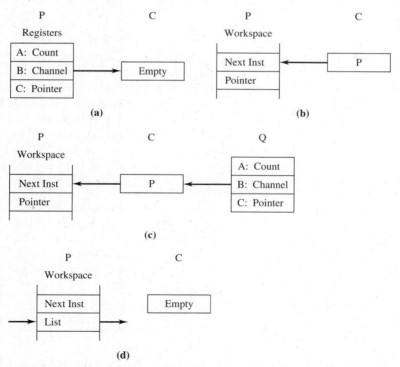

Figure 6.33 Four Stages of Communication Between the Processes on the Same Transputer (Courtesy of SGS-Thomson Microelectronics Ltd., formerly INMOS Ltd.)

list. The channel C and the process P remain in this state until a second process Q executes an output instruction on the channel, as shown in (c). The message is copied, the waiting process P is added to the scheduling list, and the channel C is reset to its initial state, as shown in (d).

EXTERNAL CHANNEL COMMUNICATION
For two processes running on separate transputers, the process making a request to send data out through a channel to another transputer is descheduled. Hardware determines when the other transputer is ready and then transfers data using direct memory access (DMA). When all data have been transferred, the process is rescheduled.

At the machine code level, hardware links appear identical to internal channels, and the same instructions are used for both. The only thing that distinguishes between them is that, for external communication, the address of the channel word passed as a parameter to an input or an output instruction is specified as one of the first few reserved locations in the memory. The microcode detects that the address is one of these reserved locations and passes their parameters on to the link hardware for the link associated with that address.

When a message is passed via an external channel, the processor delegates to an autonomous link interface the job of transferring the message and deschedules the process. When the message has been transferred, the link interface causes the processor to reschedule the waiting process. This allows the processor to continue the execution of other processes while the external message transfer is taking place.

Each link interface uses three registers: a pointer to a process workspace, a pointer to a message, and a count of bytes in the message. In the Figure 6.34(a), processes P and Q executed by different transputers communicate using a channel C; P outputs, and Q inputs. When P executes its output instruction, the registers in the link interface of the transputer executing P are initialized, and P is descheduled. Similarly, when Q executes its input instruction, the registers in the link interface of the process executing Q are initialized, and Q is desheduled, as shown in (b). The message is now copied through the link after which the workspaces of P and Q are returned to the corresponding scheduling lists, as shown in (c). The protocol used on P and Q ensures that it does not matter which of P and Q first becomes ready.

SUPPORT FOR CONCURRENCY
The processor provides the support for the Occam model of concurrency and communication. It has a microcoded scheduler that enables any number of concurrent processes to be executed together, sharing the processor time. This removes the need for a software kernel. The processor does not need to support the dynamic allocation of storage as the Occam compiler allocates space to concurrent processes.

At any time, a concurrent process may be:

active   –   being executed
               –   on a list waiting to be executed
inactive   –   ready to input
               –   ready to output
               –   waiting until a specified time

6.7 EXAMPLE SYSTEMS

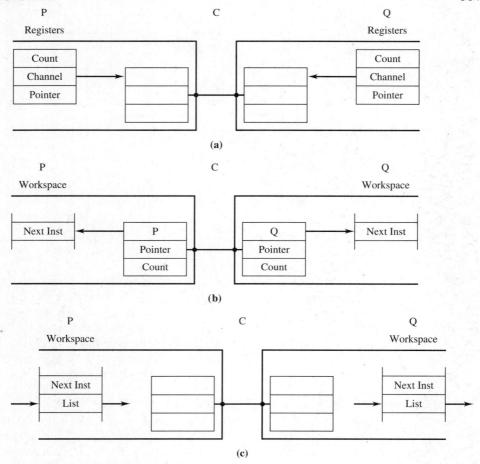

Figure 6.34 Three Stages of Communication Between Transputers (Courtesy of SGS-Thomson Microelectronics Ltd., formerly INMOS Ltd.)

The scheduler operates in such a way that inactive processes do not consume any processor time. The active processes waiting to be executed are held on a linked list of process workspaces implemented using two registers, one of which points to the first process on the list and the other to the last.

In Figure 6.35, S is executing, and P, Q, and R are active, awaiting execution. A process is executed until it is unable to proceed because it is waiting to input or output, or waiting for the timer. Whenever a process is unable to proceed, its instruction pointer is saved in its workspace and the next process is taken from the list. Actual process switch times are small, as a small amount of state information needs to be saved and it is not necessary to save the evaluation stack on rescheduling.

The processor provides a number of special operations to support the process model. These include *start process* and *end process*. When a parallel construct is executed, start process instructions are used to create the necessary concurrent processes. A start process instruction creates a new process by adding a new workspace

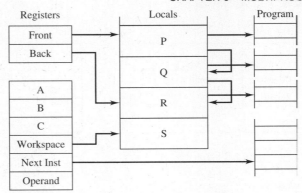

Figure 6.35 Process Activity (Courtesy of SGS-Thomson Microelectronics Ltd., formerly INMOS Ltd.)

to the end of the scheduling list, enabling the new concurrent process to be executed together with the ones already being executed.

The correct termination of a parallel construct is assured by use of the end process instruction. This uses a workspace location as a counter of the components of the parallel construct, which have to still terminate. The counter is initialized to the number of components before the processes are started. Each component ends with an end process instruction that decrements and tests the counter. For all but the last component, the counter is nonzero and the component is descheduled. For the last component, the counter is zero and the component continues.

INTERFACING WITH PERIPHERALS

There are three methods by which the transputers communicate with the peripherals: 1) by employing peripheral transputers, 2) by employing link adaptors, and 3) by memory mapping the peripheral. (See Figure 6.36.) In all these methods, the peripheral driver interfaces to the rest of the application via Occam channels. Therefore, any peripheral device can be simulated as an Occam process.

In the first method, peripheral transputers (e.g., for disks or graphics) are employed. The central transputer connects directly with the peripherals. The interface to the transputer is implemented by special purpose hardware within the transputer. The application software in the transputer is implemented as an Occam process and controls the interface via Occam channels linking the processor to the special purpose hardware.

In the second method, link adaptors are employed to convert between a link and a specialized interface. The link adaptor is connected to the link of an appropriate transputer, which contains the application designer's peripheral device handler implemented as an Occam process.

In the third method, the peripheral is mapped onto the memory bus of a transputer. The peripherals are given PORT addresses. The transputer accesses the peripheral devices by issuing the PORT addresses of the particular device. The application designer's peripheral device handler provides a standard Occam channel interface to the rest of the application.

6.7 EXAMPLE SYSTEMS

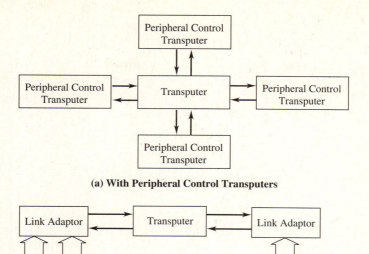

(a) With Peripheral Control Transputers

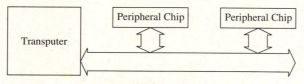

(b) With Link Adaptors

(c) Memory-Mapped Peripherals

Figure 6.36 Peripheral Interface (Courtesy of SGS-Thomson Microelectronics Ltd., formerly INMOS Ltd.)

OCCAM

Occam enables a system to be described as a collection of concurrent processes that communicate with each other and with peripheral devices through channels. Occam programs are built from three primitive processes:

```
1. v := e    assign the value of expression e to variable v
2. c ! e     output the value of expression e to channel c
3. c ? v     input a value from channel c to variable v
```

These primitive processes are combined to form the following three constructs:

```
1. seq (sequential)   components executed one after another
2. par (parallel)     components executed in parallel
3. alt (alternative)  component first ready is executed
```

A construct is itself a process and may be used as a component of another construct. Conventional sequential programs can be expressed in terms of variables and assignments combined with sequential constructs. IF and WHILE looping constructs are also provided.

The following examples illustrate various features of Occam. Refer to manufacturers manuals for further details.

EXAMPLE 6.11

The following process inputs a value for X from the channel IN, adds 1 to it, and outputs it to the channel OUT.

```
chan IN, OUT:
var X:
seq
    IN?X
    X := X + 1
    OUT!X
```

The first statement declares two channels IN and OUT, and the second declares the variable X. The three statements indented below the keyword *seq* are executed in sequence.

EXAMPLE 6.12

The following process repeatedly performs the increment operation until the TEST value is false.

```
chan IN1, IN2, OUT:
var X, TEST:
seq
  IN2?TEST
  while TEST
  seq
      IN1?X
      X := X + 1
      OUT!X
      IN2?TEST
```

EXAMPLE 6.13

The following code illustrates two processes, executing in parallel, each receiving the data from a channel, incrementing it, and sending it to another channel.

```
chan IN1, OUT1:
chan IN2, OUT2:
par
  -- First Process
  var X:
  seq
      IN1?X
      X := X + 1
      OUT1!X
```

6.7 EXAMPLE SYSTEMS   305

```
    --Second Process
    var X:
    seq
        IN2?X
        X := X + 1
        OUT2!X
```

Note that the statements corresponding to the two processes are indented at the same level following the keyword *par*. The statements within each process are executed sequentially. The statements beginning with -- are comments.

EXAMPLE 6.14

The following code illustrates two processes communicating via the link COMMON.

```
chan IN, OUT:
chan COMMON:
par
  --First Process
  while TRUE
  var X:
  seq
      IN?X
      X := X + 1
      COMMON!X
  --Second Process
  while TRUE
  var X:
  seq
      COMMON?X
      X := X + 1
      OUT!X
```

This example illustrates a one-way communication. If two-way communication is required, another channel would be used sending the data from the second process to the first.

EXAMPLE 6.15

The following code segment shows alternate processes.

```
    --Declarations
    alt
        --First Process
        (VALUE>0) & IN?X
            seq
                X := X + 1
                COMMON!X
```

```
  --Second Process
(VALUE<0) & IN2?X
  seq
    X := X + 7
    OUT!X
```

The first process is executed when VALUE > 0 and the data arrives on the channel IN. The second process is executed when VALUE < 0 and data arrives on the channel IN2. Thus, the execution order depends on the guard conditions attached to each process.

APPLICATIONS

Transputer-based systems are currently being used in a wide range of applications. They include fluid flow; image analysis; image generation including animation, finite element analysis, electrical and mechanical design analysis and simulation; molecular modeling; high-performance database management; and information retrieval and artificial intelligence.

6.7.4 Thinking Machines Corporation's Connection Machine 5 (CM-5)

The CM-5 is a hybrid MIMD/SIMD multiprocessor system. The number of processors can be scaled from 32 to 16,384, providing an observed peak performance of 20 GFLOPS. Optionally, four vector units can be added to each processor, resulting in a peak performance of 2 teraflops. The CM-5 is controlled by one or more front-end workstations (Sun Microsystems's SPARC 2, Sun-4, or Sun-600) that execute the CM-5 operating system CMost. These front-end workstations (control processors) are dedicated to either PE array partition management or I/O control, and control all the instructions executed by the CM-5.

Figure 6.37 shows the system block diagram of the CM-5. There are three independent network subsystems—the data network, the control network, and the diagnostic network. All system resources are connected to each of these networks. Processing nodes are not interrupted by network activity, which permits message routing and computational tasks to be performed in parallel. The control processor broadcasts a single program to all the nodes. Each node runs this program at its own rate, utilizing the control network for synchronization. The library primitives provided with the machine, allow the implementation of synchronous communications for data parallel parts and asynchronous communications for the message-passing parts of the program.

The data network provides for data communications between CM-5 components. It has a fat tree topology. Each set of four processing or storage nodes has a network switch connecting them together. This switch provides for the data communication between the four nodes and to the upper layers of the network. Four of these groups of processing or storage nodes are in turn connected by a higher level switch. Four of these larger groups are in turn similarly connected to provide an aggregate bandwidth of 1280 Mbytes/second. At the bottom layer, each node is connected to its corresponding network switch by two bidirectional links of 5 Mbytes/second capacity.

6.7 EXAMPLE SYSTEMS

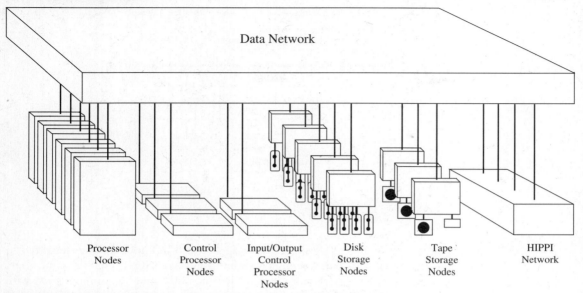

Figure 6.37 CM-5 System Block Diagram (Reprinted by permission of Thinking Machines Corporation, 1991.)

The control network subsystem coordinates the processor interactions required to implement interprocessor broadcasting and synchronization. It also provides the interface between the CM-5 front-end processors and the corresponding processor nodes and provides protection against multiuser interference.

The diagnostic network subsystem provides the interfaces required to perform internal system testing of device connectivity and circuit integrity. It can also access machine environmental variables (temperature, airflow, etc.) for detection of failure conditions.

Each processing node consists of a 22-MIPS SPARC microprocessor, 32 Mbytes of memory, four 32-MFLOP vector-processing units (64-bit operands) each with 8 Mbytes memory, and a network interface (Figure 6.38). The vector units implement a full floating-point instruction set with fast divide and square root functions. The SPARC is the control and scalar processing resource of the vector units. It also implements the operating system environment and manages communication with other system components via the network interface.

The scalable disk array is an integrated and expandable disk system that provides a range of 9 Gbytes to 3.2 terabytes (Tbytes) of storage. Data transfers between CM-5 and the disk array can be sustained at 12 Mbytes to 4.2 Gbytes per second. The disk array is an array of disk storage nodes. Each node contains a network interface implemented by a RISC microprocessor controller, disk buffer, four SCSI controllers, and eight disk drives. The scalable disk array features are implemented via the vendor's CM-5 scalable file system (SFS) software, which executes on a SPARC-based I/O control processor.

The I/O nodes are the third class of computational resources in a CM-5 system. These nodes include magnetic tape and network communications facilities. The inte-

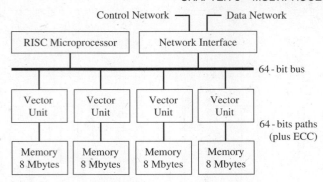

Figure 6.38 Block Diagram of a Processing Node (Reprinted by permission of Thinking Machines Corporation, 1991.)

grated tape subsystem is implemented via a specialized I/O node that has local buffer memory and a pair of Small Computer System Interface (SCSI) channel controllers that can connect to a maximum of seven devices per controller. Communication with other computers is provided by the High Performance Parallel Interface (HIPPI) I/O node. Serial and parallel Transmission Control Protocol/Internet Protocol (TCP/IP) and user HIPPI style interfacing through sockets is provided by the HIPPI subsystem. CM-5 also supports Ethernet and Fiber Digital Data Interface (FDDI) communications.

CMost provides the integrated user interface in the form of the X-Window System and OSF/Motif. The software environment integrates the debugging, performance analysis, and data visualization facilities into the integrated user interface. The following languages are available: C*, CM Fortran, and *LISP, which are respective supersets of C, Fortran 90, and LISP.

6.7.5 Cray Research Inc.'s T3D

The Cray T3D system (Kessler and Schwarzmeier, 1993; Koeninger et al., 1994) is the first massively parallel processor (MPP) from Cray Research, Inc. It integrates industry-leading microprocessors with a Cray-designed system interconnect and high-speed synchronization mechanisms to produce a balanced scalable MPP.

The MPP section of the T3D system (Figure 6.39) contains hundreds or thousands of DEC Alpha 21064 microprocessors, each associated with its own local memory. It is connected to a parallel vector processor (PVP) host computer system (either Cray Y-MP or Cray C90). All applications written for the T3D system are compiled on the host. The scalar- and vector-oriented parts of the application run on the host while the parallel portions run on the MPP. The MPP consists of three components: processing element nodes, interconnect network and I/O gateways.

PROCESSING ELEMENT NODES
Each processing element (PE) contains a microprocessor, local memory, and the support circuitry. The local memory is 16 or 64 Mbytes of dynamic random access memory (DRAM) with a latency of 87 to 253 nanoseconds and a bandwidth of up to

6.7 EXAMPLE SYSTEMS   309

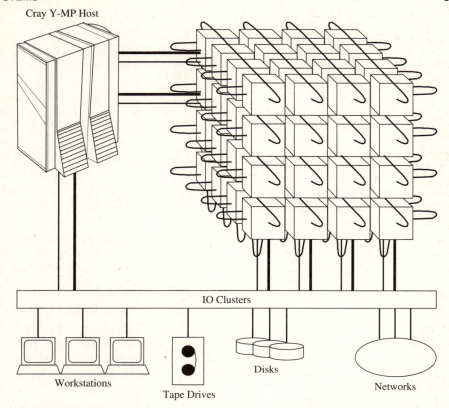

Figure 6.39 Cray T3D System (Koeninger et al., 1994) (Reprinted with permission from Digital Technical Journal.)

320 megabytes per second. Remote memory is directly addressable by the processor with a latency of from 1 to 2 microseconds and a bandwidth of over 100 megabytes per second. The total size of memory in a T3D system is the number of PEs times the size of each PE's local memory. The support circuitry extends the control and addressing functions of the microprocessor and facilitates data transfers to or from local memory.

Each processing element node contains two PEs, a network interface, and a block transfer engine (BLT). The two PEs in the node are identical but function independently. Access to the block transfer engine and network interface is shared by the two PEs.

The network interface formats information before it is sent over the interconnect network to another processing element node or I/O gateway. It also receives incoming information from another processing element node or I/O gateway and steers it to the appropriate PE in the node.

The BLT is an asynchronous direct memory access controller that redistributes system data between local memory in either of the PEs and globally addressable system memory. The BLT can redistribute up to 65,536 64-bit words of data without interruption from the PE.

INTERCONNECT NETWORK

The interconnect network provides communication paths among the PE nodes and the I/O gateways. It is a three-dimensional matrix of paths that connects the nodes in the X, Y, and Z dimensions. It is composed of communication links and network routers.

A communication link transfers data and control information between two network routers. Each network router connects to a processing element node or an I/O gateway node. A communication link connects two nodes in one dimension and consists of two unidirectional channels. Each channel contains data, control, and acknowledge signals.

The interconnect network is a bidirectional torus in which a link connects the smallest numbered node in a dimension directly to the largest numbered node in the same dimension. This type of connection forms a ring where information can transfer from one node through all of the nodes in the same dimension and back to the original node.

The network uses the dimension-order routing. That is, when the message leaves a node, it travels through the network in the X dimension first, then through the Y dimension, and finally through the Z dimension to the destination node.

I/O GATEWAYS

The I/O gateways transfer system data and control information between the host system and the MPP or between the MPP and an input/output cluster. An I/O gateway can transfer information to any PE in the interconnect network.

The T3D system provides three mechanisms for hiding the start-up time (latency) of remote references: prefetch queue, remote processor store, and block transfer engine.

PREFETCH QUEUE

The DEC alpha instruction set contains an opcode (FETCH) that permits a compiler to provide a hint to the hardware of an upcoming memory activity. The T3D shell hardware uses FETCH to initiate a single word remote memory read that will fill a slot that is reserved by the hardware in the external prefetch queue. The prefetch queue acts as an external memory pipeline. As the processor issues each FETCH instruction, the shell hardware reserves a location in the queue for the return data and sends a memory read request packet to the remote node. When the read data returns to the requesting processor, the shell hardware writes the data to the reserved slot in the queue. The processor retrieves the data from the queue by executing a load instruction from a memory-mapped register that represents the head of the queue. The data prefetch queue can store up to 16 words, so the processor can issue up to 16 FETCH instructions before executing any load instruction to pop the data from the head of the queue.

REMOTE PROCESSOR STORE

The Alpha processor stores to remote memories need not wait for the completion of a single store operation. This is an effective communication mechanism when the producer of the data knows which PEs will immediately need to use the data. The Alpha processor has four 4-word write buffers on chip that try to accumulate four words (a cache line) of data before performing the actual external store. This feature increases the effective bandwidth. In the T3D system, a counter is set up in the PE shell circuitry. Each time the processor issues a remote store, the counter is incremented and each time a write operation completes, the counter is decremented. The processor can read the counter and determine when all the write operations are completed.

BLOCK TRANSFER ENGINE (BLT)
The BLT is an asynchronous direct memory access controller used to redistribute data between remote and local memory. The BLT operates independently of the processors at a node. The processor initiates BLT activity by storing individual request information in the memory-mapped control registers. The overhead is significant in this setup work, and hence, the BLT is most effective for large data block moves.

The T3D system provides four hardware synchronization primitives: barrier, fetch and increment, lightweight message, and atomic swap. These facilitate synchronization at various levels of granularity and support both control parallelism and data parallelism.

In summary, the major characteristics of the T3D system are:

1. high-speed microprocessors,
2. distributed shared memory,
3. high-speed interprocessor communications,
4. latency hiding,
5. fast synchronization, and
6. fast I/O capabilities.

The T3D system is scalable from 32 to 2048 processors, from 4.2 to over 300 GFLOPS peak performance, and from 512 Mbytes to 128 Gbytes of memory.

PROGRAMMING MODEL
The system uses CRAFT, a Fortran programming model with implicit remote addressing. It provides a standard, high-level interface to the hardware, both the traditional data parallel and message-passing MPP programming capabilities, and the work-sharing capability between the host and the MPP. Parallelism can be expressed explicitly through message passing library calls or implicitly through data parallel constructs and directives, taking advantage of the compiler to distribute data and work.

OPERATING SYSTEM
The UNICOS MAX operating system was designed to reuse Cray's UNICOS operating system, which is a superset of the standard UNIX operating system. UNICOS MAX is a multiuser operating system that provides a powerful supercomputing environment that enhances application development, system interoperability, and user productivity.

UNICOS MAX is a distributed operating system wherein functions are divided between the MPP and the UNICOS operating system on the host. The bulk of the operating system runs on the hosts with only microkernels, such as application data storage and processing, running on MPP processors.

PERFORMANCE

A 256-processor T3D system was the fastest MPP running NASA/Ames parallel benchmarks. Although the Cray C916 PVP system ran six of the eight benchmarks faster than the T3D, the price-to-performance ratio is better for T3D, because the cost of C916 is about three times that of T3D. It is expected that a 512-processor T3D will outperform C916 in six of the eight benchmarks.

6.8 SUMMARY

The basic architectural models for MIMD systems were introduced in this chapter. Problems involved in designing these systems, concepts of programming such systems, and performance evaluation were also discussed. Details of five commercial multiprocessor systems were provided.

The field of multiprocessor systems has been a dynamic one recently in the sense that several experimental and commercial MIMD systems have been built, brought to market, and discarded. Two recent casualties of the commercial MIMD system market are the Alliant FX series and the BBN Butterfly series. At this writing (1994), Japan's NEC Corporation has announced a multiprocessor system (SX-4) with 512 processors providing a peak operating capacity of 1.024 teraflops.

The hardware technology of today allows the development of large MIMD systems, but tailoring the applications to take advantage of the parallelism in hardware is still nontrivial. Parallel programming languages and corresponding compilers and software development support environments are still evolving.

Some of the problems with MIMD system application are:

1. Selecting the proper model of parallel computation.
2. Parallel programming languages that allow easy representation of task creation, deletion and synchronization, and send/receive message-passing primitives.
3. Reduction of overhead by overcoming data dependencies of tasks, optimal allocation of processors, minimizing contention for resources and idle waiting, and optimal scheduling of tasks.
4. Scalability.
5. The control of software development and operational control of the MIMD system is also complex. A primary concern is how the development of application software for a multinode computing system should be approached. Much work has been done concerning the need for maintaining control of software developed for SISD computers. With the N-fold complexity of concurrent architectures, the concern of software development control becomes paramount. More sophisticated software development environments are needed if a multitude of programs are to be developed within reasonable cost and time constraints. Williams (1990), Brawer (1989), and Perrott (1987) provide further details on these topics.

Obviously, the single processor architecture is the most efficient solution if the performance requirements of the application can be met. If not, an SIMD solution might be evaluated. If the application does not suit the SIMD solution, the MIMD solution would be appropriate. In addition to the performance and cost constraints, the application characteristics dictate the selection of architecture. It is observed that only parallel processing architectures will be able to meet the grand computational challenges of the 1990s and beyond.

REFERENCES

Adam, T., K. Chandy, and J. A. Dickson. 1974. Comparison of list schedulers for parallel processing systems. *Communication of ACM* 17 (December) 685–690.

Agarwal, A., R. Simoni, J. Hennessy, and M. Horowitz. 1988. An evaluation of directory schemes for cache coherence. *Proceeding of Fifteenth Annual International Symposium on Computer Architecture,* June, 280–289.

Agrawal, D. P., K.V. Janakiram, and G. C. Pathak. 1986. Evaluating the performance of multicomputer configurations. *IEEE Computer,* May, 23–37.

Ajmone, M. M., G. Balbo, and G. Conte. 1989. *Performance models for multiprocessor systems.* New York: McGraw-Hill.

Alamasi, G. S., and A. Gottlieb. 1989. *Highly parallel computing.* Redwood City, CA: Benjamin/Cummings Publishing Company.

Alliant Computer Systems Corporation. 1988. *Alliant product summary.* Littleton, Mass.: Alliant Computer Systems Corporation.

Alliant Computer Systems Corporation. 1988. *FX/Series architecture manual.* Littleton, Mass: Alliant Computer Systems Corporation.

Anderson, T. 1990. The performance of spin lock alternatives for shared-memory multiprocessors. *IEEE Transaction on Parallel Distributed Systems* 1(1): 6–16.

Annaratone, M., and R. Ruhl. 1989. Performance measurements on a commercial multiprocessor running parallel code. *The 16th Annual IEEE International Symposium on Computer Architecture,* May-June, 307–314.

Asbury, R., et al. 1985. Concurrent computers ideal for inherently parallel problems. *Computer Design* 24(9) (September 1): pp. 46–49.

Bashir, A., G. Susarla, and K. Karavan. 1983. A statistical study of a task scheduling algorithm. *IEEE Transactions on Computers* C-32 (8): 774–777.

Barnes, J., and C. Whitby-Strevens. 1988. High-performance Ada using transputers. *Defense Computing* (September-October): 45–49.

Bawerjee, P., et al. 1990. Algorithm based fault tolerance on a hypercube multiprocessor. *IEEE Transactions on Computers* 39 (9): pp. 960–969.

Benes, V. E. 1965. *Mathematical theory of communication networks and telephone traffic.* New York: Academic Press.

Benes, V. E. 1967. On rearrangeable three-stage connecting networks. *The Bell System Technical Journal* (September): 1481–1492.

Bhuyan, L. N., and D. P. Agrawal. 1984. Generalized hypercube and hyperbus structures for a computer network. *IEEE Transactions on Computers* C-33 (1): pp. 426–439.

Brawer, S. 1989. *Introduction to parallel programming.* New York: Academic Press.

Burns, A. 1988. *Programming in Occam 2* Reading, Mass.: Addison-Wesley.

Carmona, E. A. and M. D. Rice. 1991. Modeling the serial and parallel fractions of a parallel algorithm. *Journal of Parallel and Distributed Computing* 2(2): pp. 221–229.

Censier, L. M. and L. Feautrier. 1978. A new solution to coherence problems in multicache systems. *IEEE Transaction on Computers* C-27 (December): pp. 1102–1114.

Chnafas, D. N., and H. Steinman. 1990. *Supercomputers.* New York: McGraw Hill.

Clos, C. 1953. A study of nonblocking switching networks. *The Bell System Technical Journal* (March): 406–424.

Crowther, W., J. Goodhue, R. Gurwitz, R. Rettberg, and R. Thomas. 1985. The butterfly parallel processor. *IEEE Computer Architecture Technical Committee Newsletter* (September-December): 18–45.

Deital, H. M. 1990. *Operating systems.* Reading, MA: Addison Wesley Publishing Company.

Desrochers, G. R. 1987. *Parallel and multiprocessing.* New York: Intertext (McGraw Hill).

Dinning, A. 1989. A survey of synchronization methods for parallel computers. *IEEE Computer* 22 (7) 66–77.

Eggers, J. S and R. H. Katz. 1988. Evaluating the performance of four snooping cache coherency protocols. *Proceedings of Sixteenth Annual IEEE International Symposium on Architecture* 17 (June): 3–14.

El-Rewini, H. and T. G. Lewis. 1990. Scheduling parallel program tasks onto arbitrary target machines. *Journal of Parallel and Distributed Computing* 1(6)(June): pp. 610–615.

Feng, T-Y., 1981. A survey of interconnection networks. *Computer* 14 (December): 12–27.

Gallant, J. 1991. Cache coherency protocols. *EDN* 36 (March 14): 41–50.

Ghezzi, C., M. Jazayeri. 1982. *Programming language concepts.* New York: John Wiley & Sons.

Goke, G., and G. J. Lipovsky. 1983. Banyon networks for partitioning multiprocessor systems. *First Annual Symposium on Computer Architecture.* December, 21–28.

Goodman, J. R. 1983. Using cache memory to reduce processor memory traffic. *10th International Symposium on Computer Architecture,* June.

Graunke, R. and S. Thakkar. 1990. Synchronization algorithms for shared-memory multiprocessors. *IEEE Computer* 23 (6): 175–189.

Gupta A. and V. Kumar. Performance properties of large scale parallel systems. *Journal of Parallel and Distributed Computing,* 19 (3): pp. 110–116.

Gustafson, J. L. 1992. The consequences of fixed time performance measurements. *Proceedings of the 25th Hawaii International Conference on System Sciences* III: 113–124.

Johnson, T., and T. Durham. 1986. *Parallel processing: The challenge of new computer architectures.* Ovum Inc.

Hagersten, E., A. Landin and S. Haridi. 1992. DDM—A cache-only memory architecture. *IEEE Computer* 25 (9): 44–54.

Hwang, K. and F. A. Briggs. 1984. Computer architecture and parallel processing. New York: McGraw Hill.

Hwang, K. and D. Degroot. 1989. Parallel processing for supercomputers and artificial intelligence. New York: McGraw Hill.

IEEE Spectrum. 1992. Special issue on supercomputers, September.

Indurkhya, B., H. S. Stone, and L. XiCheng. 1986. Optimal partitioning of randomly generated distributed programs. *IEEE Transactions on Software Engineering* SE-12 (3): 483–495.

INMOS Limited. 1989. *The transputer applications notebook: Architecture and software.* Bristol, UK: INMOS Limited.

REFERENCES

INMOS Limited. 1989. *The transputer databook*. Bristol, U.K: INMOS Limited.

Intel Corporation. 1988. Processing on Intel concurrent supercomputers: A technical seminar.

Kallstrom, M. and S. S. Thakkar. 1988. Programming three parallel computers. *IEEE Software* 5 (1): 11–22.

Kessler, R. and J. Schwarzmeier. 1993. Cray T3D: A new dimension for Cray Research. *Proceedings of COMPCON,* 176–182.

Koeninger, R. K., M. Furtney, and M. Walker. 1994. A shared memory MPP from Cray Research. *Digital Technical Journal* 6(2): 8–21..

Knuth, D. E. 1971. An empirical study of fortran programs. *Software Practice and Experiences.* 105–133.

Krajewski, R. 1985. Multiprocessing: An overview. *BYTE* 10 (5): 171–181.

Kuck, D. et al., 1986. Parallel supercomputing today and the Cedar approach. *Science* (28 February).

Kumar, V. and A. Gupta. 1991. Analyzing scalability of parallel algorithms and architectures. *Technical Report 91–18.* Computer Science Department, University of Minnesota.

Levitan, S. P., 1987. Measuring communication structures in parallel architectures and algorithms. *Characteristics of parallel programming.* Cambridge, Mass.: MIT Press.

Marinescu, D. C. and J. R. Rice. 1991. On high level characterization of parallelism. *Technical Report CSD-TR-1011.* Computer Science Department, Purdue University.

Mitchell, D. A. P., J. A. Thompson, G. A. Manson, and G. R. Brookes. 1990. *Inside the Transputer*. New York: Blackwell Scientific Publications.

Perrott, R. H. 1987. *Parallel programming*. New York: Addison-Wesley.

Pountain, D. and D. May. 1987. A tutorial introduction to Occam programming. New York: BSP Professional Books.

Rattner, J. 1992. Parallel supercomputers tackle tough research questions. *R&D Magazine* (July): 48–52.

Rodney, G. L., and G. J. Lipovsky. 1973. Banyan networks for partitioning multiprocessor systems. *Proceedings of First Annual Symposium on Computer Architecture,* 21–28.

Shiva, S. G. 1991. Computer design and architecture. Glenview, IL: HarperCollins.

Siegal, H. J. 1985. *Interconnection networks for large-scale parallel processing.* Lexington, Mass: Lexington Books.

Stone, H. S. 1971. Parallel processing with the perfect shuffle. *IEEE Transactions on Computers* C-20 (February): 153–161.

Sun, X. H. and L. M. Ni. 1993. Scalable problems and memory-bounded speedup. *Journal of Parallel and Distributed Computing* 19 (September): 27–37.

Tang, C. K. 1976. Cache system design in a tightly coupled multiprocessor system. *Proceeding of AFIP National Computer Conference.*

Tang, Z., and G. J. Li. 1990. Optimal granularity of grid iteration problems. *Proceeding International Conference on Parallel Processing.* Vol. I, 111–118.

Thinking Machine Corporation. 1993. *CM-5 desktops-to-teraOps supercomputing*. Cambridge, Mass: Thinking Machine Corporation.

Thinking Machine Corporation. 1991. *CM-5 Product Specifications*. Cambridge, Mass: Thinking Machine Corporation.

Wexler, J. 1989. *Concurrent Programming in Occam 2*. London: Ellis Horwood Limited.

Williams, S. A. 1990. *Programming models for parallel systems*. New York: John Wiley & Sons.

Wu, C-L., and T-Y. Feng. 1980. On a class of multistage interconnection networks. *IEEE Transactions on Computers* C-29 (8): 694–702.

Yeh, P. C., J. H. Patel and E. S. Davidson. 1983. Shared cache for multiple stream computer systems. *IEEE Transactions on Computers* (January) C-32 (1): 64–69.

PROBLEMS

6.1. It is required to design a general purpose multiprocessor system using processor and memory elements. Identify the minimum set of characteristics that each element needs to satisfy.

6.2. Four 16-bit processors are connected to four 64K × 16 memory banks through a crossbar network. The processors can access 64K memory directly. Derive the characteristics of the crossbar network to efficiently run this multiprocessor system. Show the hardware details. Describe the memory mapping needed. How is it done?

6.3. Study any multiprocessor system to which you have access to answer the following:
  a. What constitutes a task?
  b. What is the minimum task switching time?
  c. What synchronization primitives are implemented?

6.4. The fetch and add can be generalized to fetch and op (a, b), where a is a variable and b is an expression. This operation returns the value of a and replaces it with $(a$ op $b)$. What would be the advantages of this operation over the synchronization primitives described in this chapter?

6.5. Analyze the matrix multiplication algorithm of this chapter to derive the optimum partitioning and storage of matrices A and B so that all the spawned tasks can run simultaneously.

6.6. Consider the following computation:

$$z_i = a_i * b_i + c_i * d_i$$

where $i = 1$ to N. Write a high-level program for this computation using (a) fork/join, (b) parbegin/parend, and (c) doall primitives.

6.7. Estimate the computation time for the program of (a) in the above problem assuming the following time characteristics:

Operation	Execution time
Addition	1
Multiplication	3
Fork	10
Join	4

Assume that the tasks start execution as soon as they are spawned and there is no waiting time.

6.8. What is the ideal task granularity in problem 6.7 (i.e., when will the computation time be a minimum) if the number of processors is four?

6.9. An algorithm requires access to each row of an $N \times N$ matrix. Show the storage of matrix to minimize the access time if the multiprocessor consists of N processors and N memory banks interconnected by (a) crossbar and (b) bus.

6.10. Repeat problem 6.9 if the algorithm accesses both rows and columns of the matrix.

6.11. Consider two concurrent processes X and Y each executing the following sequence of statements:

```
WAIT(A)
WAIT(B)
SIGNAL(B)
SIGNAL(A)
```

where A and B are binary semaphores.
a. Can these processes deadlock? If so, when?
b. If X is not changed, but Y is changed to execute:

```
WAIT(B)
WAIT(A)
SIGNAL(A)
SIGNAL(B)
```

How does the deadlock condition change?

6.12. Consider the following program:

```
for i = 1,n
  for j = 1,m
    c[i] = c[i] + a[i,j] * b[i,j]
  endfor
endfor
```

a. Determine dependencies among the statements.
b. Interchange i and j loops and determine dependencies among the statements.
c. Which of the above two programs would you prefer to achieve each of the following implementation goals: vectorization, shared memory MIMD, message passing MIMD?

6.13. Consider an MIMD with N processors and N memories. It is required to compute the row sum of an $N \times N$ matrix using this system. Show the storage format of the matrix among the N memories and the corresponding time to compute the row-sum if the following interconnection networks are used:
a. crossbar and
b. single-bus.

6.14. Study the Multibus II and VME bus architectures. What support do they provide for configuring multiprocessor systems?

6.15. Assume that the synchronization and communication overhead in an N processor system is 10N instruction cycles. Plot the speedup offered by this system as a function of the number of processors if synchronization and communication is required every 100, 1000, and 10,000 instructions.

CHAPTER 7

Dataflow Architectures

The basic structure underlying all the architectures described so far in this book is the one proposed by von Neumann. Parallel and pipeline structures were used to enhance the system throughput and overcome the limitations of the von Neumann model. Over the last few years, other types of architectures have evolved. The dataflow and reduction architectures introduced in Chapter 2 are two among many such experiments.

Recall that the von Neumann architectures are **control driven,** and in them, data are passive and fetched only when an instruction needs them. That is, the operation of the machine is dictated by the instruction sequence (i.e., the program). Dataflow architectures, on the other hand, are **data driven** because the readiness of data dictates the operation of the machine. That is, data are operated upon when they are available. Reduction architectures are **demand driven** in the sense that data are fetched when the evaluation of a function requires (i.e., demands) them. This chapter concentrates on dataflow architectures because they have received much wider attention compared to other experimental architectures.

Dataflow architectures can be used advantageously for computation-oriented applications that exhibit a fine grain parallelism. Examples of such applications are image processing, automated cartography, and scene analysis. Studies conducted by the National Aeronautics and Space Administration (NASA) have shown that this architecture type is suitable for aerodynamic simulation. Jack Dennis and the researchers at MIT have demonstrated that a dataflow computer can substantially increase the simulation speed over control flow computers. Consider, for instance, the weather forecasting application in which a weather prediction model is used to predict

7.1 DATAFLOW MODELS

the weather at some future time based on current and historical observations. A model implemented on a Control Data Corporation (CDC) 7600 took about 2 minutes to simulate 20 minutes of real-time weather. A dataflow model consisting of 256 processing elements, 128 addition units, 96 multiplication units, 32 memory modules, and a total memory of 3 Mbytes met the goal of 5 seconds for the same simulation.

Dataflow concepts have been utilized in the design of various processors. The CDC 6600 series of machines is an example. Some Japanese manufacturers have recently introduced processor boards that utilize dataflow structures. Yet, after almost 20 years of experimentation, there are no major commercially available dataflow machines. Extensive hardware requirements and lack of progress in programming language and operating system development have been cited as the reasons.

The two common models of dataflow architectures are introduced in the next section. Section 2 extends the description of dataflow graphs provided in Section 1. Section 3 introduces dataflow programming languages. Section 4 briefly describes several experimental dataflow systems, and Section 5 outlines performance characteristics.

7.1 DATAFLOW MODELS

As mentioned earlier, in a control flow architecture, the total control of the sequence of operations rests with the programmer. That is, a processor undergoes the instruction fetch, decode, and execution phases for each instruction in the program. The data manipulation involves the transfer of data from one unit to another unit of the machine. Data are stored as variables (memory locations), taken to functional units, and operated upon as specified by the programmer; then the results are assigned to other variables.

A dataflow program, on the other hand, is one in which the sequence of operations is not specified but depends upon the need and the availability of data. There is no concept of passive data storage, instruction counter, variables, or addresses. The operation of the machine is entirely guided by data interdependencies and availability of resources. The architecture is based on the concept that an instruction is executable as soon as all its operands are available. As such, the data dependencies must be deducible from the program. Also because the only requirement for operations to occur is the availability of operands, multiple operations can occur simultaneously. This concept allows the employment of parallelism at the operator (i.e., the finest grain) level. In fact, all dataflow architectures to date have employed instruction level parallelism.

EXAMPLE 7.1

Figure 7.1 shows a Pascal program to calculate the roots of the quadratic equation $ax^2 + bx + c = 0$. In conventional architecture, the execution follows the sequential structure of the program, and on a single processor machine, the following eight steps are required:

```
Program find roots(input,output);
var
        a,b,c:real;
begin
        writeln(" Give the values of a,b,c");
        readln(a,b,c);
        a:= 2 * a;
        c:= b * b - 2 * a * c;
        c:= sqrt(c);
        c:= c/a;
        b:= -b/a;
        a:= b + c;
        b:= b - c;
        writeln(" The roots of the equation are");
        writeln(a,b);
end.
```

Figure 7.1 Pascal Program to Find the Roots of Equation $ax^2 + bx + c = 0$

```
1>  a:=2 * a              ; must wait for input a
2>  c:=b*b - 2 * a * c    ; must wait for input b and step1
3>  b:= -b/a              ; must wait for step1
4>  c:= sqrt(c)           ; must wait for step2
5>  c:=c/a                ; must wait for step4
6>  a:=b + c              ; must wait for step5 and step3
7>  b:=b - c              ; must wait for step5 and step3
8>  output(a,b)           ; must wait for steps 6 & 7.
```

The number of steps can be reduced from eight to six if multiple processors are available, because steps 2 and 3 and steps 6 and 7 can be performed simultaneously. The important characteristic of this program is that the sequence of operations is dictated by it.

Now consider the **dataflow graph (DFG)** in Figure 7.2 representing the same computation. Here the nodes (circles) represent operators (processors) and arcs represent paths that carry either data or control values between them. For example, node 1 computes the square of its input operand "b" and its output becomes the input for node 6. Node 3 negates "b," and its output is one of the inputs to node 5. Node 2 multiplies its inputs "2" and "a," and its output "2 * a" is placed on three arcs that become inputs to nodes 4, 5, and 8.

A node *fires* as soon as data are available on all its input arcs and its output arcs are free of data. The effect of node firing corresponds to removing the data from the input arcs, performing the node computation, and placing the result on the output arc.

As soon as the values for a, b, c, and the constant 2 are available, nodes 1, 2, and 3 fire simultaneously; nodes 4 and 5 fire as soon as they receive the output of node 2; node 6 fires after receiving data from nodes 1 and 4; and so on. Thus, arcs imply the data dependency of operations, and each node starts computing as soon as data arrive

7.1 DATAFLOW MODELS

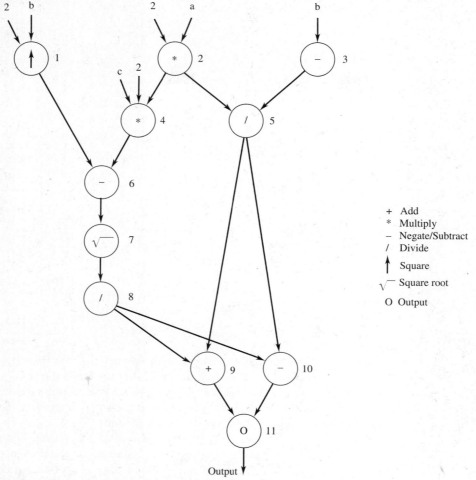

Figure 7.2 Dataflow Graph for the Solution of $ax^2 + bx + c = 0$

on all its inputs. No other time or sequence constraints are imposed, and several nodes can be active simultaneously. The important point to note is that there is no explicit representation of control flow in a DFG. The operations occur as and when data are ready.

Figure 7.3(a) shows a schematic view of a dataflow machine. The machine memory consists of a series of **cells**. A cell shown in (b) provides all the information needed for an operation to occur (at an appropriate node in the DFG). It consists of an operation code, number of input arcs (NI), number of output arcs (NO), NI input data slots, and NO output slots. Each data slot contains the data field and a flag that indicates whether the data value is ready or not. Each output slot points to a cell that receives the result of operations of that cell. When all the input operands are ready, a cell is firable. The instruction fetch unit consists of multiple fetch units operating in parallel looking for firable cells in the memory. They fetch firable cells and convert them into instruction packets and enter them into the instruction queue. When a

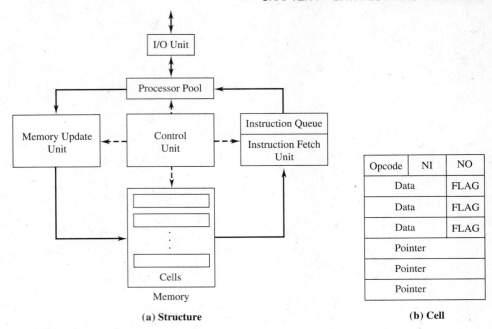

Figure 7.3 Static Dataflow Model

processor becomes available, it executes an instruction from this queue and presents the output to the memory update unit, which in turn sends the results to appropriate memory cells based on the output pointers. This process continues until there are no firable cells. The I/O unit manages the interaction with external devices, and the control unit coordinates the activities of all the units.

Now consider the details of the firing of a (multiplier) node shown in Figure 7.4. Here the availability of the data on an arc is indicated by the presence of a **token** on the arc (Rumbaugh, 1977). When a node has a data token on each of its input arcs, it fires and generates a data token on each of its output arcs. That is, when a node fires, the tokens on input arcs are removed and each output arc gets a token.

There are two node firing semantics commonly employed in a DFG: static and dynamic. In the **static** model, a node fires only when each of its input arcs has a token and its output arcs are empty. Thus, an acknowledgment of the fact that a subsequent node has consumed its input token is needed before a node in a static DFG can fire. The dataflow model of Figure 7.3 represents the static architecture. Here each node

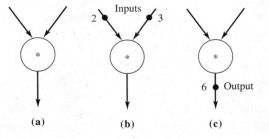

Figure 7.4 Node Firing

7.2 DATAFLOW GRAPHS

receives as one of its input a control tag from the subsequent node indicating that the subsequent node has consumed the data on the output arc.

In the **dynamic** model, a node fires when all its inputs have tokens and the absence of tokens on its outputs is not necessary. Thus, it is possible to have multiple tokens on an arc. A tagging scheme is employed in dynamic DFGs to associate tokens with the appropriate data set. The tag carries the information as to when and how a token was generated and which data set it belongs to.

Figure 7.5 shows a dynamic dataflow machine. This is similar to the one in Figure 7.3 except for the token matching section. Here the processors operate on the operands that have similar tags and the memory update unit uses the tags to update cells belonging to the same data set.

Note that a high throughput can be achieved by dataflow architectures, because the algorithms are represented at the finest grain parallelism and, hence, the maximum degree of concurrency possible. This fine grain parallelism also poses a major challenge in the design and coordination of activities of various subsystems in the machine.

7.2 DATAFLOW GRAPHS

As seen by Figure 7.2, a DFG is a directed graph whose nodes represent operators and whose arcs represent pointers for forwarding the results of operations to subsequent nodes.

Figure 7.6 shows the three common types of operators in a DFG. The arithmetic and logical operators implement the usual binary operations. The array handling

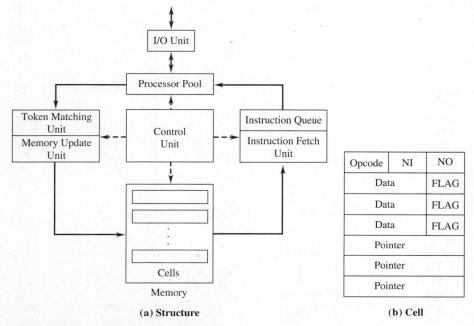

Figure 7.5 Dynamic Dataflow Model

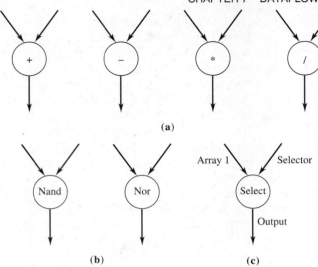

Figure 7.6 DFG Operators

operator selects and outputs a particular element of the array based on the value of the selector input.

Figure 7.7 shows the structure of two control operators (nodes). In the **switch** node, the control input selects the output arc to which the input token is transmitted. In the **merge** node, the control input selects one among the data inputs to be placed on the output. In these cases, it is not necessary that the inputs not selected have a token before the nodes fire.

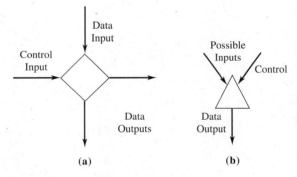

Figure 7.7 DFG Control Operators

EXAMPLE 7.2

Figure 7.8 shows a loop construct implemented as a DFG. The *condition* operator evaluates the loop control condition and generates the control input for the switch node, which either allows the continuation of the loop or exits from it.

7.2 DATAFLOW GRAPHS

The classical dataflow model is represented by the **cyclic** graphs of the type shown in Figure 7.8 (while the functional model is represented by the **acyclic** graph notation). A major problem of cyclic graphs is the *race* condition, as illustrated by the following example.

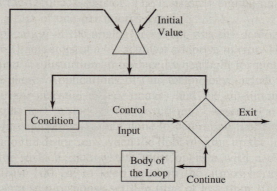

Figure 7.8 Cyclic Graph for Loop Control

EXAMPLE 7.3

In the graph shown in Figure 7.9, two computations produce the values A and B. These values are used by a node, which also receives the values X and Y produced by another set of two nodes. Ideally, A needs to be combined with X and B with Y. If the node producing A as the output takes longer than the one that produces B, then B meets with X and A meets with Y, which is not desirable. To eliminate this problem, labels are attached to the data in order that only those that belong to a certain label can pair together. A checking procedure is then needed in the computations to ensure that both the operands carry the same label.

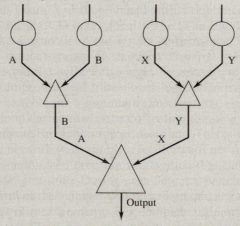

Figure 7.9 Race Condition in a Dataflow Graph

7.3 DATAFLOW LANGUAGES

The primary goal of a high-level language for the dataflow computers is the representation of parallelism and the dataflow as depicted by a DFG. The best-known dataflow languages are Irvine Dataflow language, or Id, (Arvind, Gostelow, and Plouffe, 1978) and Value-Oriented Algorithmic Language, or VAL, (Ackerman, 1982). Other dataflow languages are HASAL (Sharp, 1985); Lapse (Glauert, 1978); and SISAL, or Streams and Iterations in Single Assignment Language, (Gaudiot, 1989). There have been attempts to use conventional languages to program dataflow machines (as in a Texas Instruments' design that used Fortran). On the other hand, the goal of languages like SISAL was to define a universal language for programming multiprocessor systems.

The essential features of a dataflow language are:

a. The language should be functional. The term *functional* implies a language that operates by applications of functions to values. In a functional language, all control structures are replaced by combining operators that manipulate functions directly without ever appearing to explicitly manipulate data. A functional programming (FP) system consists of a set of objects, functions, functional forms and definitions, and a single operation (i.e., application). The power of an FP system is due to its ability to combine functions to form new functions. An example of a functional language is (pure) LISP.
b. The language should allow a nonsequential specification. That is, the order of the function definitions should not be related to their order of execution, which is a fundamental property of the dataflow system.
c. The language should obey the single assignment rule. That is, the same variable name cannot be used more than once on the left-hand side of any statement. A new name is given for any redefined variable, and all subsequent references are changed to the new name.

EXAMPLE 7.4

The sequence of statements:

```
X := A + B
Y := A - B
X := X * Y
```

has to be changed to the following:

```
X := A + B
Y := A - B
Z := X * Y
```

The single assignment rule facilitates the detection of parallelism in a program and offers clarity compared to repeated use of the same name. Tesler

7.3 DATAFLOW LANGUAGES

and Enea (1968) proposed this rule, and it was applied in the development of the French dataflow computer LAU and the Manchester, England, dataflow machine. (The optimizing compilers on conventional machines also perform this transformation.)

d. There should be no side effects, because a node in a dataflow graph is self-contained and there is no global data space of values or use of shared memory cells.

Dataflow languages differ from conventional languages in several aspects:

a. The concept of variables is much different in dataflow languages compared to that in a control flow language. The variables are not assigned values in the sense that a value is routed to a specific memory location reserved for that variable. That is, all variables are values (including arrays) and not memory locations. Operations merely produce new values. Names are assigned to values instead of values being assigned to names. The names are for the convenience of the programmer. Because the values produced by a computation are to be used immediately after they are produced, they can be simply sent to the next computation for which they are intended.

b. Dataflow languages are *applicative* in nature. That is, values are operated on to produce more values. These values, in turn, are used for other operations until the given task is completed.

c. One property of dataflow languages is the *locality* of effect. When data is produced by one node of the dataflow graph, it is used by some other node but does not influence the computation performed by another node. Because of this property, temporary names can be used in a mutually exclusive section of a program. Different sections may use the same name and still execute concurrently without influencing the computations performed by other sections. This is true of any block-structured language.

d. Because of the data driven mode of execution, go to constructs of conventional languages are not required in dataflow languages. The DFG contains all the information necessary to execute the program.

e. The iteration structures of dataflow languages are somewhat unusual because of *no side effects* and *single assignment* properties. These languages are not particularly suited to execute loops, and usually only one type of iteration structure is allowed.

Dataflow languages can be classified as either **graphical** or **textual.** The DFG notation used so far in this chapter represents graphical languages while VAL and Id are examples of textual languages.

There are two graphical notations: **cyclic** and **acyclic.** The classical model of dataflow is represented by the cyclic graph notation while the functional model is represented by the acyclic graph notation.

As noted in earlier chapters, efficient manipulation of data structures is a difficult task for any parallel environment. It poses special problems in dataflow machines because of the use of functional languages (with no side effects and no updatable storage), data-driven computation, and a high degree of parallelism.

All dataflow machines have utilized the concept of a structure store that holds the values of the elements of the data structure while labels carry their addresses. Different machines allow different types of operations on these structure stores.

7.3.1 Value-Oriented Algorithmic Language (VAL)

This section highlights the major characteristics of VAL, which is designed to operate on dataflow structures although it incorporates many features from modern imperative programming languages.

The data types in VAL are the same as the ones in conventional languages: integer, real, character, and Boolean. Other types may be formed using the structured operators: array, record, and one of. An error value exists for each of the data types.

Being a dataflow language, VAL works only on values. Values are assigned to variable names, and they cannot be changed within the function or block in which they are defined. Arrays and records are considered to be functionally equivalent to single scalar values. That is, an array or record is not a collection of individual values but a single value to be operated upon: thus, it cannot be changed once it is assigned a value. However, the values can be accessed and used to create new arrays.

VAL is purely applicative in nature and hence does not contain statements similar to the ones in Pascal or Fortran. But, expressions and functions are present.

The IF-THEN-ELSE construct in VAL is shown below:

```
conditional:: = IF expression THEN expression
        {ELSEIF expression THEN expression}
        ELSE expression ENDIF
```

Parallelism is represented in VAL by a parallel expression consisting of three parts: a range specification, an environment expansion, and a result accumulation. The range specification identifies which range of values in the named value construct will be used. The environment expansion area identifies the operating environment of the expression, such as the binding of the variable names. The result accumulation portion identifies how the results of the body of the expression will be combined and returned.

The definition of the parallel expression forall is:

```
forall-expression ::=
FORALL name IN [expression] {, name IN
    [expression]} [declaration-definition part]
        forall-body-part {forall-body-part} ENDALL
forall-body-part ::=
CONSTRUCT expression | EVAL forall-op expression
forall-op ::= PLUS | TIMES | MIN | MAX | OR | AND
```

Two examples are given below:
```
FORALL J IN [1,N]
    EVAL PLUS J * J + J
ENDALL
FORALL J IN [1,4]
    X: REAL := Nth POWER ( REAL(J), J);
        CONSTRUCT J,X
    ENDALL
X: ARRAY [REAL] :=
    FORALL I IN [0,M+1]
        CONSTRUCT
            IF I = 0 | I = M + 1 THEN A[I]
            ELSE 0.5 * (A[I - 1] + A[I + 1])
            ENDIF
        ENDALL
```

7.4 EXAMPLE SYSTEMS

This section provides a brief description of several experimental systems implementing the static and dynamic dataflow models. These systems have been implemented in one of the two forms: **ring** and **network.**

In a **ring architecture,** the processors are connected by a ring. All the processors execute tasks independently and produce results. The results are sent to the control unit, which assigns them to subsequent operations and generates new tasks that are passed around the ring. The architecture may contain either a single ring or multiple rings connected together in parallel layers. In the latter case, a switch is provided to enable communication between the rings. Also the control function may be distributed between different layers.

In a **network architecture,** a separate control unit is not used. The processing nodes themselves perform the control task and are interconnected by a network.

7.4.1 Static Architectures

In the static dataflow model, only one data token is allowed to exist on an arc at any given time. Also control tokens are needed for proper transfer of data tokens from node to node. The MIT static architecture, the data-driven processor (DDP) of Texas Instruments Incorporated (TI), and the French LAU system are the popular static architectures.

MIT STATIC ARCHITECTURE
A schematic view of the MIT static architecture is shown in Figure 7.10. It consists of five major blocks connected by channels through which information flows in the form of packets. The memory contains the cells representing the nodes of a DFG. It receives the data tokens from the distribution network and control tokens from the

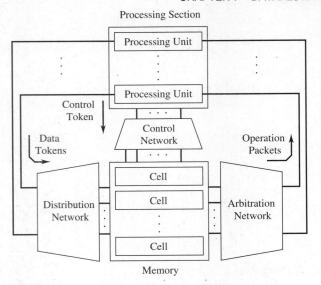

Figure 7.10 MIT Static Dataflow Machine

control network. When all the operands in a cell have arrived, the cell becomes an operation packet (i.e., enabled instruction). The arbitration network transfers the operation packets to the processing section. The processing units in the processing section perform functional operations on data tokens. The results of the execution are transferred to the memory through the distribution and the control networks. They become the operands for subsequent instructions.

TEXAS INSTRUMENTS' DDP SYSTEM

The architecture of the TI-DDP shown in Figure 7.11 is based on the MIT architecture. It was designed to execute Fortran programs in a dataflow fashion. The host processor compiles Fortran programs into program graphs. A cluster detection algorithm is used to partition the program graph into subgraphs, which are loaded into the memory units of processing elements. Each node stored in the memory represents an operation. A counter called the *predecessor counter* is used to determine whether a node is enabled for firing or not. A node can generate a maximum of 13 operands to a maximum of 13 destination addresses. An enabled node is executed in the ALU of the processing element. The results generated from the node firing will be forwarded to successor nodes in the processor's memory or to another processing element. Communication between processing elements is in the form of (34-bit) packets over the E-bus interconnection network. Each processing element contains a single ALU, and the enabled instructions are held in a queue awaiting execution. Similarly, there are queues at the inputs to the memory. The maintenance controller enables the loading and dumping of the contents of the memory, monitors the performance of the processor, and diagnoses the processor when faults occur.

7.4 EXAMPLE SYSTEMS

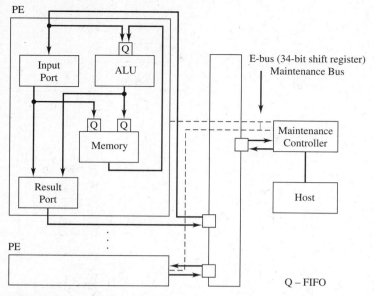

Figure 7.11 TI's DDP System

A DDP with four processing elements was built by TI. A number of benchmarks were run, and the results indicated that the performance could be improved in a linear manner by adding more processors. Although the DDP system is not commercially marketed, a follow-up with Ada as the programming language is being considered for military applications.

THE FRENCH LAU SYSTEM

A prototype of the LAU system was built at the Department of Computer Science, ONERA/CERT, France. It contains four major blocks (shown in Figure 7.12): the memory unit, the execution unit, the control unit, and the host interface. Programs are compiled by the host to produce dataflow graphs, which are represented as cells in the memory. Each node in the dataflow graph can have a maximum of two input arcs and several output arcs. The enabled nodes are presented to the execution unit through the instruction ready queue. The execution unit consists of up to 32 processors interconnected by a number of buses. Each processor executes the instruction assigned to it by reading the operands from the memory unit. The generated results are written into the memory.

7.4.2 Dynamic Architectures

The main characteristic of dynamic architectures is that many data tokens can exist on the same arc at any time. These data tokens need to be tagged so that only those tokens that belong to the same pair can be operated on. These tags can be either labels or colors, and there is no need for control tokens acknowledging the transfer of data

332 CHAPTER 7 DATAFLOW ARCHITECTURES

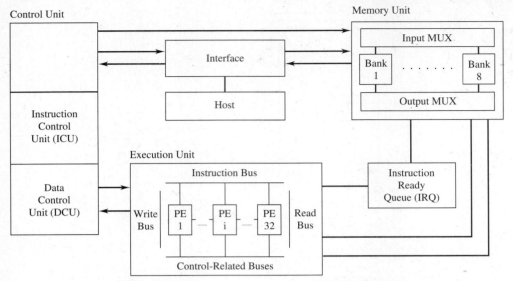

DCU-32k × 1 Pseudoassociative Memory
ICU-32k × 3 Pseudoassociative Memory

Bank i – two sections of 4k × 32 for instructions;
32k × 56 for data and links.
IRQ-FIFO with 128 entries. Each entry is 64 bits long.

Figure 7.12   French LAU System

tokens between the nodes. Tagging of data tokens and their matching requires extra hardware. Irvine dataflow machine developed by Arvind (Hwang & Briggs, 1984); the Manchester dataflow machine developed by Watson and Gurd at Manchester, England; the Data-Driven Machine (DDM) proposed by Davis; the Epsilon dataflow processor of the Sandia National Laboratories; the Experimental system for Data Driven processor array (EDDY) of Japan; and the MIT Monsoon system are examples of dynamic architectures.

MANCHESTER DATAFLOW MACHINE (MDM)

The MDM, shown in Figure 7.13, is organized as a circular pipeline. The I/O switch is capable of supporting seven pipelines and also communicates with the external environment. There are four independent units forming the circular pipeline. Tokens move in the form of *Token packets*.

The token packets first enter the token queue, which is used to smooth out the uneven rates of the generation and consumption of tokens. The token queue consists of three pipeline buffer registers surrounding a first-in-first-out (FIFO) circular store with a capacity of 32K tokens and with an access time of 120 nanoseconds. The width of the store and the registers is 96 bits, and the clock period is 37.5 nanoseconds. The maximum throughput of the queue is 2.67 million tokens/second.

The tagged token matching is done in the matching unit, which matches the tokens with the same tags (i.e., the token pairs designated for the same instruction). The single operand instructions bypass this unit. The matching utilizes a hardware hashing mechanism and consists of an associative memory capable of holding up to

7.4 EXAMPLE SYSTEMS

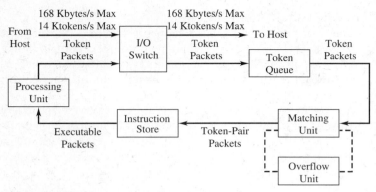

Figure 7.13 Manchester Dataflow Machine

1.25 million unmatched tokens awaiting their partners. This unit has eight buffers and twenty 64K-token memory boards, which also contain a comparator. The incoming token has a 54-bit matching key where 18 bits indicate the destination and 36 bits are for the tag. This will be hashed to a 16-bit address corresponding to the same cell on each board. Each board compares the key of the token stored at that address against the matching key of the incoming token. If a match is found, the two tokens are combined into a 133-bit group package and will be sent to the instruction store; if no match is found, the incoming token is written at that address on one of the 20 boards. Thus, the system can concurrently accommodate 20 tokens that hash to the same address. The subsequent tokens are sent to the overflow unit to continue their search.

The instruction store is a buffered random access memory with a capacity of 64K instructions. The memory access time is 150 nanoseconds, and the clock period is 40 nanoseconds, providing a maximum rate of 2 million instruction fetches/second.

The instructions are fetched from the store and executed by the processing unit resulting in the production of new tokens, which may reenter the queue. The token package entering and leaving the processing element is 96-bits wide and consists of 37 bits of data, 36 bits for the tag, and 23 bits for destination address, input port number, and the number of tokens that are needed to enable the destination instruction.

The processing unit consists of a homogeneous bank of 15 microcoded functional units. Each functional unit has 51 internal registers and 4K words of writable microcoded memory. The internal word length is 24 bits.

The dataflow graphs that are executable on this machine are generated by a compiler from the high-level language *Lapse*, a Pascal-like language.

The prototype of this machine had a single processing element and two structure stores (structure rings) connected to a host (VAX 11/780) with an I/O switching network. The speed of the link connecting the host was 168 KB/second (14K tokens per second). The two structure store modules hold a total of 1 million data values with an access rate of 0.75 million reads/second and nearly half as many writes/second. Arrays and other data structures were stored in this memory as *I-structures*, which improve the parallelism and efficiency of computations involving data structures by allowing these structures to be created incrementally. This enables the production and consumption of a data structure to proceed concurrently.

IRVINE DATAFLOW MACHINE

The Irvine dataflow machine shown in Figure 7.14 aims to exploit the potential of VLSI to provide a high-level, highly concurrent computation environment. This system was first developed at the University of California, Irvine, by Arvind and his group and was later transferred to the Massachusetts Institute of Technology. It utilizes the dataflow programming language Id.

In this architecture, a number of PEs are connected to a switching network using bit-serial connections. Each PE consists of a program memory for storing the code associated with the nodes, a data memory (I-structure) to store arrays, a waiting-matching store to match tokens, a 32-bit ALU, and a token output module. The output module also manipulates the tag part of the token.

DATA-DRIVEN MACHINE (DDM)

The DDM (Davis, 1978) is a recursively structured machine composed of asynchronous modules and can dynamically assign concurrent tasks to the available pro-

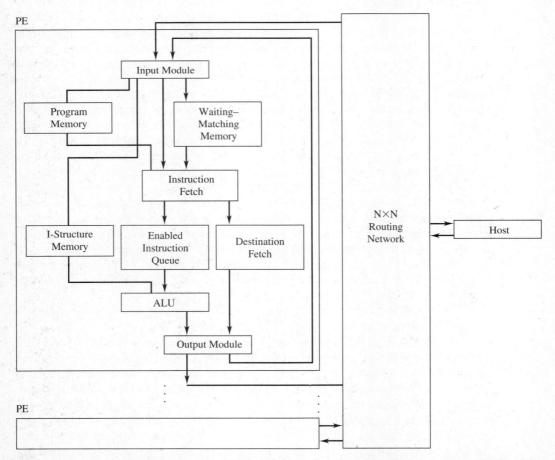

Figure 7.14 Irvine Dataflow Machine (Srini, 1986) (Reproduced with permission from IEEE.)

7.4 EXAMPLE SYSTEMS

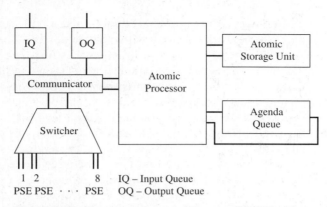

Figure 7.15 Processor Storage Element of DDM

cessing and storage elements. Several instances of a node in a program graph can be concurrently executed. The system uses FIFO queues instead of tagged tokens for keeping the data items of different computations distinct. Figure 7.15 shows the details of each node (called as a processor storage element—PSE). Each PSE has a switch, a processor, a storage unit, and queues for input and output tokens.

THE EPSILON DATAFLOW PROCESSOR

The Epsilon dataflow processor, developed at the Sandia National Laboratories (Davidson et al., 1989), aims at scalability and simplicity. It can not only be used as a high speed uniprocessor but also can be used for parallel operation as a multiprocessor system. Figure 7.16 shows the block diagram of the prototype Epsilon processor.

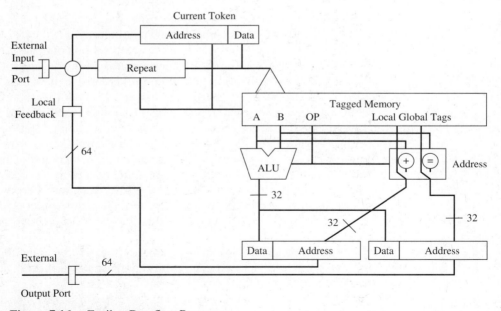

Figure 7.16. Epsilon Dataflow Processor

Each processor in this architecture has a fast ALU and its own tagged memory and shares the network resources with other processors. The tagged memory contains either idle or partially enabled instructions out of which only one can be enabled during a given clock cycle. The A and B fields shown in the figure make up the two operands of the instruction whose arrival enables the execution of the instruction. The results can be sent to either the local tagged memory or to other processors through the network. These routings are done through an FIFO, and the address for these routings comes from the LOCAL and the GLOBAL fields of the instruction. The instruction tag indicates the presence of the operands.

An FIFO buffered (input) port exists between the host and the processor, and a similar (output) port connects the processor to the host. Communication with the host and other processors and peripherals is performed by memory-mapped transfers through these FIFO ports. Local feedback of intermediate results is accomplished through another FIFO buffered port. This allows the design to effectively utilize the locality in computation to advantage. Both the feedback to the local tagged memory and the output to the external unit pass through an input stage and are written into the Epsilon's tagged memory. This process allows the matching tags to be checked and updated in a single clock cycle. The data from the tagged memory are sent to the address and arithmetic calculation units where they are processed. Depending on the action of the conditional unit, the generated results may be written into one, both, or neither of the output ports.

The Epsilon prototype is organized as a five-stage, nonblocking pipeline. A 10 MFLOPS CMOS/TTL processor prototype is currently operational, and its performance is being evaluated with several benchmarks.

EDDY

The Experimental system for Data Driven processor array (EDDY), developed in Japan as a scientific dataflow machine, is shown in Figure 7.17. It consists of a 4×4 array of processing elements and two broadcast control units (BCUs).

Each PE consisting of two Z8001 microprocessors is connected directly with eight other neighboring PEs. The broadcast control is capable of loading or unloading the programs to or from all the PEs by column or by row at the same time.

The PE is custom designed and consists of an instruction memory section, an operand memory section, an operation section, and a communication section. As each operand token arrives, the instruction memory fetches its operation node and sends both the fetched instruction and operand data to the operand memory section. If the incoming data is an operand for a two-operand operation, the operand memory will search for its paired partner associatively. When the paired operand is found, an operation packet will be constructed and sent to the operation section. If no paired operand is found, the arrived data token will be stored in the operand memory with a key attached.

All the data tokens are tagged so that at any time there can be more than one token on any given arc. The tagging control is decentralized and optimized for extracting maximum amount of parallelism.

The EDDY design concept uses a unique strategy of mixing static tagging and dynamic tagging. Static tagging refers to the situation in which execution environments are predefined and a unique tag will be assigned to each of them. Dynamic

7.4 EXAMPLE SYSTEMS

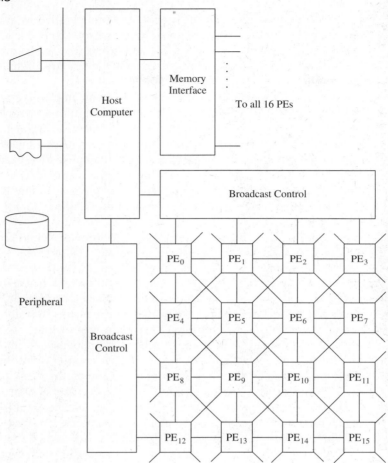

Figure 7.17 EDDY Dataflow Machine

tagging refers to a situation in which tags are assigned to each environment dynamically. An execution environment would be represented by the tag name. The environment name and the opcode are used as keys for the associative search.

MIT/MOTOROLA MONSOON SYSTEM
The Monsoon dataflow multiprocessor (Hicks, Chiou, Ang, and Arvind, 1992), built jointly by MIT and Motorola, is a small shared memory multiprocessor. The motivation behind building this research prototype was to demonstrate the feasibility of general purpose parallel computers, suitable for both numerical and symbolic applications. The main goal of this project was to show that one could easily write parallel programs in an implicitly parallel programming language (such as Id) and that these programs would run efficiently. Several programs written in Id previously were implemented on the Monsoon system with eight processors and achieved speedups of more than seven. Because the Monsoon processor consists of an eight-stage interleaved pipeline, an 8-processor Monsoon requires at least 64-fold parallelism to achieve 100% utilization.

As detailed earlier, there are three levels of parallelism: processor level, consisting of procedure activations on separate processors; thread level, consisting of multiple threads active on each processor; and instruction level, consisting of instructions within a thread. The Monsoon system, being a dataflow architecture, tries to exploit all three types of parallelism.

Id, the language used on Monsoon, is an implicitly parallel language—the compiler merely exposes the parallelism implicit in the program. The programmer is not required to write a program for a specific machine architecture or configuration. In fact, to a degree, the programmer does not even have to be aware of the parallelism in the program. Id programs on Monsoon are compiled to be executed in parallel—the same object code runs on any number of processors. Id is a high-level declarative (functional) language with extensions for single assignment data structures (called I-structures) and for updatable data structures with fine grain synchronization (called M-structures).

The nonstrictness of Id permits the execution of a child procedure to begin even before all of its arguments have been computed. It also allows loops to unfold dynamically, constrained only by data dependencies. Id, via I-structures and M-structures, also allows fine grain producer-consumer parallelism between parent and children procedures and between sibling procedures. In fact, because of all these properties, Id tends to expose too much parallelism, often exhausting machine resources, especially frame memory, if not controlled. A simple way to limit the amount of resources required is bounded loops, where a bound is specified to indicate how many loop iterations can occur in parallel. In a current version of Monsoon, the user must input the loop bounds either as parameters or by computing them at run time.

Interprocessor communication in multiprocessor systems generally takes much longer than local communication. For example, fetching data from a frame usually is much faster than fetching data from remote memory. However, a processor may hide the latency of a remote request by doing other work while the request is in progress. In order for this latency toleration to be successful, the processor must be able to switch between activities quickly and it must be able to deliver a response to the activity that made the request. Furthermore, the program must have sufficient parallelism for the processor always to have something to do while a request is in progress.

In the dataflow model, remote requests are structured as split-phased transactions so that multiple requests may be in progress at one time. An instruction issues a request to the processor or memory module containing the desired data and then executes other instructions that do not depend upon the result of the request in progress. The request carries a tag (continuation) indicating the procedure activation and the instruction at which the computation should be continued when the response arrives. In a Monsoon dataflow model, a tag, or context, is composed of an instruction pointer (IP), a frame base pointer (FP), and a node number. Because responses to requests from a processor can be reordered due to the network and synchronization, tags are essential to match requests and responses correctly.

When processors communicate, they also need to synchronize to ensure that valid data is used and to avoid race conditions. Id I-structures and M-structures provide high-level semantics for fine grain synchronization and can be implemented efficiently by providing a few presence bits for each word of memory. An I-structure has a property where a read-request that arrives before the write to that location is deferred until that element has been written. A deferred request can be memorized simply by saving its continuation (the return tag). Once the value is present, it can be sent to the requesters using the saved return tags. Because of this synchronization, the latency of a request may be much longer than the actual network delay. However, this synchronization allows writing of deterministic programs, and the split-phased nature of remote requests allows hiding the extra latency, given enough parallelism in the program.

In order for split-phased transactions to be effective in hiding latency, the overhead of issuing a remote request must be low. Most commercial microprocessors have poor network interfaces, and it can take hundreds of cycles just to put the message, corresponding to the first-phase of a split-phased memory request, on the network. On the other hand, dataflow architectures have network interfaces that blend seamlessly with the processor pipeline and can produce a message for the network basically every cycle.

On a conventional processor, if some needed data is not available, the processor must either wait for the data to arrive or switch to another thread, occasionally polling for the data arrival or waiting for an interrupt announcing the arrival of the data. On a parallel computer, more than one thread may have to be executed while a request is in progress in order for the processor to stay busy. This adds the additional constraint that thread switching must have low overhead and that there must be a mechanism for resuming the execution of a thread when the required response arrives. Commercial microprocessors generally have large context switching time and expensive interrupts due to large processor state. Dataflow architectures solve these problems by executing all instructions in a data-driven manner, and by making threads lightweight. The state of a dataflow thread is just a single token: a data value along with its continuation. Lightweight threads together with hardware management of thread queue allows threads to be switched in a single cycle. However, as can be expected, the small state of a thread in a pure dataflow machine is detrimental to good sequential performance.

For split-phased transactions to work efficiently, the overhead of synchronizing the response with the consumer must also be low. High-performance sequential computers make some use of split-phased transactions by allowing a load instruction to issue a request and continuing execution until an instruction that makes use of the register that was the target of the load is encountered. In this case, synchronization of the response and the consumer is done through the hardware register scoreboard and is efficient. But these systems typically do not allow load requests to complete out of order. Furthermore, these techniques are of little use when the data to be read may be missing; the requesting task has to release the processor to avoid deadlocks in case of a synchronizing read.

The largest Monsoon multiprocessor constructed is made up of eight processing elements (PE) and eight I-structure processors (IS) connected by a two-stage, packet-switched, butterfly network composed of switches. Each PE in the current implementation runs at 10 MHz and is capable of processing up to ten million tokens per second. It has 128 kilowords of instruction memory where each instruction word is 32 bits; 256 kilowords of frame memory, where each data word is 64 bits; plus three presence bits and eight type bits, the last of that are currently not used. It also has two token queues that can hold up to 32K tokens each. (A token is roughly twice the size of a data word.) The current implementation of Monsoon's processor has no caches and thus is implemented using SRAMs exclusively.

Global memory on Monsoon is implemented with I-structure processors. Access to global memory always occurs over the network, and every global read or write is a split-phased operation. A PE may also access the frame memory of another PE by sending split-phased requests to that processor. Global addresses are interleaved across the IS nodes. Each IS contains 4 megawords of 64-bit data memory with associated presence and type bits and is implemented using DRAMs.

The network interface to each node (which is either a PE or an IS) has a bandwidth of 100 Mbytes per second. This translates to about four million tokens per second for each node. When Monsoon's network is unloaded, a token takes about 13 cycles to go from one node to another. Monsoon's network interface is capable of delivering a token to the network every cycle though the network is not capable of delivering that many tokens at a sustained rate. Token formation, that is, packaging up the destination and the value, is performed automatically in most cases. Though token formation and delivery to the network interface is extremely efficient, compiled code rarely, if ever, saturates the network.

The Monsoon processor has an eight-stage pipeline as shown in Figure 7.18. It consists of an instruction fetch stage, an effective-frame-address computation stage, a presence-bits operation stage, a frame operation stage, a three-stage ALU, and a

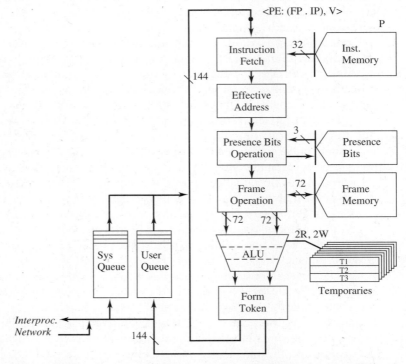

Figure 7.18 Monsoon Processing Pipeline (From Hicks et al., 1992)

form token stage. The instruction fetch, effective-frame-address, and ALU stages perform the tasks specified by their names. The presence-bits operation stage can read, modify, and write presence bits in one cycle. The frame operation stage either reads a value from a frame, writes a value in a frame, exchanges a value (takes two cycles), or does nothing. The form-token stage generates zero, one, or two tokens each cycle.

Tokens are kept in token queues while waiting to be processed. Each PE has two token queues, one for system tokens and the other for user tokens. The system token queue is needed to ensure that some critical tokens, such as a token to halt the system, can always be processed.

During each cycle, the processor tries to execute a recirculating token coming from the bottom of its pipeline. If no recirculating token was produced the last cycle, it pops a token from its own token queues to execute. Execution results in either zero, one, or two tokens at the end of the eighth cycle. These result tokens are either: (1) circulated to the head of the pipeline, (2) sent to the network to be delivered to either another processor's system queue or an I-structure board, or (3) enqueued in either the local processor's system or user token queue, depending on the operation. If no token is produced, then one is taken from the system or user queue to be executed next. If no token is available, then the processor idles for one cycle.

The eight tokens being processed at any given time are independent of each other—that is, no token in the pipeline could have created another token that exists in the pipeline at the same time. This is so because the next instruction is not computed until the eighth cycle of the pipeline. Thus, keeping an eight-processor Monsoon busy (nonidle) requires at least 64-fold parallelism.

Because Monsoon accepts only one token at a time for processing, the first token of a two-input instruction to arrive will cause the execution unit of the processor to idle. Because the second token could not have arrived yet, there is no work for the processor to do other than to store away the value from the first token. This idling of the execution stages is called a bubble in the pipeline. Bubbles are unavoidable whenever synchronization is implemented as a stage of a pipelined machine that takes only one token per cycle.

Monsoon can execute a sequential thread of instructions that are scheduled at every eighth cycle. Except for the first instruction, each instruction in this sequence must take only one input token, which comes from the previous instruction in the thread (via the recirculating path). Furthermore, each instruction except the last must be annotated as critical, which ensures that another thread cannot enter the original thread's pipeline slot. In the absence of the critical annotation on an instruction, a network token can displace the original thread from its pipeline beat. Such critical threads are broken by either synchronization points, trap instructions, or split-phased transactions. An instruction in the middle of a critical thread can produce two output tokens, but only one of the output tokens can be critical. The other token must be pushed onto the token queue or sent to the network. Only a restricted subset of Monsoon's instruction set can be used in critical threads.

To enhance the performance of such critical sequential threads, each Monsoon processor has eight register sets of three temporary registers each. Each register set is associated with one of the eight interleaved threads. Registers are not saved or restored implicitly and can only be used within an unbroken, critical thread of instructions. Currently, only run time system (RTS) code makes use of these registers. Notice, if a single, sequential thread of computation is executed on Monsoon, the pipeline utilization would be 12.5% because seven of the eight pipeline stages would be idle. Again this utilization is true for any processor pipeline design with fixed interleaving and fixed stages.

It is possible to simulate I-structure operations in the Monsoon processor's frame memory because it also has presence bits. This allows the compiler and the run time system to allocate some heap objects locally. Reading and writing to I-structures located in processor memory requires the second phase of the split-phased transaction to be executed on the processor containing the structure.

In addition to join and I-structure and M-structure types of synchronization, Monsoon supports synchronization through spin-locks. If an instruction attempts to acquire a spin-lock on a location that is already locked, a token to reexecute the same instruction is recirculated in the pipeline until the lock is freed. Only the frame and heap managers spin-wait because, if used improperly, spin-waiting can cause deadlocks. Eight threads simultaneously spin-waiting on one processor will cause a livelock in the pipeline because no thread will ever be able to unlock any of the locations on which they are spinning. However, spin-waiting in some instances is much more efficient than M-structure synchronization.

Because of limited board space and resources, Monsoon has a structural hardware hazard that affects token movement to and from its token queues and network interface. Essentially, the path from the token queues to the top of the processor pipeline and the path from the bottom of the processor pipeline to the network queues are the same path—the implementation uses a single bus for both paths. If an instruction generates two tokens, one that will recirculate and one that goes to the network, everything is fine. On the other hand, if an instruction generates a single token destined for the network, it must get a token from the token queues in order to keep the processor busy. Because the path to the network is the same as the path from the token queues, the processor cannot send a message to the network while pulling off a token from the token queue. The network token always has higher priority for the shared bus because results from the pipeline will be lost if the network token is delayed and a token from the queue is fetched first. Thus, when an instruction produces a single token that goes to the network, the pipeline must idle for one cycle in which the token is delivered to the network interface. A token is then read from the token queue in the next cycle unless the next instruction in the pipeline also excites the hardware hazard.

The maximum number of idles that can be caused by the hardware hazard is 50% of the total cycles. A similar hazard exists when the network tries to put a token into a token queue.

Most reads destined for the I-structure processors generated by the Id compiler create a network token but no local token, forcing the structural hazard to insert an idle cycle in the processor pipeline.

Monsoon has hardware instrumentation for performance measurement. Each processor has 64 statistics counters, and each cycle of execution on Monsoon is accounted for by incrementing one statistics counter. The decoded instruction specifies the statistics register to be incremented. In order to account for every cycle of execution time, idle cycles also increment a statistics counter.

Monsoon's instrumentation also allows the definition of between 1 and 64 groups of procedures, where each group is called a color. Procedures can either be specified to be in a specific color or to inherit the color of the procedure that called it. Statistics for each color are collected independently; thus, statistics divided into separate categories for each procedure group can be generated.

For statistics collection, Monsoon's instructions are divided into a small number of categories described next.

The system has the standard integer and floating-point operation categories. The fetch-and-store categories refer only to the cycle in which an instruction issues remote memory requests. Tag operations are instructions that manipulate continuations, such as for sending arguments to and results from a called procedure. Identity operations include moves (frame fetches and stores), jumps, forks, and joins. Miscops instructions consist of control flow, data conversion, and control register operations. The remaining cycles on Monsoon may be classified into four categories: idle cycles, bubbles, second-phase operations, and recirculate cycles.

Idle cycles occur when the first stage of the pipeline does not get a token to execute. The idle cycles are caused either by empty token queues or by the hardware hazard that prevents a token from entering the pipeline.

Bubbles are caused by the arrival of the first token of a dyadic operation. The instruction cannot execute until the second token arrives, so the first value is stored into the frame and the rest of the pipeline does nothing for this particular token.

Second-phase cycles are due to the handling of read-and-write requests for the I-structures stored in a Monsoon processor's frame memory. Accesses to these objects cause the second-phase of the instruction also to be executed on the Monsoon processor. Normally, the second phase executes on the I-structure board.

Recirculate cycles are due to the spin-lock instructions. The cycle in which the instruction acquires the lock is counted as a fetch instruction, but all the other cycles are counted as recirculate cycles. These cycles, which are devoted to busy waiting, are like idle cycles.

COMPILING ID FOR MONSOON

The Id compiler for Monsoon compiles each procedure and loop in the source code into a separate dataflow graph; instances of procedures are connected together at run time by dynamic dataflow arcs according to some calling convention. The compiler assigns a frame for each procedure. A frame is a contiguous block of memory and has the matching locations used by tokens of a particular procedure invocation. A frame is also used for storing constants and loop invariants.

Code executing on Monsoon is divided into code blocks corresponding to procedure bodies or loop iterations. The compiler may also split a procedure into several smaller code blocks to reduce code-block size or inline procedures to create larger code blocks. All tokens belonging to the same code block invocation have the same frame pointer, which is the base address of the block. A frame always resides in the local memory of a single processor, and thus, all instructions belonging to a code block invocation are executed on the PE where the frame is allocated.

The code generator for Monsoon has to satisfy a number of constraints imposed by the hardware. For example, instruction fanout is limited to two in most cases and one in other cases. The compiler must add fanout or fork instructions to explicitly distribute a value if too many instructions require the output of an instruction. The instruction encoding also constrains the location in instruction memory of a destination instruction relative to its source instruction. A destination instruction can be at most 512 instructions away from its source instruction. For instructions that allow two destinations, one of the destinations is further constrained to reside at the instruction address immediately following the source instruction. In some cases, the compiler must insert jump instructions to generate correct code for large procedures or loop bodies. The compiler also splits large code blocks in order to satisfy this constraint.

The run time system (RTS) for Id consists of a frame manager and a heap manager. The frame manager allocates and deallocates the activation frames in which code blocks are executed, and the heap manager allocates and deallocates dynamic storage for tuples, arrays, and other aggregate objects.

When a procedure calls a child procedure, the parent procedure first executes a get context instruction. The get context instruction traps to an exception handler that allocates a frame, possibly on another processor, and returns a continuation consisting of the instruction pointer (IP) of the procedure's entry point and the node and base pointer of the newly allocated frame. This continuation is sometimes called a context. The frame manager chooses the processor on which to allocate the frame so that the distribution of the workload does not have to be specified in the compiled code. The frame manager also colors the child's context for statistics gathering before returning it to the parent procedure. Procedure invocation then continues with the parent procedure sending the required arguments to its child procedure using the context. Each argument is directed to a specific instruction by some preset procedure-calling convention.

In order to minimize external fragmentation, only a limited number of frame sizes are provided. For each frame requested, the smallest available frame large enough to satisfy the request is returned. The current frame manager has sixteen different frame sizes, each a multiple of 64, and employs a version of the quick-fit algorithm. Each quick-list contains free frames of a specific size, linked together through the first word of each frame. Because Monsoon has eight-way interleaved pipeline, up to eight independent frame requests per processor can be active at the same time, and thus contention is possible. An investigation of frame managers that have eight sets of resources per processor revealed that, although the frame managers rarely waited for a critical resource, they had difficulty sharing resources between the different sets. For maximum efficiency, the frame allocator is written in threaded style in Monsoon assembly language and uses some instructions written specifically for the frame manager.

The frame manager is also responsible for partitioning work among the processors on a code block granularity. Currently, the frame manager distributes work in a round-robin fashion. Each processor has a set of round-robin counters, one for each frame size, that it uses to distribute work to other processors. Because each processor has its own round-robin counters, work distribution decisions can be made locally. Such a distributed approach to load balancing does not ensure a globally even distribution of work. However, because many frames are allocated during the execution of most programs and the amount of work done in each frame is relatively small, a round-robin scheme will balance the load reasonably well.

7.4 EXAMPLE SYSTEMS

Requests for heap memory, like requests for frame memory, are made by special instructions that trap to run time system procedures. These run time system procedures are written in Id. The same heap manager code runs on the various configurations of Monsoon.

The Id run time system places all aggregate object storage (such as arrays and tuples) on the I-structure processors. This storage is interleaved so that adjacent logical addresses are actually on different I-structure processors. Interleaving is used to reduce the contention on individual I-structure processors and hence the average latency of access. I-structures can also be allocated in a Monsoon processor's local memory. These local I-structures, however, are not interleaved.

Each processor manages its own partition of I-structure storage in order to reduce RTS contention and to improve throughput. The current heap allocator uses the quick-fit algorithm to manage each partition, and keeps 15 quick-lists for object sizes of 2 through 16 words. Larger objects are managed by the first-fit algorithm.

I-structure objects have presence bits associated with each word. These presence bits are initially empty on all words of an object and are set to full by I-store operations. In our implementation, the presence bits of a piece of storage are cleared when that storage is first cut off from the tail (pool of unused memory) and then cleared again whenever the storage is returned to the heap manager for reuse. The heap manager keeps around storage that has been cut from the tail rather than returning it to the tail. Presence bits are cleared upon deallocation in order to minimize the latency of subsequent allocation requests.

Even though each processor has a heap manager, if too many requests to allocate or release heap objects come bunched together in time, the heap manager can still become a temporary bottleneck.

The eventual goal is to have both parallelism and storage management be implicit in Id. Such an Id program will contain no user annotations to direct where to exploit parallelism or how to manage storage. In the current system, the Id compiler and RTS cannot run a program efficiently without some user help. Two kinds of annotations are added to programs to control the amount of parallelism and the amount of resources used by them. The first annotation, loop bounds, controls how many iterations of each loop are executed in parallel. The second annotation causes heap storage to be reclaimed when it is no longer needed. Currently, the user must specify loops as either sequential, bounded, or unbounded. The compiler generates specific code for each kind of loop. A sequential loop executes one iteration at a time and uses only one frame. A bounded loop executes a specified number of iterations in parallel and uses frames. An unbounded loop is compiled into a recursive call so all loop iterations can potentially execute in parallel. The sequential loop schema incurs less overhead than the bounded loop, which has to allocate and initialize more frames. However, it also exploits less parallelism than a bounded loop. It is usually used for the innermost loops where it is more important to achieve smaller instruction counts than parallelism. Parallelism is, instead, provided by the outer loops.

Each iteration of a loop that is executing in parallel consumes a frame, and perhaps some heap storage. By controlling the number of iterations executing in parallel, one can control how much storage is used. Generally, the number of iterations executing in parallel must be large enough to keep the machine busy but small enough not to exceed the storage available on the machine.

Categorizing loops as sequential, bounded, or unbounded and determining how many bounded loop iterations to execute in parallel is currently perhaps the only tedious part of achieving good performance on Monsoon. It is partly due to the relatively small size of Monsoon's frame memory.

Section 5 provides some performance details on the Monsoon system. Modifying an existing high-speed processor to support dataflow paradigm is the focus of the next project at MIT. *T (pronounced *Start*), being built in collaboration with Motorola, will use 88,110 processing nodes that have a fast network interface incorporated as a functional unit on the chip. While this is not optimal, it is still very fast. *T will also have hardware support for handling continuations. These are similar to token queues on Monsoon but are an improvement in that they allow a certain degree of software control over scheduling.

The architecture of *T was driven in part by observations of Monsoon's architectural drawbacks. *T will have good single thread performance because threads are not interleaved in the processor pipeline. This will, among other things, cut down RTS latencies and RTS critical section bottlenecks. Furthermore, the *T processor will be based on a RISC core so threads will be able to make better use of registers than they could on Monsoon. Plans have been made for a 512 processor *T machine to be built by the end of 1994.

7.5 PERFORMANCE EVALUATION

Little data is available on the performance of dataflow machines in practical or commercial applications. Most of the dataflow machines have been built only in part, and tests are being conducted on them. The results are comparable and in most of the cases better than the machines based on the control flow architectures. This section provides some details on the performance evaluation of MDM (Watson, 1983); Epsilon (Grafe et al., 1989); and Monsoon (Hicks et al., 1992).

7.5.1 MDM

Many programs of various types and structures, having both regular and irregular parallelism, were executed (Chambers et al., 1989) on a single ring MDM with 1 to 12 processing elements. The results are presented in Figure 7.19. The speedup is almost linear while the number of processing elements is less than 8. The bandwidth limitation of the ring pipeline is approached as the number of processors exceeds 8 and the speedup is no longer linear. The store sizes in the ring were expanded allowing execution of more realistic programs. The results did not deviate much from the above.

The performance of the multiring structure is being investigated using a Motorola 68000-microprocessor-based system. A 4-ring system is currently operational and is proposed to be extended to 20 rings.

All presently available results indicate that the dataflow architectures should be capable of producing efficient high-speed parallel computers although there are some differences of opinion regarding this conclusion.

7.5 PERFORMANCE EVALUATION

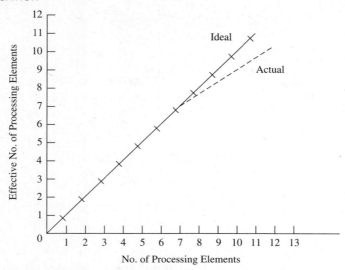

Figure 7.19 Performance Characteristics of Manchester Machine

7.5.2 Epsilon

The performance evaluation on Epsilon (Davidson et al., 1989) involved comparing the Epsilon with comparable control flow processors. Because it is difficult to define precisely what characteristics make a dataflow processor comparable to a control flow processor, two sets of comparisons were made.

In the first set, representative benchmarks were used to compare Epsilon's performance to that of control flow processors performing the same function. Here it was assumed that single board computers built on the basis of both architectures are available and have the same amount of board space, cost the same, and are built with the same level of technology.

In the second set, representative benchmarks from scientific problems were used. This set compares Epsilon's absolute performance to that of control flow processors optimized for scientific computing.

ARITHMETIC DIAGNOSTIC BENCHMARK

These are a set of simple arithmetic diagnostics originally developed to test the floating-point capabilities of control flow processors. These are tight loops where computation of a complicated function of a loop index is carried out. The function reduces algebraically to a known value, and hence, the results of each iteration can be checked. A sample arithmetic diagnostic loop of this type is shown in Figure 7.20.

This diagnostic test was performed to show the ability of Epsilon's high-speed execution on problems with a lower degree of parallelism. A small arithmetic loop was taken, and four of these diagnostics were run to emphasize different arithmetic operations: square root, multiply and divide, add and subtract, and a mix of these. These were coded in C for control flow processors and translated to the graph representation for the Epsilon. To make the experiments comparable, the Epsilon processor was restrained to execute only one iteration at a time.

```
#define MAX 1000000
#define MAXERR 0.1
main ( )
{ int i;
    float error = 0, j, jsdq1, jsqd2,
    oneoverj, shouldbej, shouldbe0;

    for (i = 0; i < MAX; i++)
    { j            = (float)i;
      jsqd1        = j * j;
      jsqd2        = j * j;
      oneoverj     = j / jsdq2;
      shouldbej    = jsqd1 * oneoverj;
      shouldbe0    = shouldbej - j;
      if (shouldbe0 > MAXERR)
          printf("\nERR, i = %d", i);
      if (shouldbe0> error)
          error = shouldbe0;            }
    printf("max error = %f", error); }
```

Figure 7.20 Sample Arithmetic Diagnostic Loop (Davidson et al., 1989)

The average execution times were: 6.9 seconds for the Epsilon running at 10 MHz, 10 seconds for an INMOS T800 at 20 MHz, and 85 seconds for a Sun 3/260 at 16.7 MHz. These results indicate that the single processor dataflow machines are not inherently slower than comparable control flow processors even at a lower degree of parallelism.

When all four diagnostics were run together, the (total) execution times were: 14 seconds for Epsilon, 40 seconds for INMOS, and 340 seconds for Sun. The control flow processors execute the independent loops in a sequence while the Epsilon executes them in parallel. These results illustrate the speed advantage of Epsilon and its ability to exploit the maximum amount of parallelism.

SCIENTIFIC COMPUTING BENCHMARK

Figure 7.21 compares the performance of Epsilon on six Lawrence Livermore kernels with that of Convex C1. In this evaluation, Epsilon was allowed to execute several iterations in parallel as long as the data dependencies were observed.

The control flow vector computer C1 was significantly faster than the Epsilon on the kernels where the algorithm vectorizes well, but its performance fell drastically when vector parallelism was not available. Epsilon's performance was almost similar on all the kernels because it is determined only by the ratio of floating-point operations to integer and control operations. The C1, on the other hand, demonstrates more sensitivity to the type (vector) and the degree of parallelism present.

Sustained performance of these machines on these kernels gives a better indication as to what can be expected on a typical scientific computing workload. Figure 7.22 shows the harmonic mean of the performances shown in Figure 7.21 along with that for the Cray 1S on the same kernels. This comparison indicates that a single Epsilon

7.5 PERFORMANCE EVALUATION

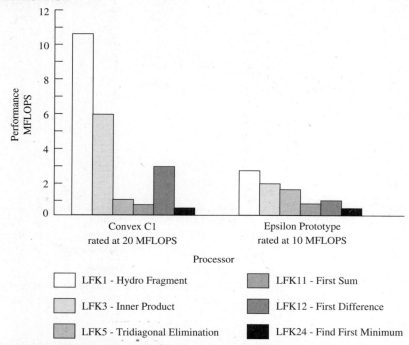

Figure 7.21 Measured Performance on Selected Livermore Fortran Kernels (Davidson et al., 1989)

processor would sustain higher throughput than the Convex C1 and about one-fourth the throughput of the Cray 1S for a typical workload.

7.5.3 Monsoon

This section provides details on four benchmarks on Monsoon: Matrix-Multiply, Gamteb, Simple, and Paraffins (Hicks et al., 1992.) In addition to these benchmarks, one of the largest Id applications currently being developed is a version of the Id compiler written in Id; another is the Monte Carlo Neutron Photon (MCNP) application being written at the Los Alamos National Laboratory. The Matrix-Multiply benchmark was written in Id, C, and Fortran by experts in each of these languages. Simple and Gamteb were originally written in Fortran. These programs were ported to Id by programmers familiar with both Id and the applications. Paraffins was originally written in Id and was then ported to C.

MATRIX-MULTIPLY

This benchmark creates two matrices with double-precision floating-point numbers, multiplies them, and returns the sum of the elements of the product matrix as its result. The Id version of Matrix-Multiply is written as a straightforward triple-nested loop. In early versions of this benchmark, the innermost loops of the matrix creation, multiplication, and summation routines were all unfolded ten times by the compiler to ameliorate the overhead of loop iteration. Recent compiler improvements have

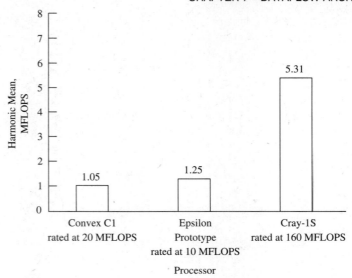

Figure 7.22 Harmonic Mean of Performance on Fortran Kernels (Davidson et al., 1989)

reduced the overhead of loop iteration by a large amount. The unfolding is scaled down to four times as further unfolding increases code and frame sizes without providing much improvement in performance.

The Matrix-Multiply program is invoked by supplying a matrix size and several loop bounds. The Matrix-Multiply runs are of size 500 by 500. The loop bounds control how much parallelism is exposed in the outer loops of the matrix creation, multiplication, and summation routines.

This benchmark has been coded in C to compare the performance of Id with the performance of C. The Id code implementing Matrix-Multiply is about 130 lines long, including comments. The corresponding C code is 152 lines long.

Another version of this benchmark is written in both C and Id in a blocked style. This version simultaneously computes the value of 16 elements that form a block in the final matrix. The net effect is to reduce the number of fetches performed on the two source matrices. Thus, each time the innermost loop is executed, 8 matrix elements are fetched, 4 from each source matrix, in order to update 16 elements of the product matrix. The unblocked version needs 32 fetches to support the same computation. Blocking in this manner reduces the number of fetches by a factor of four. Although the numbers reported here for Id are obtained by changes to the source code, work is underway to have the compiler automatically perform this transformation as an optimization.

GAMTEB

Gamteb statistically simulates the trajectory of particles (photons) through a carbon rod that is partitioned into cells. Each particle is statistically weighted to emphasize particles that are in the rightmost cells. Each particle can be simulated in parallel.

7.5 PERFORMANCE EVALUATION

Gamteb was written by researchers from Los Alamos National Laboratories as a standard supercomputer benchmark derived from MCNP, a real application.

There are two versions of Gamteb, corresponding to two different rod geometries. In the first version, gamteb-2c, which corresponds to the Fortran benchmark code, the rod is divided into 2 cells with 4 surfaces. In the second version, gamteb-9c, the rod is divided into 9 cells and 11 surfaces. The second version is much more computationally intensive than the first because each particle is split many more times.

The simulation considers particles independently where typical problem sizes are 40 thousand to several million particles. Particles enter the simulation through the front surface and may exit the simulation in one of four ways: escaping through the cylindrical surface, backscattering through the front surface, transmitting through the back surface, or dying due to lack of statistical significance. The result is three histograms of the energies of the particles that exited plus counts of particles that underwent various processes.

This program is storage intensive. It operates on particles and counts functionally so whenever a new particle or count of events is needed a new 9-tuple is allocated. This code has been hand annotated with storage reclamation pragmas that direct the compiler to insert heap deallocation calls.

The Gamteb runs are of 40 thousand particles, which is a small but standard benchmark size. Real program runs would be in the millions or tens of millions of particles. The Id code implementing Gamteb is about 750 lines long including comments. The Fortran code is 720 lines long.

Gamteb is actually an *embarrassingly parallel* program, and is expected to show excellent speedups on Monsoon. It does so achieving a 92% efficiency on eight processors with a speedup of 7.35.

SIMPLE

This application is a hydrodynamics and heat conduction simulation program known as the Simple code. The Simple document, along with the associated Fortran program, was developed as a benchmark to evaluate various high-performance machines and compilers. Although Simple is supposed to reflect some *real applications,* it is contrived to reflect a more complex mix of numerical methods than the usual problems in that class.

The simulation is performed a specified number of cycles. Simple runs reported here are of 100 cycles with a grid size of 100 times 100. The Id and Fortran codes implementing Simple are about 1000 and 2400 lines long, respectively. The best speedup achieved for Simple is a factor of 6.2 on an 8 processor configuration, giving an efficiency of 78%.

PARAFFINS

The Paraffins benchmark enumerates all of the distinct isomers of each paraffin of size up to n. Paraffins are molecules with the chemical formula C_nH_{2n+2}, where C and H stand for carbon and hydrogen atoms, respectively, and $n > 0$. A paraffin is essentially an unrooted four-array tree. Thus, the problem of generating distinct paraffins is the same as the problem of detecting isomorphism in labeled free trees. The number of paraffins grows exponentially with n.

Paraffins are an example of a nonnumeric program. The program generates lists of paraffins and finally returns an array filled with the number of distinct paraffins of each size up to and including the maximum size specified by the user.

Paraffins runs are of size 22, meaning paraffins up to and including those of size 22 are generated. This came up to a total of 3,807,508 paraffins. The Id code implementing paraffins is about 300 lines long. The C code is 370 lines long.

The paraffins runs had speedups of 7.25 for eight processors, giving an efficiency of 91%.

Table 7.1 shows the speedup results for all these benchmarks, for 1, 2, 4, and 8 PE configurations. Here the critical path is defined as the total number of cycles executed by the processor that starts and ends the execution of the program. All other processors will execute fewer instructions because they must start after and end before the first processor.

Table 7.2 gives the detailed breakdown of the dynamic instruction counts for the Matrix-Multiply benchmark. It shows the total dynamic opcode mix on all four machine configurations. The column for each configuration shows the sum of the statistics, including idles, from all of the processors in the configuration.

COMPARISON WITH MIPS R3000

This section presents an experiment comparing the execution efficiency of Id on Monsoon with that of Fortran and C on a MIPS R3000 processor. Each Fortran program was compiled with the DEC Fortran (f77) compiler with full optimization ($-O4$) while the C programs were compiled using the MIPS cc compiler with full optimization ($-O3$).

Because commercial processors do not have hardware support to count the number of instructions a program executes, the pixie tool was used for gathering this information on the MIPS R3000 processor. The R3000 executables were preprocessed by the pixie program provided by MIPS. The programs were then run on a DEC Station 5000, which contains an R3000 processor, and the resulting data was processed by the program pixstats, which is also provided by MIPS.

TABLE 7.1 MONSOON SPEEDUP RESULTS FOR FOUR BENCHMARKS

Configuration / Program	1 PE		2 PE		4 PE		8 PE	
	$\frac{1\ PE}{1\ PE}$	$\times 10^6$ Critical path	$\frac{1\ PE}{2\ PE}$	$\times 10^6$ Critical path	$\frac{1\ PE}{4\ PE}$	$\times 10^6$ Critical path	$\frac{1\ PE}{8\ PE}$	$\times 10^6$ Critical path
4 × 4 Blocked-MM 500 × 500	1	1057	1.99	531	3.90	271	7.74	137
Gamteb-2c 40000 particles	1	590	1.95	303	3.81	155	7.35	80.3
Simple 100 iters, 100 × 100	1	4681	1.86	2518	3.45	1355	6.27	747
Paraffins $n = 22$	1	322	1.99	162	3.92	82.2	7.25	44.4

(From Hicks et al., 1992)

7.6 SUMMARY

TABLE 7.2 MONSOON BLOCKED-MATRIX-MULTIPLY OPCODE MIX

Configuration Op Category	1 PE		2 PE		4 PE		8 PE	
	Cycles $\times 10^6$	Fraction %	Cycles $\times 10^6$	Fraction %	Cycles $\times 10^6$	Fraction %	Cycles $\times 10^6$	Fraction %
Intop	77.0	7.28	77.0	7.25	77.1	7.11	77.2	7.06
Floatop	250.3	23.66	250.3	23.55	250.3	23.07	250.3	22.90
Fetch	62.8	5.93	62.8	5.91	62.8	5.79	62.9	5.76
Store	1.5	.14	1.5	.14	1.6	.14	1.6	.15
Identity	289.4	27.36	289.4	27.23	290.0	26.73	290.7	26.60
Tag	0.5	.05	0.5	.05	0.7	.06	0.9	.08
Miscop	7.5	.71	7.5	.71	7.7	.71	7.9	.72
Bubble	269.2	25.45	269.2	25.34	269.6	24.85	270.0	24.70
Second Phase	0.1	.01	0.1	.01	0.2	.02	0.4	.04
Recircs	0.0	.00	0.0	.00	0.0	.00	0.0	.00
Idles	99.5	9.41	104.2	9.81	125.1	11.53	131.1	12.00
Total	1057.7	100	1062.5	100	1084.9	100	1093.0	100
Speedup	1.00		1.99		3.90		7.74	
Efficiency	100.0%		99.5%		97.5%		96.8%	

(From Hicks et al., 1992)

Table 7.3 includes both cycle counts and run times for MIPS and Monsoon runs of each program. On the MIPS processor, cycle counts are produced by pixstats and run times are the sum of user and system times as measured by the Unix time command. When using Unix time, the original binary is run, not the pixie-processed one. On Monsoon, the total cycle count is measured by Monsoon's hardware statistics counters, and run times are calculated by dividing the total cycle count by 10^7 because Monsoon issues instructions at 10 MHz. Both sets of cycle counts are in millions of cycles while the run times are in seconds.

This comparison is not very meaningful because it compares two different systems that include different source languages, compilers, RTSs, and hardware. Aside from the algorithms, which stay the same, all the other system components are changed at the same time. For further details refer to Hicks et al., (1992).

7.6 SUMMARY

The concept of dataflow architecture is introduced in this chapter in contrast with the conventional (control flow) architectures. Associated dataflow representations, such as dataflow graphs and dataflow languages, are also discussed. Details of representative static and dynamic architectures are provided. Performance evaluation strategies for dataflow systems are outlined.

TABLE 7.3 MIPS R3000/MONSOON COMPARISON

Program	MIPS R3000		1PE Monsoon	
	($\times 10^6$ cycles)	seconds	($\times 10^6$ cycles)	seconds
Matrix-Multiply, 500 × 500				
double precision	1198	202.3	1768	176.8
single precision	915	153.1	–	–
4 × 4 Blocked-MM, 500 × 500				
double precision	954	61.4	1058	105.8
single precision	741	44.9	–	–
Gamteb-2c				
40000 particles	265	11.1	590	59.0
Simple, 100 iters, 100 × 100				
double precision	1787	86.5	4682	468.2
single precision	1745	84.1	–	–
Paraffins				
$n = 22$	102	12.0	322	32.2

(From Hicks et al., 1992)

Dataflow research has received wide attention. The most notable efforts are at MIT (Jack Dennis and his research associates on static architectures and Arvind and his group on dynamic architectures); at the University of Manchester, England, by John Gurd and Ian Watson, which lead to the development of the Manchester dataflow machine, one of the earlier dataflow architectures; at Sandia National Laboratories, New Mexico; at the University of Utah; and in France and Japan. The Ministry of International Trade and Industry of Japan has sponsored dataflow research, and Hitachi Ltd. is privately funding research at the University of California at Berkeley.

The major reasons for this architecture not being a commercial success are extensive hardware complexity, complexity of representation schemes, and difficulty in developing and compiling languages and other representation schemes. There is much controversy regarding the viability of this architecture type. Some feel that this type of architecture is just a laboratory curiosity and can never be implemented in a cost-effective manner. Others argue that, with the availability of faster VLSI components and the advances in dataflow representation techniques, it is possible to build cost-effective dataflow machines.

Japanese manufacturers seem to be leading the field in dataflow hardware technology. One of the earliest machines is the SIGMA-1 from the Electrotechnical Laboratory (ETL) in Tsukuba. The development of the EM series of machines began in 1981 at ETL. The current version EM-5 employs a hybrid architecture composed of dataflow and control flow concepts. It is expected that a 1000 processor machine will be built by the end of 1993. The aim of the EM project is to develop a general purpose machine with 16K, 80 MIPS processors.

In 1991, Japan's Sharp Corporation announced a data-driven processor (DDP), produced jointly with Mitsubishi. This is a 1024-node architecture and uses a C-like programming language.

The Enhanced Data-Driven Engine (EDDEN) of Sanyo Electric Company is also a 1024-node architecture interconnected by a two-dimensional torus network. The nodes are based on a 32-bit custom-designed processor. The commercial version of this architecture (Cyberflow) announced by Sanyo in 1992 is a desktop system with 4 to 64 nodes and a peak rating of 640 MFLOPS.

Srini (1986) provides an exhaustive comparison of dataflow architectures. The books by Sharp (1985) and Gaudiot and Bic (1991) provide further details on these architectures.

REFERENCES

Ackerman, W. B. 1982. Data flow languages. *IEEE Computer* 15(2): 15–25.

Almasi, G. S., and A. Gottlieb. 1989. *Highly parallel computing.* Redwood City, CA: The Benjamin/Cummings Publishing Company, Inc.

Arvind, D. E. Culler, and G. K. Maa. 1988. Assessing the benefits of fine-grained parallelism in dataflow programs. *The International Journal of Supercomputer Applications* 2(3): 10–36.

Arvind and R. S. Nikhil. 1990. Executing a program on the MIT tagged-token dataflow architecture. *IEEE Transactions on Computers* 39(3): 300–318.

Arvind, and R. S. Nikhil. 1989. Can dataflow subsume von Neumann computing? Proceedings ACM. 262–272.

Bic, L. 1989. AGM: The Irvine Data flow Database Machine. In *High level language computer architecture.* Ed. by V. M. Milutinovic. New York: Computer Science Press, Inc.

Brinch-Hansen, P. 1978. Distributed processes: A concurrent programming concept. *Communications of the ACM,* November, 934–941.

Brownbridge, D. R., P. C. Treleaven, and R. P. Hopkins. 1982. Data driven and demand-driven computer architectures. *ACM computing surveys* 14(1): 93–143.

Davidson, G. S., V. G. Grafe, J. E. Hoch, and V. P. Holmes. 1989. The Epsilon data flow processor. *Proceedings 16th Annual International Symposium on Computer Architecture,* 36–45.

Davis, A. L. 1978. The architecture and system method of DDM1: A recursively structured data driven machine. *Proceedings 5th Annual Symposium Computer Architecture,* New York, 210–215.

Dennis, J. B. 1980. Data flow supercomputers. *IEEE Computer* 13 (November) 48–56.

Dennis, J. B. 1983. Maximum pipelining of array operations on static data flow machines. *Proceedings International Conference Parallel Processing.* Bellaire, Michigan, August.

Dennis, J. B., G. Gao, and K. W. Todd. 1984. Modelling the weather with a data flow supercomputer. *IEEE Trans. Computers* C-33(July): 592–603.

Gaudiot, J. 1989. Data flow machines. In *High level language computer architecture.* Ed. by V. M. Milutinovic. New York: Computer Science Press, Inc.

Gaudiot, J., and L. Bic. 1991. *Advanced topics in data-flow computing.* Englewood Cliffs, N.J.: Prentice Hall.

Ghosal, D., H. Jiang, L. N. Bhuyan, and S. K. Tripathi. 1989. Analysis of computation-communication issues in dynamic data flow architectures. *Proceedings 16th Annual International Symposium on Computer Architecture.* 325–335.

Glauert, J. 1978. A single assignment language for data flow computing. Master's thesis, University of Manchester.

Gurd, J., and I. Watson 1980. Data driven systems for high speed parallel computing. Parts 1 & 2: Hardware design. *Computer Design* (June and July): 91–100 and 97–106.

Hicks, J., D. Chiou, B. Ang, and Arvind. 1992. Performance studies of the Monsoon dataflow processor. CSG Memo 345-2. Cambridge; Mass.: MIT.

Horowitz, E. 1984. *Fundamentals of programming languages.* New York: Computer Science Press, Inc.

Hwang, K., and F. A. Briggs. 1984. *Computer architecture and parallel processing.* New York: McGraw-Hill.

Johnson, D. 1980. Data flow machines threaten the program counter. *Electronic Design* 28 (November 22): 255–258.

Kahaner, D. K., and U. Wattenberg. 1992. Japan: A competitive assessment. *IEEE Spectrum* 29(9) 42–47.

Kirkham, C. C., I. Watson, and J. R. Gurd. 1985. The Manchester prototype data flow computer. *Communications of the ACM* 28(1): 34–52.

Kirkham, C. C., I. Watson, J. R. Gurd, and J. R. W. Glauert. 1984. The data flow approach. In *Distributed processing.* Ed. by Fred B. Chambers et al. Boston: Academic Press, Inc.

Padua, D.A., and M. J. Wolfe. 1986. Advanced compiler optimizations for supercomputers. *Communications of the ACM*, December.

Papadopoulos, G. M. 1992. *Implementation of a general-purpose dataflow multiprocessor.* Research Monograph on Parallel and Distributed Computing. Cambridge, Mass: MIT Press.

Patil, S., R. M. Keller, and G. Lindstrom. 1978. *An architecture for a loosely coupled parallel processor.* Report UUCS-78-105. University of Utah, July.

Rosenblatt, A., and G. Watson. 1991. Computers and ICs: Leading in notebooks, laptops, memory chips. *IEEE Spectrum* 28(6): 32–34.

Rumbaugh, J. 1977. A data flow multiprocessor. *IEEE Trans. Computers* C-26 (2): 1087–1095.

Sakai, S., Y. Yamaguchi, K. Hiraki, Y. Kodama, and T. Yuba. 1989. An architecture of a dataflow single chip processor. *Proceedings of the 16th Annual International Symposium on Computer Architecture*, Jerusalem, Israel, 46–53.

Sharp, J. A. 1985. *Data flow computing.* Ellis Horwood Series on Computers and Their Applications, New York: John Wiley & Sons.

Shaw, A. 1993. Implementing data-parallel software on dataflow hardware. Master's thesis, MIT, EECS, Laboratory for Computer Science.

Stone, H. S. 1987. *High performance computer architecture.* Reading, MA: Addison Wesley Publications.

Shiva, S. G. 1991. *Computer design and architecture.* Glenview, IL: HarperCollins.

Srini, V. P. 1986. An architectural comparison of dataflow systems. *IEEE Computer* 19 (March): 68–88.

Tesler, L. G., and H. J. Enea. 1968. A language design for concurrent processes. *Proceedings of AFIPS Spring Joint Computer Conference* 32, 403–408.

Yasuhara, H., M. Kishi, and Y. Kawamura. 1983. DDDP: A distributed data driven processor. *Communication of the ACM.*

PROBLEMS

7.1. Construct dataflow graphs for the following conventional programming statements:
   a. $Z = (A - B) * (B - C)/(D - A)$
   b.
```
for i = 0 step 1 until m
    sum = sum + X[i]
endfor
```
   c.
```
while (x > 0) do
    s = s + 1;
    x = x - 1;
endwhile
```
   d.
```
if (a > b)
    then
        z = z + 2
    else
        z = z - 2
endif
```

7.2. Develop dataflow graphs for the following vector operations. Compare the speed characteristics of the dataflow machine to that of SIMD and MIMD structures for these applications:
   a. $C[i] = A[i] + B[i]$ $i = 1$ to n.
   b. $C = A * B$ where A, B, and C are $(N \times N)$ matrices.

7.3. Develop a DFG for a number generator that generates all the integers between two input values x and y.

7.4. Develop a DFG to compute the following Fibonnaci sequence:
$$f(x) = x \quad \text{for} \quad x = 1, 2$$
$$= f(x - 1) + f(x - 2) \quad \text{for} \quad x > 2.$$

7.5. Explain how the DFG in the above problem is executed on a) MIT Static architecture, b) Manchester single-ring MDM, and c) Manchester multiple-ring MDM.

7.6. Examine the following aspects of the von Neumann structure:
   a. Memory access delays during instruction fetch and execute phases.
   b. Instruction wait time until it is fetched after a program counter update.
   c. Semantic gap.
   How does the dataflow architecture minimize these effects?

7.7. Develop detailed operating specifications for the Instruction Fetch Unit in Figure 7.3, assuming only one fetch mechanism is used.

7.8. Expand the solution for Problem 7.7 assuming a fetch unit with multiple fetch mechanisms operating in parallel.

7.9. How is the memory system of Figure 7.3 different from the memory system of conventional machines?

7.10. List the detailed characteristics of an operating system needed for static and dynamic dataflow machines.

CHAPTER 8

Current Directions

The primary goal of the innovative architectures described in this book is either a dramatic improvement in the cost-to-performance ratio compared to existing designs or a highly scalable performance along with a good cost-to-performance ratio. In general, there are two approaches to achieving the highest performance with the least cost. The first one is an **evolutionary** approach that attempts to improve the performance of the single processor system to its possible limit (the topic of Chapters 1 and 4), and the second is the **revolutionary** approach that uses a large number of processors and minimizes the overhead involved to achieve linear speedup (the topic of Chapters 5 through 7).

The first approach is mainly a result of advances in hardware technology yielding powerful processors at low cost. The advantage of this approach is that the applications and algorithms remain unchanged although changes to compilers and operating system may be needed to accommodate the new hardware. As and when the new hardware is available, there will be a market for it because users tend to update their systems with new ones in an incremental fashion. For instance, the Cray series of supercomputers have followed this strategy whereby the number of processors in the system is kept relatively low (up to 16 in the Cray Y-MP series) while the processors are made increasingly powerful in terms of their performance.

Some believe that silicon technology has almost reached its physical limits in yielding the performance and that newer technologies are needed for the evolutionary approach to be viable. The Cray-3, for instance, is a gallium arsenide-based system and boasts severalfold performance enhancement over its silicon counterparts without any drastic changes to the architecture.

As of this writing, the Japanese supercomputer manufacturers seem to be leading the field in this approach with vector processors such as NEC Corporation's SX-3 (24.6 gigaflops peak rating); Hitachi's S-3800 (32 gigaflops peak); and a gallium arsenide processor chip from NEC (0.2 gigaflops).

The advantage of the second approach is that the hardware (processors, memories, and interconnection networks) can be simply replicated. But this massively parallel processing (MPP) strategy requires a rethinking of application algorithms and data structures to effectively utilize the multiprocessor architecture. There have been successful efforts to devise languages that represent parallelism explicitly, compilers that retain the parallelism expressed by the code, and operating systems that manage the multiprocessor system resources efficiently. Even with the availability of these, the redesign of applications is not trivial.

Several multiprocessor architectures have been proposed over the years, some for general purpose applications and some for special purpose applications. For the general purpose designs to survive, the development cost should be recuperated by the sale of a large number of systems while the special purpose application should justify the cost of architecture development. Nevertheless, new and more powerful architectures are being introduced at a fast rate while the time to recuperate costs has grown shorter and shorter. These cost recuperation aspects have contributed to a large turnover in the computer manufacturing industry. The debate continues as to whether we need massively parallel computers or not. Will the fast sequential processors be able to solve all the computing problems? Lewis (1994), in his article titled "Where Is Computing Headed?", states that "we can expect multiprocessing to become widely accepted in the practical world of everyday computing. Multiprocessor systems with four, eight, and 16 processors will be integrated into desktop personal computers . . . (However) the lack of software will keep massively parallel computers outside the mainstream of computing and the lack of good parallel processing software languages, tools and environments makes for fertile areas of research." Furht (1994), on the other hand, argues that "we need fast and inexpensive sequential machines which will solve about 99 percent of today's problems. For the remaining one percent, small multiprocessors or sequential machines connected and distributed on networks should achieve satisfactory solution."

The most significant commercial developments in massively parallel architectures are Thinking Machine Corporation's Connection Machine (CM) series; DARPA/Intel Teraops (10^{12} operations per second); and Touchstone projects resulting in the Paragon series of machines. The CM-200 benchmarked at 9.03 gigaflops while the CM-5 is rated at 128 Mflops on double precision data. It is anticipated that the final prototype of the Touchstone program (SIGMA) will scale to at least 2048 processors and provide aggregate performance exceeding 150 gigaflops and 100,000 MIPS.

There are other commercial efforts to produce massively parallel architectures, such as the recent collaboration of Digital Equipment Corporation (DEC) with MasPar Corporation. Even Cray Research Corporation, a staunch advocate of vector architectures with a limited number of processors, has switched over to building MPP architectures, the first of which is their T3D system described in Chapter 6. The T3D supports both SIMD and MIMD styles. In addition, it can be coupled with Cray Y-MP systems to combine MPP with vector processing architectures.

Another significant system introduced recently by Japan's Fujitsu is the Vector Parallel Processor (VPP) 500. Each processor in VPP-500 is rated at 1.6 gigaflops, which is achieved by coupling a RISC processor with a vector processor. Up to 222 of such coupled processors are interconnected by a crossbar network. Japan's NEC Corporation recently introduced a 512 processor MIMD system (SX-4) offering a peak speed of 1.024 teraflops.

It appears that the SIMD and MIMD paradigms are being combined to build high-performance MPP systems, as in Thinking Machine's CM-5 and Intel's Paragon series. Thinking Machine Corporation now delivers vector processing units to be interfaced to CM-5, thus combining SIMD, MIMD, and vector processing styles (along the lines of Cray T3D) to achieve high performance. Table 8.1 summarizes the characteristics of the major commercial MPP architectures.

There are several other experimental efforts to build high-performance machines that are not covered in this book. Some of those are IBM GF-11 (Beetem et

TABLE 8.1 CHARACTERISTICS OF THE MAJOR MPP ARCHITECTURES

System	Type	Interconnection structure	Node processor	Peak rating (double precision MFLOPS)
Intel Paragon XP/S	MIMD	2-D Mesh	i860	50
nCUBE 2S	MIMD	Hypercube	Custom 64-bit	2.4
Kendall Square	MIMD	Hierarchy of rings	Custom RISC	40
Meiko Scientific Corp. Computing Surface	MIMD	Variable topology	i860 or Sun Sparc	40
Parsytec GC	MIMD	3-D mesh Variable topology	Transputer (T9000)	25
Thinking Machines CM-5	MIMD/SIMD	Fat Tree	Sun Sparc	128
MasPar MP-1	SIMD	2-D Mesh X-net	32 custom 4-bit processors per chip	1.2 per 32 processors
Wavetracer DTC	SIMD Attached processor	3-D Mesh	Custom serial processor	-
Cray Research T3D	MIMD	3-D Torus	DEC Alpha	-

al., 1987), an SIMD; Purdue University's CHip (Snyder, 1986), a systolic architecture; shared memory MIMDs, such as New York University's Ultracomputer (Gottlieb et al., 1983), IBM Research Parallel computer (RP3) (Hester et al., 1986), Paradigm (Cheriton et al., 1991), and Hector (Vranesic et al., 1991); multiple SIMD designs, such as Columbia University's NON-VON (Shaw, 1984), University of Texas' Reconfigurable Array Computer (TRAC) (Lipovski and Malek, 1987), and Purdue University's Partitionable SIMD/MIMD (PASM) (Siegel et al., 1987); and very long instruction word (VLIW) architectures, such as Multiflow Inc.'s TRACE (Wallich, 1987).

Gordon Bell (1989) predicted that computer systems that are capable of sustaining one million MFLOPS (teraflops) will be constructed by the late 1990s, either using MIMD structures with a large number (4K to 32K) of nodes or using a connection machine with millions of processors. He also predicts that these teraflop machines would utilize a small (less than 100) number of data streams. Dan Hillis of Thinking Machine Corporation predicts that the largest machines of the late 1990s will utilize a large number (more than 1000) of data streams.

The thrust of the MPP architectures is *super number crunching* as evidenced by the machines listed in Table 8.1. When efficient resource sharing, rather than super number crunching, is the criteria, computer networks offer an advantage. With the availability of versatile workstations and desktop systems, computer networking has emerged as a popular architecture style. Section 1 introduces networks and the associated concept of distributed processing. Section 2 describes the fifth generation computer systems (FGCS) project of Japan, which was aimed at building *knowledge processing* machines (inspired by the field of artificial intelligence). Section 3 introduces one sixth generation architectural concept, the neural computers. As mentioned earlier, optical technology has enhanced the performance of computer systems through fast data transmission rates of optical fibers and massive storage capabilities of optical disks. There have been numerous efforts to build optical computing devices with some recent successes in building optical switching devices. Section 4 provides a brief description of optical computing. These descriptions are necessarily brief, and the reader is referred to the books and journals listed at the end of this chapter for the latest on these and other architectures.

8.1 COMPUTER NETWORKS AND DISTRIBUTED PROCESSING SYSTEMS

Pinfold (1991) identifies three areas in which conventional SIMD and MIMD approaches fall short:

1. They are not highly scalable and hence cannot be easily expanded in small increments.
2. They employ only one type of general purpose processor and hence are not suitable for environments with an array of specialized applications.
3. They employ fixed interconnection topology, thereby restricting the users when the applications dictate a different, more efficient topology.

The Touchstone program, for instance, addresses the first two shortfalls to a certain extent because the last prototype is envisioned to use heterogeneous processing nodes and to be scalable up to 2048 nodes. As can be expected, the future architectures would merge the SIMD and MIMD concepts. In fact, the evolution of the Thinking Machine's CM series illustrates this. The earlier machines in the series were SIMDs while the CM-5 can operate in both modes.

A new breed of versatile network architectures is now surfacing as an answer to the above shortfalls. Figure 8.1 shows the structure of a computer network. It is essentially a message-passing MIMD system except that the nodes are loosely coupled by the communication network. Each node (host) is an independent computer system. The user can access the resources at the other nodes through the network. The important concept is that the user executes an application at the node he or she is connected to as far as possible. The user submits a job to other nodes when resources to execute the job are not available at his or her node.

A distributed processing system utilizes the hardware structure of the network shown in Figure 8.1. It is more general in its operation in the sense that the nodes operate in what is called a *cooperative autonomy*. That is, the nodes cooperate to complete the application at hand and all the nodes are equal in capability (i.e., there is no master-slave relationship among the nodes). In a distributed system, the hardware, data, and control (operating system) are all distributed.

Figure 8.2 shows an example architecture, the Computing Surface from Meiko Scientific Corporation. It initially allows the design of systems with single processor and scales the system to as many processors as needed in an incremental fashion. Up to 800 processors have been used so far. It supports the use of three processors simultaneously (Intel i860, Sun Microsystems' SPARC, and Inmos' T800 transputer) to take advantage of strong characteristics of each. It is a true multiuser, multitasking system. For instance, a 64-node computing surface can be partitioned simultaneously

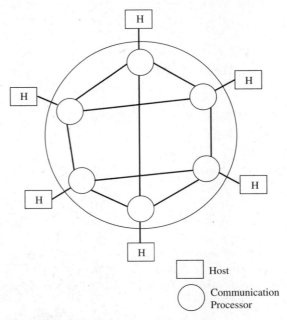

Figure 8.1 Computer Network

8.2 JAPAN'S FIFTH GENERATION COMPUTER SYSTEMS (FGCS) PROJECT

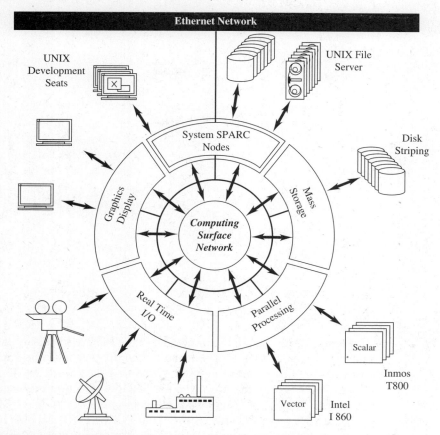

Figure 8.2 Meiko Scientific's Computing Surface (Pinfold, 1991)

into a 32-processor subsystem for numerical application, a 24-processor subsystem for simulation application, and two 3-processor and two single processor subsystems for other applications.

8.2 JAPAN'S FIFTH GENERATION COMPUTER SYSTEMS (FGCS) PROJECT

The goal of this project was to create, by 1990, a prototype FGCS, which was intended to unify the concepts from knowledge-based expert systems, very high-level programming languages, decentralized computing, and VLSI technology. This unification was intended to result principally in new knowledge-based expert systems with applications in such fields as computer-aided design (CAD), computer-aided engineering (CAE), computer-aided instruction (CAI), office automation, and robotics.

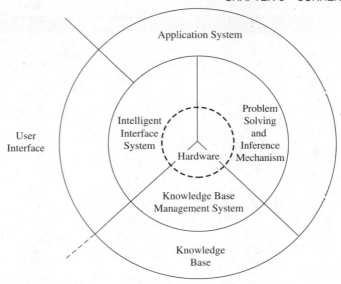

Figure 8.3 Elements of the Fifth Generation Computers (Bishop, 1986)

Figure 8.3 provides a top level view of the FGCS. The heart of the system is the problem-solving and inference machine. The inference machine interacts with a user through the intelligent interface system, accessing the knowledge base as necessary to obtain those facts required to solve a particular application problem. Underlying the whole system is a complex hardware foundation embedded in VLSI devices.

Figure 8.4 gives a detailed view of the FGCS. The basic operating mode of this computer is logical inferencing. All system software, from machine language to the high level Knowledge Base Enquiry Language, was to be based on logic programming, and Prolog was selected as the initial language. The target performance of the system was 50 to 1000 million logical inferences per second (MLIPS). This represented about a 1000-fold increase over the technology of the 1980s. The knowledge base management system was slated to support a capacity of 1000 gigabytes.

The project was broken up into three phases. Phase 1 (1982 to 1984) was devoted to feasibility studies and tool design. Prolog was selected as the fundamental software tool, and the dataflow paradigm was targeted as the fundamental hardware architecture. Thus, the intent was for all subsystems to be based on some logic programming language, such as Prolog, and to embed that language in hardware, making rapid concurrent advancements in VLSI architecture essential. Phase 2 (1985 to 1989) was dedicated to building and testing the inference machine and the knowledge base machine as separate entities. Phase 3 (1989 to 1991) was to combine all subsystems into the prototype FGCS.

Two prototype machines were developed in the first phase. The first prototype was the Personal Sequential Inference computer (PSI), which was similar to the workstations of the day. The second machine was a relational database machine, DELTA, which was intended to serve as a machine to resolve queries from the PSI

8.2 JAPAN'S FIFTH GENERATION COMPUTER SYSTEMS (FGCS) PROJECT 365

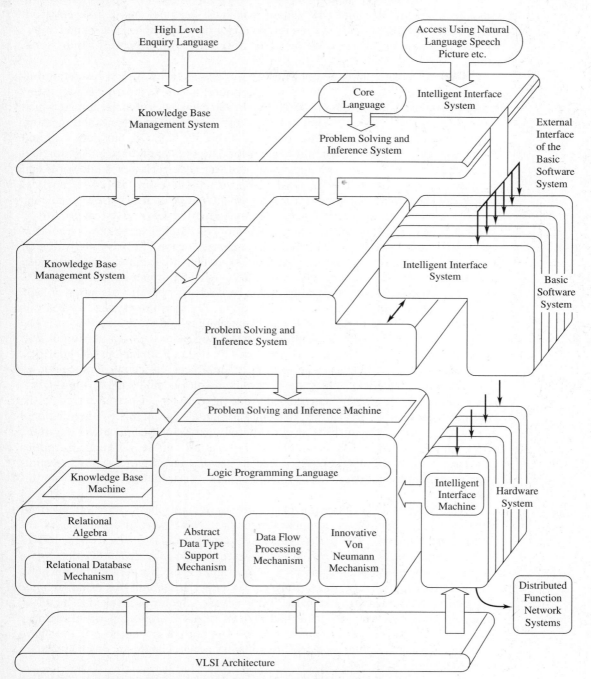

Figure 8.4 Basic Configuration of the Fifth Generation Computer (Courtesy of Japan Information Processing Development Center)

class of machines on a network. These machines were not much different from machines of the same period and offered no major breakthroughs in computer architecture. However, their design influenced the fifth generation project efforts to a great extent.

The PSI is essentially a sophisticated workstation with a high-resolution bit-mapped display with 1200 × 900 pixels, a mouse, and a keyboard. It was distinguished from the workstations of 1985 by having 80 megabytes of main storage, which was a large amount of memory for 1985 because 1-megabit and 4-megabit memory chips were not yet being produced. It was a 40-bit machine (32-bits data field and 8-bits tag field). The tag field could be used for data typing, garbage collection, and for other aspects of high-level languages. There were two caches of 4 kilowords and an address translation unit to translate 32-bit virtual addresses into 24-bit physical addresses. The PSI was microprogrammed with a writable control store to enable the research team to explore the effects of different instruction sets and system primitives. This machine was a sequential machine and offered no parallelism besides the concurrent input/output operations. The machine language for the PSI was a derivative of Prolog called Kernel Language 0 (KL0), and system programming was provided through Extended Self-Contained Prolog (ESP), an object-oriented extension to KL0. There was also the KL1, a concurrent Prolog derivative for parallel execution of logic programming for the next generation workstation. The operating system for PSI was SIMPOS (Sequential Inference-Machine Programming and Operating System). The successor of PSI (PSI-II) was essentially a faster and more compact version of PSI. The performance of PSI-II was roughly three times that of PSI or about 100 kiloLIPS.

The DELTA machine has a network interface processor, a control processor for three relational engines, 128 megabytes of main memory, and 20 gigabytes of auxiliary memory. Once a query is received from the network, it is transferred to the control processor that breaks the query into primitives executable by the relational engines. The primitives are high-level relational operations such as SORT, UNION, JOIN, and RESTRICT. One or more of the engines can be assigned operations concurrently, and the operations proceed in parallel unless consistency restraints force sequential executions. Thus, a limited amount of parallelism was built into this machine.

The Multi-PSI machines, developed in the second phase, were intended for research into parallelism in computer languages. There were two versions of the Multi-PSI: the PSI/V1, which was based on PSI, and the PSI/V2, based on the PSI-II. In these architectures, several PSI machines were connected with a lattice network in which each network branch contains two-way signal lines. Network communication was performed by message passing. The network interface circuit was installed in the PSI internal bus and controlled by the PSI firmware, which was invoked as a built-in predicate. Each processing element had its own memory and independent memory address space. Shared memory architecture was not chosen because it may have serious performance problems caused by memory access contention when applied to large scale multiprocessor systems.

There was also a great deal of research on programming systems, including intelligent user interfaces, intelligent programming where the language could represent a graph similar to dataflow graphs, and user interfaces capable of manipulating the Japanese character set. On a lower level, there were studies into problem solving, inference system processing problems, and knowledge-based management systems, which would accumulate and manage the knowledge in the system. Also the programming system of the research machines was to be used to create simulations for prototypes of parallel inference machines.

Perhaps the most important result of the project was the impact it had on the rest of the world. Other nations established fifth generation research programs of their own, some with direct government involvement and funding as in Europe and the United Kingdom, others more informal as in the United States, Taiwan, and India. The Japanese model of a *logical* computer represented a significant break with traditional thinking and presaged the direction of future generations of computers.

8.3 THE SIXTH GENERATION

The Real World Computing project of Japan can be considered a sixth generation computer system project, extending the work done under the FGCS project. In 1985, the Japanese Ministry of Science and Technology (STA) released a report proposing advanced research in knowledge science. Translated in one incarnation as "Promotion of Integrated Research and Development of Information and Electronic Technologies concerning Systems to Substitute or Augment Intelligent Functions of Human Beings," this report was quickly dubbed the *sixth generation* by the Japanese press.

The thrust of this project is flexible, or intuitive, information processing (i.e., similar to the way human beings absorb information and make decisions). The structure of the machines envisioned under this project comprise both massively parallel computing systems and neural networks. Optical technology is also being investigated both for interconnection and processing aspects.

The dataflow paradigm seems to be guiding the massive parallel structure in this project. In the first phase, it is anticipated that several architectures with as many as 10,000 processors would be developed. In the second phase, the best of these architectures would be selected as the basis for a million-processor system. The goal of the project is also to develop a neural network composed of 1000 subnetworks of 1000 neurons each, providing a speed of 10 trillion connection updates per second.

The Japanese have decided to make the sixth generation project an international cooperative effort and have invited other countries to participate in it. The emphasis of the project is massively parallel processing, optical computing, and new software techniques.

In addition to the Japanese efforts, several other sixth generation concepts have evolved over the last few years. A brief description of one such concept (neural networks) follows.

8.3.1 Neural Networks

Neural networks or artificial neural networks (ANN) are suitable for solving problems that do not have a well-defined algorithm to transform an input to an output. Rather a collection of representative examples of the desired transformation is used to *train* the ANN, which in turn *adapts* itself to produce the desired outputs when presented with the example inputs. In addition, it will respond with an output (a good guess) even when presented with inputs that it has never seen before. That is, during the training mode, the information about the problem to be solved is encoded into the ANN and the network spends its productive mode in performing transformations and *learning*. Thus, the advantage of the ANN approach is not necessarily in the elegance of the particular solution but in its generality to find a solution to particular problems, given only examples of the desired behavior. It allows the evolution of automated systems without explicit reprogramming. This section provides a brief description of the state of the art in neural network technology.

ANNs resemble their biological counterparts in terms of their behaviors of learning and recognizing and applying relationships between objects. Biological neural networks consist of a large number of computational elements called neurons. A **neuron** is composed of the cell body, a number of extensions called **dendrites** that serve as inputs, and a long extension called an **axon** that serves as the output. **Synapses** connect the axon of one neuron to dendrites of other neurons. The neurons are arranged in layers. In general, neurons in one layer receive their inputs from those in another layer and send their outputs to the neurons in a third layer. Depending on the application, it is possible that the neurons in a layer receive inputs from and provide outputs to the neurons in the same layer. Neurons undergo a constantly changing state of biochemical activity. The composite state of all the neurons in a layer constitutes the representation of the world. The connections between the neurons have weights associated with them. These weights (called coupling weights) represent the influence of one neuron over the other connected to it. If two neurons are not connected, the corresponding coupling weight is 0. Each neuron essentially sends its state information (i.e., value) multiplied by the corresponding coupling weight to all the neurons it is connected to. All neurons sum the values received from their dendrites to update their state.

ANNs are thus based on a threshold processing circuit or neuron (shown in Figure 8.5) at which the weighted inputs are summed. Here the weighting functions have been relabeled as attenuators. In practical implementations, the inputs to a neuron are weighted by multiplying the input by a factor that is less than or equal to one (i.e., attenuated). The value of the weighting factors are determined by the

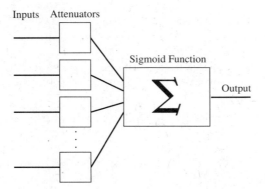

Figure 8.5 Neuron Model

8.3 THE SIXTH GENERATION

learning algorithm. The attenuated inputs are summed using a nonlinear function called a sigmoid function. If the output of the summing function exceeds a built-in threshold, the neuron *fires,* generating an output.

Figure 8.6 shows the layered model of an ANN consisting of a large number of neurons. Each neuron has multiple inputs, and its output is connected to a large number of other processors' inputs. As mentioned earlier, in the normal operating mode of the ANN, data presented as input will cause a specific output pattern to be generated. The input-to-output relationship is determined during the *training mode,* when a known input is presented along with the expected output. The training algorithm adjusts the weighting of inputs until the expected output is attained.

IMPLEMENTATION TECHNOLOGIES

Note that the neurons in Figure 8.6 have a modest computational complexity and they normally communicate only with the nearest neighbors, making the interconnections simple and repetitive. Because of these characteristics and the capabilities offered by the VLSI technology, it is now possible to cost effectively build ANNs with a large number of processors.

There are two types of connectivity models encountered in the practical implementation of ANNs. The first, the Hopfield model illustrated in Figure 8.7, is a fully connected model in which the output of every neuron is an input to every other

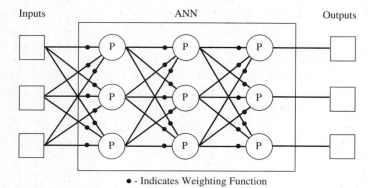

● - Indicates Weighting Function

Figure 8.6   ANN Structure

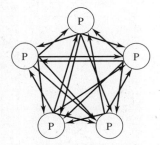

Fully Connected
Every Processor Has Input From All Others   **Figure 8.7**   Hopfield Model

neuron. This is the most difficult model to implement because of the exponential increase in network complexity as the number of neurons grows. The second is the layered model illustrated in Figure 8.6. This model requires fewer attenuators and interconnections and enables multichip implementations. The number of layers and the number of neurons found in each layer varies from design to design.

Several technologies have been used in implementing ANNs. These include digital electronics, analog electronics, analog/digital (hybrid) designs, optical technology, and simulation.

The main reasons for digital implementation are the ability to readily program weights, high noise immunity, and flexibility for signals to be transmitted between chips. But digital implementations occupy a large silicon area because of the synaptic multipliers. Figure 8.8 illustrates the basic elements that comprise a digital ANN and a few implementation techniques. Parallel input data (usually 8 to 16 bits) is clocked into a register, which is then multiplied with the synaptic weight (stored digitally) and accumulated using some form of digital adder mechanism. The digital storage of synapse weights are stable over a long period and do not suffer from temperature variations. It is relatively easy to load or retrieve trained configuration data to and from the circuitry.

A disadvantage of digital implementations is that, due to the more extensive circuitry required, the number of neurons per package is much less compared to analog designs. Digital ANNs must be clocked through their multiply and accumulation cycles, which greatly reduces the throughput as compared to analog implementations. Another problem is that inputs to digital ANNs must be presented in the form of digital data. This requires converting analog data sources to a digital form compatible with the ANN design.

In analog implementations, the synapse is implemented as a variable resistor and the neuron is implemented as a multi-input summing amplifier. The methods employed to implement these elements are almost as numerous as the number of designs. Figure 8.9 illustrates several representative ones.

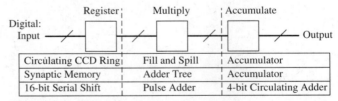

Figure 8.8 Digital Implementations

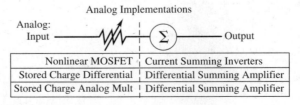

Figure 8.9 Analog Implementations

The advantages of analog over digital implementations are: the analog circuitry is much smaller; the number of circuit elements required to implement an analog synapse, or neuron, is much lower; and the connectivity between neurons requires a single path as opposed to multiple lines required in digital technology. Thus, a much greater packaging density may be achieved in analog implementations. Also because the circuitry is simple, on-chip training is easier to achieve. Other advantages include direct sensor interface and higher throughput. On the negative side, analog implementations suffer from long-term memory instability because of the charge leakage in synapse storage. Circuit fabrication and temperature sensitivity may also contribute to errors. Also the input interface is inflexible because all inputs to a specific analog implementation must be conditioned and scaled to match the performance requirements of the design.

Hybrid implementations combine digital and analog circuitry in the same design. A set of digitally selected resistors (Fisher, et. al., 1991), or MOSFETs (Khachab, 1991), are used to implement the synapse weighting, thus utilizing the digital advantage of reading and writing synaptic weights combined with the greater density of analog designs.

Optical implementations are not as well developed as other approaches yet they offer the greatest potential for future growth in ANN systems. Figure 8.10 illustrates an optical approach in which holograms are used to implement the synaptic function. In optical implementations, connectivity is achieved via light. Because crossing light beams do not interfere, one of the greatest problems in implementing high density ANNs is eliminated. Optical ANNs have the potential of achieving the highest connectivity and density of all the approaches. Another advantage of optical ANNs is that the highest throughput is achieved. The greatest difficulty in practical implementation is interfacing to a variety of input types and generating holographic attenuators.

Other implementations of ANN systems include simulations executed on SIMD (Iwata,1989) and MIMD architectures (Zitti, 1989). While these approaches generally outperform simulations on conventional computer architectures, their throughput does not match that of hardware implementations.

A PROGRAMMABLE ANALOG NEURAL NETWORK PROCESSOR

This section provides a brief description of an analog neural network breadboard consisting of 256 neurons and 248 programmable synaptic weights (Fisher, et. al., 1991). The breadboard has been used to demonstrate the application of neural network learning to the problem of real-time adaptive mirror control. The processor was

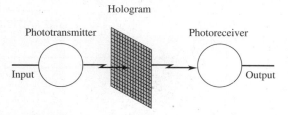

Figure 8.10 Optical Implementations

designed to maximize its analog computational characteristics and flexibility. It can be used to study both feedforward and feedback networks or as a massively parallel analog control processor. It consists of an array of custom programmable resistor chips assembled at the board level.

The analog neural network processor shown in Figure 8.11 consists of 256 operational-amplifier-based neural circuits with a total of 2048 programmable resistors physically located on 16 boards (neuron boards). The resistors, which are programmed via a personal computer (PC), provide a means of training the analog neural network. The C programming language was used to write an extensive library of routines that can be used as part of specialized programs within an overall system shell. The input to the neuron boards can be from analog sources or from 12-bit digital sources converted to analog. The digital sources can be provided by the PC or from external sources. Thus, it is possible to test an application using simulated data from the PC or from external sources. The outputs can be monitored with a set of 256 analog-to-digital converters.

The digitally programmable analog resistor chip was produced using a commercial analog gate array process. Each channel of the chip consists of a buffered source follower operational amplifier connected to five polysilicon resistors through bipolar analog switches. The values range from 8 to 128 Kohms. Hundreds of these resistors are connected in parallel without placing too large a load on either the external summing amplifier or the input circuit. The data word is latched within the chip; hence, no refresh is required.

The interconnection crossbar structure, the weights (or resistors), and the operational amplifiers are on a single board. The processor is on a separate board. This design approach allows the system to be expanded in a modular fashion; the complexity expands linearly with the number of required output neurons. The interconnect boards are problem specific while the rest of the analog processor is general purpose.

The neuron board can be configured to have as few as 7 inputs to each of the 16 neurons or as many as 128 inputs to a single neuron. One channel per resistor chip is used to program the feedback resistor. By using a programmable resistor from the

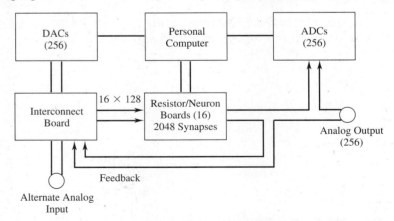

Figure 8.11 Analog Network Processor (Fisher, 1991) (Reprinted with permission from IEEE.)

package for the feedback resistance, the neuron gain becomes independent of the actual value of the internal package resistance. The gain is dependent only on the ratio of the resistances within the package. These can be controlled more closely than the package-to-package variation. The board may be set up as an integrator by installing a capacitor across the feedback resistor. The resistor (weights) on the board may be reprogrammed at a rate of one per microsecond.

The first application of the analog processor was the demonstration of neural network control of 21 actuators of a 69-actuator adaptive mirror. The purpose of such a system is to correct for distortions introduced when light forming the image passes through the atmosphere. Applications of this technology include the correction of solar and other bright celestial object images and the up-linking of laser beams through the atmosphere. The slope of the wavefront is measured at a large number of points and a best-fit calculation is then done to determine the position of actuators, which will then undo the distortions when the light making up the image reflects from the adaptive mirror surface. The system must operate with a closed-loop control bandwidth of at least 100 Hz to keep up with the atmospheric changes. This is equivalent to having a step response settling time of less than 10 ms.

The overall system includes a wavefront sensor that provides the input signals to the system through a set of digital-to-analog converters. The output of the neuron boards drives the integrators, whose output is amplified to drive the adaptive mirror. A STAR array processor is used as a diagnostic to evaluate the performance of the system.

In order to implement the sparsity of the control matrix method, 16 programmable resistors and 2 operational amplifiers were required per actuator. Because the operational amplifiers are used in an inverting mode, the first takes inputs that have positive coefficients and the second inputs that have negative coefficients. In order to obtain a type one servo, the output of the neuron boards is fed to a set of integrators. A software controlled switch is used to open and close the control loop.

A laser and beam expander was used to direct a beam into the adaptive mirror. An image from the mirror reflects from the back side of a beam splitter onto the wavefront sensor. This beam is also combined with a reference beam to produce an interferogram image on a CCD array focal plane. The interferogram provides an independent, real-time diagnostic of the system performance.

There are two distinct stages of training. The first stage produces the best possible open-loop control coefficients, and the second modifies these control coefficients to obtain improved real-time closed-loop performance.

The best set of weights for a minimum time solution are the weights that are optimal for an open-loop correction or the correction that one gets if just one frame of data is used to compute the new actuator positions. This is the type of correction one would have if the network were simply a feedforward network. In order to obtain this set of weights, an automated program was written that can supply a test voltage to each of the actuators at a time. During each actuator *punch,* each of the resistors connected to the control of the actuator was turned on one at a time and the response was recorded. This set of measurements is a complete training set. While these data could be used with a traditional neural network training routine such as the LMS algorithm to obtain a control matrix, it is more straightforward to calculate the pseudoinverse of the data. Such an inversion is possible because the data set is guaranteed to be complete and nondegenerate. Such is not the case for randomly sampled data typically used for training. The resulting control matrix did have contributions to nonnearest neighbor connections not implemented in the hardware. However, the largest contributions were at the nearest neighbors that had been prewired. Contributions to unwired elements of the control matrix were ignored. The resistor values were then scaled to be within the 5-bit range of the resistor chip. The gain-determining resistors were adjusted to maximize the closed-loop gain while avoiding oscillation on any of the 21 actuators. There was more than a factor of 3 margin on the range of gain from a critically damped signal with a damped oscillation with a decay time of less than one second. Finally, the values of the resistors for the feedback connections were set to the value of the gain resistor divided by the number of the nearest neighbors. The values of these resistors are determined from the interconnectivity and cannot be larger without causing interactuator oscillations.

The first test of the flexibility of the system came when the optical alignment difficulties within the wavefront sensor limited the number of actuator measurements such that the control was valid only for the inner 21 actuators. Although the system had been wired for 69 actuators, only software modifications and changes in the control matrix values were required to reduce the analog control to the smaller number. This illustrates the advantage of the programmable resistor design.

APPLICATIONS AND HARDWARE

Neural networks have been used to match patterns, make generalizations, merge new situations into old experiences, mirror the structures in their environment, and find the best fit among many possibilities. The future trend in neural networks can be gauged from the few examples presented below.

Intel Corporation released an analog neural network chip in August 1990. This is a fully interconnected 64-neuron neural network based on EPROM technology that is well suited to replace a single layer in a multilayer network. While extremely dense, the synapses require a complex programming circuit and synapse-specific training, and the analog throughput must be halted during programming. The chip is best suited to ultrafast execution of problems that require infrequent retraining.

A wave of neural net research has spread through the laboratories at AT&T, TRW, Texas Instruments, IBM, General Electric, NASA's Jet Propulsion Laboratory, and others. The scientists at AT&T Bell Laboratories are testing a chip that has 512 neurons. NHK Science and Technology Laboratories of Japan is working on a neural network that recognizes typewritten characters. SAIC Technology Research offers a circuit board that can be added to a conventional computer to simulate a neural network. It can update the connections between the neurons at the rate of two million per second. Several other add-on boards are quickly appearing.

Researchers at Allied Signal have trained a neural net to recognize underwater targets from the object's reflections of sonar signals. After only three hours of training, the neural network was able to outperform humans and a conventional computer program that took more than ten months to design.

The University of Pennsylvania has built an optical neural net that stores how radar signals reflect from various types of vehicles. It can match the correct one from as little as 10% of the complete radar pattern.

NestorWriter from Nestor, Inc. employs a neural net type of design and can be run on a PC. It reads handwritten characters written on a pen-sensitive pad. Nestor has also a network-based program that can recognize any of the 2500 handwritten Japanese characters.

Neural networks and learning algorithms that better reflect the human brain must still be developed. It is also unknown how the current designs with a relatively small number of neurons will operate when enlarged to contain a huge number of neurons.

8.4 OPTICAL COMPUTING

Optical computing has been an active area of research over the last few years as an alternative to electronic digital computing to design high-speed computer systems. Data communication through optical fibers has already proven to be more versatile and cost-effective than that through the electronic media. Optical interconnection networks are widely being investigated (Brenner, 1988; Eichmann, 1987; Goodman, 1984; and Jahns, 1988). Optical interconnections between the components on an integrated circuit chip would save the chip area occupied by the interconnect silicon and eliminate the signal interference problems. Several analog computer-like structures based on optical devices have also been in use in image processing applications. But the technology has not yielded any practical equivalent to current day electronic digital computers yet. The AT&T Bell laboratory has recently announced the invention of a practical optical transistor. This has led to the speculation that optical computers may be around the corner.

Recall that the speed characteristics of electronic computational structures are functions of device speeds and the architecture. There is a large disparity between the speed of the fastest electronic switching component and the speeds of the fastest digital electronic computers. The switching speeds of transistors are as high as 5 picoseconds while the fastest computers operate at clock periods of the order of a few nanoseconds. The limitations of electronic technology that cause this speed disparity are (Jordan, 1988): electromagnetic interference at high speeds, distorted edge transitions, complexity of metal connections, drive requirements for pins, large peak power levels, and impedance-matching effects.

Electromagnetic interference is the result of the coupling of inductances of two current-carrying wires. Sharp edge transitions are a requirement for proper switching. But higher frequencies attenuate greater than lower frequencies, resulting in edge distortions at high speeds. The complexity of metal connections on chips, circuit boards, and between-system components introduces complex fields and unequal path delays. The signal skews introduced by unequal path delays are overcome by slowing the system clock. Large peak power levels are needed to overcome residual capacitances. Impedance-matching effects at connections require high currents and, in turn, cause lower system speeds.

There are several advantages to using free-space optics for interconnections (Jordan, 1988). By imaging a large array of light beams onto an array of optical logic devices, it is possible to achieve high connectivity. Because physical interconnects are not needed (unless fibers or waveguides are used), connection complexity and drive requirements are reduced. Optical signals do not interact in free space (i.e., beams can pass through each other without any interference), and hence, a high bandwidth can be achieved. There is no feedback to the power source as in electronic circuits, and hence, there are no data dependent loads. The inherently low signal dispersion of optical signals implies that the shape of a pulse as it leaves its source remains virtually unchanged until its destination. Another advantage of optics over electronics is communication. Optical devices can be oriented normal to the surface of an optical chip such that light beams travel in parallel between arrays of optical logic devices rather than through pins at the edges of chips as in electronic integrated circuits. Lenses, prisms, and mirrors can convey an image with millions of resolvable points in parallel.

It is important to note the differences in basic characteristics of electrons and photons. Electrons easily affect each other even at a distance, thus making it easy to perform switching. But, this ease of interaction complicates the task of communication because the signals must be preserved. Because it is difficult to get two photons to interact, it is difficult to get two optical signals to interact. Thus, optics is bad for switching but good for communications. A solution may be to stay with hybrid technology where electronics perform all the computations and the optics perform all the communication.

There are several problems associated with optical technology. Most of these problems stem from an inability of optical signals to interact and thus perform switching. Electronics technology is mature and cost-effective, and it allows the fabrication of high-density switching components. Photonics, on the other hand, is less mature and requires tight imaging tolerances and constant power consumption for modulator-based optical devices. Optical devices can be spaced a few microns apart on optical chips but require several centimeters of interaction distance for lenses, gratings, and other imaging components. Micro-optic techniques are being investigated as solutions to this problem.

The lack of a suitable optical memory has been another problem. The development of optical memories has followed the requirements imposed by the modified finite state machine, which is a serial structure, rather than the classical parallel model. The parallelism offered by optics was thus ignored, and the emphasis was to incorporate an addressing mechanism. This required beam deflectors, page composers, and detector arrays, which were slow, awkward, and expensive. Also note that in a modified finite state machine the memory elements are required to preserve their contents indefinitely because they are addressed in random order. (In the classical finite state machine, the storage elements need only preserve their information for one cycle). It has been difficult to fabricate such an optical device. An optical disk device provides this capability but is hardly satisfactory as a main memory element.

A number of research efforts were started in the early 1960s to build digital logic devices utilizing the semiconductor laser diodes and the nonlinear phenomena of saturable absorption. The infancy of optoelectronic technology and a critical study of power dissipation versus speed for optical logic led to the conclusion that the inherently higher switching speeds of optical phenomena could not be exploited to build optical computers that can offer the performance of electronic technology. The early 1980s saw rapid improvements in optoelectronic technology. New materials, such as multiple quantum wells (MQW), and device configurations, such as self-electro-optic effect devices (SEED) and optical logic etalons (OLE), were developed.

8.4 OPTICAL COMPUTING

Many approaches have been proposed for forming general purpose optical computers (Smith, 1986) although none of them has been completely implemented. One among them is Huang's Symbolic Substitution (Huang, 1983), which is based on binary pattern substitution. The general idea is to search for a two-dimensional pattern in a binary grid and to replace that pattern with another pattern everywhere the search pattern is found.

Consider the example shown in Figure 8.12. The search pattern is the left-hand side (LHS) of the transformation rule, and the pattern that replaces the LHS is the right-hand side (RHS) as shown in (a). In (b), the LHS of the rule is satisfied at two locations. The RHS is written at those locations, and the cells that do not contribute to the LHS disappear after the rule is applied.

A number of rules can be applied either in series or in parallel over a number of iterations to realize complex functions. Transformation rules can be customized to perform specific functions, such as addition or subtraction, or they may be made to perform Boolean logic primitives in which case the configuration of the grid is customized to implement specific functions.

A schematic diagram of an optical setup for a single transformation rule with four cells in the LHS and four cells in the RHS is shown in Figure 8.13. Here a two-dimensional input pattern is combined with a two-dimensional control image (produced by imaging light through a mask) onto the optically nonlinear OR-array A. The feedback path from array A is split into four identical copies that are shifted and superimposed onto the AND-array B to implement the LHS of the rule. Array B performs a threshold operation and normalizes the signals. The output of array B is split into four copies that are shifted and superimposed onto array A to implement the RHS of the rule, normalize signals, and provide an output. Figure 8.14 shows a time sequence of symbolic substitution using this setup. Here the input image (A) contains one binary pattern that matches the LHS of the rule. It is split into four identical copies (B), which are each shifted (C) and superimposed (D) according to the positions of the bits in the LHS. Each of the bits in the LHS is one position away from the center cell in the x and y directions, and hence, each image is shifted according to its distance from the center cell. A threshold operation (E) sets all cells to 0 except those cells that have the original intensity after the images are superimposed. The array (F) is then

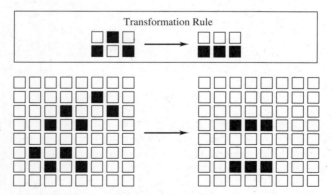

Figure 8.12 Symbolic Substitution (Huang, 1983) (Reprinted with permission from IEEE.)

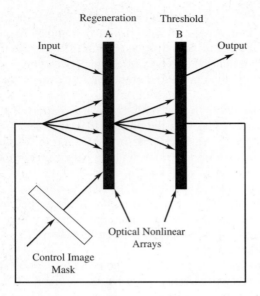

Figure 8.13 Schematic of Optical Implementation of Symbolic Substitution (Huang, 1983) (Reprinted with permission from IEEE.)

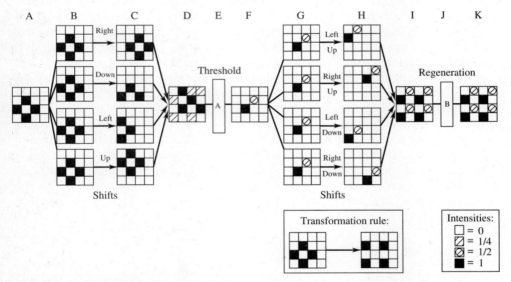

Figure 8.14 Time Sequence of Symbolic Substitution for a 4 × 4 System (Huang, 1983) (Reprinted with permission from IEEE.)

split into four identical images (G), which are shifted (H) and superimposed (I) according to the RHS pattern. The intensity values in the final image are restored by regeneration element B (J). This mechanism will locate in parallel all such areas that contain such a pattern.

It is possible to apply several rules in parallel. Figure 8.15 shows a setup for implementing four rules with two cells in the LHS and RHS of each rule (Brenner, et.

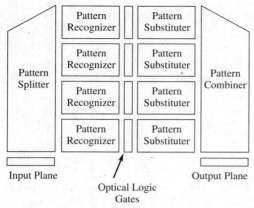

Figure 8.15 Optical Implementation of Four 2 × 2 Symbolic Substitution Rules (Huang, 1983) (Reprinted with permission from IEEE.)

al., 1986). The input image is passed through a cascade of beam-splitters to produce four copies. Each copy is passed to a pattern recognizer/substituter pair, and the signals are regenerated by an array of optically nonlinear logic gates. The outputs are then combined on the output plane through a cascade of beam-combiner.

While quite different from the current approach for computing, the symbolic substitution technique is quite general and powerful. Refer to Huang (1983) for further details.

For further details on optical computing, refer to the book by Murdocca (1990), and to the excellent surveys on various aspects of optical computing in Feitelson (1988); Goodman (1985), and Bell (1986). For details on optical methods of implementing neural networks, refer to Abu-Mostafa (1987) and Athale (1989).

REFERENCES

Abe, S., T. Bandoh, S. Yamaguchi, K. Kurosawa, and K. Kiriyama. 1987. High performance integrated Prolog Processor—IPP. *Proceedings of 14th Annual International Symposium on Computer Architecture,* 100–107.

Abu-Mostafa, Y. S., and D. Psaltis. 1987. Optical neural computers. *Scientific American* 256 (April): 88.

Agranat, A. J., C. F. Neugebaur, R. D. Nelson, and A. Yariv. 1990. The CCD neural processor: A neural network integrated circuit with 65536 programmable analog synapses. *IEEE Transactions on Circuits and Systems* 37(8): 820–829.

Allman, W. F. 1989. *Apprentices of wonder, inside the neural network revolution.* New York: Bantam Books.

Amano, A., T. Aritsuka, N. Hataoka, and A. Ichikawa. 1989. On the use of neural networks and fuzzy logic in speech recognition. *Proceedings of the IEEE International Joint Conference on Neural Networks,* vol. 2.

Annartone, M., E. Arnould, T. Gross, H. T. Kung, M. S. Lam, O. Mezilcioglu, K. Sarocky, and J. A. Webb. 1986. Warp architecture and implementation. *Proceedings of 13th International Symposium on Computer Architecture,* 346–356.

Arbib, M. A. 1989. Schemas and neural networks for sixth generation computing. *Journal of Parallel and Distributed Computing* 6(2): 185–216.

Athale, R. A. 1989. Optical implementations of neural computing. In *Optical Computing*. Vol. 9, p. 2. Technical Digest Series. Washington, D.C.: Optical Society of America.

Beetem, J., M. Denneau, and D. Weingarten. 1987. The GF11 parallel computer. In *Experimental parallel computing architectures*. Amsterdam: North-Holland.

Bell, C. G. 1989. The future of high performance computers in science and engineering. *Communications of ACM* 32(September): 1091–1101.

Bell, T. E. 1986. Optical computing: A field in flux. *IEEE Spectrum* 34(August).

Bishop, P. 1986. *Fifth generation computers: Concepts, implementations and uses.* Chichester, U.K.: Ellis Horwood Ltd.

Brenner, K. H., A. Huang, and N. Streibl. 1986. Digital optical computing with symbolic substitution. *Applied Optics* 25(February): 120–127.

Brenner, K. H., and A. Huang. 1988. Optical implementation of the perfect shuffle interconnections. *Applied Optics* 27(January). 135.

Chapman, R. E. 1986. Intelligent computing (the sixth generation): A Japanese initiative? *Proceedings of the IEEE International Conference on Systems, Man, and Cybernetics*, vol. 2, 1019–23.

Cheriton, D. R., H. A. Goosen, and P. D. Boyle. 1991. Paradigm: A highly scalable shared-memory multicomputer architecture. *IEEE Computer* 24(2): 76–90.

Chiueh, T., and R. M. Goodman. 1991. Recurrent correlation associative memories. *IEEE Transactions on Neural Networks* 2(2): 201–207.

DeWitt, D. J., R. Finkel, and M. Solomon. 1984. The CRYSTAL multicomputer: Design and implementation experience. *Computer Sciences Technical Report No. 553*. University of Wisconsin, Madison, Wis.

Donlin, M. and J. Child. 1992. Is neural computing the key to artificial intelligence? *Computer Design*, 31(10): 87–104.

Elder, J., A. Gottlieb, C. K. Kruskal, K. P. Mcauliffe, K. Randolph, M. Snir, P. Teller, and J. Wilson. 1985. Issues related to MIMD shared-memory computers: The NYU ultra-computer approach. *Proceedings 12th International Symposium on Computer Architecture*, Boston, Mass., 126–135.

Feitelson, D. 1988. *Optical computing.* Cambridge, Mass.: The MIT Press.

Fisher, W. A., R. J. Fujimoto, and R. C. Smithson. 1991. A programmable analog neural network processor. *IEEE Trans. on Neural Networks* 2(2): 210–216.

Freeman, J. A. and D. M. Skapura. 1991. *Neural networks: Algorithms, applications, and programming techniques.* New York: Addison–Wesley.

Fuchi, K., and K. Furukawa. 1987. The role of logic programming in the fifth generation computer project. *New Generation Computing* 3(5): 3–23.

Fuchi, K., and K. Furukawa. 1987. The role of logic programming in the fifth generation computer project. *New Generation Computing* 3: 5.

Furht, B. 1994. Parallel computing: Glory and collapse. *IEEE Computer* 27(11): 74–75.

Gajski, D., D. Kuck, D. Lawrie, and A. Sameh. 1983. Cedar—A large scale multi-processor. *Proceedings International Conference on Parallel Processing*, 524–529.

Galler, B. A. 1986. The influence of the United States and Japan on knowledge systems of the future. *Proceedings of the IEEE International Conference on Systems, Man, and Cybernetics,* vol. 2, 1024.

Gehringer, E. F., D. P. Siewiorek, and Z. Seghall. 1987 *Parallel processing: The Cm experience*. Bedford, Mass.: Digital Press.

Goto, A., A. Matsumoto, and E. Tick. 1989. Design and performance of a coherent cache for parallel logic programming architectures. *Proceedings of the ACM Annual Conference*, 27.

Gottlieb, A., B. D. Lubachevsky, and L. Rudolph. 1983. Basic techniques for the efficient coordination of very large numbers of cooperating sequential processors. *ACM Transactions on Programming Languages and System* 5(2): 164–189.

Graf, H. P. et al. 1986. VLSI implementation of neural network memory with several hundreds of neurons. *AIP Conference Proceeding, Neural Networks for Computing,* 182–187.

Habata, S., et al. 1987. Cooperative high performance sequential inference machine: CHI. *Proceedings of the IEEE International Conference on Computer Design: VLSI in Computers and Processors,* 601–604.

Hecht-Nielson, R. 1986. Performance limits of optical, electro-optical, and electronic neurocomputers. *Optical and Hybrid Computing* 634(3): 277–306.

Hecht-Nielson, R. 1987. Counter propagation networks. *Proceedings IEEE First Annual International Conference on Neural Networks,* June 21–24 San Diego, Calif.

Hester, P. D., R. O. Simpson, and A. Chang. 1986. The IBM RT PC ROMP and memory management unit architecture. IBM Publication No. SA23-1057. Armonk, NY: *IBM RT Personal Computer Technology,* 48–56.

Hochet, B., V. Peiris, S. Abodo, and M. J. Declercq. 1991. Implementation of a learning Kohonen neuron based on a new multilevel storage technique. *IEEE Journal of Solid-State Circuits* 26(3): 246–249.

Hockney, R. W., and C. R. Jesshope. 1988. *Parallel computers-2, architectures, programming and algorithms.* Bristol, England: Adam Hilger Ltd.

Hollis, P. W., and J. J. Paulos. 1990. Artificial neural networks using MOS analog multipliers. *IEEE Journal of Solid State Circuits* 25(3): 320–326.

Hopfield, J. J., and D. W. Tank. 1986. Computing with neural circuits: A model. *Science* 233 (August): 625–633.

Hosokawa, M., S. Omatu, and M. Fukumi. 1989. A new approach for pattern recognition by neural networks with scramblers. *Proceedings of the IEEE International Joint Conference on Neural Networks,* vol. 2.

Huang, A. 1983. Parallel algorithms for optical digital computing. *IEEE 10th International Optical Computing Conference,* Cambridge, Mass.

IEEE Spectrum. 1992. Special issue on supercomputers. September.

Intel Corporation. 1990. Toward TeraFLOP performance: An update on the Intel/DARPA Touchstone Program. *Supercomputer Systems Division Report.*

Intel Corporation. 1991. Neural networks: Computing's next frontier. *Microcomputer Solutions.* March/April.

Iwata, A., Y. Sato, N. Suzumura, S. Matsuda, and Y. Yoshida. An electronic neurocomputer using general purpose floating-point digital signal processors. Department of Electrical and Computer Engineering, Nagoya Institute of Technology, Showa-ku, Nagoya, Japan.

Jewell, J. L., M. J. Murdocca, S. L. McCall, Y. H. Lee, and A. Scherer. 1989. Digital optical computing: Devices, systems, architectures. *Proceedings of The Seventh International Conference on Integrated Optics and Optical Fiber Communication,* July 18 Kobe, Japan.

Jewell, J. L., A. Scherer, S. L. McCall, A. C. Gossard, and J. H. English. 1987. GaAS-AIAs monolithic microresonator arrays. *Applied Physics Letters* 51(2): 94.

Jhans, J., and M. J. Murdocca. 1988. Crossover networks and their optical implementation. *Applied Optics* 27(15): 31–55.

Jordan, H. F. 1988. Report of the workshop on all-optical, stored program, digital computers. *Technical Report,* Department of Electrical and Computer Engineering, University of Colorado at Boulder.

Kahn, R. 1985. A new generation computing. In *Next generation computers,* ed. by Edward A. Torrero. New York: IEEE Press.

Kaneda, Y., et al. 1986. Sequential prolog machine PEK. *New Generation Computing* 4(1): 51–66.

Kawanobe, K. 1984. Current status and future plans of the fifth generation computer system project. In *Fifth generation computer systems,* ed. by ICOT. Amsterdam: North-Holland.

Khachab, N. L., and M. Ismail. 1991. A new continuous-time MOS implementation of feedback neural networks. Solid-State Laboratory, Ohio State University.

Lerner, E. J. 1985. Data-flow architecture. In *Next-generation computers,* ed. by Edward Torrero. New York: IEEE Press.

Lewis, T. G. 1994. Where is computing headed? *IEEE Computer* 27(8): 59–63.

Lipovsky, A. G., and A. Tripathi. 1977. A reconfigurable varistructure array processor. *Proceedings International Conference of Parallel Processing,* 165–174.

Lipovsky, G. J., and M. Malek. 1987. *Parallel computing: Theory and comparisons.* New York: John Wiley.

Lovett, T., and S. Thakkar. 1988. The symmetry multiprocessor system. *Proceedings International Conference of Parallel Processing,* University Park, Penn., 303–310.

Matsuoka, T., H. Hamada, and R. Nakatsu. 1989. Syllable recognition using integrated neural networks. *Proceedings of the IEEE International Joint Conference on Neural Networks,* vol. 2.

Mullender, S. 1993. *Distributed processing: From theory to practice.* Berlin: Springer–Verlag.

Murdocca, M. 1990. *A digital design methodology for optical computing.* Cambridge, Mass.: The MIT Press.

Murray, A. F., and A. V. Smith. 1988. Asynchronous VLSI neural networks using pulse-stream arithmetic. *IEEE Journal of Solid-State Circuits* 23(3): 688–697.

Myers, W. 1991. Caltech dedicates world's most powerful supercomputer. *IEEE Computer* 24 (7): 96–97.

Pfister, G. F., W. C. Brantley, D. A. George, S. L. Harvey, W. J. Kleinfekder, K. P. Mcauliffe, E. A. Melton, V. A. Norton, and J. Weiss. 1985. The IBM research parallel processor prototype (RP3): Introduction and architecture. *Proceedings 12th International Symposium on Computer Architecture,* June, 764–771 Boston, Mass.

Pinfold, W. 1991. Meiko Scientific's computing surface: A highly scalable parallel processor for C^3I. *Military and Aerospace Electronics* 2(4): 37–38.

Sakai, H., S. Shibayama, H. Monoi, Y. Morita, and H. Itoh. 1987. A simulation study of a knowledge base machine architecture. *Proceedings of Database Machines and Knowledge Base Machines,* 585–598.

Salam F. M., and Y. Wang. 1991. A real time experiment using a 50-neuron CMOS analog silicon chip with on-chip digital learning. *IEEE Transactions on Neural Networks* 2(4): 370–382.

Sawchuk, A. A., B. Jenkins, C. S. Raghavendra, and A. Varma. 1987. Optical crossbar networks. *IEEE Computer* 20(6): 50–60.

Siegal, H. J., T. Schwederski, J. T. Kuehn, and N. J. Davis. 1987. An overview of the PASM parallel processing system. In *Tutorial—Computer Architecture.* New York: IEEE.

REFERENCES

Siviolotti, M. A., M. R. Emerling, and C. A. Mead. 1986. VLSI architectures for implementation of neural networks. *AIP Conference Proceedings,* 408–413.

Smith, P. W. 1986. Digital optics: Progress towards practical applications. *Proceedings of the International Optical Computing Conference.*

Soucek, B., and M. Soucek. 1988. *Neural and massively parallel computers: The sixth generation.* New York: John Wiley & Sons.

Tanenbaum, A. S. 1991. *Computer Networks.* Englewood Cliffs, NJ: Prentice-Hall.

Treleaven, P. C., and I. G. Lima. 1982. Japan's fifth generation computer systems. *IEEE Computer* 15(8): 79–88.

Umemura, M., et al. 1986. AI oriented computer. *NEC Technical Journal* 39(8): 11–17.

Yagi, T., Y. Funahashi, and F. Ariki. 1989. Dynamic model of dual layer neural network for vertebrate retina. *Proceedings of the IEEE International Joint Conference on Neural Networks,* vol. 2.

Woodrow, B. 1962. Generalization and information storage network of adeline neurons. In *Self organizing systems.* Washington, D.C.: Spartan Books.

Zarri, G. 1984. A fifth generation approach to fifth generation intelligent information retrieval. *Proceedings of the ACM Annual Conference,* 30.

Zitti, E., D. Caviglia, G. Bisio, and G. Parodi. 1989. Neural networks on a transputer array. Department of Biophysical and Electronic Engineering, University of Genoa, Italy.

Zvonko, G. V., M. Stumm, D. M. Lewis, and R. White. 1991. Hector: A hierarchically structured shared-memory multiprocessor. *IEEE Computer* 24(1): 36–43.

INDEX

Alliant Computer Systems
      Corporation's FX series, 248, 277
Amdhal's law, 158
architecture
  control-driven (control-flow), 59
  data parallel, 61
  data-driven (data-flow), 59, 73, 318
  demand-driven (reduction), 59
  direct execution language (DEL), 22
  distributed memory, 242
  language corresponding, 22
  message passing, 71, 241
  MIMD, 61, 240
  MIMD/SIMD, 82
  MISD, 59
  nonuniform memory (NUMA), 71, 242
  reduction, 71
  shared memory, 240
  SIMD, 60, 169
  SISD, 53, 60
  systolic, 81, 218
  taxonomy, 52
  tightly-coupled, 240
  uniform memory (UMA), 70, 240
  VLIW, 129
  wavefront array, 83
arithmetic/logic unit, 12
array processor
  attached, 133, 137
  synchronous, 168
associative processor, 77, 168
attached array processors, 133, 137
average latency, 105
axon, 368

bandwidth, 5, 137
barrier synchronization, 262
BBN butterfly, 248
benchmark
  arithmetic diagnostic, 347
  dhrystone, 25
  kernel, 25

Lawrence Livermore loops, 25
local, 25
parallel, 26
partial, 25
PERFECT, 25
recursive, 25
scientific computing, 348
SPECmarks, 25
SLALOM, 27
Stanford small programs, 26
synthetic, 25
Unix utility and application, 25
whetstones, 25
binary tree network, 187
bitonic, 195
bitplane array processing, 77
branch history, 116
branch-prediction, 114
broadcasting, 176
Burroughs Scientific Processor (BSP), 178
bus
  network, 189, 249
  snooping, 246
  watching, 246
  window, 250

C*, 210
cache coherence, 245
cache flushing, 246
cache only memory architecture (COMA), 242
Carnegie Mellon University
  Cm*, 248
  C.mmp, 248
Control Data Corporation (CDC)
  6600, 119, 124
  STAR-100, 124, 132
Cedar, 285
chaining, 147
chime, 148
CHip, 361
circuit switching, 183
CISC, 22
coarse grain, 239

collision vectors, 102
CM-2, 202
CM-5, 248, 306
CM-200, 359
complete interconnection, 187
complex instruction set computer (CISC), 22
computer networks, 361
control driven (control-flow) architectures, 59
control unit, 16
Convex Computer Corporation
  C1, 132, 151
  C120, 151
  C2, 132, 151
  C3, 132, 151
cost factor, 27
Cray Computer Corporation
  Cray-1, 132, 151
  Cray-2, 132, 151
  Cray-3, 132, 151
  Cray-4, 132
Cray Research Corporation
  T3D, 248, 308
  X-MP, 141
  Y-MP, 132, 141
critical section, 259
crossbar networks, 190, 252
cut-through routing, 184

DADO, 248
DARPA, 359
data alignment network, 170
data driven machine (DDM), 334
data flow
  dynamic, 323
  graphs, 320, 323
  languages, 326
  performance evaluation, 326
  static, 322
data interlocks, 102
data parallel architectures, 61
deadlock, 263
decode history table, 116
degree of parallelism, 53, 239
DEL architecture, 22

INDEX

delayed branching, 114
demand-driven (reduction)
    architectures, 59
dendrite, 368
dhrystone, 25
Digital Equipment Corporation (DEC)
  Alpha, 28
  VAX-11, 23
distributed memory, 242
distributed processing systems, 361
DOALL, 270
Duncan's taxonomy, 64

EDDY, 336
enhanced data-driven engine
    (EDDEN), 355
Epsilon data flow processor, 335, 347
evolutionary approach, 358

fast fourier transform, 217
fat tree, 250
FETCH_AND_ADD, 263
fifth generation computer systems, 363
fine grain, 239
floating-point
  addition, 95
  multiplication, 96
Flynn's taxonomy, 58
forall, 267
FORK, 256, 268
FPS 5000, 132, 154
French LAU System, 331
Fujitsu
  Vector Parallel Processor (VPP
    500), 360
  VP-200, 132

Gamteb, 350
generations of computer systems, 2
GFLOPS, 23
Goodyear Aerospace Corporation, 168
grand challenges, 5
granularity, 54, 239

Harvard architecture, 12
HASAL, 326

hazard, 100, 109
Hector, 361
high level language (HLL)
    architectures, 9, 21
Hitachi
  S810, 132
  S3800, 359
hypercube, 206

Id, 326, 343
ILLIAC-IV, 200
indivisible, 260
INMOS Limited Transputer, 295
instruction deferral, 118
Intel Corporation
  iPSC Series, 248, 285
  iPSC/1, 287
  iPSC/2, 287
  iPSC/860, 294
  i860, 36
  iWarp, 218
  Teraops, 359
interconnection networks
  average distance, 181
  bandwidth, 181
  connectivity, 181
  cost, 181
  fault tolerance, 182
  hardware complexity, 181
  latency, 181
  place modularity, 182
  regularity, 182
  reliability, 182
  topologies
    Benes, 253
    binary tree, 187
    bus, 189, 249
    complete interconnection, 187
    crossbar, 190, 252
    dynamic, 189
    fat tree, 250
    hypercube, 188, 251
    loop, 251
    mesh, 185, 251
    multistage, 252

nearest neighbor, 185
omega, 252
perfect shuffle, 191
ring, 184
star, 26, 186
static, 184
switching, 191
internal forwarding, 110
International Business Machines (IBM)
360/91, 120
801, 23
RP3, 248, 361
GF-11, 248, 360
I/O subsystem
channels, 17
direct memory access, 18
front-end processors, 18
I/O processors, 19
interrupt mode, 18
programmed, 18
Irvine data flow machine, 334

JOIN, 256, 268

language corresponding architecture, 22
lapse, 333
latency, 6
latency sequence, 102
Lawrence Livermore loops, 25
level of parallelism, 54
linear array network, 184
*Lisp, 210
lock, 260
loop
distribution, 163
fusion, 162
jamming, 162
unrolling, 131, 162
loop network, 175, 184
loosely coupled, 242

Manchester data flow machine (MDM), 332, 346
Mandelbrot set, 217

MasPar Corporation
Fortran (MPF), 215
MP Series, 212
programming environment (MPPE), 215
programming language (MPL), 215
massively parallel processor (MPP), 6, 168
memory
bandwidth, 14, 158
banked, 243
cache, 15
high-order interleaving, 15, 243
latency, 6, 14
low-order interleaving, 15, 243
multiport, 15
virtual, 16
mesh network, 185
message passing architecture, 241
MFLOPS, 23
microtasking, 264
MIMD
distributed memory, 242
memory organization, 243
operating system, 255
organization, 240
performance evaluation, 271
performance models, 273
programming, 266
scalability, 272
synchronization, 258
MIMD/SIMD architectures, 82
MIPS Computer Systems
R3000, 352
R40000, 42, 126
MISD, 59
MIT static architecture, 329
MIT/Motorola Monsoon system, 337, 349
MLIPS, 23
Monsoon, 337, 349
MOPS, 23
multicomputer systems, 242
multiprocessor systems, 242
multitasking, 264
mutually exclusive, 259

nCUBE systems, 248
NEC
  SX-4, 360
  SX-3, 359
network (*see* interconnection networks)
neural networks, 367
neuron, 368
NEWS grid, 207
NON-VON, 248, 361
NUMA (non uniform memory access), 242

Occam, 303
openness, 24
optical computing, 375
ownership protocol, 247

packet switching, 183
paradigm, 2, 56
Paraffins, 351
parallel array processors, 133
parbegin, 269
parend, 269
Paris, 209
PASM, 361
peak rate, 24, 159
perfect shuffle, 191
pipeline
  arithmetic, 95
  conditional branches, 113
  control, 99, 103
  dynamic, 118
  instruction, 92
  model, 89
  multifunction, 106
  nonlinear, 99
  performance, 99, 103
  performance evaluation, 123
  static, 98
  types, 92
pipelined vector processors, 132
private-address-space, 242
process, 238
processes
  heavy-weight, 263
  light-weight, 263
processing paradigms, 56
  completely serial, 56
  serial-parallel-serial, 57
processor-time product, 198
PSI, 364

receive, 270
reduced instruction set computers (RISC), 9, 22
reduction architectures, 71
reservation table, 93
revolutionary approach, 358
ring, 184, 251
RISC-I, 23
R-to-C ratio, 239
routing protocols, 183

Saxpy MATRIX-1, 227
scalability, 24, 195, 198, 272
scalar expansion, 161
scalar renaming, 161
scheduling, 265
semantic gap, 11
semaphores, 261
send, 270
Sequent Balance and Symmetry, 248
shared memory, 240
shared-address-space, 71, 242
SIGMA, 359
SIGNAL, 261
SIMD
  arithmetic/logic processors, 171
  control processor, 171
  data storage techniques, 174
  instruction set, 171
  interconnection network, 171
  memory organization, 170, 174
  organization, 169
  performance evaluation, 171, 195
  programming, 199
  scalability, 195, 198
SIMD/MIMD, 361
simple, 351
SISAL, 326

SISD, 53, 60
sixth generation, 367
skewed storage, 174
Skillcorn's taxonomy, 64
space-time diagram, 90
SPECmarks, 25
speedup, 3, 91
staging register, 89
Stanford small programs, 26
star, 26, 186
STAR-100, 124, 132
STARAN, 79
start-up time, 134
store and forward, 183
straight storage, 174
strip mining, 146
subprogram inlining, 163
superliner, 196
superpipelining, 44, 129
superscalar, 44, 129
sustained rate, 24
switching networks, 191
supervisor/worker, 57
SYMBOL, 22
systolic arrays, 81, 133, 218

task, 238
taxonomy
   Duncan's, 75
   Flynn's, 58
   Skillcorn's, 64
teraflops, 23
TEST_AND_SET, 260
Texas Instruments DDP system, 330
Thinking Machine Corporation
   Connection Machine 2 (CM-2), 202
   Connection Machine 200
      (CM-200), 359

Connection Machine 5 (CM-5), 248, 306
thread, 238
tightly-coupled architecture, 240
token ring, 251
Tomosulo's algorithm, 120
topology (*see* interconnection networks)
torus, 185
Touchstone, 359
TRAC, 361
TRACE, 361
trivial parallelism, 4, 56
two-dimensional mesh, 185, 251

UMA (Uniform Memory Access Architecture), 240
uniprocessor model, 9
unlock, 260

value oriented algorithmic language (VAL), 328
vector processor
   models, 133
   performance evaluation, 157
   programming, 159
virtual processor, 198
VLIW, 129
von Neumann model, 11

WAIT, 261
wavefront array architectures, 83
waves of computing, 2
whetstone, 25
wormhole switching, 183
write-back, 245
write-once, 247
write-through, 245